AF574858

30126 00279648 7

Foreword

Twelve months after the appearance of the first bound volume of Warships in Profile the time has come round to present Volume Two. The success of the first series has been matched in the following twelve Profiles, and we can look forward to even greater success in the next series.

This second series marks two bold departures. For the first time a modern warship has been included, the giant nuclear-powered aircraft carrier, the USS *Enterprise*. There will always be a limit to the amount of information that can be divulged about an up-to-date fighting ship, but in common with Aircraft and AFV Profiles, the Warship Profiles must record whatever details can be disclosed without infringing security. The second innovation is the double-foldout colour spread for the German battleship *Bismarck* and her unfortunate opponent, HMS *Hood*. Both ships were over 800 feet long, and the high standard of Profile artwork would have been hard to maintain if the normal page size had been retained. The result is a truly magnificent pair of views.

For the first time a warship of the Italian Navy has been included, the heavy cruiser *Zara* which was sunk at the Battle of Cape Matapan in 1941. In this Profile and in the *Hood* and *Bismarck* Profiles we are privileged to see unique photographs from the authors' collections. This underlines one of the great attractions of a Warship Profile; it gathers together the cream of the available views of the chosen ship, and because the quality of reproduction is so high, the Profile forms a compact visual record. Add to this authoritative texts written by authors who are hand-picked for their special knowledge of the subject and you have a combination which meets the exacting requirements of the ship-modeller and the enthusiast. As with any subject covered by a Profile series, the standard must always be that of the most fanatical enthusiast. If the details were not right the general comments would lose their point, and the author's opinions would be devalued.

In other respects this bound volume follows the lead set by Volume One. The warship-types represented include carriers, battleships, cruisers, destroyers and submarines, and by including the German battle cruiser *Seydlitz* the ships of World War I are represented. Once more it has been necessary to cover a complex ship by allocating double the amount of space to her; this time the British carrier *Furious* has been done at greater length to give due attention to her unique metamorphosis from battle cruiser to seaplane carrier, and then to fleet carrier.

In passing I must pay tribute to the great work done by my predecessor, John Wingate, who started the Warship series and saw it through its birth-pangs to its present vigorous state. As you enjoy the pages that follow give a thought to the co-ordination of effort needed between artists, authors and the various members of the production team. Comments and criticisms are always welcome, and authors will be happy to see any new information or photographs which turn up.

THE EDITOR

Contents

Acknowledgements

Profile Publications Ltd are grateful to the Trustees, Directors and Head Librarians of the following authorities: The National Maritime Museum, Greenwich; The Imperial War Museum; The Public Record Office; The Ministry of Defence; The National Portrait Gallery; The Naval Library and Historical Section; The City of Southampton Public Library; The Hampshire County Library; The Winchester Library; The London Museum Library; The Illustrated London News & Sketch Ltd; US Navy; US Air Force; The National Archives of the United States; Bibliothek für Zeitgeschichte, Stuttgart; Bundesarchiv/Militarchiv, Freiburg. Without the patience and unfailing courtesy of their historical and photographic staffs, the Warship Profiles could not have been produced. In addition, the Publishers wish to thank all those who have so generously given of their experience and time in the compilation of the Warship Series.

ERRATA

Page 2 Column II lines 3-4—*Cumberland* and *Suffolk* had 8—8in guns as built, in common with the rest of the class.

Page 2 Column II, lines 29-30—'Sir William Berry, Director of Naval Construction'.

Page 5 Column II, line 47—for 'runways' read 'catapult'.

Page 6 Column I, line 40 et seq—The Hawker Osprey was armed with one fixed machine-gun only. The engine was a Rolls-Royce Kestrel, with moderate supercharging.

Page 6 Column II, lines 5-8—Supermarine-built 281 Walrus aircraft and Saunders-Roe-built 460.

Page 6 Column II, line 14 et seq—Characteristics of Walrus should be as follows: 775hp Bristol Pegasus 9-cylinder radial; Span: 45′ 10″ (17′ 6″ when folded); Length: 38′; Height: 16′ 10″ (on wheels); Wing Area: 610sq ft; Max speed: 135mph at 4750ft; Absolute Range: 512 statute miles at 98mph; Service Ceiling: 18,500ft; Weight: 4900lb (empty) 7200lb (loaded).

Page 11 Caption to photograph—for 'runways' read 'catapult'.

Page 14 Column I, lines 16-21—should read, ' "Flank Marking" enables the fall of shot of two units with a wide angular displacement from the same target to be corrected for range as well as line (bearing). Tactically it divides the enemy's return fire and, in this instance, enabled the 6in and 8in guns to open fire at their optimum ranges instead of a compromise range'.

Page 15 Column II, line 15—for 11in read 8in shells.

Page 16 Column I, line 11—for 11in read 8in shells.

Page 22 Column I, lines 9-10—for *de Ruyter* read *De Ruyter;* for *de Witt* read *Witte de With;* for *Kortenear* read *Kortenaer.*

Page 34 Caption to photograph at top of page—A reader has identified this as the torpedo-flat, and the numbers are therefore the inventory numbers of spare torpedoes.

Page 50 Column II, lines 19-21—The *Yorktown* class was the first group of large American carriers built from the keel up.

Page 52 Column II, lines 22-23—First *American* combatant vessel which could not transit the Panama Canal.

Page 58 Column II, lines 3-4—TACAN (TACtical Air Navigation Beacon) more correctly provides aircraft with range and magnetic track (uncorrected for wind).

Page 67 Right-hand photograph—The horns are for catching the catapult bridles, not for extending the catapult.

Page 71 Caption to photograph—The aircraft on deck should read from the bow as A-4s, F-8s, F-4s and A-5s, not as shown.

Page 114 Column I, line 4—For 'six Fulmars and the four Albacores' read 'six Albacores and four Swordfish'.

Page 136 Column II, lines 5-13—The two-colour bands were identification markings, contrasting in order that one or other would be visible under most light conditions. The turret-tops were painted yellow just before the last sortie.

Page 140 Column I, line 14—*Hood* was hit on the boat deck, not on the stern.

Page 140 Column II, lines 18-22—The Swordfish were unescorted, and dropped their torpedoes, making a maximum of nine in only one attack.

Page 142 Column II, lines 16-19—The first *German* use of radar for surface gunnery control.

Page 143 Column I, lines 35-37—*Rodney* was not hit by German shellfire, according to Admiralty records.

Page 161 Column II, line 7—Type 279 radar was not fitted to *Hood*, and neither of the photographs showing her foremast post-March 1941 reveal the large array which would indicate 279.

Page 170 Caption to photograph—The radar on the director is Type 284, which was a gunnery radar, not air-warning.

Page 179 Column II, line 23—The Resonant Cavity Magnetron was developed by a team from Birmingham University, assisted by naval scientists; it was developed for production by the Telecommunications Research Establishment and first used in a radar set for the RAF.

Page 216 Caption to photograph—for 1943 read 1942.

Page 217 Caption to photograph—shows *Tennessee* in 1942.

HMS Exeter

by Randall A. R. Tonks MA

The Post War Navy

At the end of World War I, the formidable strength of the Royal Navy lay in 70 capital ships, 120 cruisers, and 466 destroyers manned by 438,600 officers and men.

Demobilisation began in 1919 at the same time that the Admiralty were prescribing, for the maintenance of the supremacy of British seapower, a fleet of 41 capital ships, 60 cruisers and 352 destroyers. In order to sustain the efficacy of this fleet an extensive shipbuilding programme was required, to replace obsolete ships and those worn out by war.

But the continuing parlous state of the national economy; a widespread desire for disarmament as expressed in the Ten Years Rule of 1919, renewable annually, that the British Empire would not be engaged in any great war for ten years; and international agreements to curb any naval arms race severely restricted the Admiralty's programmes of ship construction. Only two battleships and 14 cruisers were laid down in the 1920s providing a fleet in 1932 of 15 capital ships, including six carriers, and 52 cruisers.

The Washington Conference 1921-22

To prevent an Anglo-American arms race, and to restrain the threatening increase of Japan's naval power, a naval conference was convened at Washington.

Agreement was reached on quotas of capital ships and carriers, Britain reluctantly accepting parity with America and Japan yielding to a three-fifths ratio.

But Britain refused to entertain any limitations on her total strength of cruisers which long experience and the war had shown to be so vital for the protection of trade and communications with her overseas territories, as well as in fleet work.

However, the conference accepted a British proposal that cruisers should not exceed 10,000 tons with 8in guns, which not surprisingly ensured the building of much larger cruisers with much larger calibre guns than any then in commission.

This proposal coincided with current thinking in American circles where the possibility of war with Japan involving vast distances between US Pacific bases was a cogent consideration.

Full speed trials after commissioning. Note the very high masts (*Captain Dallmeyer*)

The Geneva Naval Conference 1927

This conference foundered largely on Britain's adamant refusal to accept any limitations in her cruiser strength but in 1930 at the London Naval conference she surrendered to American pressures. In 1929 Mr Ramsay MacDonald came to power with a Labour Government that was committed to policies that would cut down armaments. Britain agreed to reduce her cruiser strength from 70 to 50 in return for an American reduction of her Washington Treaty cruiser strength from 24 to 18: Japan was persuaded to accept a 5:5:3 ratio in cruisers. Understandably this agreement was a factor in the improvement in Anglo-American relations but, at the approach of war in 1939 the British Commonwealth could muster only 62 cruisers many of which, having been in commission for more than 16 years, were in the 'over-age' category.

Subsequent Cruiser Policy

Faced with Japan's immediately expressed intention to build eight 10,000 ton 8in gun cruisers and every indication that America, France and Italy were entering the 'Washington Treaty' cruiser race, the Admiralty proposed an ambitious cruiser-building programme. In 1924 five of these large 8-8in gun 'A' Class or County Class Cruisers, *Berwick, Cornwall, Kent, Cumberland,* and *Suffolk* (the last two had 8-6in guns) were laid down; four more, *Devonshire, London, Shropshire* and *Sussex* in 1925, followed by *Dorsetshire* and *Norfolk* in 1926.

Thereafter the increased gravity of the economic situation, as well as differences of opinion in the Admiralty on the optimum size of cruisers, led to a severe cut-back in their construction programme. One, *York,* alone of the three included in the 1926-1927 programme, was laid down in 1927 and only *Exeter* was authorised for 1928. These two 8400 tons 'B' Class or Cathedral Class cruisers represented the first attempt of a Washington Treaty power to break away from the 10,000 cruiser as well as a victory in the Admiralty for those who advocated the smaller, more lightly armed, cruisers. Not only were they considered more useful, as events subsequently proved correct, for the protection of our sea routes and convoys, but, being less costly to build, it was hoped that more could be afforded. The 7000 ton *Leander* Class cruisers, the next to be built with 8-6in guns were hailed as 'a return to sanity': these ships, *Leander, Neptune, Orion, Achilles* and *Ajax,* were launched between 1931 and 1934.

Some Features in Design and Equipment

Like *York,* the *Exeter* was designed by Sir William Barry, Chief of Naval Construction, and differed from her sister ship in several features. She was one foot broader in the beam, had a slightly larger displacement and was to cost more. It was originally intended that both ships should have three raking funnels but their foremost funnels were trunked into the second in order to improve conditions on the bridges and to economise in space and weight. *Exeter's* funnels were built straight in order to improve her appearance and were shorter than *York's*. Because 'B' turret proved insufficiently strong to take the aircraft catapult and runway, as had been planned, they were repositioned abaft the funnels. This decision came too late to alter *York's* bridge and funnels but *Exeter's* bridge was lowered so that the director was only 60ft above the water. *Exeter* was provided with unique arrangements for launching her aircraft, her twin runways in a V pattern enabling two planes to be carried and catapulted from either side of the stack.

HMS *Dorsetshire* and *York.* Much weight was saved in *York* and *Exeter* by eliminating half the No. 1 deck accommodation provided in the County Class cruisers which were also 50ft p.p. longer. Clearly illustrated are *York*'s high bridge, raked funnels and extended sideplating (*Captain Dallmeyer*)

Exeter on trials, before the aircraft runways were fitted and her sideplating was extended. Note the low freeboard abaft the bridge. Compare the bridge and funnels with those of *York* (*Captain Dallmeyer*)

Design Specification 'B' Class Cruisers

The design specifications for the 'B' Class cruisers finally approved on 20 July 1926, were:

Length:	(between perpendiculars) 540′ overall 575′	
Breadth:	(extreme) 57′	
Draught:	(forward) 16′ (aft) 18′	
Standard Displacement		8400 tons
General Equipment		490 tons
Armament		890 tons
Machinery		1770 tons
Hull and Armour		5250 tons
		8400 tons

Freeboard forward:	30′ 6″ (c.f. 'A' Class 32′ 3″)
Draught:	light 17′ deep load 20′ 6″
Armour:	3″ side 2½″ and 1″ bulkheads 1½″ deck 1″ on gunhouse roof and sides
Armament:	6-8″ guns 4-4″ HA guns 6-21″ torpedo tubes 1 aircraft
Machinery:	four shafts geared turbine engines 80,000 shaft horsepower
Fuel Capacity:	1900 tons

The use of superheated steam in *Exeter's* boilers was another innovation, requiring a special distilling plant on board to ensure that the water used was entirely pure. Her torpedoes used enriched air which added 25% to their range, the liquid oxygen required being manufactured on board. *Exeter's* searchlights, two being fitted on a platform between the funnels and a third aft of the mainmast, were controlled by the new ARL (Admiralty Research Laboratory) system. The beams of the lights were synchronously focused on the target with binoculars fitted on the bridge.

Building and Launching

In Devonport Dockyard on 1 August 1928, Lady Bentinck, wife of the Commander-in-Chief Plymouth, started the motor that drew the first keel plate into position and the Mayoress of Exeter, Mrs A. E. Brock, drove in the first rivet. The building of the cruiser proceeded without impediment under the direction of Mr C. J. Butt, Naval Constructor, with Mr J. Bennett as foreman. Less than a year later the cruiser, 4000 tons deadweight, was ready for launching.

On 18 July 1929, on a fine summer's day and to the accompaniment of music from the combined bands of the Commander-in-Chief, the Royal Naval

At full speed

Exeter, port side amidships. The 4in guns are covered. The torpedo tubes and searchlights are clearly shown (*NMM*)

Barracks and the Devonport Division of the Metropolitan Police, who then provided the Dockyard Police, Lady Madden, wife of the First Sea Lord, launched the *Exeter*. A running commentary of the ceremony was broadcast for the BBC by Commander Stephen King-Hall, Royal Navy.

An immediate scare that the plight of the national economy might cause suspension of work on the ship proved false and for the next three years the work of completion continued in No 5 Basin, Keyham.

Commissioning

Under the command of Captain I. W. Gibson, OBE, MVO, *Exeter* was commissioned on Tuesday 21 July 1931 and on the following Thursday proceeded to sea for acceptance trials, returning to harbour the same evening. After inspection by the Commander-in-Chief in Plymouth Sound a week after being commissioned, *Exeter* sailed for Exmouth off which resort she anchored. Civilities were exchanged between the ship and the City of Exeter whose presentations included a silver model of the Guildhall and shields for inter-divisional football and rifle shooting. After working-up exercises at sea, *Exeter* put into Portsmouth for minor repairs and modifications to be carried out before proceeding to join the Atlantic Fleet at Invergordon.

Mutiny at Invergordon

Exeter was proceeding to join the Second Cruiser Squadron, having been engaged in gunnery exercises and in cooperating with the Royal Air Force in their 'B' bomb trials, when a signal was received outlining the cuts in services' pay that the government had imposed. The Captain immediately cleared lower deck to read the distasteful news to the ship's company off duty. Their Divisional Officers then collected the names of those who would be particularly hard hit by the pay cuts and tried to alleviate their anxieties.

The ship arrived at Invergordon late in the evening of Tuesday 15 September and as she proceeded to her mooring ahead of *York*, her crew, unaware that the Atlantic Fleet was in a state of mutiny, were surprised by the unexpected enthusiastic cheering from other ships that greeted them. That evening and on Wednesday, on the afternoon of which a make-and-mend (free afternoon) was given, other ships tried to persuade *Exeter's* crew to refuse to turn-to when ordered. Although some half dozen men appeared reluctant to fall in for work on Thursday and tried to raise a cheer at the forecastle break, the ship's company by and large, 'continued to show the best

Plan of *Exeter*'s arrangement for twin aircraft runways

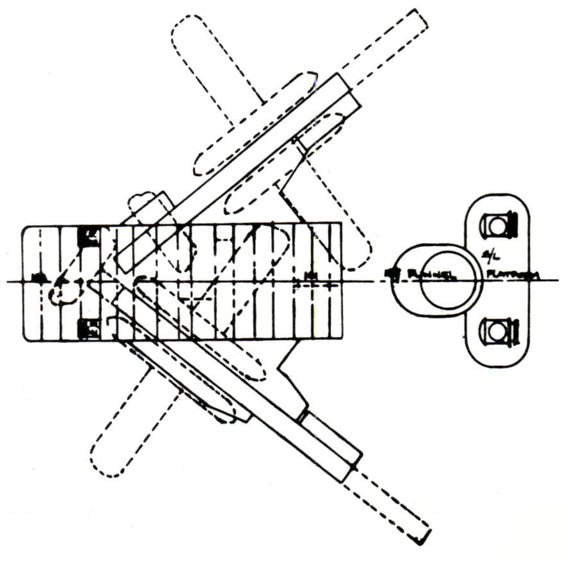

Port bow view of *Exeter*. The draught marks indicate a light load (*NMM*)

Exeter is launched at Devonport (*Sporting & General*)

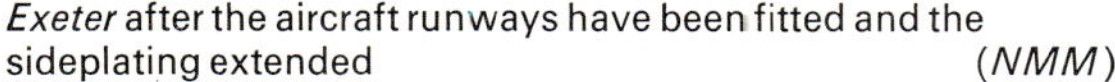

Exeter after the aircraft runways have been fitted and the sideplating extended (*NMM*)

possible spirit and loyalty'. Later that day, discipline having been restored, the ships of the Atlantic Fleet sailed for their home ports.

Structural Additions

Whilst at Devonport, not only were the catapult and the two runways fitted but also the sideplating at forecastle level, which ended at the break, was extended to the fore funnel. This modification to the structure of the ship kept the ship drier when steaming at speed or in rough weather.

'Exeter's' Aircraft

The Fairey IIIF

The Fairey IIIF was the last of the famous Fairey III biplane series, with a smooth pointed nose and streamlined fuselage. Although it might have been used for high-level bombing, it was essentially a three-seater spotter-reconnaissance plane carrying a wireless telegraphist air-gunner and naval observer in addition to the pilot. They were flown off carriers or, an especially stressed mark, catapulted from capital ships or cruisers. In all, 622 of these all metal structured, fabric covered, aircraft were built, 340 being provided to the Fleet Air Arm. The first was delivered to the FAA in 1927 and the last in September 1932. They were armed with fixed Vickers guns forward and one manually operated Lewis gun in the after cockpit. Up to 500lb of bombs could be carried below the wings.

CHARACTERISTICS

A single 570hp Napier Lion XIA water-cooled engine

Span:	45′ 9½″
Length:	34′ 4″ (36′ 4″ if fitted out as a seaplane)
Height:	14′ 2¾″
Wing area:	44½ sq. ft
Max. speed:	120mph 10,000ft
	3-4 hours endurance
	Service ceiling 20,000ft
Weight:	3923lb empty
	6301 loaded

The Hawker Osprey

The Hawker Osprey had supplanted the Fairey IIIF in all catapult flights by 1935. It was a two-seater fighter-reconnaissance biplane either flown from carriers or, modified as a seaplane, catapulted. Its structure was stainless steel and fabric covered. These aircraft were fitted with one or two fixed forward firing Vickers guns and one moveable Lewis gun over the rear cockpit.

CHARACTERISTICS

A single 640hp Rolls Royce medium supercharged engine

Span:	37′
Length:	29′ 4″ (31′ 9¾″ if fitted out as a seaplane)
Height:	10′ 5″
Wing area:	339sq ft
Max. speed:	160mph at 13,000ft
	2-3 hours endurance
	Service ceiling 22,000ft
	(Performance was greater when not modified as a seaplane)

*The Supermarine Walrus

The Supermarine Walrus, or *Shagbat* as it was popularly called, was especially designed as a naval spotter-reconnaissance amphibian. By its perfor-

A Fairey IIIF being hoisted on board by the crane
(*Captain Dallmeyer*)

mance and proven capabilities in all weathers and climates it earned naval pilots' unreserved respect. Designed by R. J. Mitchell of Spitfire fame it was first ordered for the Royal Navy after trials abroad *Nelson* in 1935. Supermarine built the first 287 Walrus until they had to concentrate on building Spitfires when they sub-contracted to Saunders-Roe who built a further 453 until production ceased. The Walrus could also be flown from carriers or catapulted and it carried a crew of three. They were armed with one Vickers K gun in the bows and one or two of the same weapon amidships, and light bombs could be fitted underneath the wings.

CHARACTERISTICS

Pegasus nine cylinder radial air cooled engine

Span:	45′ 10″ (17′ 11″ when folded)
Length:	37′ 3″
Height:	15′ 3″
Wing area:	610sq ft
Max. speed:	135mph at 4750ft
	600 miles cruising range at 95mph at 3500ft
	Service ceiling 18,500ft
Weight:	4900lb empty
	7200lb loaded

Second Cruiser Squadron, Home Fleet

In peacetime the Royal Navy not only in its military role, policed the seas and exercised a visible deterrent to would-be trouble makers but also, as an extension of British diplomacy, paid goodwill visits to foreign parts and rendered assistance in the maintenance of order and in alleviating disaster in many parts of the world. And by frequent calls to Britain's colonial territories, the ships of the Royal Navy gave tangible evidence of Britain's close association and her concern for their well-being and protection.

When she sailed to the West Indies in January 1932 with the Second Cruiser Squadron for the spring cruise, *Exeter* began to play her part in the exercise of British seapower. Having visited Trinidad, St Louis

* Aircraft Profile No. 224.

Two Fairey IIIF aircraft on their launching runway. The catapult equipment is clearly shown (*Captain Dallmeyer*)

Exeter's Osprey aircraft piloted by Lieutenant Caspar John, RN (*Captain Dallmeyer*)

A Fairey IIIF being launched (*Captain Dallmeyer*)

Exeter in the West Indies. The seamen, in tropical white uniform, have just lowered No. 2 cutter preparatory to securing to the buoy ahead of the ship. Note the two aircraft (*Captain Dallmeyer*)

and Barbados, she returned with the Squadron to Scapa Flow for the Home Fleet Regatta, in which *Exeter* won the 'Cock', an almost unknown feat in any ship's first year of commission. Then followed a cruise round the UK, visiting Liverpool, Ilfracombe and St Ives before proceeding to Portland for the Royal Review in July. In the autumn, all four ships of the squadron *Dorsetshire, Norfolk, York* and *Exeter* visited Copenhagen on the occasion of the British Exhibition there.

In 1933, before paying off in August, *Exeter* visited several Spanish ports in the spring and later, after torpedo trials in the Moray Firth, undertook a goodwill cruise of Scandinavian countries.

Crisis in the Mediterranean 1935-36

On recommissioning in October, *Exeter* joined the South American Division of the American and West Indies Squadron, 'showing the flag' round both British territories and the centres of South America and both sides of the continent.

In the hope of deterring Mussolini's overt intention to invade Abyssinia the British Government postured a threat to intervene by hastily reinforcing the Mediterranean Fleet. From Bermuda hastened *Ajax,* whilst *Exeter,* at Valparaiso, refuelled and sailed round Cape Horn in the longest passage of all the ships to the crisis area. Such was the urgency that she was required to maintain high speed all the way, causing the Captain grave anxiety whether she would have sufficient fuel to reach Alexandria non-stop. Commander T. H. Crookshank, the Engineer Commander, ventured the calculated risk that there was enough fuel to take the cruiser to Alexandria but the Captain, 'might not be able to go astern to check the way of the ship when she got there'. In the event *Exeter* safely berthed in Alexandria with less than one per cent of her fuel capacity—about 20 tons. *Exeter* remained in the Mediterranean until the crisis evaporated in 1936 after the British and French governments retracted from their position thus enabling the successful occupation of Abyssinia by the Italians.

'The Cock' won by *Exeter* in the Home Fleet Regatta at Scapa Flow (*Captain Dallmeyer*)

Exeter lit up on Midsummer Day at Karlskrona (*Captain Dallmeyer*)

Exeter returns through the Kiel Canal with her topmasts struck in order to pass under the bridges (*Captain Dallmeyer*)

Vice-Admiral Sir Henry Harwood, victor at the Battle of the River Plate and later Commander-in-Chief, Mediterranean

America and West Indies Squadron again

On 29 December 1936, *Exeter* re-commissioned under Captain H. H. Harwood OBE, who commanded the South American Division and she then sailed for Bermuda. In the course of the next two and a half years *Exeter,* in addition to the usual round of diplomatic visits and Squadron exercises, was called upon to illustrate the ubiquitous availability amid the varied calls upon the resourcefulness of the Royal Navy. In June 1937 *Exeter* steamed 1400 miles in less than 48 hours to join *Ajax* at Trinidad where there was serious rioting in the oilfields. Platoons of seamen and marines were landed to patrol the streets of Port of Spain until the troubles subsided. In January 1938 the crew were called upon to render assistance after a seriously damaging earthquake at Valparaiso. The ship returned to Devonport on 17 August 1939 to pay off.

Return to the South Atlantic

On 23 August the ship's company was recalled from leave and two days later *Exeter* sailed for Freetown where on 1 September Commodore Harwood discussed with Vice-Admiral G. d'Oyly Lyon, Commander-in-Chief South Atlantic, the function of the South America Division in the protection of trade. *Exeter* sailed the same day for Rio de Janeiro 3400 miles away, where she joined *Ajax* pm 7 September. The cruiser *Cumberland* and destroyers *Hotspur* and *Havock* were on passage from Plymouth to strengthen Commodore Harwood's Division. HMNZS *Achilles,* in the Pacific, was not yet under orders to join.

Commodore Harwood's most urgent consideration

Exeter, in her West Indies light grey paint, commissioned in 1936. The commissioning pendant streams from her mainmast (*NMM*)

was to arrange for the fuelling of his ships in the ports of neutral South America. Port Stanley in the Falkland Islands was the nearest British base, 1000 miles from Montevideo and almost 2000 miles from Rio de Janeiro, both of which were focal areas requiring protective patrols against German commerce raiders.

Having been showing the flag in the South American station for three years before the war, the Commodore was as respected as he was well known in these countries. The facilities he managed to obtain were more helpful than he had dared to hope for, in view of the restrictive clauses of the international laws governing the use of neutral ports by the warships of belligerent nations. Also the tanker *Olwen* arrived on the station to lessen the fuelling problems.

A Narrow Escape

Meanwhile, *Cumberland* left Freetown on 8 September for Rio de Janeiro on a course that unknowingly would take her through the area chosen by *Graf Spee* to hunt for prey. The German pocket battleship* had sailed out into the Atlantic on 21 August and successfully rendezvoused with her supply ship *Altmark* south west of the Canary Islands on 1 September. Whilst preparing to provision *Graf Spee* from *Altmark* on 11 September, Captain Langsdorf flew off his aircraft to patrol the the area against any surprise interruption whilst both ships were stopped. *Cumberland* was spotted by the battleship's aircraft when she altered to a course that would have taken her within 10 miles of the German ships. Captain Langsdorff decided to avoid the dangerous consequences of discovery if he engaged the enemy cruiser and, making off at high speed, avoided detection.

Patrolling off South America

Exeter was on watch in the area off the River Plate when information was received on 12 September that some Germans, who had been unable to return home from Argentina where they had been working, were planning to mount a raid on the Falkland Islands. *Ajax* was ordered to remain at the base and Commodore Harwood sailed south so that he could be in a position to cover eventualities both at the Falkland Islands and off the River Plate. His resources were further stretched when *Cumberland,* who had begun her watch off Rio de Janeiro, was ordered to Ascension Island where 'reliable information' of an intended rendezvous of German ships on 28 September was expected. *Ajax* came north to replace *Cumberland* off Rio, leaving the Falkland Islands unguarded. When it was learnt that *Achilles* would reinforce the South America Division, it was decided that she should join her sister-ship, *Ajax,* with the two destroyers to protect trade off Rio, whilst *Exeter* and *Cumberland* would form a hunting group. However, *Hotspur* and *Havock* were recalled to the Home Fleet which was critically short of destroyers, and Commodore Harwood considered that *Exeter,* who had been continually at sea since 23 August, needed a respite in Port Stanley to make repairs and rest the crew. On instructions from the Commander-in-Chief, *Exeter* continued giving protection to convoys until 26 October when *Achilles* joined her off the River Plate. Having fuelled from the *Olwen,* and her commander, Captain W. R. Parry, having conferred with the Commodore, *Achilles* sailed to join *Cumberland* who had reached Montevideo on the same day. These two cruisers then sailed for the focal area off Rio. When *Ajax* arrived off the River Plate, Commodore Harwood transferred his pendant from *Exeter* who sailed for the Falkland Islands. *Ajax's* task was to watch over the shipping lanes whilst *Cumberland* and *Achilles* patrolled as a hunting group with instructions, should they meet a German battleship raider, to shadow her by day and to attack only at night.

The consequences of Britain's agreement in 1929 to limit her cruiser strength was all too evident. Commodore Harwood was required to cover an area extending well over 2000 miles with only four cruisers, always facing the possibility of an engagement with a raiding German battleship. And in order

* See Warship Profile No. 4.

to maintain the fighting efficiency of his ships and their crews, the Commodore had to allow periods for repair and rest which meant that for most of the time only three of his cruisers were fully operational. Throughout her history of maritime warfare, Britain's cruisers have been overstretched to meet the demands made upon them. Nelson's plaint echoed over the years, *'I wrote to the Admiralty for more cruisers until I tired, and they left off answering those parts of my letters'.*

The Cruise of the 'Graf Spee'

Between leaving Wilhelmshaven on 21 August and sinking the *Clement* off Pernambuco, *Graf Spee* had already sailed to the endurance of her engines before a dockyard overhaul was required and she had narrowly missed detection by *Cumberland.* Captain Langsdorff moved south, taking three more prizes north of St Helena. Aware, from the increased allied wireless traffic, that all available enemy ships were being thrown into the hunt, he decided to search the Cape shipping lanes and, after making another rendezvous with *Altmark* to revictual and refuel, he then made a sortie into the Indian Ocean, extending the alarm by sinking the *African Shell* off Lourenço Marques. By such a manoeuvre he hoped to deflect attention from the South Atlantic through which he intended making his passage home for a much needed refit. After rejoining *Altmark* and spending a week carrying out a vital overhaul of her engines, *Graf Spee* returned into the South Atlantic. On 2 December he sank the *Doric Star* off Angola but not before the British ship had sent repeated RRR distress calls adding the word 'battleship'. After steaming only 170 miles on a south-westerly course, *Graf Spee* sank another ship who also wirelessed her distress and position. Captain Langsdorff, realising that his position was now accurately known, decided to accept the risk of marauding the focal shipping areas off South America before attempting the long, dangerously threatened return to Germany.

Closing the Ring

Since the signals from *Doric Star* and *Tairoa* had given away the position of the German battleship, still believed to be the *Admiral Scheer,* it was evident that she would make all speed to another area of operations. *But in what direction?* In case she should return to the Indian Ocean, the *Cornwall* and *Gloucester,* with the *Eagle* from Ceylon, were to patrol off the Cape whilst *Sussex* and *Shropshire, Ark Royal* and *Renown* were to position themselves south-west of St Helena in order to be available to proceed to the Cape, Freetown or the focal areas off South America. Further north, a French force of cruisers and destroyers, with the British carrier *Hermes,* watched the latitudes between Freetown and Pernambuco.

Commodore Harwood was given the news of the sinking on 2/3 December of *Doric Star* and *Tairoa,* as he sailed north from the Falkland Islands in *Ajax.* He calculated the German raider could reach the River Plate by the 12th, Rio by the 13th or the Falkland Islands by the 14th. He decided to concentrate his force off the River Plate which he considered might be regarded as the most rewarding hunting ground by the Germans.

Preparations for Battle

He thus directed that *Ajax* and *Achilles* were to be 230 miles east of Montevideo by the 10th and that *Exeter* should join them there by the 12th after completing her refit. The *Cumberland's* most urgent repairs could not be delayed and she was to arrive at the Falkland Islands on the 7th as planned but to remain 'at short notice on two shafts'. This meant that that ship could put to sea on two shafts almost

A close view of *Exeter* with her two Walrus aircraft, wings folded, on their runways (*MOD*)

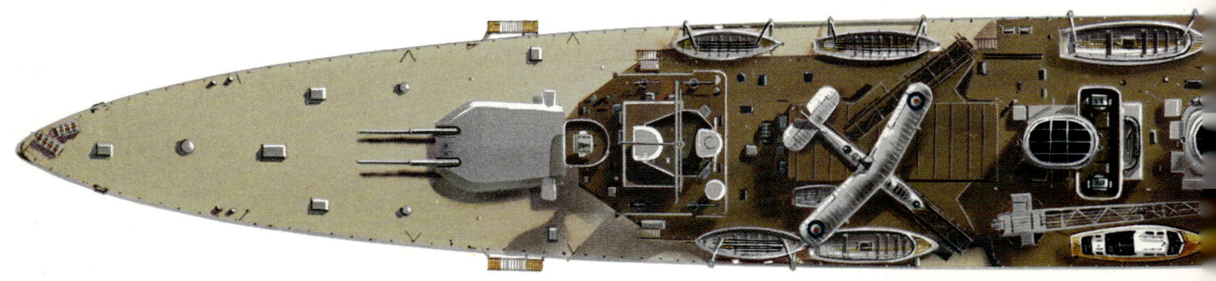

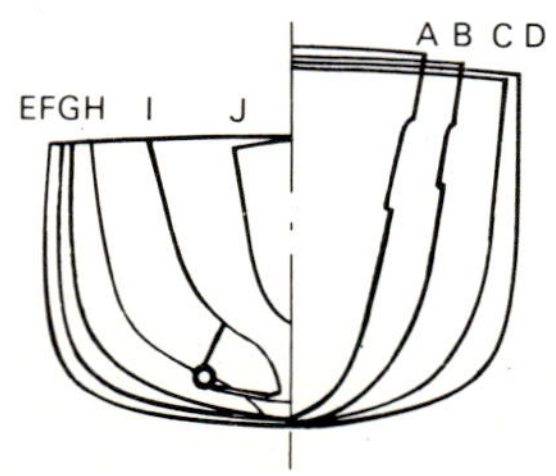

Silhouette
Silhouette of HMS *Exeter* after repair and modernisation at Devonport during 1940-1941. She appeared thus when she finally proceeded to the East Indies to meet the Japanese Fleet at the Battle of the Java Sea, 1 March 1942.

This 8in gun cruiser, whose life was both glorious and tragic, was the dissimilar sister of HMS *York,* whose name the class carried.
HMS *Exeter* is depicted as she appeared before going into action against the German Pocket Battleship, *Graf Spee* (Warship *Profile No. 4*), on 13 December 1939. The Walrus seen on the catapult had been transferred from *York* who had paid off in Chatham eight months earlier.

D C B A

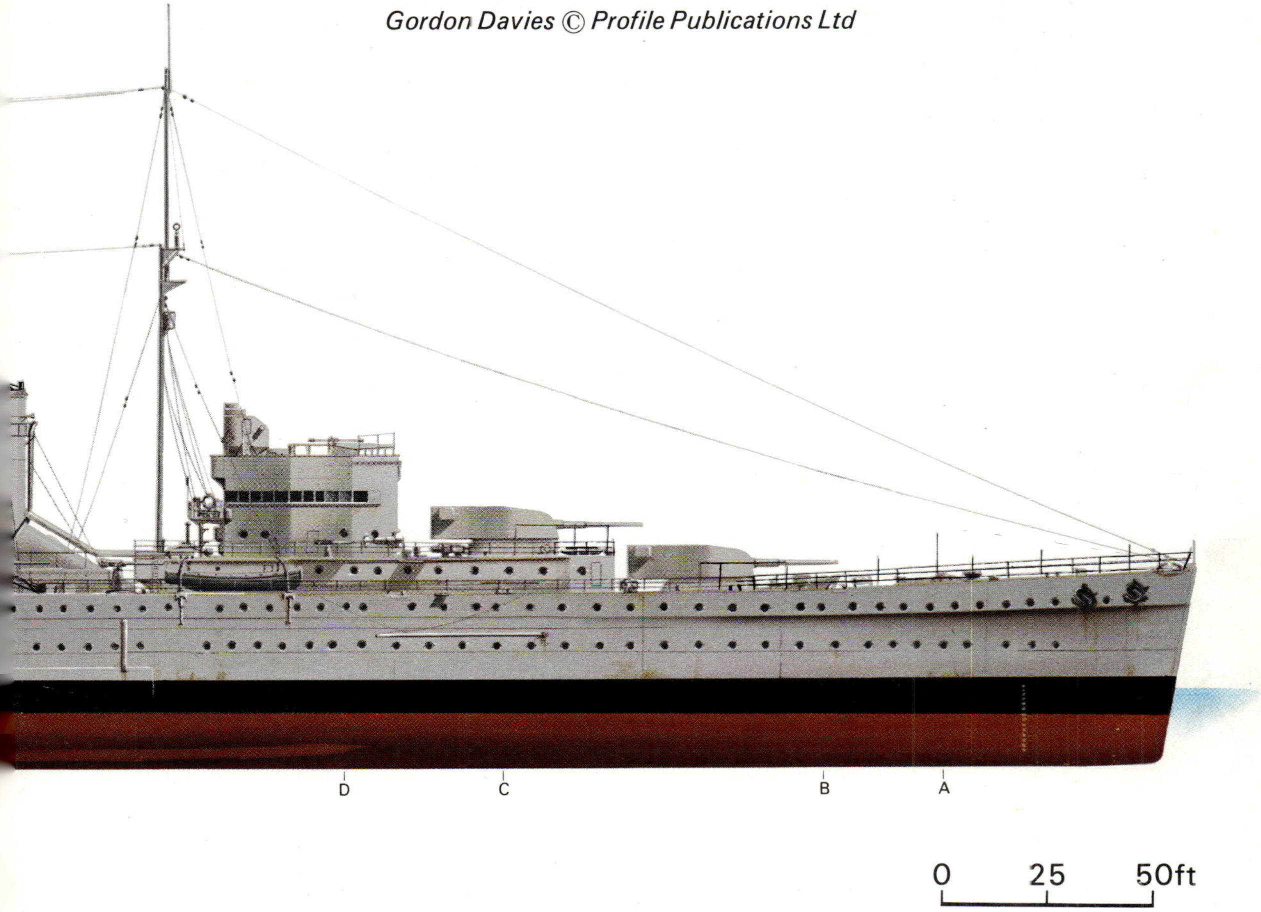

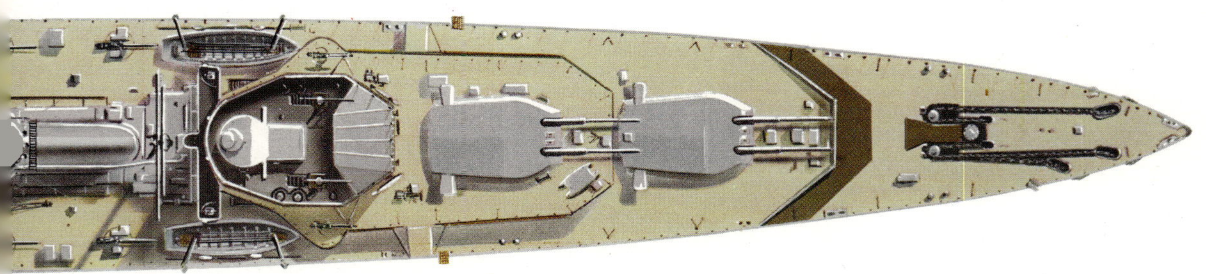

The directors and guns of *Exeter*'s main armament are all trained on a 90° bearing (Green nine-o) (*MOD*)

immediately, bringing the other two into operation whilst on passage.

When *Exeter* joined, as directed on the morning of 12 December, Commodore Harwood's plans had been made. Dividing his force into two Divisions, intending to go into action from different directions, he decided to *'attack at once by day or by night. By day act as two units. 1st Division* (Ajax *and* Achilles) *and* Exeter *diverged to permit flank marking. First Division will concentrate gunfire. By night ships will normally remain in open order . . .'.* Of the clarity and precision of these orders Captain Parry later commented, 'His intentions were so clear that practically no signals were made during the action, because we all knew exactly what to do'.

'Flank marking' meant that each Division could spot the others' fall of shot and also engage the enemy's attention on two sides. *'First Division will concentrate gunfire'* required *Ajax* and *Achilles* to fire simultaneously directed, from *Ajax.* These tactics were practised on the evening before the battle.

Battle enjoined off the River Plate*

Whilst *Graf Spee* was steaming off the River Plate on the morning of 13 December, two mast-heads were sighted at 0530 and recognised 20 minutes later as belonging to *Exeter.* The *Ajax* and *Achilles* were sighted and identified at the same time. Captain Langsdorff, realising that any attempt to elude detection was purposeless, ordered his crew to action stations and increased to full speed.

At 1614, *Exeter* was ordered to investigate smoke which is now known to have been caused by *Graf Spee's* diesels as 'they were stepped up to maximum power'. Two minutes later Captain Bell reported an enemy pocket battleship. At 1618, *Graf Spee* opened fire with her main armament on *Exeter* and with her secondary armament on *Ajax. Exeter* immediately steamed to west of the battleship and opened fire at 0620 whilst *Ajax* and *Achilles* made for *Graf Spee's* other flank, opening fire two minutes later.

The Bridge is wrecked

The first shell to strike *Exeter* passed through the ship without exploding but, within a minute, B turret was put out of action by a direct hit from an 11in

* For a full description of the battle from the German viewpoint see Warship Profile No. 4 by the late Kapitän zür See, Gerhard Bidlingmaier.

The damage to *Exeter*'s bridge when 'B' turret received a direct hit

Both 'A' and 'B' turrets have been put out of action

shell. Splinters wreaked havoc, killing or wounding all bridge personnel and wrecking the wheelhouse and its communications. Captain Bell, himself wounded by flying metal, went to the after-conning position only to discover that the steering-order transmitter and telephone were out of action. To con the ship, he gave his orders through a chain of messengers to the sailmaker and an ERA who were manning the wheel in the after steering compartment. Shells bursting short had already killed the starboard torpedo crew, riddled the searchlights, funnels, and the steel plating of the ship's side. The two aircraft were also damaged but not before petrol from their tanks had spurted aft, drenching the Captain and others at the after-conning position and adding to their hazards. The aircraft were then ditched over the side. A 12ft square hole was torn abaft the cable-holder in the bows which started fires in the paint store and other compartments.

The wreckage after the explosion in the Chief Petty Officers' flat

Crippled

As Captain Bell brought his ship round to fire his port torpedoes in an abortive attack, 'A' turret was decisively hit by an 11in shell and another, piercing the light plating of the ship's side and penetrating 65ft through bulkheads, exploded in the Chief Petty Officers' flat amidships, causing very serious damage and a furious fire. Vital electric leads were severed causing abandonment of the Transmitting Station which controlled the main armament and, as the blazing heat was endangering the 4in and 'B' turret magazines, they were flooded.

All control positions and communications systems had now been wiped out, but 'Y' turret continued to fire under local control until power finally failed due to flooding.

Withdrawal from action

At 0730, listing 7°-10° to starboard, 3ft down by the bows from water which had flooded in through splinter holes, steered by a boat compass, every gun out of action, her main mast moving perceptibly, with 61 officers and men killed and 23 wounded, *Exeter* broke off action. But, with her engines and boiler rooms undamaged, *Exeter* was still capable of steaming at 20 knots and Captain Bell did not baulk the possibility of ramming *Graf Spee.* No such opportunity occurred and the battered cruiser was made as seaworthy as was possible for the 1200 mile journey to the Falkland Islands which she reached on 16 December. Fortunately the weather remained friendly.

Damage inflicted on 'Graf Spee'

Of the 190-plus 11in shells fired by *Exeter,* three hit *Graf Spee.* The first passed through the upper part of the bridge without causing any real damage; the second pierced the armour plate of an AA gun,

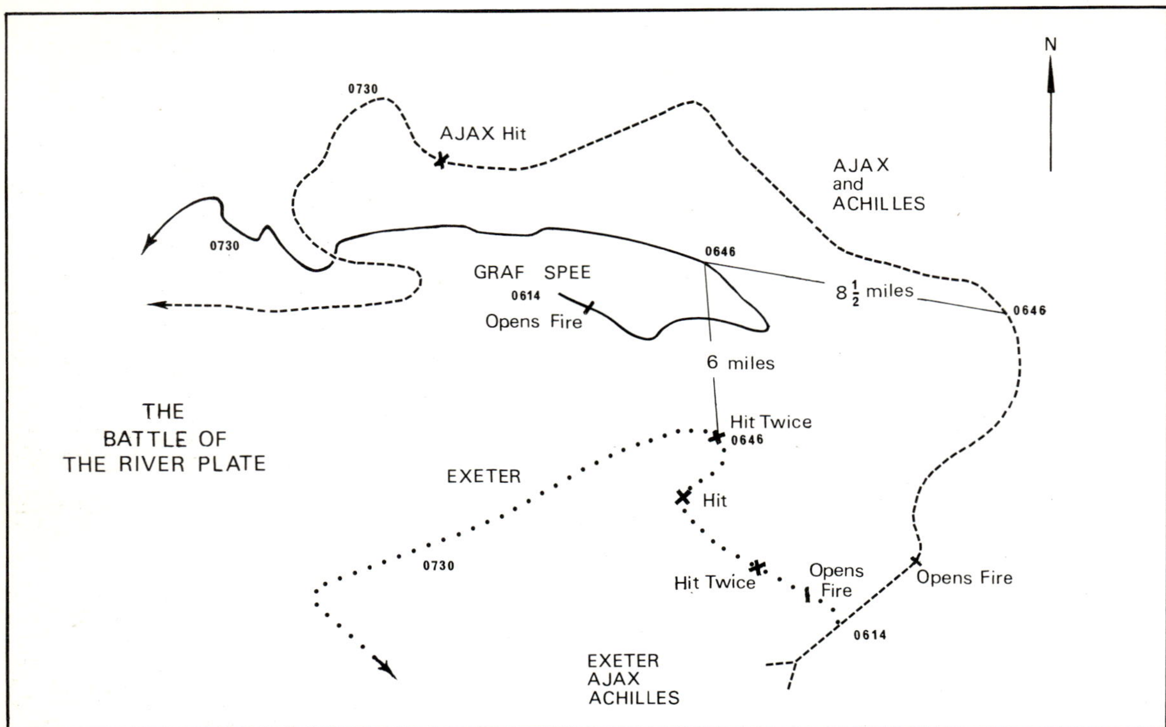

killing half the gun's crew, and went through two decks before exploding in the equipment for providing fresh water; the third penetrated the 140mm steel armoured belt and the starboard armoured longitudinal bulkhead before exploding amidships. This last shell, had it struck a metre lower, might have reached No 4 section of the engine room before exploding.

Commander F. W. Rasenack, a gunnery officer on board *Graf Spee*, commented on the surprising effectiveness of the British 11in shells which clearly belied the view that '*Graf Spee* could only be successfully fought by a battleship'.

Exeter's influence on the course of the action is measurable through the words of Captain Langsdorff, 'I knocked out her foremost guns, I smashed her bridge; yet with only one gun firing, they came at me again. One can only have respect for such a foe as that'.

The end of the Battle of the River Plate

Ajax and *Achilles* continued to harass *Graf Spee* until 0740, when Commodore Harwood broke off the action though continuing to shadow the German ship.

Captain Langsdorff decided that his ship was too severely damaged to put out into the Atlantic and proceeded to Montevideo roads where he anchored at 0500 on 14 December.

On Sunday 17 December, *Graf Spee* left harbour and 'blew herself up' six miles from the town.

Repair and return home

At Port Stanley, *Exeter's* crew plugged and patched holes, rigged jury aerials, repaired equipment and, as far as facilities permitted, made the ship ready for sea. 'Y' turret was put into full working order and all ammunition transferred to it: the forward turrets were man-handled into fore and aft positions. One rumour current was that *Exeter* would be abandoned as a rusting hulk alongside the iron steamship *Great Britain* but, as he wrote later, Winston Churchill '*was most anxious about the* Exeter, *and would not accept proposals made to leave her unrepaired in the*

Ajax after the action, showing her crew watching the last moments of *Graf Spee*. *Cumberland* is in the background (*IWM*)

After the scuttling, *Admiral Graf Spee* in flames off Montevideo

Falkland Islands till the end of the war'.

In late January 1940, leaving behind her wounded, *Exeter* began her long voyage home, first escorted by the cruisers *Dorsetshire* and *Shropshire,* then by Force H and finally by nine destroyers. On 14 February, to an enormous welcome, *Exeter* sailed into Plymouth Sound, past a cheering mass of people on the Hoe, past the men who built her, banging their hammers and dipping their cranes in salute, to her berth. There, amidst the crowd, was Winston Churchill come *'to pay my tribute to her brave officers and men from her shattered deck in Plymouth Harbour'.* The ship's company went on leave.

Honoured in the City . . . 23 February 1940

First the ship's companies of *Ajax* and *Exeter* paraded in Horse Guards' Parade where, surrounded by continuous cheering of a vast crowd, the King inspected them before investing officers and men with the orders, decorations and medals which had been awarded to them. Then the crews of the two cruisers marched past his Majesty and through dense cheering crowds all along the triumphant route to the Guildhall. There they were welcomed by the Lord Mayor and Corporation of London whose guests they were to lunch; every officer and man was presented with a leather cigarette case bearing the City's arms. Mr Winston Churchill, then First Lord of the Admiralty, replied on behalf of the guests followed by the Captains of the two cruisers.

A telegram was read from the Governor of the Falkland Islands: 'Pluck and good cheer of *Exeter's* seriously wounded are wonderful. All are doing well'. Another message from the Mayor of Auckland, New Zealand, announced that the officers and men of *Achilles* were being similarly entertained by that city on the same day.

AWARDS AND DECORATIONS

Captain Bell was appointed Commander of the Bath

Distinguished Service Order:	2 awarded
Distinguished Service Cross:	7 awarded
Conspicuous Gallantry Medal:	3 awarded
Distinguished Service Medal:	17 awarded

Repair, Refit and Modernisation at Devonport 1940-41

1. Masts shortened and strengthened with tripod struts to take new RDF aerials. However, not all RDF equipment was completed.
2. Modernisation and enlargement of the bridge.
3. The engine rooms were also modernised.
4. The 8in guns were given more elevation in order to extend their maximum range and to allow them to participate in HA barrage.
5. Twin 4in HA/LA mountings, with their own director and control systems, replaced the single 4in guns.
6. Two eight-barrelled 2 pounder pom-poms, on platforms built out from each side of the after superstructure, and twin 0·5 disc rifle HA guns were installed.
7. Additional magazines and ready use splinter-proof ammunition lockers were provided.

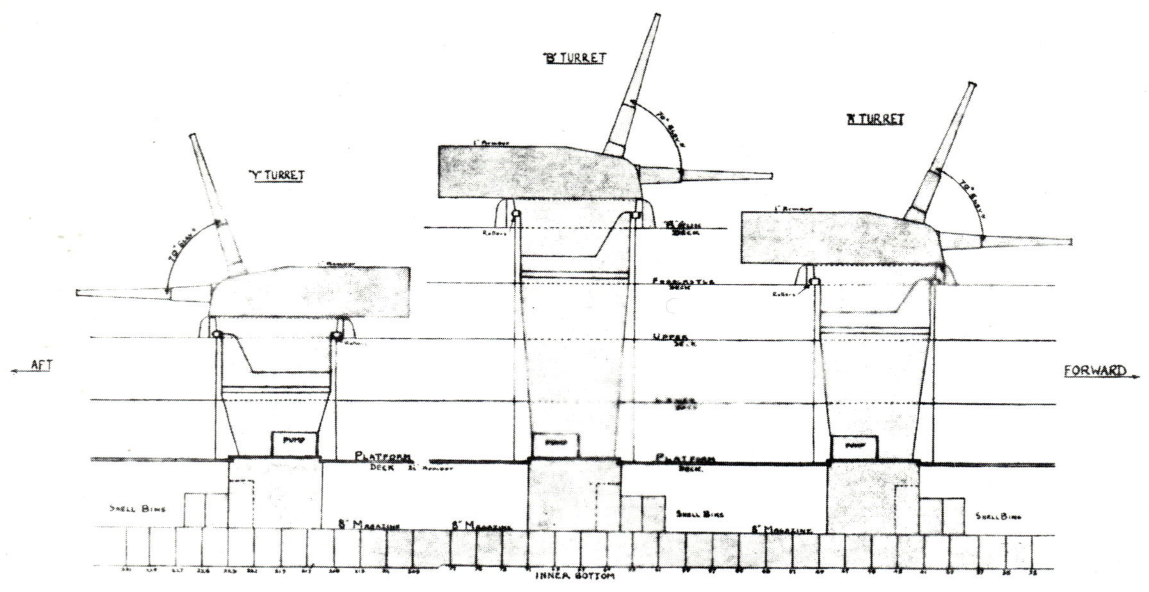

Position of 8in turrets in HMS *York*

HMS *Exeter* returns to her home port, Devonport, after the battle

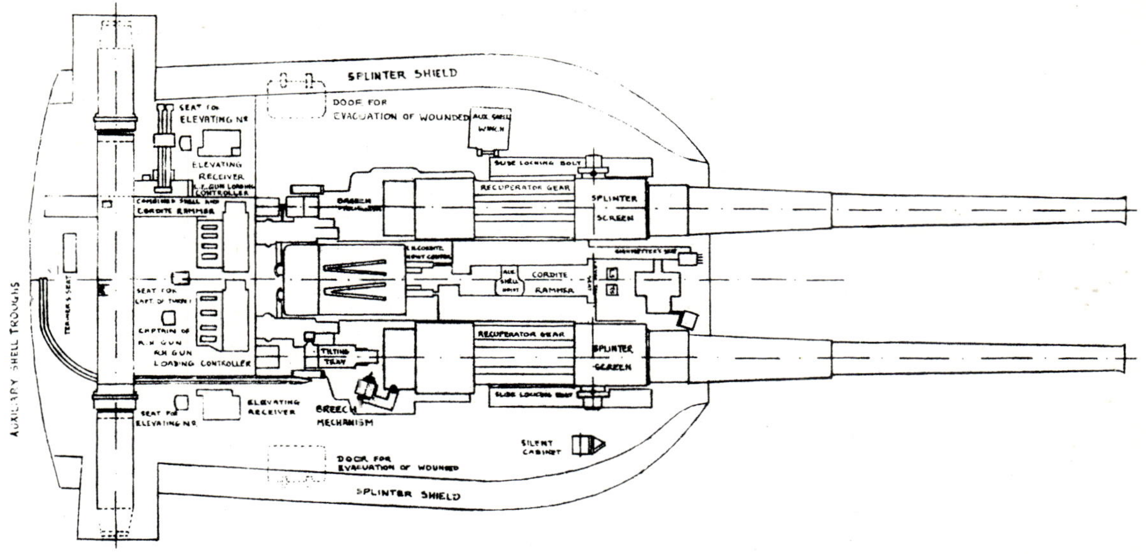

Plan view of guns

Section through fore turret

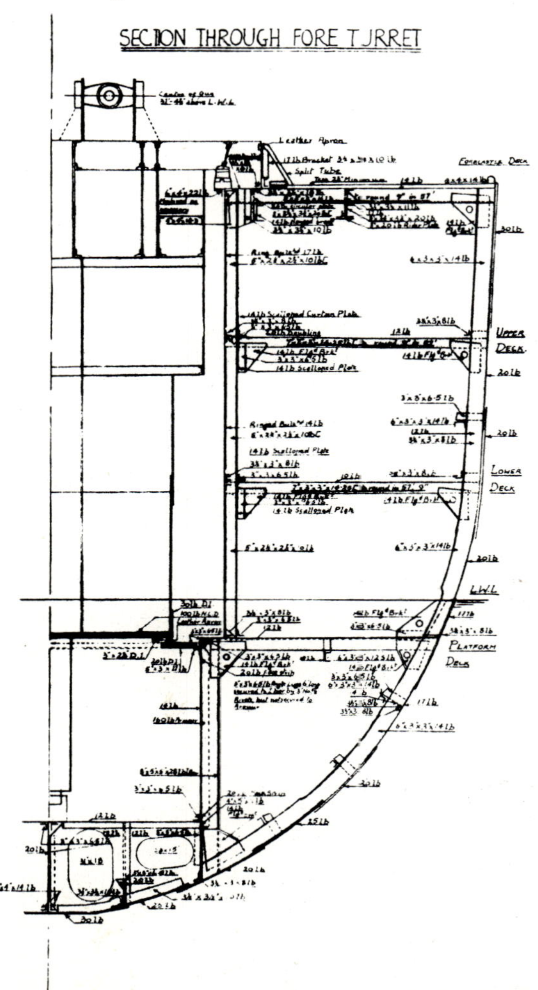

On Convoy Duty in many waters

The sudden death of Captain Beckett on the day of recommissioning was sadly unpropitious for *Exeter*. Captain O. L. Gordon took over command the following day. The hectic activity of embarking ammunition, storing and provisioning ship, was frequently interrupted by the devastating blitz on Plymouth during which *Exeter's* largely inexperienced crew fired their guns for the first time. On 24 March she sailed to join the 1st Cruiser Squadron at Scapa Flow for a period of intensive work-up, followed by a spell patrolling the Denmark Strait, before sailing for the Clyde to escort a troop convoy round the Cape of Good Hope as far as Aden.

After four months routine convoy duty in the area, *Exeter* proceeded to Colombo for docking, after which the Commander-in-Chief put the ship's company through a rigorous efficiency test before sailing her to 'show the flag' at Malé, in the Maldive Islands, and Calcutta.

After these diplomatic excursions, convoys were escorted to Rangoon during one of which the news of Japan's attack on Pearl Harbour came through. *Exeter* was immediately summoned to Singapore to join the *Prince of Wales* and *Repulse* but these two great ships were sunk before she could join them. After escorting convoys between Singapore and Colombo, often running the gauntlet of Japanese air attack against which she effectively used her 8in guns, *Exeter* sailed for Tanjong Priok, the main port of Batavia for further convoy duty.

At the time that Singapore fell on 15 February, *Exeter* was at sea in a combined force of British, American, Dutch and Australian ships, under Rear-Admiral Doorman, seeking to destroy enemy transports approaching Sundra.

As the allied fleet, unable to make contact with the

The crippled *Exeter* returns home. Note the top masts are missing and the successful results of repair and patching which have camouflaged the extensive damage (*IWM*)

Japanese ships, retired they were subjected to consistent and extremely heavy air assaults but without suffering any crippling damage. Once again *Exeter's* 8in guns startled and broke up concentrations of enemy bombers. Events moved rapidly and confusedly as the Japanese advanced relentlessly to

The officers and men of *Exeter* and *Ajax* march through Admiralty Arch on their way to the Guildhall (*The Times*)

A view from the starboard quarter showing one of the 2pdr pom-pom platforms and the twin 4in guns. Carley floats are much in evidence. A barrage balloon can be seen over the bows (*MOD*)

A view from the starboard bow. Draught marks indicate that *Exeter* is fully stored and ammunitioned (*IWM*)

The repaired and modernised *Exeter* hoisting in a Walrus aircraft. Evident are the enlarged bridge, the short tripod masts, the twin 4in gun platforms in their new positions extending over the side by the bridge and after funnel. The port 2pdr pom-pom platform is seen forward of the mainmast and the 0·5 placements are shown on top of 'B' and 'Y' turrets (*IWM*)

occupy the islands of the East Indies, with their wealth of oil as the principal objective.

The Battle of the Java Sea

Three hours after reaching Sourabaya on 25 February, *Exeter* sailed, again under Rear-Admiral Doorman, in the mixed fleet that so gallantly, yet so forlornly was to fight until its destruction in the Java Sea. The names of these ships are worthy of proud recollection—HMNS *de Ruyter, de Witt, Kortenear,* HMAS *Perth,* USS *Houston, Pope, J. D. Edwards, Alden, Paul Jones, Ford,* HMS *Exeter, Electra, Encounter* and *Jupiter.*

Throughout the brightly moonlit night, the allied fleet unsuccessfully swept the waters off Sourabaya in search of the reported enemy troop convoy. Just after dawn, Japanese reconnaissance aircraft appeared and began sporadic attacks but, as the convoy had not been sighted, Admiral Doorman turned for Sourabaya to refuel his destroyers; he reversed course when an enemy threat of four cruisers and 14 destroyers was reported 90 miles away. Just after 1600, *Electra* was fired upon and the Battle of the Java Sea had begun. Only the 8in guns of *Exeter* and *Houston* could engage at this extreme range; one Japanese cruiser was hit and she withdrew under a pall of smoke. But at 1651 *Exeter* suffered flooding of some compartments from a near miss: 15 minutes later a shell passed through the gun shield of her starboard 4in gun turret and No. 1 boiler-room ventilator down into 'B' boiler room. The shell failed to detonate but exploded on entering a boiler. Six of the cruiser's eight boilers were put out of action and a temporary loss of electric power put the main armament out of action. As speed was soon reduced to 11 knots, *Exeter* was forced to haul out of the line, throwing the allied line into confusion. In the subsequent manoeuvres

An artist's impression of the sinking of HMS *Exeter* (*Illustrated London News*)

HMNZS *Achilles,* 6in gun Cruiser; her Osprey spotter-reconnaissance sea-plane is on the catapult

to reform the line, the enemy delivered a torpedo attack which was countered by destroyers—*Kortenaer* blew up and *Electra* was sunk.

The crippled *Exeter,* now capable of 15 knots, covered by smoke from *Encounter* and *Jupiter,* and escorted by the damaged *de Witt* set course for Sourabaya which she reached at 2300, having beaten off a Japanese cruiser with broadsides from all her guns firing simultaneously.

After she went alongside at the naval base, early the following morning, everybody on board—*'You can clear the sick-bay; there are no sick from now on, and that includes the doctors'*—began clearing the debris, equalising the ammunition in each turret, carrying out repairs in the boiler and engine rooms and furiously fighting off frequent air attacks with the 4in guns. In the afternoon the dead were buried with full customary naval honours in the European Cemetery, Kembang Koening.

'It was all very tragic, the impressive ceremony, the beautiful uniforms, the immobile faces, and as background the lost cause of the Allies in the Indies', wrote a Dutch officer who was present.

Meanwhile, out at sea the survivors of Admiral Doorman's fleet were harried to destruction. *Jupiter* was blown up by an underwater explosion; *de Ruyter* and *Java* were torpedoed during the night; *Perth* and *Houston* were caught and, after a valiant fight against three cruisers and nine destroyers, were sunk whilst trying to escape through the Sunda Strait.

'Exeter's' End

At dusk on 28 February, *Exeter,* accompanied by the destroyers *Encounter* and USS *Pope,* steamed out of Sourabaya, making 15 knots to try to escape to Colombo using the Sunda Strait, since her draught prevented her passage through the shallow eastern entrance out of the port. Against the light of the setting moon the following morning, ships, who proved to be the two enemy cruisers, *Nachi* and *Haguro,* were sighted; these were shortly joined by two more *Ashigara* and *Myoko.* All were armed with ten 8in guns and had destroyers in company.

Reminiscent of an earlier *Exeter* in 1782, damaged and faced by a vastly stronger enemy *'there was nothing to be done but to fight her till she sunk'.* Weaving in and out of the smoke made by *Encounter* and *Pope,* the cruiser, now making 23 and then 25 knots, fired four or five salvoes whenever a target appeared whilst her 4in turrets harassed the enemy's spotting seaplanes. Then an 8in shell penetrated 'A' boiler room—main engines stopped, all power failed, the main armament was put out of action and fires blazed in the damaged boiler room and the officers' quarters aft.

Enemy shells now remorselessly straddled and then hit the stricken cruiser and Captain Gordon, realising that it was no longer possible to save his ship, decided to sink her. At 1135, after the seacocks and flooding valves had been opened, and the small charges, which had been placed in shaft passages in the event of such an emergency, had been exploded, the order 'Abandon Ship' was broadcast. Shortly before noon, after a mighty explosion had torn open her hull, *Exeter* momentarily, almost defiantly, righted herself then heeled over to starboard and sank. *Encounter* and *Pope* continued to engage the enemy until, battered by gunfire and dive-bombing, they were abandoned and sunk. The end of *Exeter* and her consorts was the culminating tragedy in the Battle of the Java Sea.

Survivors from these ships were picked up by the Japanese and then began their years of cruel captivity.

'EXETER'S' CAREER

21 July 1931	Commissioned at Plymouth 2nd Cruiser Sqdn. Atlantic Fleet 2nd Cruiser Sqdn. Home Fleet
10 October 1933	Re-commissioned at Plymouth American and West Indies Squadron
29 December 1936	Re-commissioned at Plymouth America and West Indies Squadron
17 August 1939	Arrived at Plymouth to pay-off
25 August 1939	Sailed for South America
14 February 1940	Return to Plymouth
10 March 1941	Re-commissioned at Plymouth
1 March 1942	Sunk

HER CAPTAINS

13 April 1931	Captain I. W. GIBSON OBE MVO
3 August 1932	Captain H. C. G. FRANKLIN
10 October 1933	Captain A. E. EVANS OBE (Commodore 2nd Class commanding S. American Division of the America & West Indies Squadron)
7 October 1935	Captain C. E. DOUGLAS-PENNANT (Flag Captain to Rear-Admiral A. E. EVANS, promoted 17 October 1935: Rear-Admiral as Second in Command 1st Cruiser Sqdn.)
17 Sept. 1936	Captain H. H. HARWOOD OBE (Commodore 2nd Class commanding S. American Division of America and West Indies Squadron)
25 August 1939	Captain F. S. BELL CB
12 December 1940	Captain W. N. T. BECKETT MVO DSC
11 March 1941	Captain O. L. GORDON CB MVO

HMS 'EXETER'

Built at Devonport

Laid down:	1 August 1928
Launched:	18 July 1929
Completed:	23 July 1931
Cost:	£1,837,415
Displacement tonnage:	8390
Length:	bp 540'; oa 575'
Breadth:	58'
Draught:	forward 20', aft 20' 3" at deep load; 17' light
Armament:	6-8" (CL) max. elevation 50°, max. range 29,000yd, 100 rounds per gun 4-4" HA (4-twin 4" HA/LA after 1940 refit) 2-0·5" machine guns 2-8-barrelled 2pdr. pom-poms fitted in 1940 6-21" torpedo tubes.
Protection:	belt, protecting machinery spaces 2-3"; deck 2"; control tower 3"; bulkheads 1-2"
Machinery:	Parsons geared tubines, 4 shafts.
Fuel Capacity:	1900 tons
Range:	10,000nm at 11-14 knots
Speed:	Max. 32 knots (but exceeded)
Complement:	630
Designer:	Sir William Berry
Constructor:	Mr C. J. Butt

The end of *Exeter,* taken from a Japanese aircraft. The ship is still underway (*IWM*)

Acknowledgements

The author is particularly indebted to Captain W. A. Dallmeyer DSO, RN (Ret'd) for giving so much of his time to recalling the early days of *Exeter*'s life and for allowing him to reproduce some of his private photographs. His thanks are also due to Miss L. Farrow of the Naval Historical Branch and to Lieutenant-Commander K. V. Burns, RN (Ret'd) of the City of Plymouth Library for their invaluable assistance. And he owes a special measure of gratitude to John Wingate for a wealth of advice, encouragement and patient forbearance without which this *Profile* would never have been started, let alone finished.

Bibliography

Naval Policy Between the Wars by Captain Stephen Roskill, Collins
The Drama of the Graf Spee and The Battle of the River Plate by Sir Eugen Millington-Drake, Davies
No Surrender by W. E. Johns and W. E. Kelly, Harrap
Fight it Out by Captain O. L. Gordon, Kimber
The Battle of the River Plate by Dudley Pope, Kimber
The Battle of the Java Sea by D. A. Thomas, Deutsch
British Naval Aircraft 1912-1958 by Owen Thetford, Putnam

Series Editor: JOHN WINGATE DSC

HMS *Ajax,* flagship, flying Commodore Harwood's broad pendant (*Courtesy, Sir Eugen Millington-Drake, KCMG*)

1913, private ship : note absence of Admiral's flag (*BfZ*)

SMS SEYDLITZ/Grosser Kreuzer 1913-1919

by Professor F. Ruge, Vice-Admiral a.D.

THE 'DREADNOUGHT' ERA

When Lord Fisher as First Sea Lord ordered HMS *Dreadnought* to be built in January 1905, he not only started a revolution in naval construction, but also unintentionally upgraded the German Navy Laws of 1898 and 1900.

The first of these laws was intended by Admiral Tirpitz, who introduced them, to put order into the plans which had been drawn up repeatedly since 1871 for a German Navy, but which had never been carried out completely. The second law considerably increased the number of ships to be built to 38 battleships, and 14 heavy armoured cruisers.

However, even a fleet of that size which would be ready by 1917, would not be excessively large for a power situated between France and Russia, who together had concluded a military alliance obviously directed against Germany. Such a fleet could never be a match for the Royal Navy.

On 1 January 1901, the figures for the largest navies were:

	Battleships	*Armoured Cruisers*
	(ready and under construction)	
England	67	61
France	37	29
Russia	26	17
Germany	19	12
USA	17	11

Tirpitz had exploited the general feeling existing in Germany against England resulting from the Boer War in order to promote his Navy Laws. At that time this was a good tactical stroke, but bad politics in the long run. The size of the French and Russian fleets and the necessity to keep open the vital ore traffic with Sweden justified a navy of considerable size.

The transition to the all-big-gun ship not only increased the displacement of the ships, but also their costs, which soon doubled. Even Great Britain could no longer afford to lay down seven big ships annually as she had been doing on average during the 10 years before *Dreadnought.* Under the German Navy Laws, three ships were to be built every year, and this rate did not change because the laws fixed only the numbers. They did not refer to the costs. The money was available in the steadily expanding German economy, particularly as the German army had scarcely increased until 1911, when political tension began to mount.

Challenge Accepted

If Lord Fisher had hoped that German industry would be unable to keep step with the all-big-gun ships, and that the additional costs for widening and deepening the Kiel Canal and several harbours would deter the German Navy, he was mistaken.

There was a gap in the launching dates between the last small and the first of the large German battleships but, from the autumn of 1909 two, and later, even three battleships were commissioned every year. This expansion to three arose from three amendments of the Navy Laws passed by the German Parliament in the years 1906, 1908 and

1914, *Seydlitz;* manning the side (*BfZ*)

1912, which increased the number of battleships to 41 and heavy cruisers to 20 (including all reserves). This Act made it necessary to lay down four large ships annually from 1908 to 1911. By then England had already concluded the *Entente Cordiale* with France. This German building programme contributed greatly to the deterioration of Anglo-German relations and the strengthening of Anglo-French ties.

Although German naval expenditure increased by over 100% between 1903 and 1913, her expenditure was less than half that of the Royal Navy.

In 1913 the naval estimates of the major powers were in the following order of magnitude: England, America, Russia, Germany, France.

The New Ships

The first four battleships, the *Nassau* class, were sturdily built with a displacement of 18,500 tons, practically the same as that of *Dreadnought.* They were armed with twelve 28cm guns in six turrets all at the same level. The battleships still had reciprocating engines and coal was mainly used as fuel. Small quantities of oil could be added for high speeds.

The successive four ships, the *Ostfriesland* class, displaced a further 3000 tons and had a main armament of twelve 30·5cm guns. The secondary battery of both types consisted of twelve 15cm guns.

Seydlitz under construction (*Bibliothek für Zeitgeschichte*)

In the next type (*Kaiser* class, ten 30·5cm guns) and in all subsequent ships, turbines were used.

The first step to the larger type in the cruiser class was not so successful. The armoured cruiser, *Bluecher,* authorised in 1906 and commissioned in 1909, was an intermediate type of 15,800 tons, with twelve 21cm and eight 15cm guns. With her reciprocating engines she could just reach 25 knots. Altogether she was too large for an armoured cruiser, but no match for a battle cruiser. This proved only too evident during the Battle of the Doggerbank on 24 January 1915, when she was sunk by the British battle cruisers under Admiral Beatty.

A new English class had been inaugurated by the three *Invincibles,* laid down shortly after *Dreadnought* and commissioned in 1908. They displaced 17,600 tons, had a main armament of eight 12in (30·5cm) guns, no secondary battery, and a speed of nearly 27 knots. On the German side, the first real battle cruiser was *von der Tann,* commissioned in the summer of 1910. Her specifications were: 19,000 tons, turbines, still mainly coal, 28 knots, eight 28cm and twelve 15cm guns. In the Battle of Jutland she destroyed her opposite number, *Indefatigable,* with 52 shells in 20 minutes.

She was built by the famous shipyard of Blohm und Voss at Hamburg who also constructed the battle cruisers, *Moltke, Goeben, Seydlitz* and *Derfflinger,* one of whom was laid down in each fiscal year. The first two were identical. They displaced 23,000 tons, had a speed of 28 knots and an armament of ten 28cm, twelve 15cm and twelve 8·8cm guns, with four submerged torpedo tubes.

SMS 'SEYDLITZ'

Seydlitz was armed in exactly the same way, but she was larger, displacing 25,000 tons. Her underwater protection was improved, with her fo'c'sle one deck higher. This increased the freeboard which probably saved the ship on her return after the Battle of Jutland.

Characteristics

Length: 200m
Beam: 28·5m
Draught: 8·24m, laden with 1000 tons of coal

When filled to her top capacity of 3600 tons her draught increased to about 9m.

Machinery

She had two sets of Parsons turbines arranged in

Seydlitz almost ready for trials (*BfZ*)

three engine rooms, and working on four propellers. Steam was produced by 27 navy type boilers in four boiler rooms. Six turbo-dynamos generated 1800kW at 220V. There were two rudders, arranged one abaft the other. During her trials, she reached 28·1 knots with 90,000hp.

In *Seydlitz*, as in a number of other ships, the material used in the boiler tubes had a tendency to pitting, and this made rather frequent re-tubing necessary. While this could be carried out on board with the means available, it was hard work for the engineers and stokers.

Watertight Integrity and Armour

The ship was very well subdivided, athwartships by 16 bulkheads, longitudinally by a bulkhead on each side and almost from stem to stern. The central part of the ship was protected by an additional armoured bulkhead (30mm) on each side, especially designed against torpedo attack. *Seydlitz* had an extensive armour belt, 300mm in the centre part of the ship tapering to 100mm near bow and stern. The fore plates of the turrets were 250mm thick. All over the central part, there was an armoured deck mainly 50mm thick.

Handling

Seydlitz was slow in turning, but otherwise she was a handy ship with good manoeuvring and sea-keeping qualities.

1914, *Seydlitz*, flag ship, Rear-Admiral's flag flying from the foremast (*BfZ*)

Ship's Company

The ship's company consisted of 43 officers and 1025 petty officers and men; the admiral's staff of 13 officers and 62 other ratings.

The admiral's and the captain's mess were each allowed 0·8 ton of provisions, the officers 10·9, the warrant officers 9·2, the midshipmen 1·1, and the ship's canteen 16·1 tons.

Armament

The range of her heavy guns was 18,100m, but was increased during the war to 19,100m by cutting away some of the armour plate protecting the gun openings in the turrets, and thus allowing a higher elevation. There were 87 shells for each heavy gun, 870 in all, and 1920 15cm shells.

She carried 11 torpedoes of 50cm diameter.

A Great Cavalryman

Seydlitz was named after General Friedrich Wilhelm Freiherr von Seydlitz (1721 to 1773) who served as a cavalry officer under the Prussian King, Frederick the Great, in the three Silesian wars. During the last—the Seven Years War—Frederick was allied with England, and Seydlitz with his regiments took a decisive part in several battles, showing great personal courage and a marked gift of making the right decisions with fast-moving forces under difficult circumstances.

Without doubt he was one of the greatest cavalry leaders in history. The name of this distinguished fighting man was well suited for a hard-hitting battle cruiser leading the van of the fleet. It was fitting that this ship was christened by General von Kleist, Inspector-General of Cavalry, when she was launched in Hamburg on 30 March 1912.

Her First Captain

Commissioned in the spring of 1913 by Captain von Egidy, an excellent sailor, *Seydlitz* was stationed at Wilhelmshaven, the chief German base on the North Sea. Here everybody took a keen interest in the fine new cruiser, including Mrs von Egidy, herself a very good sailor. It is said that when *Seydlitz* entered the lock at Wilhelmshaven at somewhat high speed (because of strong currents outside) Mrs von Egidy, awaiting the ship with many others, called up to her husband high on the bridge:

Seydlitz from the air during the war. In the upper right hand corner a torpedo-boat of the A/S screen can be seen zig-zagging (*Bundesarchiv*)

The quarter deck of *Seydlitz* (*BfZ*)

The quarter deck of *Seydlitz* awash at high speed in shallow water, 1913 (*Bundesarchiv*)

'Maurice, I think we should now go full astern on all engines.'

After training on her own for almost a year, *Seydlitz* took over her duties as Flagship Scouting Forces, which post she held until the spring, 1916. Rear-Admiral Hipper and his staff moved on board, and squadron and fleet exercises began. These were concluded by the usual training cruise to Norway in July, but this had to be broken off because of the increased political tension following the murder of the Austrian Archduke and his wife.

Conflagration: 1914

When hostilities commenced in August 1914, *Seydlitz* was rapidly made ready for action. As her crew was augmented by reservists, quarters became cramped. No one objected to this, however, as everybody expected that a decisive naval battle would be fought very soon, and that the war would be over 'by Christmas'.

In actual fact, a very different situation developed. Admiral von Ingenohl, Commander-in-Chief High Seas Fleet, was ordered by Emperor William II not to expose his battlefleet to unnecessary risks, and consequently the Admiral held back his squadrons. For this reason, *Seydlitz*, with other large ships, was not present at the fight, off Heligoland on 28 August 1914, when Beatty's forces attacked German patrols and sank three light cruisers and one torpedo-boat. Von Ingenohl at first sent only light cruisers in support, and the larger ships arrived when it was too late.

The German torpedo-boats were similar to the British destroyers, but were somewhat smaller and armed with lighter guns. They were trained more for night torpedo attack than for daylight action with guns and torpedoes. (In the account which follows, 'torpedo-boat' will be used exclusively for the German type, 'destroyer' for the British.)

The First Months

The fleet continued to wait at roadsteads, paint-scraping being the main occupation. This paint was found to be inflammable and on the older ships several layers had accumulated which now had to be removed. After some weeks, all the battle cruisers had developed boiler trouble and numerous tubes had to be replaced. In addition, *Seydlitz* had to have a turbine overhauled. As Ingenohl waited until all his ships were ready again, the fleet did not undertake any significant operation before November 1914.

By this time, the first phase of the land war was already over, and had in no way been influenced by any action on the part of the German fleet. The attempt to encircle the French armies (the famous *Schlieffen Plan*) had been foiled on the river Marne: both sides were exhausted and had dug

Seydlitz seen from the port quarter. The after steering position and the stern anchor are clearly visible (*Bundesarchiv*)

Painting the after funnel (*Bundesarchiv*)

Seydlitz at target practice. Note independent firing of each gun (*Bundesarchiv*)

themselves in, until there was a continuous front line from the Swiss frontier to the coast of Flanders.
True, the German submarine *U9* under Lieutenant Weddigen had sunk three British armoured cruisers off the Dutch coast and other submarines, as well as mines, had caused some British losses. However, the immense power of the highly-trained High Seas Fleet had not been used either to fight the Grand Fleet or to influence land operations near the English Channel. The British Fleet and its blockade, which isolated Germany from the oceans, was too far away to be attacked by surface ships with any hope of success. The German cruisers, who were in distant seas, constituted a nuisance to British shipping, but no more, and they could not be expected to last much longer. The best chance for the High Seas Fleet was to lure some of the British forces into a situation favourable to the Germans.

Attacks on the English Coasts: the First Sortie, 2 November 1914

Early on 2 November, the Scouting Forces (4 battle-cruisers including *Bluecher,* and 4 light cruisers, 1 carrying mines) left the Jade Estuary, led by Admiral Hipper in *Seydlitz.* They steamed at 20 knots to the west, and then to south-west in the direction of the Norfolk coast in order to bombard batteries and other military installations at Great Yarmouth. The German Battlefleet (14 battleships, 3 armoured cruisers, 6 light cruisers and over 50 torpedo-boats) followed at 12 knots about half way across the North Sea.
On the morning of 3 November, the Scouting Forces sighted numerous fishing vessels and merchant ships, but carried on, as they had no torpedo-boats to search them. Because of haze, the approach to the coast proved difficult. The land was shrouded in mist and important buoys had been removed. About 10 miles from shore, the British gunboat, *Halcyon,* and two destroyers were sighted and were subjected to fire. The British zig-zagged, laid a smokescreen, and escaped with only light damage.
In the meantime, *Seydlitz* engaged the three coastal batteries, the coast-guard station and the aerodrome at Great Yarmouth, the other heavy ships following suit. The closest distance was 13,000m, out of range of the batteries, which nevertheless answered though no hits resulted. Meanwhile, the light cruiser, *Stralsund,* laid her mines, most of which were too far from the coast and outside the shipping channel.
After about 20 minutes, Admiral Hipper turned away to avoid danger from submarines. This proved a right decision, as there were three British submarines in readiness at Gorleston, south of Great Yarmouth. These put to sea at once but were unable to overtake the rapidly retiring German ships. HM Submarine, *D5,* struck a mine and sank with most of her crew.
The British light cruisers, *Aurora* and *Undaunted,* and some destroyers, all of the Harwich Force, were at sea. They tried to intercept the German ships and, although they sighted them, they were soon recalled. There were no British heavy ships near the scene of the action. In order to avoid German submarines and mines, Admiral Jellicoe had taken the battleships of the Grand Fleet to Lough Swilly on the northwest coast of Ireland. Off this base on 27 October the battleship *Audacious* struck a mine laid by the German auxiliary cruiser *Berlin,* and sank after 12 hours. The battle-cruisers were stationed at Cromarty, too far to intervene.
Accordingly, the German forces returned unscathed to their bases. Their appearance off the Norfolk

Seydlitz at sea during the war (note white ring on top of A turret). She is steaming, probably in the Western Baltic, under individual training: turrets are trained on different bearings; men off watch are on deck (*Bundesarchiv*)

Seydlitz at anchor: a view of the fo'c'sle from the bridge. The white circle on A turret is a recognition signal for friendly aircraft (*Bundesarchiv*)

Heavy cruiser *Bluecher* and light cruiser, *Rostock,* and the Fifth Torpedo Boat Flotilla leaving harbour for the Dogger Bank Operation (23 January 1915) (*Author's collection*)

coast had been dramatic, but otherwise the results of the operation were meagre. There had been nothing very successful on either side. Entering port, the German armoured cruiser, *Yorck,* blundered into a defensive minefield, and sank within a few minutes with great loss of life.

Reaction of the Grand Fleet

As a direct result of the German action, the main part of the Grand Fleet returned to Scapa Flow. On 23 November, all available British forces met in the North Sea half way from the southern tip of Norway, and proceeded towards Heligoland. In excellent visibility, an advanced group of armoured cruisers and destroyers approached the island next morning. In the latter part of the night, without being aware of it, they had followed two German torpedo-boat flotillas returning from a night sweep to the north-west. Three days earlier, the German battle cruisers had made a similar daytime sweep for the benefit of *Derfflinger* (26,000 tons, eight 30·5cm guns, twelve 15cm guns) who had just joined the fleet.
The British ships were sighted at a distance of about 20 miles. The German patrols then withdrew, and the heavy guns of the island fired a few rounds. This was the only time they were used on live targets during the whole war. The distance was too great for rapid hits and the British withdrew.
The German C.-in-C. limited his countermeasures to pursuing them with two torpedo-boat flotillas. He gave his orders too late and nothing came of it. He made plans, however, for another raid on the English coast, in spite of the fact that at the end of November military correspondents were already speculating on such a move, possibly combined with an attempt at landing troops. Some German papers took up this disturbing piece of news, but von Ingenohl did not cancel his plans.

Seydlitz: the third hit from the Hartlepool shore battery. (See page 31) (*BfZ*)

The Second Sortie against the English Coast: 15 December 1914

Owing to bad weather, this operation could not start before the morning of 15 December, when the Scouting Forces (5 battle-cruisers including *Bluecher,* 4 light cruisers, 2 torpedo-boat flotillas) put to sea again led by Admiral Hipper in *Seydlitz.* After a few hours, they were again followed by the battle fleet (14 modern and 8 old battleships), screened by a large number of cruisers and torpedo-boats.
The British W/T intelligence quickly located the Scouting Forces leaving port, but not the battle fleet. Admiral Jellicoe alerted the Second Battle Squadron (6 ships under Admiral Warrender) at Scapa Flow and the battle cruisers at Cromarty. They met in the North Sea and proceeded to a rendezvous about 100 miles due east of Flamborough Head. This put them exactly on the line of the German retreat.
Admiral Hipper had orders to bombard Hartlepool, Whitby and Scarborough. Shortly after midnight, he passed a few miles ahead of the British battle cruisers, who were steering a course at right angles to his own. Both sides continued in blissful ignorance of the narrow shave they had shared.
Just before dawn, the Fouth Destroyer Flotilla on the left wing of the British force became involved with torpedo-boats screening to starboard ahead of the German battleships. Several short actions ensued, some British destroyers being slightly damaged; a German light cruiser received a single hit, and the German battle fleet turned away to the south-east and east. Again the heavy ships did not clash, and neither side enjoyed a clear picture of the

real situation. None of the light forces had sighted any heavy ships of the other fleet.

Surprised by the Dawn Patrol: Hartlepool

In the meantime, *Seydlitz,* in the van of the battle cruisers, continued her course towards the English coast. Again, visibility was bad and, to make things worse, the wind increased to a north-westerly gale. Hipper decided to send his light cruisers and torpedo-boats back with the exception of *Kolberg* who carried about 100 mines. When Whitby came in sight, *von der Tann* and *Derfflinger* steered south to bombard Scarborough. *Kolberg* followed them to lay her mines in the shipping channel near that resort, while *Seydlitz, Moltke* and *Bluecher* turned north. Off Hartlepool, they were challenged by four British destroyers who were at sea on dawn patrol. Too far away for a torpedo attack, they turned away under heavy fire, which caused some damage. Hipper decided not to follow them but to carry out the bombardment. When the German ships opened fire at a distance of about 6000m, the British batteries replied vigorously. First, *Bluecher* was hit by four 15cm shells which killed nine men and put two 8·8cm guns out of action. Then *Seydlitz* received three hits. One caused a leak under the fo'c'sle which was soon repaired. The next blew a hole in the forward funnel, and the third damaged the superstructure aft. On *Moltke* a shell destroyed several officers' cabins. Very soon afterwards the batteries were put out of action by the overwhelming fire of the three ships. The entire bombardment only lasted a quarter of an hour but, at distances decreasing to 3000m, considerable damage was inflicted upon military and industrial installations.

Scarborough and Whitby

At Scarborough and at Whitby the German fire was not answered, as the coastguard and yeomanry previously stationed there had been withdrawn. Their buildings were destroyed, and other installations such as workshops and factories were damaged. During the bombardment, *Kolberg,* rolling heavily, laid her cargo of mines as planned. The two forces then united and steamed east, shaping course for the position where the German battle fleet was awaiting them. However, after the short contact with the British destroyers in the morning, von Ingenohl had not reversed course again, but continued to steer east.

The Net Closes

This left Hipper in a dangerous situation, for it was not difficult for the British admirals to guess the approximate course the German bombardment groups would take. At the point where, according to the operational plan, the German battle fleet should have joined the ships returning from the English coast, the British battleships and battle cruisers were now disposed in a belt 35 miles wide to cut them off.

Seydlitz: Dogger Bank, 24 January 1915. The first hit (under the fo'c'sle) (*Bundesarchiv*)

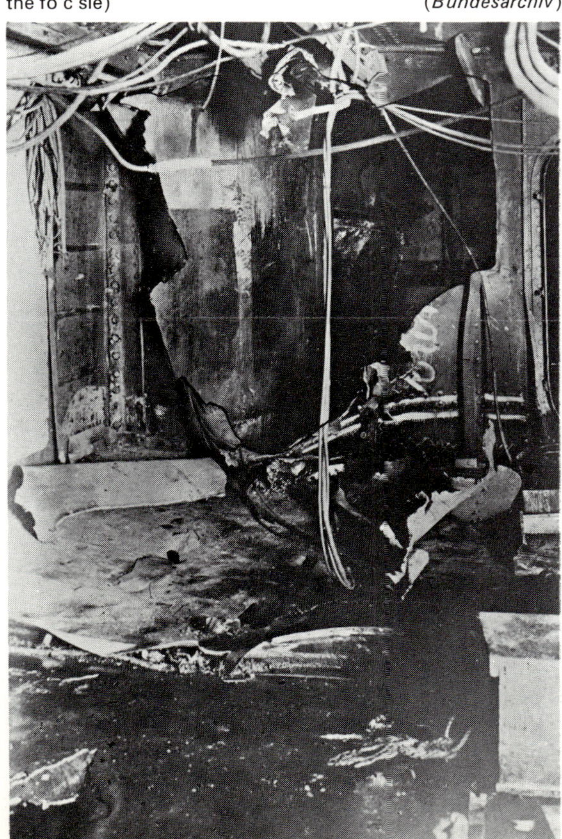

Sketch: after turrets blazing after the Battle of the Dogger Bank, 24 January 1915. The barbette of the aftermost turret has been hit by a British shell; both turrets are out of action (*Author*)

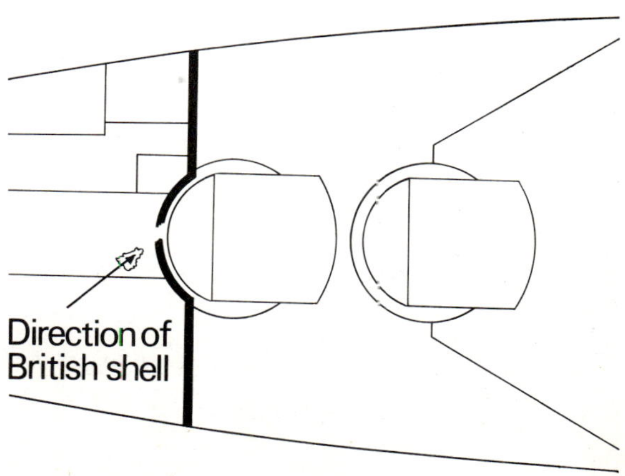

The armoured cruiser, *Bluecher,* capsizing during the Battle of the Dogger Bank, 24 January 1915 (*Author's collection*)

The German light cruisers and torpedo-boats who were sent back because of the gale, would have run head-on into Beatty's battle cruisers, but for an advanced screen of British light cruisers. In bad visibility and between rain squalls, the Germans first sighted *Southampton,* the flagship of Commodore Goodenough, and immediately afterwards, *Birmingham.* Both sides opened intermittent fire, and the Germans turned south and increased speed as much as possible. No hits were registered because accurate gunnery was impossible in the heavily rolling ships.

When Beatty saw *Southampton* opening fire, he also turned south, but soon west again because he correctly expected the German battle cruisers from that direction. *Southampton* and *Birmingham* then carried out a signal not in fact intended for them, and again took station ahead of their battle cruisers.

In this way, contact was lost with the German light forces, who hauled round to an easterly course again, and so narrowly avoided steering into the Second Battle Squadron. They passed the heavy ships on opposite courses at a distance of not more than 7-8000 metres. By using the British recognition signal, and with the help of rain squalls, the German ships succeeded in disappearing from sight before their identity became clear to Admiral Warrender. He at once turned after them, but his battleships were too slow to catch the light forces.

An Interesting Conjecture

It is impossible to say what would have been the outcome if the two vastly different adversaries had run directly into each other, the battleships pitching heavily in the short steep seas, while the light cruisers and torpedo-boats rolled and yawed. Would the 60 heavy guns have prevailed in the few minutes of contact, or would the same number of torpedoes and the fire of many light guns have been decisive?

The Emperor Wilhelm II inspecting *Seydlitz* after the Battle of the Dogger Bank (*Bundesarchiv*)

The battle-cruiser, *Moltke,* 19 August 1915: torpedo hit (see page 41) (*Author's collection*)

1915. An 8·8cm AA gun being hoisted on board *Seydlitz* (*Bundesarchiv*)

As the distance between the two battle cruiser forces diminished rapidly, another clash seemed inevitable, but now Fate intervened again. The Second Battle Squadron had mistaken the four-funnelled light cruisers for armoured ones, and Warrender informed Beatty that a German force evidently of large ships had passed him on an easterly course. This induced Beatty to reverse his course in order to overtake them, which gave Hipper enough time to draw the right conclusions from the signals and messages of his own side.

They included one from his own C.-in-C., which to his consternation put the German battle fleet more than 100 miles east of the position where he had counted on meeting it. The German battle cruisers now steered north for an hour and a half, and then northeast. In this way they passed far ahead of the two groups of British heavy ships. There were no further contacts, and all the ships returned to their ports, a number of the smaller ones being damaged by the seas.

Conclusions

Almost anything might have happened in these quickly changing and confusing situations. The German plan to overwhelm part of the Grand Fleet with the entire strength of the High Seas Fleet would probably have been successful, if the German C.-in-C. had kept to his original intention and waited at the appointed place for the return of his advanced forces. By not doing so he lost a great opportunity, and he was lucky not to lose a considerable part of his scouting groups.

On the bridge of *Seydlitz,* Admiral Hipper correctly evaluated the changing situations and directed his ships coolly and skillfully. On the British side, it was fortunate that the Second Battle Squadron did not encounter more than double the number of German battleships. On the other hand, the British were unlucky in that not a single unit of the bombardment force could be caught.

Christmas Surprise, 1914

The damage to *Seydlitz* was superficial and quickly repaired without docking. She was about to take over the normal watch in the Jade Estuary, when on the morning of 25 December 1914 a few British planes appeared. Three seaplane tenders had approached within 20 miles of Heligoland, and put 7 seaplanes on the calm seas. Two others would not operate. The planes proceeded to attack various targets in the German bases. No appreciable damage was caused but, as a Christmas surprise, the operation was most effective.

German aeroplanes and airships soon sighted and attacked the British ships. They missed all their targets, but prevented the tenders from hoisting in the seaplanes again. Their crews were rescued, some by British submarines standing by in the vicinity.

A fast German force could easily have overtaken the slow-moving seaplane tenders, but Admiral von Ingenohl decided against sending out the battle cruisers and torpedo-boats. He may have been influenced by repeated reports of the sighting of British submarines.

On 19 January 1915, a large British force approached within about 30 miles of Heligoland, but retreated again without taking any special action. At that time the strongest German battle squadron was in the Baltic for exercises, some other ships, including the battle cruiser *von der Tann,* were under repair, and the fleet as a whole was not ready for any considerable operation. Nevertheless, at the suggestion of his Chief-of-Staff, von Ingenohl decided to use the prevailing calm weather to send part of the Scouting Force (3 battle-cruisers, *Bluecher,* 4 light cruisers and 20 torpedo-boats) to the Dogger Bank. The object was to stop and search fishing and other vessels frequently sighted there, and, if possible, to surprise any British ships that might be encountered. There was indeed a surprise, but for the Germans—not the British. Quite unnecessarily, the German Fleet Command gave orders by wireless to Admiral Hipper in *Seydlitz* lying at anchor outside Wilhelmshaven. The very attentive British Intelligence service intercepted and decoded the message.

The Battle of the Dogger Bank, 24 January 1915

On the morning of 24 January 1915, when the German force approached the Dogger Bank, Admiral Beatty arrived there too. With him were the First and Second Battle Cruiser Squadrons and the First Light Cruiser Squadron, soon to be joined by

Welcoming home the commerce raider, *Moewe,* 4 March 1916. (See page 41) (*Bundesarchiv*)

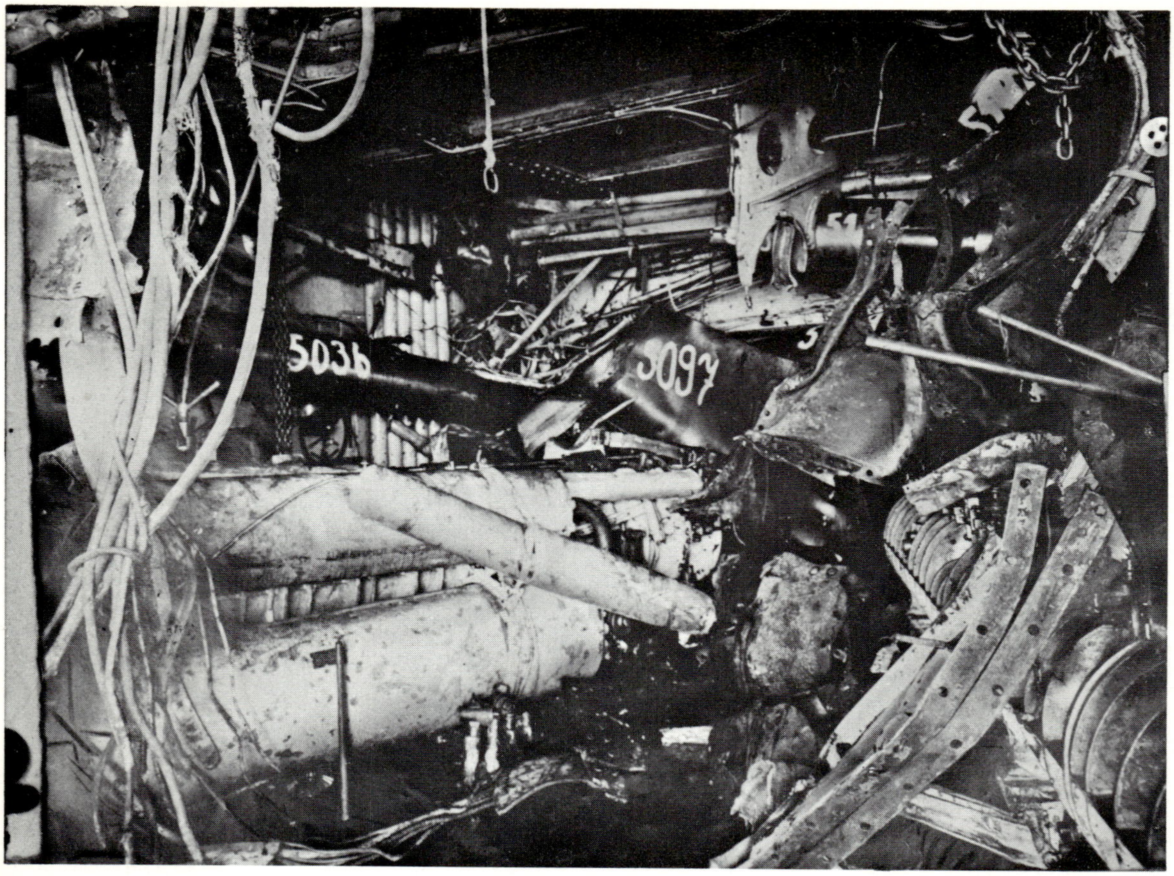

Seydlitz after mining, 24 April 1916. (No explanation of the four-figure numerals is possible) (*Bundesarchiv*)

the Harwich Force under Commodore Tyrwhitt. With 5 battle-cruisers, 7 light cruisers and 34 destroyers, the British were considerably stronger than the Germans.

A few minutes after 8 am, *Kolberg* and *Aurora* sighted each other and opened fire. Both ships were hit and both turned away to keep in touch with their neighbours. The German ship was anxious to avoid coming within range of the destroyers; and the British ship, within range of the torpedo-boats.

It was not yet full daylight, and Admiral Hipper first turned towards the direction of *Kolberg*, but he could see only gun flashes against the dark horizon. After receiving several reports on various groups of enemy ships, he turned away to gain time to form a clearer picture of the situation.

He gave orders to the light cruisers and torpedo-boats to take up station at the head of the line and to decrease their smoke. Although his speed never exceeded 21 knots, it proved difficult for the coal-burning torpedo-boats to execute both orders together.

Admiral Beatty followed on the starboard quarter of the German line, and increased speed from 24 to

Seydlitz firing, seen from the conning tower of her next-astern (*Bundesarchiv*)

Seydlitz at the Battle of Jutland, her ammunition of C turret burning after a direct hit (*Bundesarchiv*)

Seydlitz approaching Wilhelmshaven afte- the Battle of Jutland. Note her low free-board (*Bundesarchiv*)

Left:
SMS *Derfflinger*

Middle:
SMS *Moltke*

Right:
SMS *Goeben*

SMS SEYDLITZ is shown as she appeared at the Battle of Jutland on 31 May 1916. She was number three in the line which was led by Admiral Hipper in his flagship LUETZOW. SEYDLITZ was previously damaged in the battle, her draught for'd being increased by over fifteen feet.

D. Johnson © *Profile Publications Ltd.*

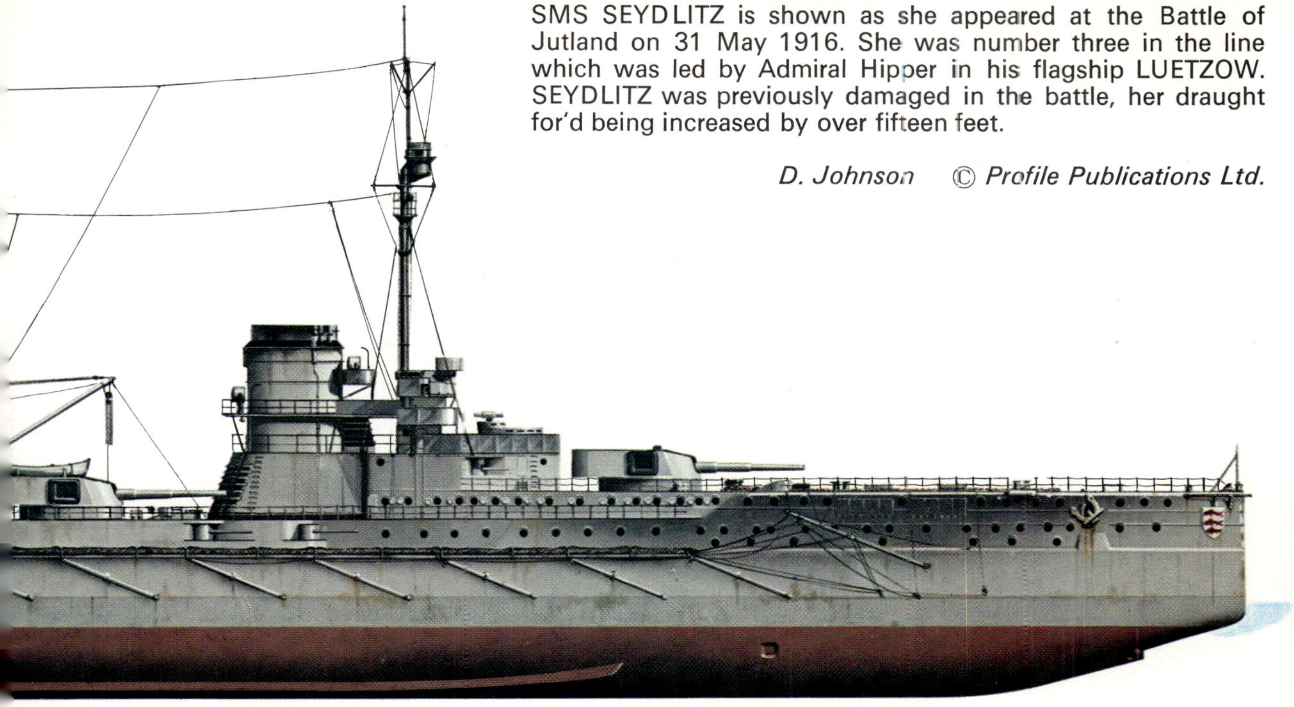

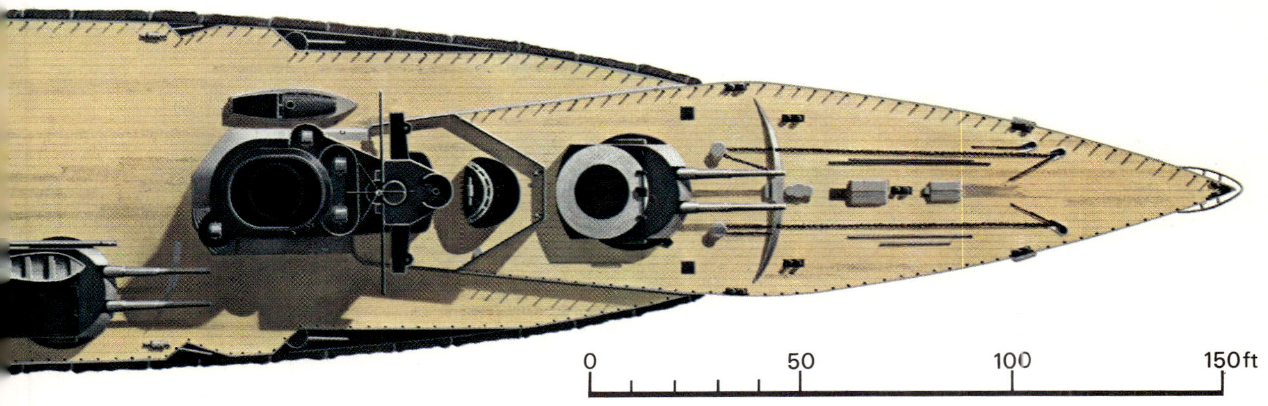

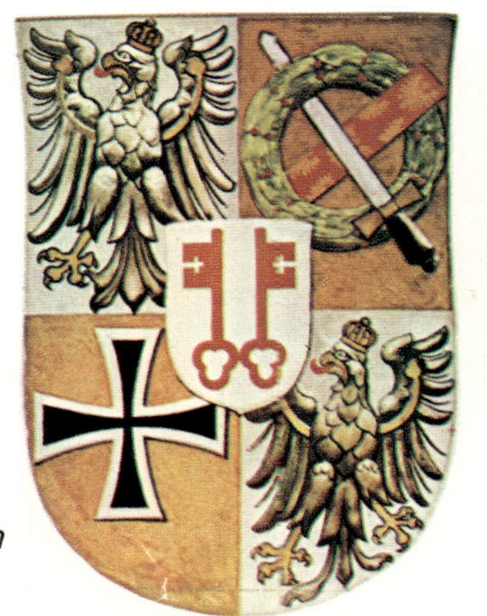

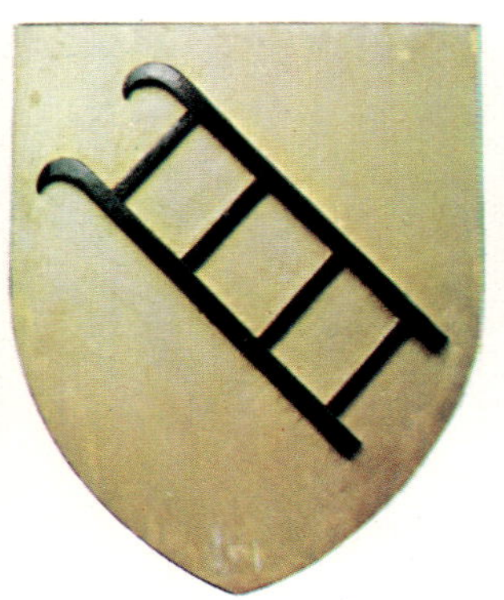

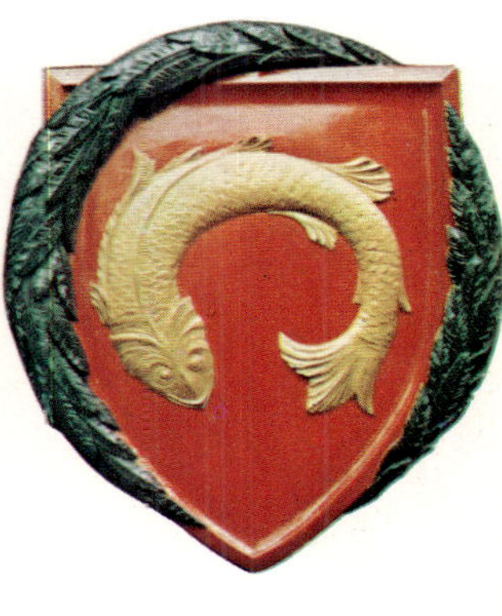

Left:
SMS *Bluecher*

Middle:
SMS *Luetzow*

Right:
SMS *Von Der Tann*

Seydlitz off Wilhelmshaven, 2 June 1916, tug and salvage steamer alongside (*Bundesarchiv*)

about 28 knots, which his older battle cruisers were unable to maintain. The distance decreased slowly, and the British ships started firing at 1000. Observation was very difficult, because a light wind from the east-north-east blew a dense pall of smoke in the direction of the British line. This was particularly unfavourable for the German gunnery, but Admiral Hipper decided to continue on this course.

The concentration of British ships was proof that the German plan had somehow leaked out, and that in all probability the Grand Fleet would not be far away. (Actually, although at sea, it was then 150 miles from the scene of action.) Hipper therefore had to try to gain time for his C.-in-C. to collect whatever was available of the battlefleet to come to his support.

In the meantime large silhouettes loomed over the horizon, and after some time, five battle cruisers could be distinguished, led by *Lion,* formed in quarter-line to port. Their fire, which they opened at a distance of 20,000m, was slow and deliberate. At first the Germans could not reply because the range was too great, but the British rapidly approached. When at 1011 Hipper hoisted the signal to open fire, only *Derfflinger* could comply with her 30·5cm battery. Immediately afterwards, *Bluecher* received the first hit on her fo'c'sle, but without significant damage. Distances now decreased, but were never less than 14,500m, and on average around 16,000m.

Seydlitz entering the Jade river after Jutland. From left to right: the pilot, Captain von Egidy, and the Officer of the Watch (injured) (*BfZ*)

DISASTER STRIKES 'SEYDLITZ'

Now *Seydlitz* received a shell on the fo'c'sle, and *Tiger* and *Lion* were also hit. Nevertheless, all ships continued to fire and to steam at high speed.

At 1043 *Seydlitz* was hit again, but this time with disastrous consequences. A 34·3cm shell pierced the barbette of the aftermost turret, and ignited some cartridges in the ammunition hoists (see plan). The crew in the loading chamber tried to escape. The flash passed through the open bulkhead door to the ammunition hoists of the next (superimposed) turret. Within seconds, 6000kg of powder caught fire, and flames shot mast high from both turrets. These were silenced and all their crews, 165 men being killed.

To the men on the bridges of the following ships and of *Seydlitz* herself, the fate of the flagship seemed to be sealed. Because he felt that she might blow up at any moment, her gunnery officer ordered *"Rapid fire"* for the remaining guns. Every 10 seconds a salvo now left the stricken ship.

In the meantime, down below, the Warrant Officer in charge of damage control and some of his assistants groped their way through heat and poisonous fumes to the valves for flooding the magazines. Already the large valves for operating them were red-hot, but the men nevertheless opened them, burning their hands severely. Sea water rushed in, and the immediate danger to the ship was over. The flames flickered over the two turrets and then disappeared, leaving smoke and steam pouring out of the blackened gun embrasures, while the watchers on the bridges shouted their relief.

The fierce fight continued, *Lion* being hit repeatedly,

although a shell that penetrated a powder magazine did not explode. Again *Lion* was hit because she offered the best target to the Germans, but it was now *Bluecher* that ran into grave difficulties.
Contrary to experience in previous operations, she was no longer able to maintain the speed of the flagship and dropped slowly astern, thus receiving heavier fire. At 1130 she was hit in her central ammunition transport installation which served all her six turrets. This unusual arrangement was unique to this ship and proved disastrous. About 40 cartridges were ignited, two turrets being put out of action immediately; most controls for handling the ship and for directing the fire of the guns were severely affected; her speed was reduced to 17 knots and subsequently to even less.
Bluecher now came under overwhelming fire and, though she still replied vigorously, she was finally halted shortly after noon.
By then *Lion* had been so heavily hit that she was compelled to slow down and haul out of the battle line. Her signal, *"Attack the enemy's rear"*, was misunderstood by the other battlecruisers, who all concentrated on *Bluecher.* This ship, still firing, put an attacking destroyer out of action, but then *Arethusa* launched two torpedoes. She only just avoided a torpedo from the *Bluecher,* who now slowly foundered after *Arethusa's* torpedoes found their target. 260 men of 1050 were picked up by the British.
For Hipper, it was a hard decision to leave *Bluecher* to her fate. However, in turning back he would probably have lost all his ships without being able to help her. He might have dealt with the battle cruisers, but he would have run into the torpedoes of the many British destroyers, and a damaged ship would have had no chance to escape. The critical state of *Seydlitz* and the fact that the German battleships had not yet left their anchorages, contributed to Hipper's decision. *Seydlitz* had, in fact, been hit twice, *Derfflinger* once, and *Moltke* not at all. *Lion* had received at least 11 hits, and *Tiger* two.
As a direct consequence of the Battle of the Dogger Bank, Admiral von Ingenohl was relieved from his position as C.-in-C. and retired. His successor was Admiral Pohl, Chief of the Admiral's Staff, an able officer but not an inspiring leader of a fleet.

Further Operations: The Baltic

Seydlitz was under repair until April 1915 and then went to the Baltic for exercises. In the North Sea, Admiral Pohl undertook several operations during the year, but he went never much more than 100 miles from Heligoland. The wireless discipline of his staff was bad, as it had been previously, in contrast to the Grand Fleet which was well served by W/T intelligence. The Grand Fleet at first put to sea whenever the Germans left port, but abandoned this practice later, when it was found that the German operations presented no threats at all.
In August 1915, the battle cruisers *Seydlitz, Moltke* and *von der Tann* were sent to the eastern Baltic. Here a force of older ships was about to enter the Gulf of Riga after thorough minesweeping. The battle cruisers were intended to give protection against fast Russian battleships, who might try to attack from the Gulf of Finland. The German crews always welcomed operations in the Baltic, although Russian mines and British submarines had to be respected there.
On 10 August, *von der Tann,* with the two other ships in the rear, destroyed Russian batteries on the island of Utoe at the entrance to the Gulf of Riga, and also fired at a Russian armoured cruiser. The latter, however, retired behind a group of rocky islands and reefs.
On 16 August, the British submarine, *E9,* sighted the battle cruisers, but was too far away to attack. On the following day, she was herself surprised on the surface, and salvoes from *Seydlitz* forced her to dive. On 19 August, HM Submarine, *E1,* fired a

Another view of *Seydlitz* in the lock at Wilhelmshaven; the absence of the guns can clearly be seen (*BfZ*)

Seydlitz after Jutland in the Wilhelmshaven lock, seen from astern (*BfZ*)

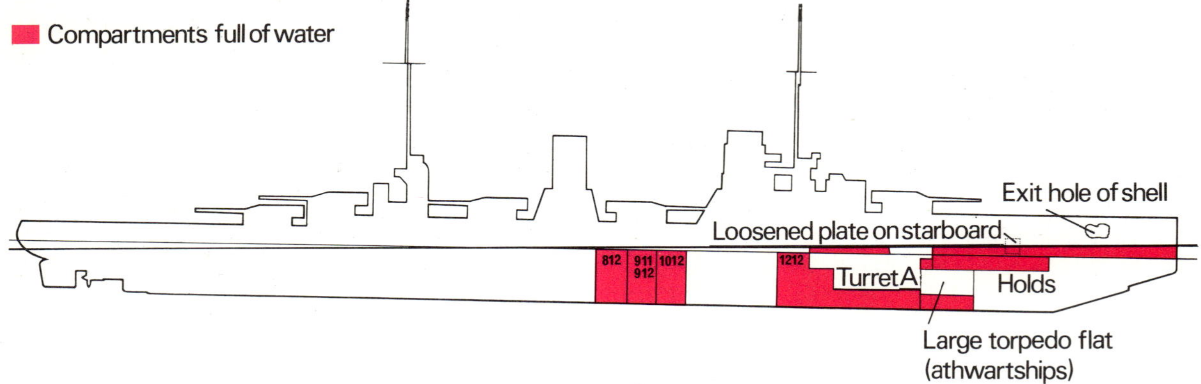

Seydlitz state on 31 May 1916 at 2300hrs after Battle of Jutland. Water in ship 2626 tons. Draught forward deeper by 2·54m. Draught aft deeper by 0·99m. Theoretical list 2° 5′ to starboard. Actual real list 2° to starboard.

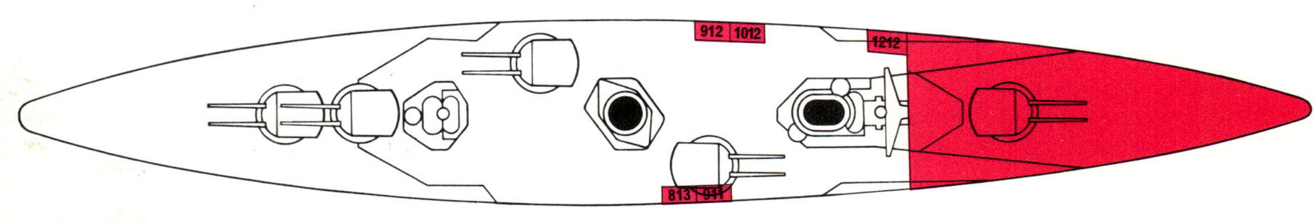

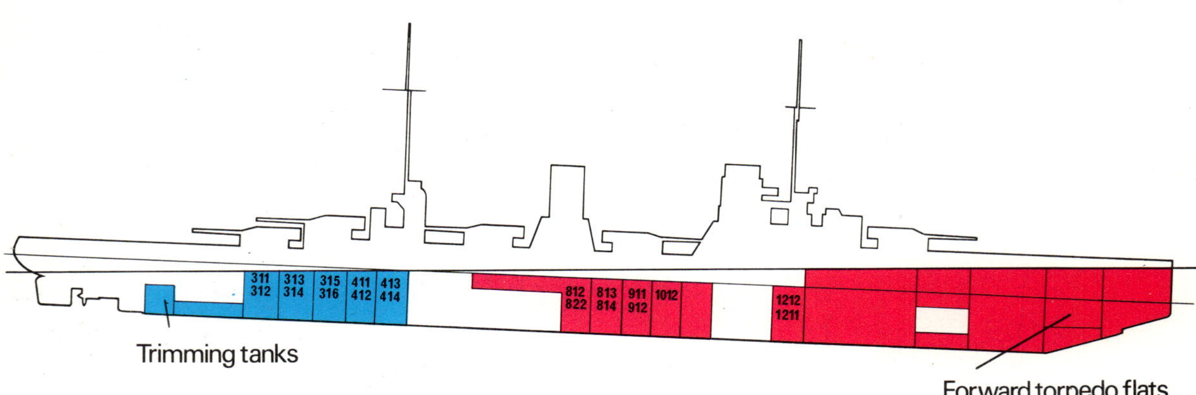

Seydlitz state on 1 June 1916 at 1900 hours. Most unfavourable state. Water in ship 5308 tons, Draught forward deeper by 4.74m. Draught aft deeper by 1·63m. Theoretical list 2° 5′ to port. Actual real list 8° to port.

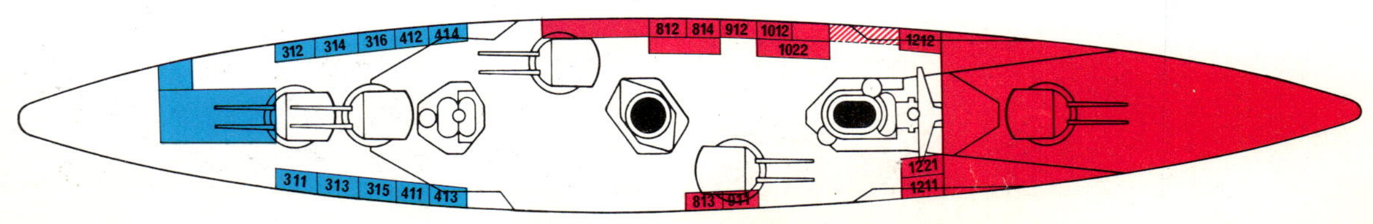

After Jutland in the lock at Wilhelmshaven: *Seydlitz* lists heavily. A battleship of the *Koenig* class is in the next lock; the battle cruiser, *Derfflinger,* is in the background, left; old ships are to the right (*Author's collection*)

Seydlitz after Jutland: hit No. 2. (*Einschussloch*=hole made by shell) (*Bundesarchiv*)

torpedo at *Seydlitz* at very close range. It passed ahead but hit *Moltke* cruising abeam of *Seydlitz. Moltke,* hit far forward, was flooded with about 1500 tons of water, but was not put out of action. Hipper took his squadron to the port of Danzig to have the damage inspected, and to replenish coal. A few days later he returned to the North Sea because the Riga operation had been broken off.

In February 1916, Admiral Pohl died of cancer. Vice-Admiral Reinhold Scheer, who had been in command of the most modern battle squadron, succeeded him. He was very popular and well known for his energy.

New Blood: Scheer Takes Over

It was therefore no surprise when Scheer decided on a more offensive use of the fleet. The Emperor at once agreed and confirmed the freedom of action of the new C.-in-C. before the assembled admirals and captains at Wilhelmshaven. A few days later, on the night of 3/4 March, Scheer sent all available forces, including *Seydlitz,* to the Horns Reef to meet the merchant raider, *Moewe.* She had suddenly returned after a long and successful cruise under Count Dohna, and the fact that Scheer did so much for the safety of a single ship made a strong impression on the whole fleet.

His next move was an operation in the southern North Sea, which coincided with a raid by three airships on British ports on the night of 5/6 March. The intention was to catch British light forces which were frequently seen in that area. This time strict wireless silence was observed, and it was not until the Scouting Forces led by Hipper in *Seydlitz,* reached the shipping route from the Netherlands to Lowestoft, that their presence was detected. The British Admiralty recalled the Harwich Force, the Grand Fleet left Scapa, but remained off the Scottish coast, and no contact was made.

Seydlitz after Jutland in the Wilhelmshaven shipyard. A crane lifts a 28cm gun (*BfZ*)

Seydlitz after Jutland: hit No. 3 under the fo'c'sle. Spt 141= frame (counting from aft); *Zwischendeck*=main-deck: *Batteriedeck*=battery deck—directly below the upper deck amidships (*Bundesarchiv*)

Seydlitz after Jutland : hit No. 4 on the fo'c'sle
(*Bundesarchiv*)

Seydlitz after Jutland : hit No. 5 *Einschuss*=entrance of shell
(*Bundesarchiv*)

Seydlitz after Jutland : hit No. 6 and torpedo hit. *Treffer*=hit
(*Bundesarchiv*)

Seydlitz after Jutland: hit No. 6. *Langaaplitterschott*= longitudinal splinter proof bulkhead. *Sprengpunkt ?*=bursting point ? *Gepanzertes Batteriedeck*=armoured battery deck. *Kasemattpanzerquerschott*=armoured transverse bulkhead of casemate (*Bundesarchiv*)

Seydlitz after Jutland : hit No. 5, below decks. The Armoured deck has been pierced (*Bundesarchiv*)

Seydlitz after Jutland : torpedo hit under the fo'c'sle, port side
(*Bundesarchiv*)

Seydlitz: B turret hit by large shell, 31 May 1916 (*Bundesarchiv*)

On 25 March 1916, the British replied with a seaplane raid on airship hangars with the Battle Cruiser and Harwich Forces in support. The British planes failed to reach their targets. Bombs from German planes hit none of the ships, but, in taking avoiding action, two destroyers collided, and *Medusa* was so extensively damaged that she had to be abandoned.

Scheer sent all available forces to sea, including the new battle cruiser, *Luetzow.* Contradictory reports by aircraft and a rising gale prevented the German heavy ships from pressing the pursuit, and only torpedo-boats gave chase. During the night the light cruiser *Cleopatra* sighted and rammed torpedo-boat, *G194. Undaunted* then ran into *Cleopatra* and was so badly damaged that she was brought back to England only with the greatest difficulty.

Seydlitz in dock after Jutland: hit No. 7, under the conning tower. On 1 or 2 June 1916, the leak was temporarily stopped with a pad of wood and soft material. The boiler and large hoses were put on board in the shipyard (*Bundesarchiv*)

Scheer did not desist. On 24 April, the High Seas Fleet left its bases for another raid on the English coast, this time to bombard Lowestoft. Hipper was ill, and Rear-Admiral Boedecker was in command of the Scouting Forces. During the afternoon, they passed through a channel which had been swept through a British minefield, but *Seydlitz* struck a mine which tore a hole of 90sq. m abreast of the torpedo flat (see plans). Admiral Boedecker transferred his flag to *Luetzow*, and carried out the bombardment without being intercepted. The Grand Fleet put to sea, but no contact was made.

Meanwhile, *Seydlitz* returned to Wilhelmshaven with 1400 cu.m of water inboard. She was still under repair when the fleet left port on 4 May, in order to forestall a move of the Grand Fleet towards Horns Reef. Again no contact was established.

On 22 May, repairs were finished but a test showed that the torpedo flat was not yet completely watertight. Since the middle of the month, Scheer had been ready for an operation to bombard Sunderland. A number of submarines were sent to strategic positions off the main British bases. Air reconnaissance was necessary and the presence of *Seydlitz* was essential.

Scheer therefore postponed the operation until 28 May, when *Seydlitz* was ready, but the weather had now become unfavourable for airships. On the other hand, the submarines were due to return on 1 June. Scheer therefore resolved to leave Sunderland for another time, and to make a sweep with light forces through the Skagerrak and Kattegat, with the battle fleet in the rear.

THE BATTLE OF JUTLAND

Early on 31 May, the Scouting Forces left the Jade, led by Hipper, this time in *Luetzow,* with *Seydlitz* as tactical number three. An hour later, the battle fleet followed, led by Scheer in *Friedrich der Grosse.* The Grand Fleet had already put to sea, because it

Seydlitz after Jutland: C turret (super-imposed), rear and front (*Bundesarchiv*)

was evident from the submarine activity and from a special code word signalled to the High Seas Fleet that something was in the wind.

In cool spring weather with a light breeze from the west, the two German groups moved northwards, with light cruisers and torpedo-boats screening ahead. Meanwhile the British Battle Fleet steered roughly east-south-east from Scapa Flow. The Battle Cruiser Force sailed from the Firth of Forth until 1415. It then turned north as pre-arranged to meet the Battle Fleet.

At a distance of about 40 miles, on slightly converging courses, Beatty and Hipper might have continued for some time. However, *Elbing,* on the extreme west of the German cruiser screen, sighted a steamer to the west and sent torpedo-boats *B109* and *B110* to investigate. When stopped the steamer, a neutral Dane, blew off steam. This was noticed by *Galatea* and *Phaeton,* on the extreme east of the British screen. The two cruisers also investigated and the first shots were exchanged. The battle cruiser forces then altered course to give support.

When they sighted each other, Hipper turned south east to draw Beatty towards the main German fleet. Hipper had 5 battle cruisers, while Beatty had 6 battle cruisers with 4 fast and powerful battleships of the *Queen Elizabeth* class somewhat in the rear. This gave Hipper the lee gauge and made conditions perfect for the gunnery of his ships; the Germans steamed in line-ahead. Beatty, eager for the fight, approached in quarterline at such an angle that he passed quickly through the range most advantageous for his heavier guns. At 1548 the range had fallen to about 15,000m, and both sides opened fire almost simultaneously.

Seydlitz fought a duel with *Queen Mary,* and, at the end of the line, *von der Tann* engaged *Indefatigable. Lion, Princess Royal* and *Tiger* were all soon hit, and *Seydlitz* then received two shells. Again C-barbette was hit, and C-turret put out of action, but the safety measures installed after the Battle of the Dogger Bank confined the damage to the stricken turret and kept down the losses of its personnel. At 1600, *Lion* received a similar hit but was saved by Major Harvey of the Royal Marines, the turret commander who, although mortally wounded, ordered the magazines to be flooded.

Three minutes later, *Indefatigable* was squarely hit by two salvoes in quick succession and blew up. However, the Fifth Battle Squadron now found the range with their 38cm guns and subjected the rear of the German line to a well-directed fire. Fumes and smoke, also coming from the cruisers and the destroyers, made observation very difficult. *Tiger* fired several salvoes at *Seydlitz,* when a shell from *Queen Mary* put a 15cm casemate out of action. *Derrflinger* then mistook *Queen Mary* for the second ship and, at distances decreasing to 13,000m, a number of salvoes from the two German ships found their target on the *Queen Mary.* At 1627 she blew up, turned over and disappeared with her propellers still turning.

Destroyers of the Thirteenth Flotilla and torpedo-boats of the Ninth Flotilla now went into the attack and met between the battle lines. In the mêlée that followed, *V27* and *V29* were sunk, as well as *Nomad. Nestor* was brought to a halt and sunk shortly afterwards by German battleships. The main German fleet was now sighted by *Southampton* who was stationed ahead of the British battle cruisers. The long line of German battleships, surrounded by numerous cruisers and torpedo-boats, came as a complete surprise to the British. As a result of faulty intelligence, it was believed that the German battle fleet was still in port. Beatty had to reverse course, and the Fifth Battle Squadron followed under very heavy fire.

Hipper also turned to take station ahead of the

Seydlitz after Jutland : hit on gun of E (port) turret (*Bundesarchiv*)

Another view of C turret after Jutland (*Bundesarchiv*)

leading battleship *Koenig* (Vice-Admiral Behncke). In doing so, the battle cruisers ran into a salvo of torpedoes from the British destroyers. *Seydlitz* avoided the first, but could not turn quickly enough when the next line of bubbles was sighted. The torpedo hit forward, again abreast the torpedo flat. The armoured torpedo bulkhead withstood the explosion, and the fighting value of the ship was hardly impaired. She could even keep up with the speed of the flagship, *Luetzow.*

Seydlitz after Jutland : hit on C turret (super-imposed) (*Bundesarchiv*)

Beatty now drew ahead to lead the Germans towards the Grand Fleet. Under difficult circumstances, Jellicoe succeeded in forming his line of battle in such a way that the German van came under tremendous fire. Visibility now favoured the British. The German battle cruisers were repeatedly hit without being able to answer. They finally turned away and, after a complete circle, again took station directly ahead of *Koenig.* While trying to finish off the disabled light cruiser *Wiesbaden,* the old armoured cruisers, *Warrior* and *Defence,* came too close to the German battle cruisers. The secondary battery of *Seydlitz* took *Defence* under fire, who at 1822 blew up in a gigantic pillar of fire and smoke. *Warrior* escaped behind *Warspite* whose helm temporarily jammed. Both ships were heavily damaged, and *Warrior* had to be towed away and finally abandoned.

Under the British fire the German van hauled slowly round from north-east to south-east. About 1830, *Invincible,* the flagship of the Third Battle Cruiser Squadron, which had joined the fight from the east, suddenly became clearly visible. Under the concentrated fire of the German battle cruisers, she blew up after a few minutes.

Admiral Scheer, now extricated his fleet by a complete battle turn of all his ships, and the fire soon ceased. Jellicoe turned by divisions to follow the retreating enemy. Scheer felt that he would find himself in a most dangerous situation if he left the initiative entirely to his able opponent. By another battle turn of his ships, he again reversed course and headed for the British line. At the same time, he ordered all his torpedo-boats to attack, and the battle cruisers to support them regardless of consequences.

In *Seydlitz,* when the captain passed this signal (well-known from exercises), to all battle stations, he was answered by a thunderous cheer from his men. With *Derfflinger* in the lead, because *Luetzow* was already too damaged to maintain her position, the battle cruisers turned towards the British gun flashes. Again they came under a terrific fire and received many hits and more near misses, which shook the great ships like gigantic hammer blows. Then, at the threat of a massed torpedo attack by 30 on-coming torpedo-boats, Jellicoe wisely turned

Seydlitz: cross-section showing details of armour, as in photograph A ; coal bunkers are shown 'dotted'

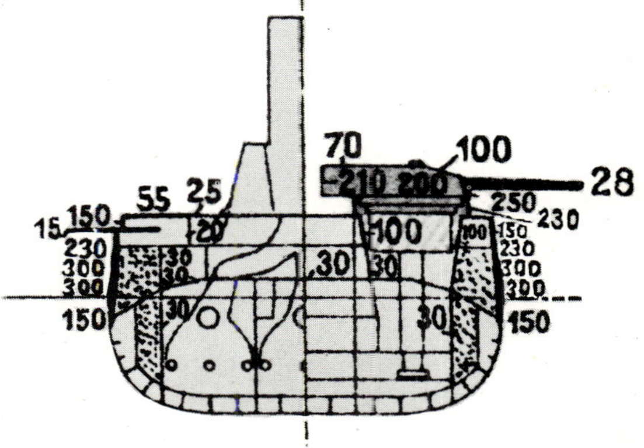

Seydlitz at anchor in the ice of the Jade, February 1917 (*Bundesarchiv*)

his divisions away. Scheer ordered a complete battle turn for the third time, the fleets separated, and the day battle was over.

At dusk there was a short contact, and *Seydlitz* was hit again. Then, on almost parallel southerly courses, both fleets took up night cruising formations, the Grand Fleet by divisions, with destroyers behind. The High Seas Fleet formed a somewhat straggling line ahead, which literally hacked its way through the British destroyers. The torpedo-boats searched in vain for the British battleships. *Seydlitz* was too damaged to keep station and proceeded on her own.

In addition to one torpedo hit, the ship had received 21 heavy and 2 medium shells. 98 men were killed and 55 wounded. Four heavy and two medium guns were out of action, and one third of her electrical capacity gone. Cables, leads, ducts, and vents were cut or broken, and the gyro compass worked only intermittently. The magnetic compass proved unreliable, and there was no electric light in many vital places. Steam was leaking, the aerials were shot through, and the torpedo net, trailing in the water, threatened to foul the propellers.

Repair parties worked their hardest. Thanks to previous battle drill carried out blindfolded (called 'blind man's buff'), specialists succeeded in finding switches in the dark. They made new connections which they improvised on the spot. The ship was still a fighting unit.

The worst headache was the great number of minor leaks from warped covers and bulkhead doors, sprung seams and loose rivets, which could not be effectively repaired. In spite of desperate efforts, the water slowly gained, and the forward part of the ship sank deeper into the sea. Speed had to be consequently reduced. On the way to Horns Reef dark shapes were suddenly made out in the calm night, which were soon recognised as British battleships.

Seydlitz, battle cruiser. Photo of an official document in the Military Archives at Freiburg; Gun calibres in centimetres; armour denoted in dark colour; armoured torpedo bulkhead denoted by diagonal lines

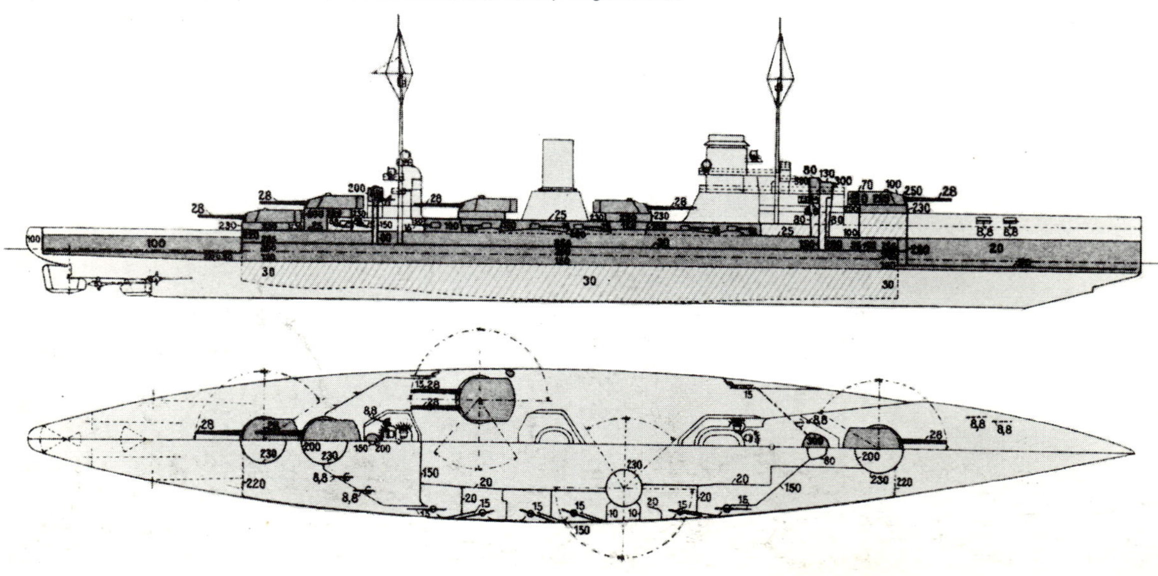

Fighting was out of the question. Captain von Egidy therefore gave the order to use the British recognition signal, 'PL', which the German torpedo-boats had picked up and reported at the first contact. It was duly answered by the British flagship, and *Seydlitz* turned away, hiding behind her own smoke, until she could resume her course.

When dawn broke, the middle 'fish' of her coat of arms could be seen 'swimming'. The smallest wave broke over the fo'c'sle, and some compartments aft had to be counterflooded to decrease the draught forward. This helped, but diminished what little buoyancy remained. Somehow, the ship reached the Horns Reef which she found by scraping over its western tip. Here she was assisted first by a light cruiser, and later by tugs and salvage vessels. In the lee of the cruiser, *Seydlitz* completed the last part of her perilous return to the Jade in a rising sea. Even taking her up the shallow river and through the locks was no easy task. On 3 June she entered the shipyard for extensive repairs which lasted until the end of September.

1917. *Seydlitz* proceeding at high speed in line ahead: the first scouting group (*BfZ*)

Last Phases of the War at Sea

Seydlitz joined the Scouting Forces again in November 1916. She therefore missed the operation in August 1916, when Scheer set out again to bombard Sunderland. However, the target was not reached because of the approach of the Grand Fleet. An incorrect report from a reconnoitring airship prevented another fleet engagement. The final result of the Battle of Jutland was the German unrestricted submarine warfare which began on 1 February 1917. However, some of the fleet were always at sea, or available at short notice in the outer anchorages. These were able to protect the minesweepers and to make certain that the submarines could penetrate the mine belt which the British had laid round the German Bight of the North Sea. No larger operations were therefore undertaken with the exception of an attempt to surprise a convoy sailing from Norway to Scotland.

The Scouting Forces, including *Seydlitz*, were in the van as usual. On the morning of 24 April 1918, in clear, calm weather they almost reached the latitude of Bergen in Norway, but there was not a single enemy ship in sight. Intelligence had been inadequate. Suddenly the battle cruiser *Moltke* broke down completely. A propeller shaft snapped, and the propeller fell to the bottom of the sea. The turbine 'ran away', and before it was automatically stopped, a large cast-iron wheel outside the turbine casing flew to pieces, smashed a condenser and cut steam and water pipes. Salt got into all the boilers, which had to be drawn and refilled with fresh water. This took many hours, and the ship of 23,000 tons had to be towed right across the North Sea. W/T silence had necessarily to be broken, but the Grand Fleet did not intervene.

SMS 'Seydlitz': An Historic Ship

Preparations for the next operation at the end of October 1918 resulted in mutinies in several ships. *Seydlitz* was not involved in this, but she was

Seydlitz on passage to her internment at Scapa Flow, November 1918 (*BfZ*)

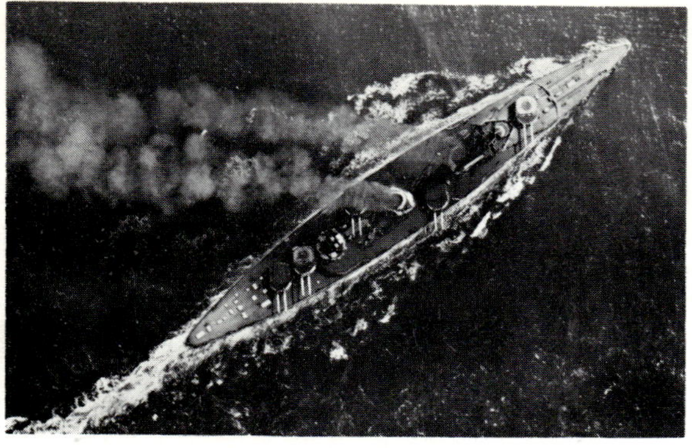

Seydlitz from above: her turrets are ready to open fire on a bearing of Green 120. September 1918 (*Bundesarchiv*)

Seydlitz scuttled at Scapa Flow (*BfZ*)

included in the 16 heavy ships interned at Scapa Flow, together with 8 light cruisers and 50 torpedo-boats. With most of these ships, *Seydlitz* was scuttled by her skeleton crew on 21 June 1919. After two hours she capsized and sank. Nine years later she was raised, towed away and broken up.
A heavy cruiser launched in 1939 was also named *Seydlitz,* but never finished. The men of the old battle cruiser who are still alive continue to keep in touch with each other and to cherish the memory of their well-loved *Seydlitz.*

Warship Series Editor: JOHN WINGATE, DSC

SMS 'SEYDLITZ'

Fiscal Year authorised	1909
Builder	Blohm & Voss, Hamburg
Laid down	4.2.1911
Launching	30.3.1912
Date of Commissioning	22.5.1913
Construction costs	44·6 million gold marks

Dimensions: Length overall 200m
Beam 28·5m

Draught: With 1000 tons coal 8·24m
With 3600 tons coal (total fuel capacity) 9m

Complement: (Including Admiral's Staff) 1143

Armour Plating: Quarterdeck 150/150mm
Side armour 0-100, 300, 100mm
Citadel 265mm

Horizontal armour plating: Upper deck and armoured deck 30-80mm with chamfers 50mm

Underwater protection: Torpedo bulkhead 45mm
SA:
Barbettes 250mm
Turrets 250-70mm
MA:
Casemates 150mm
Turret mast, forward 300mm
Turret mast, aft 200mm

Machinery: 2×marine turbines on 4 propellers
27 marine boilers (coal)
Output 67,000s.h.p.
Speed 26·5kn (during trials 89,738s.h.p.=29·12kn)

Armament: 10×28cm naval guns L/50 etc as *Moltke* class (q.v.)
12×15cm naval guns
L/45 in casemates
12, later 10, then from 1916 none×8·8cm naval guns
From 1916, 2×8·8cm
4×50cm torpedo tubes (1 port-stern, 2 side, 1 bow, all submerged)
With this single-ship class, the design of which was completed at the beginning of 1910, the conception of the *Moltke* class was maintained. With the same armament in the same arrangement, the speed was only increased by 1 knot, which resulted in increased stability. The correctness of this design was proved twice during the war. Finally the improved seaworthiness should be mentioned; a visible sign of this was the increased height of the foredeck by one deck, as compared with her predecessors.
From 1914, spotter-top on foremast. On removal of the 8·8cm naval guns, their gun-ports etc were welded shut. After that, 8·8cm HA on raised after deck. Towards the end, the heavy derricks were stowed on the upper deck and a light derrick was fitted to the after ventilator.

SMS 'SEYDLITZ': Operational History

28 August 1914	Unsuccessful counter-attack against British battle cruiser formation which had penetrated the German Bight.
3 November 1914	Shelling of Yarmouth (assault 'J1').
16 December 1914	Shelling of Hartlepool (assault 'J2').
24 January 1915	Battle of Dogger Bank (received two heavy hits, both after turrets burned out, heavy personnel losses).
25 April 1916	Struck a mine during the advance for the attack on Lowestoft/Yarmouth; retreated after shipping 1400 tons of water.
31 May 1916	Battle of Jutland, sinking *Queen Mary. Seydlitz* suffered 21 heavy, 2 medium hits, also torpedo hit by British destroyer *Petard,* D and E turrets burned out; in spite of having shipped more than 5300 tons of water, returned under own steam sailing astern; in the end, only 2·5m freeboard forward. Repaired in Wilhelmshaven; ready for action again 16 September 1916.
5 November 1916	Assault as far as west coast of Denmark.
23 April 1918	Assault as far as Stavanger.
24 November 1918-21 June 1919	Interned at Scapa Flow where she was scuttled by the crew on 21 June 1919. Raised on 2 November 1928. Broken up in Rosyth by 1930.

Enterprise in October 1961 with her crew mustered on deck with three C-1 Traders aft on the flight deck (*US Navy, PHC Mowry*)

USS ENTERPRISE
(CVAN-65) Nuclear Attack Carrier
by Commander W. H. Cracknell USN

The largest combat ship ever constructed and the first nuclear-powered surface combatant in the world, USS *Enterprise* (CVAN-65), celebrated in 1971 its tenth anniversary since commissioning. During those ten years this great ship has compiled an impressive operational record and has more than proved the many advantages nuclear power gives to a warship. She has more than justified the additional cost of nuclear power over fossil-fueled propulsion by her operational readiness, reaction speed, increased size of her air wing and less reliance on the tether of the fleet replenishment train to name but a few.

The United States Navy currently has two additional nuclear carriers under construction and is fighting for approval of a third. But in the ten year interval since *Enterprise* was commissioned two conventional carriers were built by the United States, USS *America* (CVA-66) and USS *Kennedy* (CVA-67). Although the US Navy desired these two carriers to be also nuclear-powered, a cost-conscious Department of Defense deemed it not to be—a decision that will no doubt prove to be 'false' economics.

Her eight nuclear reactors steamed *Enterprise* 200,000 miles in her first three years of commissioned service before they needed recoring. She has completed five combat tours in the waters off Vietnam, steamed around the world at high sustained speed without replenishment of any kind and suffered a fire and explosions of disastrous proportions.

Affectionately known as *'The Big E'*, as was her famous World War II namesake, *Enterprise* is a ship of superlatives. Carrying a crew and air wing of over 5000 men her versatility is even more impressive today than when she was first commissioned.

Forebears

It is the practice in the US Navy to name attack carriers after battles, famous men or famous ships in US history. It is from the latter that USS *Enterprise's* (CVAN-65) name was derived. She is the eighth ship in American naval history to be so named. Her predecessors were:

1. Sloop 'Enterprise': 12 guns

Captured by General Benedict Arnold's force from the British on Lake Champlain on 18 May 1775, the first *Enterprise* was a 70-ton sloop with a crew of 50 men. She participated in the engagement of Valcour Island and after assisting in harassing British efforts to march from Canada through New York State, she was finally burned to prevent capture on 7 July 1777.

2. Schooner 'Enterprise': 8 guns

Originally a successful privateer sailing under a *Letter of Marque* from the state of Maryland she was purchased by the Continental Congress 20 December 1776. As a Continental Navy ship this 25 ton schooner served mainly in Chesapeake Bay, convoying transports, scouting British ship movements and interdicting enemy supply traffic across the Bay. She was apparently returned to the Maryland Council of Safety in February 1777.

3. Schooner 'Enterprise': 12 guns

Built in Baltimore, Maryland at a cost of $16,240 this 135 ton schooner had a length of 84ft 7in; a beam of 22ft 6in; a depth of hold of 10ft; armament of 12 long 6-pounders; and a complement of 70.

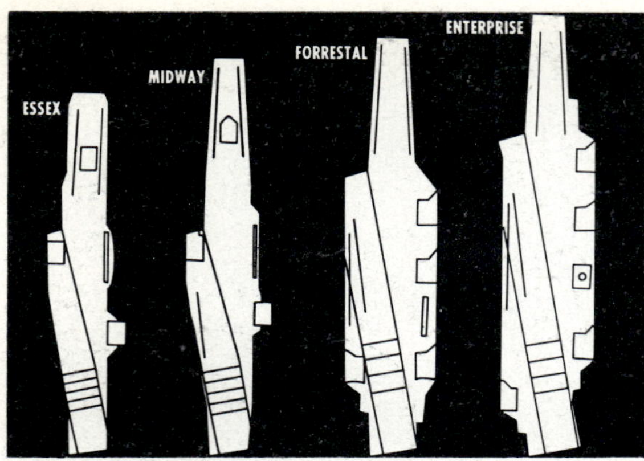

A comparative diagram of the relative flight deck sizes of all four attack carrier classes currently operating in the US Navy (*US Navy*)

Enterprise under construction at Newport News Shipbuilding and Drydock Co 17 July 1959

Known as 'The Lucky Little *Enterprise*' she served in the US Navy from 1799 until lost at Little Curaco 9 July 1823. During the Quasi-War with France (1799-1801) she recaptured eleven US merchantmen and captured eight French privateers. She served with the Mediterranean Squadron from 1801 to 1807 during which time she fought numerous engagements in the Wars with the Barbary Coast pirates. Many men who were to become famous in US Naval history served aboard 'The Lucky Little *Enterprise*' during this period—Decatur, Hull, Porter, and Lawrence, to mention a few. Rebuilt and carrying 16 guns she distinguished herself in the War of 1812 by capturing the British brig *Boxer*. It was in 1823, while serving in the Caribbean searching out smugglers, pirates and slavers, that she ran aground and was wrecked without loss or injury to her crew.

4. Schooner 'Enterprise': 10 guns
Built in the New York Navy Yard she was launched 26 October 1831. This 195 ton schooner's specifications were: length of over 88ft; beam of 23ft 5in, depth of hold 10ft; armament of ten 24 and 9 pounders; and complement of 72. She participated in suppressing the Africa Slave trade and served at various times on the Brazil, East India and Pacific Stations. She was sold in 1845.

5. Corvette 'Enterprise': 6 guns
A wooden steam corvette with auxiliary sails, she was built in the Portsmouth Navy Yard and was commissioned 16 March 1877. Her specifications were: displacement of 1375 tons; length of 185ft between perpendiculars; beam of 35ft; depth of hold of 16ft 2in; speed 11·4 knots; armament of one 11in smooth bore, four 9in broadside guns, one 60-pounder pivot and a short Gatling gun; and a complement of 184. She served with the Mediterranean, West Indies and North Atlantic squadrons. She was also used extensively in survey work and as a cadet training ship—the last seventeen years of her career she was on loan to the State of Massachusetts for this purpose. She was stricken from the Navy List and sold in 1909.

6. Motor Patrol Boat 'Enterprise': 1 gun
Originally built as a yacht, this 16 ton vessel was purchased by the Navy on 6 December 1916. She carried a single one-pounder and a machine-gun and a crew of eight. *Enterprise* number six was transferred to the Bureau of Fisheries on 2 August 1919.

7. Carrier 'Enterprise' (CV6)
'The Big E' was one of three fast carriers of the *Yorktown* Class (see Warship *Profile No. 3,* USS *Hornet*). Probably the hardest worked and the most famous ship in the US Navy during World War II, *Enterprise* number 7 was built by Newport News Shipbuilding and Drydock Company of Newport News, Virginia and commissioned 12 May 1938. With an overall length of 809·5ft, extreme width of 95·3ft, maximum draft of 29ft, standard displacement of 19,800 tons, speed greater than 30 knots and an air group of 85-100 planes, *'Big E'* and her sister *Yorktown* and near sister *Hornet* were the first large carriers built as such from the keel up. She participated in almost every major engagement of the Pacific War earning 19 battle stars (more than any other ship in the US Navy), the Presidential Unit Citation and the Navy Unit Commendation. She served as Admiral Halsey's flagship in the early part of the war and her aircraft compiled a most impressive toll of enemy ships, aircraft and shore installations. *Enterprise* was decommissioned in 1947 and sold for scrap 1 July 1958.

US Navy Carrier Classifications
Since 1 October 1952 the US Navy has classified its fast, large attack carriers as CVAs (Attack Aircraft Carriers). The CVS (Anti-Submarine Support Aircraft Carrier) classification was added 8 July 1953. The CVAN (Attack Aircraft Carrier Nuclear Powered) classification was established 29 May 1956 with the introduction of the new *Enterprise*.

All the commissioned ships of the US Navy assigned a primary mission of carrying and operating aircraft presently carry one of these three classifications.

Enterprise during final stages of completion 25 September 1960. The temporary sheds on the flight deck cover the after two catapult pits (*US Navy, PHC Olson*)

The Genesis

The US Navy came out of World War II as the largest and most powerful navy the world had ever seen. With the war won and the added insurance of the atomic bomb, the military might of the Western world was quickly demobilized. As the Cold War became a fact in the late forties, military strategists and tacticians began earnestly to look into what type of military forces were needed to deter and counter the Communist World's threat and thrust.

It was under these circumstances that the famous 'Revolt of the Admirals' occurred in 1948-49. From the experiences of the War, the United States established the Department of Defense and the Joint Chiefs of Staff. Along with this reorganization the US Air Force was established as a separate and equal partner with the Army and the Navy. A traumatic debate arose out of this reorganization, as proponents of the new Air Force pushed for control of Naval and Marine Air.

The Navy eventually won out, basing its arguments on the uniqueness of naval air operations and the absolute necessity of subordinating Naval Air to the Navy. This was required to ensure control of the airspace over the sea, a necessity if the Navy was to control the sea itself. The Navy policy makers pointed out how successful the carrier/amphibious operations were in the Pacific. It was also noted that the very policy of complete control of all military air, for which the Air Force advocates were arguing, had been disastrous for the British Fleet Air Arm while under control of the RAF from 1918 to 1937.

Arguments of History Revived

Many military strategists of this period felt that, with the advent of the intercontinental bomber and the total destructive power of the atom bomb, naval air and, in fact, navies in general were an anachronism. They argued that the day of the carrier had passed and that it was destined to follow the fate of the battleship a decade earlier. In this technological age future wars, hot or cold, would be seldom fought with the unaltered tactics or weapons of the past; but naval planners felt that the need for navies and the carrier were just as important in strategic planning as ever before.

The opponents and proponents of naval air power came together in a mighty clash in the controversey over whether the US Navy should continue to build

Three of *Enterprise*'s four screws are visible in this view taken in drydock at Portsmouth, Virginia 11 October 1969. The rudders can be seen just aft of each screw (*US Navy, PH3 Lewis*)

its first post-war carrier—the 65,000 ton USS *United States* (CVA-58). This fight for the limited military budget dollars brought the Air Force and Navy into a head-on confrontation. The Navy lost and a number of high ranking naval officers lost their positions or retired. The position that the B-36 strategic bomber force was all the deterrent the United States needed won out over the Navy's mobility and flexibility arguments. In light of the facts at the time that no other navy in the world could hope to challenge the United States' control of the sea and that no other country possessed the atomic bomb, the decision was not surprising. In 1950 the Navy's active inventory of large carriers had dropped to seven.

Carriers needed

The next year brought the outbreak of the Korean War. There is no doubt that the protective umbrella furnished by strategic bombers during the forties and fifties contributed greatly in deterring large scale war, but no B-36s dropped bombs in Korea. The peninsular position of Korea was conducive to the application of seapower and again the attack carrier proved its versatility and value. Jets were operated in combat on a routine basis from carrier decks for the first time off Korea.

The success of the carrier in the Korean War, the Soviet Union becoming a nuclear power in 1953, the emerging pattern of Communist insurgency in developing nations, and the rapidly rising Soviet submarine threat combined to give the attack carrier a reprieve.

'Forrestal' Class

On 30 July 1951 Congress approved the construction of a large carrier that was destined to become USS *Forrestal* (CVA-59). Its design benefitted from the lessons of World War II and the Korean War, the extensive design studies for the ill-fated USS *United States*, and the operational experience of the extensively modified *Essex* class carriers then serving with the Fleet.

Incorporated into her design were the angled flight deck, four steam catapults, the mirror-landing system and armored flight deck—all British innovations. Four deck-edge elevators, modular Combat Information Centers (CIC), extensive radar fits and greatly increased size and power were included to provide a platform to support foreseeable naval air operations for the next thirty years.

Forrestal was commissioned 1 October 1955. Displacing 59,650 tons, she had an overall length of 1036ft, a width of 252ft (first combatant designed that could not transit the Panama Canal), a speed of over 30 knots, rated horsepower over 200,000, a complement of 3500 (including air group), and a flight deck area of nearly four acres.

Between 1954 and 1968 four carriers of the *Forrestal* class and four near sisters of the *Kitty Hawk* class joined the US Navy.

On numerous occasions since the Korean War the

A view of *Enterprise's* spacious hangar deck looking forward (*US Navy*)

attack carrier has proven its value and usefulness—the Lebanon Crisis, the Taiwan Straits confrontation, the Cuban Quarantine, the Dominican Crisis, and the Vietnam War.

In 1967, during the peak of operations off Vietnam, the US Navy was operating a fleet of sixteen attack carriers, maintaining at least two carriers continually with the Sixth Fleet in the Mediterranean and five with the Seventh Fleet in the Far East. This force comprised the nuclear powered *Enterprise*, eight *Forrestal/Kitty Hawks*, two *Midways* (a third was undergoing extensive modernisation) and the other five were much modified members of the World War II *Essex* class.

WHY NUCLEAR POWER?

Unlimited Range at High Speed

With the highly successful application of nuclear power to the submarine, beginning with the USS *Nautilus* (SSN-571) in 1955, the Navy then considered using atomic power to propel its surface ships. The carrier was the obvious choice for the initial installation.

Although the first nuclear powered carrier was estimated to cost about half again as much as its fossil-fueled counterpart, many advantages accrued to the nuclear carrier.

The greatly increased combat effectiveness of the nuclear powered carrier is its most obvious asset. Continual high speed cruising and virtually unlimited range are its greatest advantage in both the strategic and tactical sense. The ship could move about the globe more quickly and stay on station for much longer periods of time while maintaining a high sustained speed, making it less vulnerable to detection and air or submarine attack. The power plant's superior ability to accelerate or decelerate gives the ship a much increased safety margin in combat, flight operations, and rules-of-the-road situations. Additional auxiliary power and electrical demands can be made upon the power plant with little regard to fuel consumption.

Captain Vincent P. DePoix, USN, the first commanding officer of *Enterprise* in his chair on the bridge. He's now Vice-Admiral DePoix, Commander US Second Fleet (*US Navy*)

Extra space

In a nuclear-powered carrier, the space required for black oil storage on a conventional carrier can be utilized for greater aircraft fuel storage (the *Enterprise* can carry twice as much as the *Forrestal* class), more armament and additional spares and general stores. Flight and hangar decks no longer have to give up valuable space to uptakes and stacks. This space can be utilised for aircraft handling and parking areas as well as providing more crew and shop spaces on the lower decks. The *Enterprise* carries an additional attack squadron because of this bonus. The absence of a funnel allows the installation of the highly advanced 360°, fixed, phased array, radar antenna carried by *Enterprise.*

Enterprise churning up a large wake and bow wave as she turns hard-a-starboard during her shakedown cruise 10 February 1962

(*US Navy, PH1 Williams*)

Combat servicability

Besides the protection of her larger air wing and speed and manoeuvrability potential, the nuclear-powered carrier has several other advantages in combat. The absence of vulnerable large uptakes contributes to the overall strength of the ship's structure. With no firerooms depending on volumes of outside air for operation, the ship can be completely sealed against atomic radiation, and biological or chemical attack.

Flight operations

The lack of stack gases gives pilots unobscured visibility and decreased turbulence while landing. The lack of corrosive smoke also contributes greatly to topside cleanliness. Topside surfaces do not have to be painted as frequently, and antennas and aircraft have greatly reduced corrosion problems.

The reactor can furnish all the steam necessary for the steam catapults with no effect on its ability to propel the ship.

Disadvantages

The initial installation of nuclear-power in a carrier did have several disadvantages, some of which have been overcome to a degree with the advance of technology. The costs, both initial and operational, were significantly higher. Development and research accounted for much of the initial cost increase, but larger machinery spaces and additional, more highly trained personnel were required than in a conventionally powered ship. The requirements for training, construction, and maintenance facilities to meet the particular needs of nuclear-power contributed to additional costs.

As long as nuclear ships had to operate with fossil-fuelled vessels, the nuclear ship would be tied to the fuel limitations of the conventional ships.

USS 'ENTERPRISE'

Congress approved the advance procurement items and design for the first nuclear-powered carrier in Fiscal 1957 appropriations. The Atomic Energy Commission's Bettis Atomic Power Laboratory in Pittsburgh, Pennsylvania, in co-operation with the Navy, developed the nuclear propulsion plant for the new carrier. The Westinghouse Electric Corporation of Pittsburgh was given the contract to build a reactor and steam propulsion components of the ship. A prototype (the A1W, the reactors actually installed in *Enterprise* were A2Ws) of the new ship's reactors was built at the Naval Reactor Facility, Naval Research Training Station, Idaho, for the purpose of thoroughly testing its operation and safety as well as for training the future operators.

Authorization for the construction of the carrier was included in the Congressional Fiscal 1958 new construction program. The Newport News Shipbuilding and Dry Dock Company of Newport News, Virginia was given the contract to build her on 16 August 1957. She was designated Newport's hull number 546.

At the keel laying ceremony on 4 February 1958, the then Secretary of the Navy, William B. Franke, announced that the world's first nuclear-powered aircraft carrier would be named USS *Enterprise* (CVAN-65).

Her construction went ahead at a rapid pace. One time-saving method utilized was to build her small island superstructure on the centerline and, by the time the large overhanging starboard sponson was attached, the island was moved to its rightful place on the sponson.

Enterprise underway replenishes from Fast Combat Support Ship USS *Sacramento* (AOE-1) in the Gulf of Tonkin, June 1967. The AOE is capable of operating as part of a fast carrier task force supplying fuel, munitions, and aviation and general supplies. The large box structure on the after port side sponson of the 'Big E' is the Sea Sparrow missile launcher. The starboard launcher is barely visible under the tail of the aftermost Skyhawk (*US Navy, JOC Moeser*)

A-5 Vigilantes and F-8 Crusaders undergoing maintenance on *Enterprise's* hangar deck. Note the folding tail and nose on the Vigilantes *(US Navy, PHC Bumpers)*

Launching and Commissioning

Enterprise was launched 24 September 1960 by Mrs William B. Franke, the wife of the Secretary of the Navy. From its first day at sea *Enterprise* started compiling 'firsts' and setting records. On 29 October 1961 she began her six days Builder's and Navy Pre-acceptance Trials; the first time in history that the two trials had been combined. During these trials the ship fulfilled or exceeded all design specifications including a run for a sustained period in excess of 30 knots. She returned to Norfolk with a giant broom fixed to her masthead signifying a 'clean sweep' of her trials.

Enterprise was commissioned 25 November 1961 with Captain Vincent P. de Poix, USN, commanding. Over 13,000 persons crowded the huge hangar deck for the commissioning ceremony. In his address to those assembled, Secretary of the Navy John B. Connally offered, 'She will reign a long, long time as Queen of the Seas'.

The National Ensign and Jack which were flown over the *Enterprise* at her commissioning were the last to be flown from her famous namesake, USS *Enterprise* (CV-6) of World War II fame.

Design details

The specifications of *Enterprise* are indeed impressive: full load displacement 85,350 tons, length over all 1123ft, width at main deck 133ft, extreme width at flight deck 252ft, draft 35ft, extreme height 229·5ft, and complement 4600 (including air wing). Total construction cost was about $445,000,000.

Power Plant

The nuclear power plant in *Enterprise* consists of eight A2W reactors producing approximately 200,000 shaft horsepower in four turbines which is delivered through four shafts, each turning a 64,500lb, five-bladed propeller. The resultant maximum speed is in excess of 30 knots. Four rudders of 35 tons each are placed, one behind each of the propellers, making the ship highly manoeuvrable.

Enterprise's plant comprises the largest nuclear power complex in the world. Its ten years of operation has been marked with a record of great dependability and safety. The ship's reactors comply with all the recommended radioactivity limits of the International Commission of Radiological Protection. The devices and procedures used to ensure control of radioactivity in case of failure, collision or combat casualty are considered to be as foolproof as possible.

The first uranium cores drove *Enterprise* over 200,000 miles in a three-year period before they had to be replaced. Subsequent recorings have a greater life with 'the state of the art' now advanced to cores with a 13-year life. It is considered feasible that cores will be developed in future that might last the estimated 30-year life of the new nuclear carriers. The original nuclear cores cost over $4,000,000 but the longer-lifed replacements were less costly at $3,500,000.

The Reactor Department is a separate organisation on board the *Enterprise* and its officers and men are required to undergo a most exetnsive formal training program in nucleonics before being assigned.

Armor and Armament

The main armor carried on *Enterprise* is the heavy armored flight deck. This was to prove a significant factor in the catastrophic fire and explosions that occurred on *Enterprise's* flight deck in 1969. The US Navy learned its lesson the hard way during World War II when all its carriers had only armored hangar decks. All attack carriers built since the *Midway* class have had armored flight decks.

The main armament of *Enterprise* is, of course, her air wing but she was initially designed to carry surface-to-air missiles. Space was allocated on the aft sponson on both the port and starboard side to install twin Terrier missile launchers. However, in an effort to hold down the spiralling construction costs, no missiles or guns were installed other than a pair of 3in saluting guns.

In 1966, in an effort to give *Enterprise* a close-in defense against cruise missiles and aircraft, the Basic Point Defense Missile System (BPDMS) was installed. This consists of two, eight rail, Sparrow III air-to-air missiles converted to the surface-to-air role and named Sea Sparrow. Target acquisition and initial firing information can be obtained by either radar or visual means.

The weapons for the aircraft embarked include: machine guns and cannon, air-to-air missiles such as the Sidewinder and Sparrow and air-to-surface weapons such as the Bullpup, Walleye, Snakeye, and bombs. These give the attack carrier, with its air wing, a tremendous flexibility in being able to apply power anywhere in the world to the degree national policy requires.

Flight and Hangar Decks

The flight deck comprises 4·47 acres of area and is serviced by four aluminum deck edge elevators. Each elevator measures about 4000 sq/ft. Three are placed on the starboard side and one is located aft on the port side. This arrangement, in conjunction with the angled deck, allows for bringing aircraft up from the hangar deck in preparation for launching, while simultaneously recovering aircraft and moving them down to the hangar deck.

The *Enterprise* is the first carrier to have elevators vice escalators for moving the heavily suited air crews from ready rooms to flight deck.

The hangar deck runs almost the whole length of the ship, the exception being up forward. It has a height of 25ft and, because the elevators are located along the flight deck overhang, no valuable hangar deck space is impinged upon by aircraft elevators.

Catapults and Arresting Gear

There are four C-13 steam catapults installed on *Enterprise* with a total energy potential of 60,000,000 ft/lb. Two of the catapults launch over the bow while the other two launch over the forward end of the angled deck. With all catapults operating, it is possible to launch four aircraft/minute.

The catapults are adjusted for each shot, according to the type aircraft and its gross weight. Acceleration is also controlled so that no dangerous 'G' forces are imposed on pilot or aircraft. With this system the largest shipboard aircraft, grossing more than 80,000lb, can be accelerated to 160 miles/hour in a distance of 250ft.

The arresting gear engine room of *Enterprise.* ABC B-R Hayes checks automatic lubricator. Over 200lb of grease are required each day to operate the four arresting engines. The large cylinder is for compressed air (*US Navy, PH1 Wasmer*)

Four small weapons elevators are provided for bringing missiles and bombs to the flight deck.

The advent of the angled deck allowed a great reduction in the number of arresting wires used on the straight-deck carriers of World War II, and the elimination of the retracting wire barrier.

Arrester Wires

Enterprise has four automatic compensating arresting wires. These come under tremendous strain in halting heavy aircraft, with a landing speed of 100 to 140 knots, in a matter of some tens of feet. This strain is increased by the method generally required for landing jet aircraft on a carrier. Because of the small time lag from applying throttle until the engine responds, it is necessary to have throttle on in case of a 'bolter' (no tail-hook engagement) to have sufficient flying speed to get airborne again. To achieve this, the normal practice is to apply throttle the instant the wheels touch the deck and

An early view (24 October 1962) of *Enterprise*'s island before higher mast and additional yardarm were installed. Venerable A-1 Skyraiders of Attack Squadron 65 are shown loaded with twelve 250lb bombs and one 500lb. Primary flight control juts out over the flight deck just above the bridge
(US Navy, L/Cdr Dutch)

to chop the throttle back as soon as arrestment is completed.

No fixed crash barriers are installed but a temporary nylon webbing barrier can be erected quickly if an aircraft with damaged landing gear or arresting hook has to be recovered. The barrier is designed to bring an aircraft to a halt with little or no damage resulting.

Island

Because of its lack of stacks and its unique fixed radar antenna, the *Enterprise's* island is small with a distinctive square appearance. It is located aft of amidships on the starboard side, well out over the water on a supporting sponson.

'The Big E' departs Norfolk, Virginia 29 October 1962 with six tugs pushing her bow. Note the positions of her deck edge elevators (*US Navy*)

The 'turban' topped, slab sided, square appearance of the island is a result of the Hughes fixed-array radar antenna systems. These systems give a 360° three dimensional radar presentation with a greater scanning rate than rotating antenna systems. This also assists greatly in the detection and tracking of airborne targets at increased ranges. The fixed antenna increases reliability and decreases maintenance compared to rotating antennas. A similar system is installed on the nuclear-powered cruiser USS *Long Beach* (CGN-9).

Above the radar array is the flag bridge; on the next level the navigation bridge; and, above that and overhanging the flight deck, is the primary flight control.

Atop the 'turban' is a short pole-mast with two cross-arms which supports the signal halyards, navigating radar, TACAN (gives aircraft distance and bearing to carrier) and the other antenna required for the numerous communications systems carried aboard. Also carried are LORAN and Satellite Navigation Systems. Approximately fourteen, long whip antenna are located along the flight deck edge, mounted on pivots so they can be swung out horizontally when flight operations are underway.

Command and Control

Spaces are provided aboard for a flag staff. This includes accommodations for the Admiral and his staff, a flag bridge, flag plot and flag communications. Normally the Admiral will be a carrier division commander who also will be often 'double hatted' as a task group or task force commander.

The ship carries a full range of communications equipment for maintaining contact with aircraft, ships, fleet commanders and the seat of government. Her internal telephone system has 1800 'phones.

NTDS

Enterprise was one of the first ships to have the Naval Tactical Data System (NTDS) installed. This multi-unit computer system can process and evaluate enemy threats fed into it from various sources and recommend counter-moves in micro-seconds. It can exchange data by data-link circuits with other shipborne or airborne platforms so equipped, thus enabling a task force to be co-ordinated almost as a single unit.

CDR George Talley in an F-8 makes the first landing on *Enterprise* 17 January 1962 (*US Navy*)

The computer digests information from all available sources; such as radar, sonar, other NTDS or airborne systems, and instantly displays the surface, air and subsurface picture with recommended 'answers' on scopes in the CIC. Command personnel can then make the necessary decisions and issue the required commands to meet a multitude of threats simultaneously. Not only does the task force commander have the complete tactical picture but it can also be maintained by individual unit commanders.

IOIS

Almost all of the US Navy's attack carriers, including *Enterprise*, have been equipped with the Integrated Operational Intelligence System (IOIS). This system was developed to meet the need for speed, flexibility, accuracy and rapid retrieval of stored intelligence data. Included is the capability to return rapidly newly gathered raw intelligence to the intelligence center, processed and ready for use.

The complete system comprises the RA-5C Vigilante reconnaissance aircraft and the computer and stored data in the Integrated Operational Intelligence Center (IOIC). The RA-5C can gather intelligence day or night in any kind of weather at supersonic speeds. These aircraft have a wide variety of collection capabilities. The IOIS can process and analyse this, take as well as store, retrieve and utilise information received from other sources and agencies having intelligence functions.

'Enterprise' joins the Fleet

After commissioning and fitting out, *Enterprise* was assigned to the operational control of Commander Naval Air Force, US Atlantic Fleet. She went through the de-perming (demagnetizing) crib 4-5 January 1962 and put to sea as a commissioned ship for the first time 12 January 1962. On 17 January

This stern view shows the crew rigging the crash barrier between number 3 and 4 arrestor wires. Two F-9 Couger training jets are on the flight deck (*US Navy*)

Commander George C. Talley, Jr, Commander of Air Group One in an F8U Crusader, made the first arrested landing on *Enterprise*.

Shakedown

Enterprise departed Norfolk for Guantanamo Bay, Cuba, 5 February 1962 for her shakedown cruise. She called at Mayport, Florida en route to load A3J Vigilantes of VAH-7, (the first operational squadron with this aircraft) and the F4H Phantom IIs of VF-102. These two squadrons were in addition to the embarked aircraft of CAG-1. She returned to Norfolk 5 April having completed her shakedown with the high score of 90·3.

President Kennedy with a group of congressmen and foreign diplomats arrived on board 14 April and witnessed a display of air and surface firepower by

Enterprise immediately after commissioning with her first aircraft aboard, 17 January 1962 (*US Navy*)

USS ENTERPRISE
CVAN-65

CVW "FORTUNA FAVET FORTIBUS" 14

65

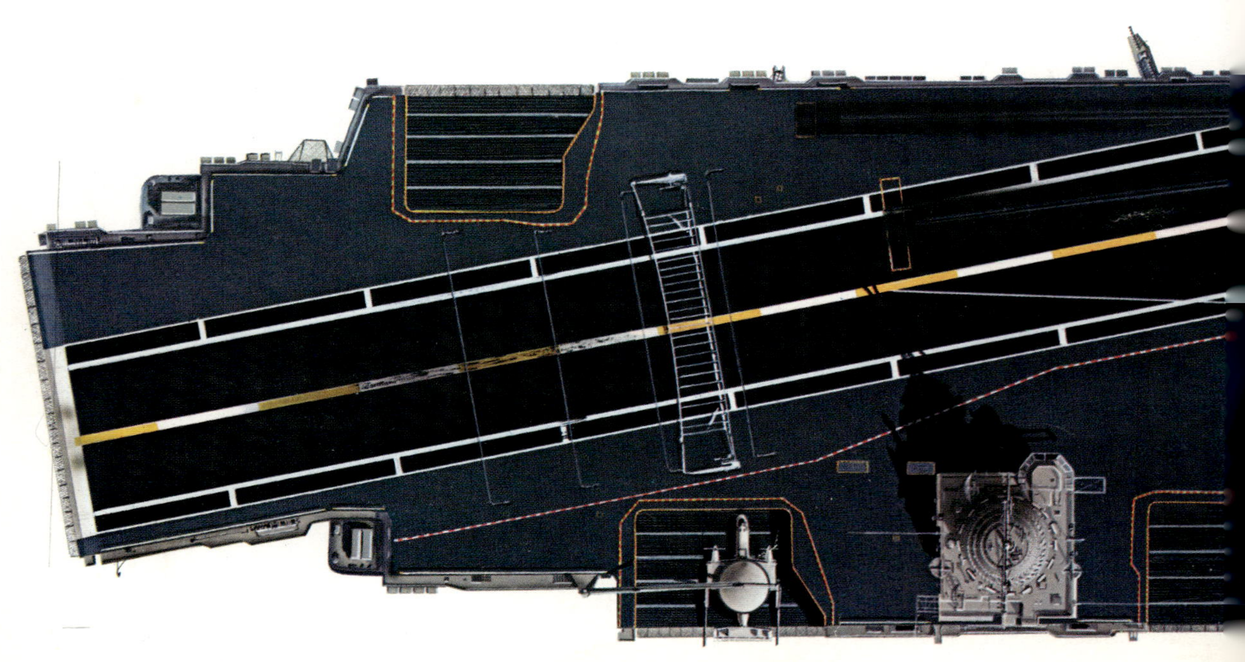

U.S.S. *Enterprise*

At left are the insignias of *Enterprise* and her current attack carrier attack wing, CVW-14. The illustration below shows an E-2 on the after starboard elevator. In the overhead view the nylon crash barrier is rigged; this is installed across the flight deck only when an emergency requires its use. The red and white dotted lines painted at various angles on the flight deck are boundary lines within which parked aircraft must be kept in order to maintain clearance while flight operations are being conducted on that particular area of the deck. The smaller red and yellow dotted lines border deck areas that could be hazardous to personnel and aircraft, such as elevators, elevator life lines, jet blast shields, ammunition elevators and refueling points.

Gordon Davies

The McDonnell F-4 Phantom II flown by Fighter Squadron (VF) 143; the F-4 is also flown from *Enterprise* by VF-142. Originally designed for the US Navy this two seat fighter is now in use or ordered by the USMC, USAF, RN, RAF, Israel, and several other countries

The Douglas EA-3 Skywarrior flown by Detachment 4 of Tactical Electronics Warfare Squadron (VAQ) 130. Besides its ECM mission this type aircraft is also used as an in-flight refueler. Most of the combat aircraft in the US Navy can be equipped as in-flight refuelers

The Ling-Temco-Vought A-7 Corsair II, flown by Attack Squadron (VA) 97; the A-7 is also operated from *Enterprise* by VA-27. This attack aircraft is also flown by the USAF

The Grumman E-2 Hawkeye flown by Carrier Airborne Early Warning Squadron (VAW) 113. This turbo-prop aircraft has a crew of five and a 24ft revolving radar disc. It patrols the approaches to the fleet providing radar early warning, strike and traffic control, area surveillance, search and rescue guidance, navigational assistance and communications relay services

The Grumman A-6 Intruder flown by VA-196; a versatile all-weather, two seat attack aircraft

The North American RA-5 Vigilante flown by Heavy Reconnaissance Squadron (VAH) 9. Originally designed as a heavy attack aircraft the two-seat supersonic Vigilante carries a multitude of reconnaissance sensors

units of the Second Fleet. She completed a post shakedown yard period 19 June. She officially joined the Second Fleet 25 June and, with CAG-6 embarked, conducted type-training exercises in the Atlantic. *Enterprise* made her first official port of call in Boston, Massachusetts for the Independence Day celebration on 4 July 1962. From 5 to 12 July she participated in fleet exercises as a unit of Task Force 24 returning to Norfolk to prepare for her first deployment.

Sixth Fleet

Enterprise departed Norfolk 3 August for her initial assignment with the Sixth Fleet in the Mediterranean. En route she participated in her first NATO exercise, RIPTIDE III. During this exercise foreign aircraft operated for the first time from her deck when British carrier aircraft came aboard.

On 16 August *'The Big E'* not only became the first nuclear-powered surface vessel to enter the 'Med' but she also introduced for the first time the Phantom II and the Vigilante. She participated in her first amphibious landing exercise on 23 August furnishing close air support for the Marines landing on Sardinia. She made her first foreign port of call with an eight-day visit to Cannes, France.

After conducting six days of flight operations, *Enterprise* arrived 10 September at Naples, Italy and there received her first foreign Chief of State, President Antonio Segni.

Upon departing Naples she headed for the Aegean Sea for a NATO exercise involving units of the United States, United Kingdom, Greek and Turkish Navies. She completed her short 'Med' deployment returning to Norfolk 11 October 1962.

During her tour with the Sixth Fleet *Enterprise* recorded her 8000th arrested landing.

Cuban Crisis

The day after she returned home *'The Big E'* became flagship for Rear Admiral John T. Hayward, Commander Carrier Division Two (COMCARDIV 2). Evidence was growing that the Soviets intended to place strategic missiles in Cuba and *Enterprise* was ordered to Cuban waters, a week after her arrival home from the Mediterranean.

When President Kennedy announced the situation to the world and proclaimed the Cuban Quarantine, *Enterprise* was on station and remained there with

The fresnal landing light system on *Enterprise,* located port side amidships on the flight deck. This system automatically advises the pilot that his approach is too high, right on, or too low on the prescribed glide path. US attack carriers are currently being equipped with an automatic landing system, that will allow pilots to make hands-off landings in most any weather condition *(US Navy)*

A montage of the type aircraft *Enterprise* carried in 1963 surround her as she makes a wide wake while operating with the Sixth Fleet in the Mediterranean. Clockwise from the top: F-8 Crusader, F-4 Phantom, A-1 Skyraider, E-1 Tracer, C-1 Trader, A-5 Vigilante, A-3 Skywarrior and A-4 Skyhawk *(US Navy)*

other units of the Second Fleet enforcing the Quarantine until the Soviets backed down. She returned to the Norfolk area 7 December 1962 where she conducted carrier suitability trials with the A6A Intruder attack aircraft and the E2A Hawkeye early warning aircraft, two new aircraft types, planned for carrier use.

One Year of Operation

As *Enterprise* completed her first year of commissioned service, she had steamed over 65,000 miles, made more than 10,000 arrested landings, and during the Cuban Crisis had on board over 100 aircraft.

With COMCARDIV 2 and CAG 6 embarked, she headed for her second Mediterranean deployment on 6 February 1963. On the seventh she was joined by the first nuclear-powered frigate, USS *Bainbridge* (DLGN-25). On the thirteenth, while south of the Azores, her combat air patrol intercepted a Russian Bear bomber and escorted it as it overflew *'The Big E'*.

She re-entered the 'Med' on 16 February. During her six months with the Sixth Fleet she participated in a number of national and NATO exercises and made port calls to Athens (where she entertained the King and Queen of Greece), Palermo, Naples, Cannes, Beirut and Genoa. *Enterprise* arrived back at Norfolk on 4 September 1963.

While back in home waters she earned the Navy

Enterprise leaves Pearl Harbor, Hawaii 23 November 1966 with her deck crowded with aircraft (*US Navy, PH2 O'Brien*)

Battle Efficiency and Readiness 'E'; participated in several Second Fleet exercises while working up her air group and passed her Operational Readiness Inspection (ORI) with flying colors.

Back Again

Enterprise departed for her third tour with the Sixth Fleet 8 February 1964, relieving *Independence* (CVA-62) in Golfo de Palma 22 February. The Mediterranean routine was started once again; national, bi-lateral and NATO exercises of every type and scope; port visits to Istanbul, Naples, Cannes and Majorca.

While on this deployment *'The Big E'* cruised 14-21 March off Cyprus during one of the periods of extreme political tension on that island. On 6 April with *Rigel* (AF-58) she set a Sixth Fleet replenishment record by receiving stores at the rate of 194 tons/hour. On 13 May 1964 *Enterprise, Long Beach* and *Bainbridge* formed the first nuclear-powered task force and extensive tests and evaluations were carried out to test the capabilities of their unique power plants and the NTDS in task force operations. The nuclear-powered submarine *Seawolf* also participated in these exercises. During this period *'The Big E'* set another Sixth Fleet replenishment record when on 16 May she received JP-5 jet fuel at the rate of 437,000 gallons/hour from oiler *Mississinewa* (A0-144). She was relieved from her Sixth Fleet duty 29 July 1964.

OPERATION SEA ORBIT

Enterprise, Longbeach and *Bainbridge* were designated Task Force One on 31 July and, as they steamed out of the Straits of Gibraltar, the force embarked on a history-making world tour—a 30,565 mile, 65 day cruise without replenishment of any kind—OPERATION SEA ORBIT.

Dignitaries from countries along the route were flown out to the force to inspect the ships and view fire power demonstrations. Countries so honored were Morocco, Senegal, Sierra Leone, Liberia, Ivory Coast, Kenya, Pakistan, India, Australia, New Zealand, Argentina, Uruguay, Brazil and Puerto Rico.

Beach fly-overs were made at Abidjan, Perth, Freemantle, Melbourne, Wellington, Christ Church, Rio de Janeiro and Recife. Port calls were made at Karachi, Sydney and Rio de Janeiro.

While rounding the Cape of Good Hope on 10 August the task force rendezvoused with units of the South African Navy and air demonstrations were performed. On 28 August 1964 south of Indonesia the task force conducted an air defense exercise with HMS *Victorious.*

The task force crossed the equator four times and *Enterprise* elevated 4300 men from the status of 'Pollywog' to 'Shellback'—an indication of the great number of new hands in the crew. The force transitted the South Pacific at an average speed of 25 knots.

On 2 October 1964 Air Wing Six launched all aircraft for home—the fact that no 'hangar queens' were left behind was an excellent indicator of the

'The Big E' alongside Pier 12 at the Naval Operating Base, Norfolk, Virginia, 15 June 1965, with USS *America* (CVA-66) tied up next to her (*US Navy*)

Enterprise in October 1965 bow on (*US Navy*)

level of readiness maintained during almost 75,000 miles of steaming in the eight months *Enterprise* had been away from home port.

Fittingly a tremendous welcome awaited *'The Big E'* on her arrival back in Norfolk. Secretary of the Navy Paul Nitze told the crew it was '. . . *the most significant naval voyage in modern naval history.*' During OPERATION SEA ORBIT her air wing had flown 1590 sorties for a total of 2372 flight hours, dropped 240 bombs, launched 2766 rockets and fired 12,500 rounds of 20mm ammunition. The whole voyage was conducted without receiving any fuel, food, ammunition or other stores enroute.

Overhaul, October 1964—February 1965

Enterprise again earned the coveted Battle 'E' in fiscal year 1964. In October 1964 she entered drydock at Newport News to undergo her first overhaul since commissioning three years earlier. She had steamed over 200,000 miles on her original nuclear core and completed 42,000 arrested landings.

It was during this overhaul that the IOIC and Satellite Navigation System was installed. The mainmast was raised 10ft and a second smaller yardarm installed to handle the new antenna. *Enterprise* also received an oil-fired boiler to provide power for heating, lighting and air-conditioning when the reactors were shut down during long in-port or yard periods.

All four shafts were removed and two replaced. The unused port Terrier missile sponson was converted to living compartments, increasing the design complement by 280 men. Holes were cut in the flight and hangar decks to remove the old fuel cores and new longer-life cores were installed. The electronic shops were modernised and numerous other repairs and modifications were made as a result of operational experience or to keep pace with the rapid technological advances.

A crewman mans the catapult controls in preparation for launching an A-7. This view of the island shows it after the new topworks were installed (*US Navy, PH3 Henderson*)

Off to War

Enterprise moved out of drydock 17 February 1965 to complete her nuclear refueling and on 22 June she got underway for sea trials and carrier qualifi-

Enterprise steaming through the South China Sea. This view off the starboard bow shows the large overhang of the flight deck on both sides of the ship (*US Navy, JOC Moeser*)

An E-2 early warning aircraft is lowered onto one of *Enterprise*'s four elevators (*US Navy, PH2 Husted*)

An *Enterprise* A-4 painted in green camouflage taxis forward past a tight pack of her sisters after returning from a strike against North Vietnam 30 March 1966 (*US Navy, JO1 Falk*)

cations off the Virginia Capes. She steamed to Guantanamo Bay, Cuba, for work-up and to conduct her ORI. On return to Norfolk she embarked Carrier Wing Nine (CAW-9) with seven squadrons and three air detachments. On 26 October, as flagship for Rear Admiral Henry L. Miller, COMCARDIV 3, she departed for Vietnam via the Virgin Islands for air wing work-up, thence around the Cape of Good Hope.

On 8 November during night flight operations a crewman was blown off the flight deck by jet blast and he could not be found—*Enterprise* had lost her first crewman.

Dixie and Yankee Stations

After a three day stop in the Philippines '*The Big E*', in company with the nuclear-powered frigate *Bainbridge* and destroyers *Barry* (DD-933) and *Roberts* (DD-823), headed for the coast of Vietnam.

On 2 December 1965 *Enterprise* launched her first combat sorties from Dixie Station against Viet Cong positions in all four corps areas of South Vietnam. Commander O. E. Krueger, C.O. of VA-94, in an A-4 Skyhawk became the first pilot from

Enterprise turns into the wind in preparation for launching a strike against North Vietnam 28 May 1966. Bomb laden Skyhawks line up at the waist catapults. A Vigilante is parked just forward of the island, a Tracer under the island overhang; immediately aft are a Phantom and two Skywarriors (used primarily for in-flight refueling and electronics countermeasures during the Vietnam War) (*US Navy, JO1 Falk*)

LT. JG. G. L. Hausmann examines his flak damaged A-4 after returning from a strike against North Vietnam 13 May 1967 (*US Navy*)

Crewmen wash down the port anchor and chain as *Enterprise* prepares to depart Sasebo, Japan 23 January 1968. The horn like structures projecting from the forward end of the flight deck are over runs for the catapult shuttle (*US Navy*)

'The Big E' to enter combat. Over 167 tons of ordnance was dropped by 125 strike sorties that first day. On 11 December *Enterprise* set a record for a single carrier, launching 165 strike sorties in a single day.

The ship moved to Yankee Station on 16 December and began hitting the heavily defended targets in North Vietnam. Flying combat sorties from 'on the line at the Tonkin Gulf Yacht Club' had its frustrations. For political reasons US forces were restricted as to location and what type targets could be hit. Although the approved target list was expanded slowly as the war progressed, in the early stages pilots were prevented from hitting surface-to-air missile sites, airfields (with their potentially dangerous MIG fighters), any military targets located within population centers (the North Vietnamese naturally took advantage of this) and the storage areas, docks and shipping in the one major port of Haiphong. Soviet Bloc merchant ships steamed by the task force unhindered carrying the supplies of war to North Vietnam. Because of these restrictions enemy anti-aircraft weapons, the greatest concentration in history, were deployed only in approved target areas.

It was during her first around-the-clock combat operations that *Enterprise's* systems and flexibility proved their worth far beyond expectations.

The Routine

On 22 December her aircraft participated in the strike that knocked out the big Uong Bi powerplant near Hanoi. The Christmas Truce came and went and operations were resumed. *'The Big E'* got a short respite in Subic Bay, Philippines, from 15 January to 3 February 1966. Her aircraft ranged over targets in both North and South Vietnam—the Bai Thuong Barracks and a storage area near Vinh on 20 February, troop concentrations and storage areas in the 'Demilitarised Zone' on the twenty-third.

She returned to Subic for a ten-day stay on 24 February, and then departed for a joint air exercise with the Chinese Nationalists off Taiwan. *Enterprise* was back on Yankee Station on 16 March at the peak of the monsoon. Sorties were continued in dirty weather and low visibility. She was back in Subic from 14 to 20 April. During the week of 22 April her squadrons pounded the enemy supply areas around Vinh. The railway, roads and coastal barge traffic in the North Vietnam panhandle received most of the attention during this period.

The 100th day of combat and 10,000th sortie was recorded on 28 April 1966. She returned to Subic 15 to 22 May, then back to Yankee Station. This was the routine of an attack carrier in the Seventh Fleet, about three weeks 'on the line' conducting operations and a week's respite in Subic with an occasional deployment along the Asiatic coast to the waters off Taiwan or Japan.

Heading Home

On 5 June 1966 *Enterprise* headed for her new home port at Naval Air Station Alameda in San Francisco Bay. Since entering combat on 2 December 1965 she had spent 170 days 'on the line', launched 13,020 combat sorties, dropping 8966 tons of ordnance on Communist targets.

As *'The Big E'* steamed under the Golden Gate Bridge the morning of 21 June, she was greeted by a tumultuous welcome. Traffic on the Bridge was backed up for miles and people, with signs and streamers, crowded the rails. With her mast clearing the bridge by a few feet, she was escorted in the Bay by geysering fireboats, by a multitude of small craft and to the accompaniment of the blasts of ships' whistles.

She tied-up at Alameda where her men were reunited with the families whom they had not seen for almost a year.

San Francisco Naval Shipyard received *Enterprise* 30 June 1966 for a two-month yard period. Her catapults were completely overhauled, her point defense Sea Sparrow missile system was installed and her electronics shops re-equipped to maintain

Enterprise departs Sasebo, Japan 23 January 1968, showing her broad, flat stern. In this view can be seen the following types of aircraft: A-3, F-4, A-5, A-6 (*US Navy*)

the new Grumman A-6A Intruder and the E-2A Hawkeye aircraft.

Back to the Far East, December 1966

'The Big E' returned to Alameda 2 September and went through a period of refresher training. On 19 November 1966 she departed the Golden Gate en route to Hawaii and points further west.

After task group exercises in Hawaiian waters *Enterprise*, in company with escorts *Bainbridge, Turner Joy, McKean* and *Gridley*, departed for Southeast Asia 28 November. She arrived at Subic Bay 8 December and was back on Yankee Station 18 December. Her Intruders, Phantoms and Skyhawks hit targets near Vinh, Thon Hon and Ha Tinh.

Short holiday truces were observed 24 through 26 December and over New Year's Day. The Intruders gave a new dimension to strike missions. This aircraft, equipped with a terrain avoidance radar and a sophisticated bomb-navigation system with a bombardier-navigator to man it, could strike accurately from low altitudes at small targets unseen due to weather or darkness.

After the first of the year, railroad facilities at Vinh, Thien Linh Dong, Thuong, Than Hoa, Pho Can, Qui Vinh and Ninh Binh received the attention of *Enterprise's* aircraft. From 8 to 14 February a truce was declared for the Vietnamese Tet Holiday. The night of 24 February, strikes were made against the power plants at Bac Giang and Hon Gai, within the deadly flak and missile umbrella of the Hanoi-Haiphong complex.

The Ha Tou Naval Supply complex was removed from the restricted list and blasted for several days commencing 23 March 1967.

Enterprise continued the grinding pace of continuous operations in the Gulf of Tonkin with short respites in Subic Bay. Noteworthy targets attacked during this time were: Bac Gian power plant and Thia Nguyen steel plant, the Chi Ne Barracks 7 May, Haiphong (East) power plant 13 May, and Da Chong petroleum depot. Four MIGs were eliminated on a strike on Kep Airfield 21 May, the Haiphong (West) power plant on the twenty-sixth and the Hon Gia railroad and supply depot was hit 12-13 June.

Enterprise departed for Alameda 25 June arriving home 6 July 1967. She had steamed 67,630 miles had flown 13,400 combat missions with the Seventh Fleet. She won the Navy Unit Commendation during this deployment.

Return to San Francisco

Upon arrival home *Enterprise* went into overhaul. In the fall she re-embarked CAW-9 at San Diego and conducted refresher training exercises with the First Fleet off the California coast. A new aircraft had joined the air wing inventory, the A4F Skyhawk, an improved version of the diminutive, reliable jet attack plane that had been in the fleet since 1954.

The night of 10-11 November *'The Big E'* hosted President Johnson, Secretary of Defense Robert McNamara and Chief of Naval Operations Admiral Thomas Moorer.

Back to Westpac

Enterprise weighed anchor at Alameda on 3 January 1968 for her third Western Pacific cruise. En route she participated in the large First Fleet exercise BLUE LOTUS off Midway Island and completed her yearly ORI.

A-7 Crusaders line up for launch on the starboard catapult as an A-3 Skywarrior is prepared for launch from the port 'cat'. Note the blast deflectors in the raised position (*US Navy, PH2 Ryan*)

In company with the new nuclear-powered frigate USS *Truxton* (DLGN-35), *Enterprise* arrived at Sasebo, Japan 19 January. This first visit of nuclear-powered surface ships to Japan sparked violent demonstrations by left wing elements in the country. However, the five day visit produced no incidents between crew and demonstrators.

USS 'Pueblo'

'*The Big E*' got underway for Vietnam on 23 January 1968. That afternoon the North Koreans seized the American electronics reconnaissance ship USS *Pueblo* on the high seas off Wonsan, North Korea. The carrier, then in the East China Sea, was ordered north to the coast of North Korea.

There she remained for a month as flagship of the specially created Task Force SEVENTY-ONE in a role of 'watchful waiting'.

Return to Tonkin Gulf

On 22 February 1968 the squadrons of *Enterprise* commenced their third combat tour from Yankee Station. The ship and air wing fell into the pace of action hitting now familiar targets in North Vietnam.

A typical heavy day for CAG-9 aircraft was 15 March when they ranged across North Vietnam hitting Kien An Airfield, a battery plant at Van Dien, power facilities at Hon Gai and Cam Pha, a petroleum storage area at Cam Pha and shipping points near Haiphong and Thanh Hoa.

Enterprise participated in the massive air effort that broke the long siege around the US Marine base on Khe Sanh near the DMZ.

In April President Johnson, in a gesture to get peace talks started, announced that bombing of North Vietnam would be limited to the lower panhandle. *Enterprise* interrupted her operations for a quick rest and recuperation visit at Hong Kong the end of May.

United States Bound

'*The Big E*' completed her third combat tour 26 June 1968 arriving back in Alameda 18 July. She arrived at the Bremerton Naval Yard, Washington for a short yard period departing 28 September.

After a period of underway training *Enterprise* steamed out of San Francisco Bay 6 January 1969 on the way to her fourth war cruise. The plan was to conduct her annual ORI off Hawaii en route.

The aftermath of *Enterprise*'s disastrous fire 14 January 1969, off Hawaii. The remains of several F-8s and an A-3 can be seen in this view of the after portion of the flight deck (*US Navy, PH2 Henderson*)

One of the nine large bombs that exploded during the fire aboard *Enterprise* in January 1969 is responsible for this hole in her armored flight deck (*US Navy, PH3 Sates*)

An A-4 Skyhawk is launched from the port waist catapult on a strike against North Vietnam 21 August 1966 as *Enterprise* operates on Yankee Station in the Gulf of Tonkin (*US Navy, JO1 Falk*)

DISASTER

The ship was struck by disaster on 14 January 1969. While steaming in Hawaiian waters a fire was caused by the explosion of a rocket on the after section of the flight deck among a number of aircraft loaded for launching. In the holocaust that followed nine major-caliber bombs were detonated as fire swept the fantail.

The fire was brought under control but 28 crewmen lost their lives, 15 aircraft were destroyed and the after portion of the flight and hangar decks were damaged.

It has been estimated that *Enterprise* could have resumed scheduled flight operations, if required, in a matter of hours. She returned to Pearl Harbor for repairs and was ready for sea trials 5 March.

Fourth Vietnam Combat Tour

After a short stay at Subic Bay *Enterprise* returned to Yankee Station and commenced her fourth combat tour off Vietnam on 31 March 1969.

Her back-breaking combat operations were abruptly halted when she was ordered once again into the Sea of Japan. A US Navy EC-121 reconnaissance aircraft was shot down by the North Koreans on 16 April. On 20 April *Enterprise* arrived off North Korea joining three other carriers and their task groups. She again became flagship of the reinstated Task Force SEVENTY-ONE—the largest task force assembled in more than 25 years. When the force was reduced at the end of April, *'The Big E'* remained conducting special flight operations.

The Second Refuelling

Enterprise returned to Alameda in July 1969; during *'The Big E's'* fourth combat tour CVW9 had recorded 3779 missions with 4351 tons of ordnance expended. Her stay was short, however, for she set course at once for Norfolk, Virginia via the Cape of Good Hope, stopping at Rio de Janeiro en route.

In August she entered Newport News Shipbuilding and Drydock Company's yard for an extended overhaul of 16 months and a second recoring of her nuclear plant.

In January 1971 she conducted sea trials and in February departed Norfolk for the West Coast. Again she stopped at Rio de Janeiro en route where she was visited by Chief of Naval Operations Admiral Elmo Zumwalt. *Enterprise* arrived back home in Alameda having been 19 months away from her home port.

'The Big E' with Carrier Air Wing FOURTEEN commenced an intensive workup training program in preparation for the ship's fifth deployment to Vietnam. As this Warship *Profile* is being written, *Enterprise's* aircraft are supporting combat operations in South Vietnam.

Since the United States is fast reducing its military forces in the Vietnam War, this will no doubt be *Enterprise's* last period of active participation in that conflict. However, she has another 15-20 years of active service ahead which will find her plying the 'Seven Seas'; hopefully, as a maintainer of peace but ready to apply the necessary power when required.

Enterprise steaming in the Mediterranean 2 July 1963. The flag and dates are comprised of 1352 men of her crew and commemorate the 4th of July that year. The aircraft on deck from bow aft are F-4s, F-8s, A-4s and A-5s

(*US Navy*)

Special Acknowledgements

I wish to express my gratitude to the following, for without their efforts this *Profile* would not have been written: Vice Admiral E. B. Hooper, USN (Ret.) *Director of Naval History and his Staff.* Miss Anna Urband, *Office of Information Department of the Navy.* Lieutenant Commander C. D. Crow, Public Affairs Officer, USS *Enterprise* (CVAN-65). Mr Fred Baker, *Naval Air Systems Command.* US Navy Photographic Center.

Bibliography

AIRCRAFT CARRIERS by Norman Polmar, *Macdonald and Co Ltd.*

DICTIONARY OF AMERICAN NAVAL FIGHTING SHIPS, Office of the Chief of Naval Operations, Naval History Division, *Department of the Navy.*

ENTERPRISE COMMISSIONING, Newport News Shipbuilding and Dry Dock Co.

EVOLUTION OF AIRCRAFT CARRIERS by Scott MacDonald, *Office of the Chief of Naval Operations, Department of the Navy.*

NUCLEAR PROPULSION FOR NAVAL SURFACE VESSELS, Hearings before the Joint Committee on Atomic Energy, Congress of the United States, First Session, Eighty-Eighth Congress.

US NAVAL INSTITUTE PROCEEDINGS (various volumes), *US Naval Institute.*

US NAVAL AVIATION NEWS (various issues). Office of the Chief of Naval Operations and Naval Air Systems Command. L/Cdr Paul Mullane, Editor.

Artist's conception of the two new nuclear powered carriers presently being built for the US Navy. Left is USS *Nimitz* (CVAN-68) and top is USS *Eisenhower* (CVAN-69). Because of advanced technology these two ships only require two nuclear reactors vice the eight in *Enterprise* (*US Navy*)

'ENTERPRISE'—SPECIFICATIONS AND FACTS

Builder:	Newport News Shipbuilding and Dry Dock Co, Newport News, Virginia
Displacement:	Full load: 85,350 tons Standard: 72,500 tons
Number of reactors:	8
Horsepower:	Over 200,000
Speed:	Close to 35 knots
Length over-all:	1123ft
Length between perpendiculars:	1040ft
Width at main deck:	133ft
Extreme width at flight deck:	252ft
Depth at C/L flight deck:	99ft 4in
Contract date:	15 November 1957
Keel laid:	4 February 1958
Christening:	24 September 1960
Delivery:	25 November 1961
Contract delivery date:	31 January 1962
Height (keel to mast top):	250ft (25 story building)
Area of flight deck:	4·47 acres
Number of crew (incl. air wing):	over 5000
Meals served aboard daily:	over 15,000
Number of compartments and spaces:	over 3200
Number of rudders:	4
Weight of rudders:	about 35 tons each
Weight of anchors:	30 tons each
Weight of links in anchor chain:	360lb each
Number of propellers:	4 (five blades each)
Height of propellers:	21ft each
Weight of propellers:	32·25 tons each
Number of telephones:	over 1800
Number of designers required:	915
Number of drawings made:	16,100
Miles of blueprints issued:	2400
Number of plane elevators:	4 (all deck edge)
Size of plane elevators:	approximately 4000sq/ft
Number of catapults:	4
Capacity of air conditioning plants:	1225 tons (enough to serve over 400 homes)
Daily capacity of distilling plants:	280,000 gallons (enough to supply daily needs of over 1400 homes)
Structural steel required:	60,923 tons
Weld metal used in construction:	3,400,000lb
Aluminum used in construction:	3,014,266lb
Length of ventilation and heating ducts aboard, about:	37 miles
Length of electrical cable:	about 625 miles
Length of $\frac{1}{4}$in welding:	4080 miles
Length of pipe and tubing (from $\frac{1}{4}$in to 2ft in diameter:	230 miles
Material received at Newport News:	equal to more than 3000 rail carloads
Estimated number of tubes, transistors and diodes:	about 1,000,000
Total power of auxiliary motors:	about 30,000 horsepower
Area covered by switchboards:	approximately 7000sq/ft
Potential electric generating capacity:	enough to supply the needs of a city of over 2,000,000 persons
Total number of lighting fixtures:	25,000

Warship Series Editor: JOHN WINGATE, DSC

A mixed bag alongside a submarine depot ship. From right to left, HMS Unison, *HMS* Upright, P 614 *(originally being built for the Turkish Navy), an early 'U' class and an 'S' class. Note the saddle tanks of the 'S' class* *(IWM)*

HM S/M Upholder

by Captain M. L. C. Crawford DSC* RN (Ret'd)

DEVELOPMENT OF SUBMARINES

From the earliest times the advantages of making a warship invisible by submerging had been recognised and numerous craft were produced by inventors, whose names are well known to students of submarine matters, such as Van Drebbel, Bushnell, Fulton, Day, Bauer, Nordenfelt, Gustave Zede and Holland.

Up until the last quarter of the nineteenth century, designers of submarines for military use were faced with two major problems. Firstly, they still had to rely on manpower to propel the submarine when submerged; secondly, no suitable weapon had yet been devised which could explode at the target without endangering the submarine.

Towards the end of the century electric motors powered from large batteries were introduced for propelling when submerged; and steam or internal combustion engines were used on the surface and for re-charging the batteries. At about the same time Whitehead produced his locomotive torpedo which could be fired at the target from a safe range. From this moment onwards progress in the development of submarines as a military weapon was rapid and at the turn of the century the American, Holland, produced the class of submarine named after him which was driven by a gasoline engine and electric motors and was armed with the Whitehead torpedoes.

British Interest

The British Government had shown little interest in submarine craft until Fulton brought his submarine *Nautilus* to England early in the nineteenth century. A committee, of which Pitt was a member, was set up to examine his design. Earl St Vincent, who was First Lord of the Admiralty, said at the time, 'Pitt is the greatest fool that ever existed to encourage a mode of warfare which those who command the sea do not want and which if successful, will deprive them of it'. This was to be the basis of British policy towards the submarine throughout the nineteenth century.

By 1900 a number of countries were building submarines and it was felt in this country that counter measures to this potential threat could not

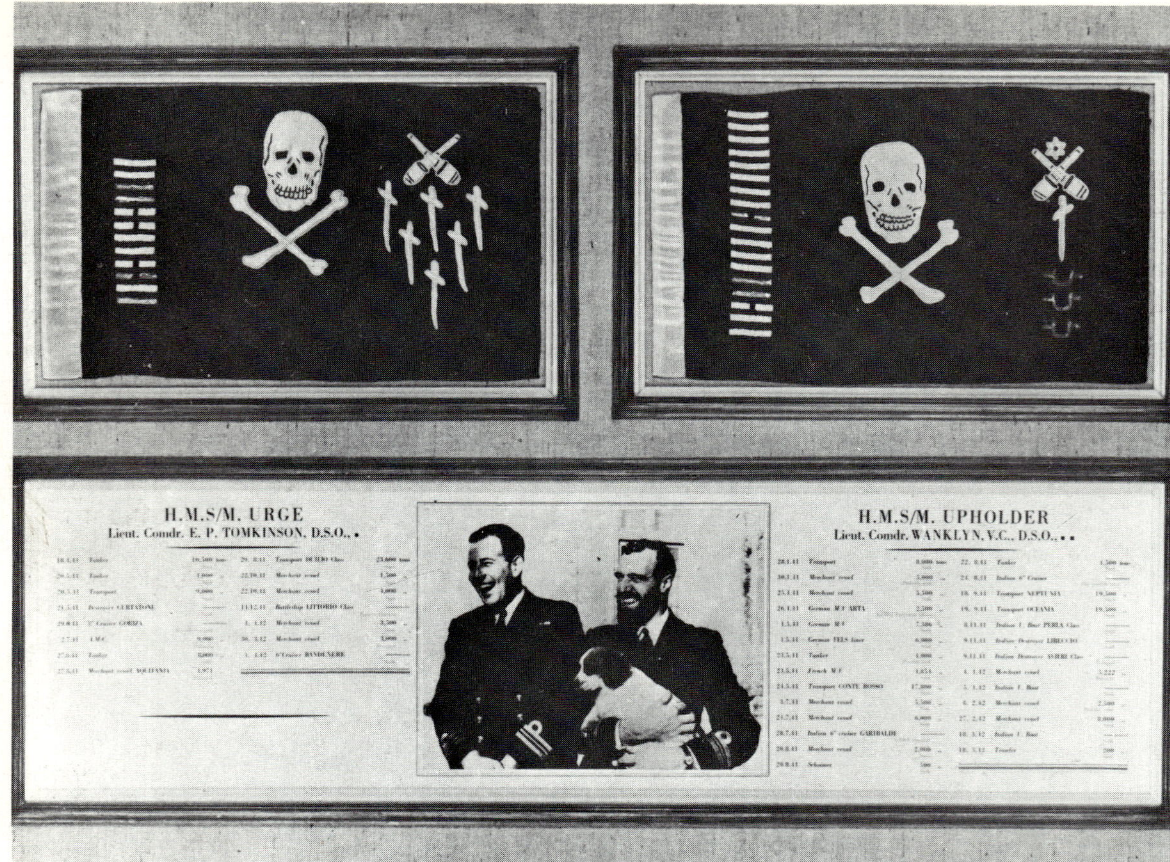

Lieutenant-Commanders Tomkinson (left) and Wanklyn with their Jolly Rogers and success boards (Author's collection)

be devised without practical experience of the capabilities of a submarine. However, the policy laid down by St Vincent in 1804 had been followed, with the result that no British designs of submarines were available. Fortunately the US Government allowed Holland to supply his drawings and five Holland boats were laid down at Vickers, Barrow, in 1901.

Few British officers at this time saw much future for submarines beyond extending our coast defences but fortunately Admiral Fisher had foresight and, when he became First Sea Lord, he ensured that submarines were built to a steady programme.

Offensive Operations

The size and endurance of submarines gradually increased with the British designed *'A'*, *'B'* and *'C'* classes but the next major change came with the *'D'* class in 1908. The Diesel engine was fitted for surface propulsion and habitability was improved by placing the ballast tanks external to the pressure hull in 'saddle' tanks. Wireless was also installed.

D 1 demonstrated the offensive capabilities of these submarines in a Fleet exercise in 1910 by steaming from Portsmouth to the west coast of Scotland, patrolling for three days off an 'enemy' base without her presence being suspected and then torpedoing two cruisers as they left harbour.

First World War

Submarines proved themselves fully capable of offensive operations during the First World War with operations in the Baltic, North Sea, the Adriatic and the Dardanelles. Names of submarine captains such as Holbrook, Layton, Dunbar-Nasmith, Little, Laurence and Max Horton have gone down in history.

The war brought with it the requirement for a variety of specialised submarines and either existing designs were modified or a new design was produced. These included a mine-laying submarine, a submarine with high surface speed for operating with the Fleet and an anti-submarine submarine with high submerged speed and a salvo of six torpedoes, for attacking enemy U-boats.

Post War Years

The war had shown that the submarine in the hands of our enemies might bring this country to its knees as foreseen by St Vincent. As a result, the Government of the day took every opportunity of pressing for the abolition of the submarine, but no support was forthcoming from other countries.

Many submarines were scrapped after the war and the submarine branch was left with two types of patrol submarine, the short range *'H'* class and the larger *'L'* class, both of which were war-time designs based on operational experience.

The Submarine Base at Malta known as HMS Talbot, *showing a submarine berthed alongside under the officers' quarters. The building was formerly used as a quarantine hospital. Boat laying smoke screen to hide submarines during an air raid* (IWM)

Upholder's *ships company taken in Malta about September 1941* (*Author's collection*)

Building of submarines was virtually at a standstill until the mid-1920s apart from an experimental cruiser submarine, the *X1*, with a surface displacement of 3000 tons and armed with four 5·2in guns in twin turrets and with six torpedo tubes. She was not a success because of constant engine trouble but much valuable design information was gained.

Other experiments at this time were the conversion of *M 2* into a seaplane carrier to extend the reconnaissance of the fleet and *M 3* into a minelayer to carry 100 mines. *M 2* was lost while exercising the aircraft launching procedure.

NEW CONSTRUCTION

In the mid-1920s, when it was realised that war against Japan was a possibility submarines of greater endurance were considered essential. The *'O'* class were designed and were followed by the improved *'P'* and *'R'* classes. The added endurance was obtained by carrying fuel in external tanks above the ballast tanks but great difficulty was experienced in keeping these tanks oil-tight; in addition, the engines in these submarines gave trouble.

Once again the need for specialised submarines was raised and a mine-layer and a fleet submarine were designed. Based on experience with *M 3*, five mine-layers of the *Porpoise* class (double-hull) carrying 50 mines, were built from 1932 onwards. The fleet submarine was provided by three submarines of the *Thames* class (double-hull) with a surface speed of 22½ knots given by supercharged Diesel engines. They never had a serious trial with the fleet as their introduction coincided with the increase of the capital ship speed to 28 knots.

The problem of maintaining external fuel tanks free from leaks led to the decision that in future all fuel was to be carried within the pressure hull and at about the same time it was decided to standardise on two main types of patrol submarine. These decisions led to the design of the *'S'* and *'T'* classes.

The *'S'* class which were built from 1932 onwards, were of 735 tons displacement with a bow salvo of six torpedoes and with a 4in gun. They had an endurance of 3700 miles at 10 knots on the surface. An improved version of this design was built throughout the war and proved very successful in service.

The *'T'* class were not as large as the *'P'* and *'R'* classes and had a lower endurance but they were considerably better armed. It was felt that improvements in A/S equipment fitted in surface ships would force submarines to attack from longer ranges and so a larger torpedo salvo was arranged. In addition to the six internal tubes they were fitted with four forward facing external tubes giving a full bow salvo of 10 torpedoes. They were also armed with a 4in gun. These submarines were built from 1938 onwards throughout the war.

Finally, just before the war, a requirement was seen for a short range small patrol submarine for operations in northern waters and in the Mediter-

Another view of the Submarine Base, Malta, showing 'T' class submarines nearest to camera and to left, as well as several 'U' class submarines (IWM)

ranean and which would be economical, particularly in manpower, for training our A/S forces. This need was met by the *'U'* class.

'U' CLASS

The first three submarines, *Unity, Undine* and *Ursula,* were fitted with four internal torpedo tubes and two external tubes within a high bow. *Ursula* had a gun mounted just forward of the bridge. Experience with these submarines showed that they were difficult to control when near the surface in any sea and that when firing a full salvo of six torpedoes it was extremely hard to prevent the submarine from breaking surface.

These shortcomings were discussed at a meeting in January 1940 and it was decided to omit the external tubes and to fit a gun in all *'U'* class. To avoid delays in construction the next six, of which *Upholder* was one, retained the high bow but omitted the external tubes and a 12pdr gun was fitted. Thereafter a flush bow was designed and a 3in gun was fitted.

One other point in this design over which there was some juggling was the position of the Wardroom, which in some submarines was in the Control Room and in others at the forward end of the Accommodation Space. War experience finally dictated that the Wardroom should be in the Control Room.

'UPHOLDER'—CHARACTERISTICS

Hull

The design was a single hull with internal frames and the sections were riveted. The overall length was 191ft with a maximum beam of 16ft and the safe diving depth was 200ft. The surface displacement was 630 tons, giving a positive buoyancy of 90 tons on the surface.

Six internal Main Ballast tanks (MBTs) were fitted for diving the submarine. All had hydraulically operated vents at the top of the tank which were controlled from the diving panel in the Control Room. The two end tanks had free flood holes in the bottom but the four centre tanks were fitted with hand operated Kingston valves. For quick diving, a tank ('Q' tank) fitted with hydraulically operated vent and Kingston valve was situated under the forward end of the Accommodation Space. The forward and after MBTs and 'Q' tank were fitted with direct HP (High Pressure) Air blows.

Control Surfaces

To control the depth of the submarine when dived, two sets of hydraulically operated hydroplanes were fitted. The forward set were above the waterline when on the surface and, to prevent damage in rough weather, they were designed to fold flat against the side of the casing. The after set were below the surface on either side of the rudder.

Diving

When diving, the positive buoyancy of the submarine was destroyed by filling the six MBTs and 'Q' tank. The hydroplanes were put to dive and the speed of the submarine to at least 7 knots. As the submarine submerged, 'Q' tank was blown empty and the submarine levelled off at periscope depth (27ft) or the depth ordered. Trim was then adjusted by admitting or pumping water from a number of compensating tanks throughout the submarine, until a level depth could be maintained at slow speed with the minimum use of the hydroplanes. Ideally the submarine should then be able to stop and remain at that depth in a neutrally buoyant condition.

Surfacing

While dived, the vents on the MBTs were kept shut, ready for surfacing and so that they could be blown empty in the event of loss of control. When ordered to surface, the forward and after MBTs were emptied by the HP Air blows and the hydroplanes were put to rise. Once the Conning Tower hatch was opened an LP blower was connected to all MBTs until they were emptied. In fine weather under operational conditions the MBTs were normally kept partially flooded in order to speed up the Diving process in case of emergency.

Casing

A light metal casing with free flood holes covered the

HMS Ursula. *Note the W/T mast in the raised position and the two external torpedo tubes which were omitted in later submarines of the class* *(Museum Curator, HMS* Dolphin)

Captain G. W. G. Simpson who commanded the Malta Submarine Flotilla. He was later promoted to Flag rank and served as Flag Officer Submarines from January 1952 to January 1954 *(IWM)*

top of all except the after part of the curved pressure hull and this included the bridge structure which covered the Conning Tower and periscope tubes. Apart from giving protection to the Bridge personnel when on the surface, the casing was for the convenience of men when handling berthing wires, anchoring, loading torpedoes or for entering and leaving the submarine.

Watertight Subdivision

The pressure hull was of circular cross-section bounded by two flat bulkheads tested to the same pressure as the hull, namely 70lb/sq. in. The submarine was divided into six compartments by bulkheads fitted with doors for access through the submarine along a passage on the starboard side which ran forward of the Control Room, and amidships abaft this compartment.

Access into the pressure hull was either through the Torpedo Loading hatch (or Fore Hatch) into the Crew Space, through the Engine Room hatch at the forward end of the Engine Room or through the upper and lower Conning Tower hatches. The Engine Room hatch was fitted as an Escape hatch for the after part of the submarine. For those forward, a separate Escape hatch was situated towards the forward end of the Crew Space.

Escape

The method of escape from submarines was known as Compartment Escape and could be carried out from the Torpedo Stowage Compartment and the Engine Room. A canvas trunking was lowered from the Escape hatch and secured to the deck. The trunking when extended left enough space for each man to bend down and enter it. The compartment bulkheads were shut off and then the compartment was flooded while the men donned Davis Submarine Escape Apparatus (DSEA). This consisted of a nose clip and a mouthpiece connected by a tube to an oxygen bag.

As the compartment flooded, the air pressure increased until flooding ceased, leaving an air pocket at the top of the trunking. The first man who entered the trunking opened a vent which allowed the trunking to fill completely. He then opened the hatch and rose to the surface; each man in turn then followed him. Depending on the depth of the submarine and therefore the pressure under which escapers were breathing, there was only a limited

The underground workshops at the Submarine Base, which were manned by naval ratings and Maltese civilians (*IWM*)

time for escaping before the onset of oxygen poisoning.

As an alternative to Compartment Escape, the Conning Tower could be used as an Escape Chamber by two men at a time. At least one escape was successfully carried out through the Conning Tower during the last war.

Accommodation

The designed complement was 4 Officers, 4 Petty Officers, 4 Engine Room Artificers and 15 junior ratings. Operational conditions led to the addition of 1 Petty Officer and 3 junior ratings making a total of 31.

The junior ratings all lived and slept in the Torpedo Stowage Compartment between the four re-load torpedoes. This meant that after firing a salvo of torpedoes their whole living quarters had to be removed in order to re-load the tubes.

The Officers and Petty Officers each had a small mess in the forward part of the Accommodation Space; the galley for the whole complement was at the after end of this compartment. The Engine Room Artificers mess was at the forward end of the Control Room. Three WCs and three hand-basins comprised the sanitary arrangements in the submarine.

Armament

The main striking power of the submarine consisted of eight 21in torpedoes, only four of which could be fired together. The re-loads were carried in racks in the Crew Space. The only other offensive weapons were a 12pdr gun forward of the bridge and two machine-guns which could be carried on to the bridge.

Machinery

The submarine was propelled by a Diesel/electric drive. The twin propellers were turned by two tandem pairs of motors. The motors received their power, when on the surface, from two generators each coupled to a 400hp Paxman Diesel engine and, when dived, direct from the Main Battery. When on the surface, the generators also provided power for recharging the Main Battery.

The Main Battery consisted of two sections, each of 112 high capacity cells giving a nominal pressure of 230 volts, situated in large tanks under the Control Room and the Accommodation Space.

The propelling machinery gave the submarine a maximum surface speed of 12 knots and a dived speed of 2 knots for about 60 hours with a maximum speed of 8 knots. The surface endurance at 10 knots was just under 4000 miles.

Periscopes

Two periscopes, with the eye-pieces in the Control Room, were fitted in tubes through the bridge structure. They could be raised hydraulically through a distance of about 12ft so that the upper lens was just above the surface at a keel depth of 44ft. This meant that the highest part of the bridge structure was only 12ft below the surface.

The Search periscope, which was bi-focal and fitted with a high and low magnification lens, had a large diameter top tube and needed careful use when near the enemy. The Attack periscope had a thin upper tube; it was monocular and fitted with a low magnification lens only.

Asdics

An Asdic set was fitted into the forward end of the keel, with the operating controls in the Control Room. This was normally operated in a passive mode, like a hydrophone, but it could be used actively to obtain the range of a target or to communicate with another submarine or surface ship. Hydrophones were also fitted.

Communications

An aerial secured to the jumping wire enabled the submarine to receive messages while dived at a shallow depth. Additionally the W/T mast could be raised whilst dived for receiving and passing messages. While on the surface, reception was no problem and messages could be transmitted to shore stations world-wide.

PART II—OPERATIONAL

Upholder was ordered in 1939 and was launched at Vickers, Barrow, on 8 July 1940. Her short life was then as follows:

August	1940	Commissioned
September	1940	Completed
October/ November	1940	Operational work-up in the Clyde area
10 December	1940	Sailed from UK for Mediterranean
23 December	1940	Arrived Gibraltar
3 January	1941	Sailed for Operation Excess (Reinforcement of Aircraft for Middle East) and Malta
10 January	1941	Arrived Malta
10 January	1941 }	Carried out 25 patrols from
14 April	1942 }	Malta
14 April	1942	Sunk by Italian A/S forces north of Tripoli. No survivors.

A Search periscope being serviced in the periscope workshop. Note the smaller tube of an attack periscope at extreme right (IWM)

Work-Up

On completion of building, *Upholder* was sailed for the Clyde, carrying out engine trials on passage. After a satisfactory dive in the Gareloch, Wanklyn, who had joined the ship in August, accepted the submarine on behalf of the Admiralty from the builders.

An intensive period of training exercises followed in which the ship's company were put through every evolution and breakdown that they were likely to meet until Wanklyn was satisfied that they were an efficient team.

Passage to Malta

Upholder sailed for Gibraltar on 10 December, making the passage, dived by day and surfaced at night. Very bad weather was experienced.

An unfortunate accident occurred to Chief Engine Room Artificer Baker during a particularly heavy roll. To retain his balance, he had grabbed at the jamb of the bulkhead door and at the same time the heavy door broke free from the retaining catch and smashed on to his hand almost severing the tops of three fingers.

Wanklyn here demonstrated that he was a man of many talents as, with infinite patience and a very delicate touch, he sorted out the mangled fingers and strapped them up, having first given Baker the necessary injections to ease the pain. For the next four days he painstakingly dressed the injured fingers until Baker could be transferred to the Military hospital at Gibraltar. It was entirely due to Wanklyn's skill and patience that, apart from a slight malformation of one finger, Baker regained the full use of his hand.

After re-storing and making good minor defects, *Upholder* sailed for Malta on 3 January 1941. While on passage *Upholder* patrolled off the western end of Sicily with the aim of intercepting any Italian surface forces that might venture forth from Naples or Palermo to attack a convoy passing through the Sicilian Straits. Various explosions were heard, presumably the bombing attacks on the convoy, but nothing was seen and *Upholder* arrived at Malta on 12 January where she berthed at the submarine base in Lazaretto Creek.

War Situation

Since Italy entered the war in June 1940 the Allies position in the Mediterranean had worsened. The battle front in North Africa surged back and forth along the African coast. The Axis powers gained air superiority in the Central Mediterranean. Their supply lines to Africa were measured in hundreds of miles compared with the Allies long haul round the Cape of 12,000 miles. Furthermore the Axis supply lines were about 1000 miles from Allied Fleet bases at Gibraltar and Alexandria.

Obviously 1941 was going to be a critical year for the Allies in the Mediterranean. It was imperative to reduce the Axis flow of reinforcements and supplies between Italy and Africa. Aircraft operations from Malta were being hampered by continuous air raids and by the difficulty of getting spares and ammunition for the aircraft. Surface forces could not be used effectively without air support.

The ratings mess deck in the Submarine Base (*IWM*)

In the last half of 1940 our submarines, some operating from Malta as an offshoot of the First Submarine Flotilla at Alexandria, had achieved very little success and had suffered the loss of nine submarines. This was in part due to a restricted 'sink at sight' area imposed on submarines and also to the size and age of the submarines, most of which were the large *'O'*, *'P'* and *'R'* classes recalled from the Far East. A further cause of the casualties was the intensive mine-laying campaign carried out by the Italians.

By the beginning of 1941 Malta was already feeling the effects of the frequent air raids and the scarcity of convoys. Although food and drink was reasonably plentiful, ammunition, torpedoes and heavy spare gear were scarce and continued to be in short supply until the siege was raised in August 1942. At times torpedoes had to be transferred from a submarine returning from patrol in order to complete the outfit of a submarine sailing for patrol. Yet Malta was ideally situated as a base for operations aimed at cutting the Axis supply lines to Africa.

It was against this background that *Upholder* was deployed to Malta as one of 10 *'U'* class submarines to be based there. The larger submarines were withdrawn to Alexandria and operated along the African coast and in the approaches to the Aegean. In February the 'sink at sight' zone was greatly enlarged and submarines were able to patrol close to the Tunisian coast along which most of the Axis convoys passed.

First Patrol

In preparation for the first patrol a short visit to the Dockyard was necessary. This coincided with some particularly heavy air attacks on 16 and 19 January. These attacks had as their main target the aircraft carrier *Illustrious* who had been damaged while escorting the convoy mentioned above; *Upholder* was in the next berth and was in action with her machine guns, but with little effect even though the enemy aircraft dived very low. Some submarines in the dockyard suffered some minor damage but *Upholder* was unscathed.

Upholder sailed on 24 January to patrol to the west of Tripoli and it was not long before the first target was sighted. At 0130 on 26 January while surfaced, a supply ship, escorted by a destroyer, was attacked

Loading a torpedo at the Torpedo Depot in Msida Creek, Malta. Note the guard protecting the propellers during loading (*IWM*)

with two torpedoes. While evading the destroyer another supply ship was sighted and two more torpedoes were fired but all four missed.

Two days later, again when on the surface, two more supply ships were sighted. After the experience of the earlier attacks, Wanklyn closed in to 900 yards before firing two torpedoes of which one hit a 8000 ton ship believed to be the German *Duisburg.* After sunrise this ship was still visible but it was felt she would soon sink.

On the afternoon of 30 January, the Asdic operator reported hydrophone effect of a convoy to the west and it was not long before the convoy and its escorts were sighted through the periscope. After manoeuvring into position, the remaining two torpedoes were fired at a 5000 ton ship and one hit was claimed. A fairly heavy and noisy depth charge attack followed but Wanklyn listened to reports from the Asdic operator and quietly manoeuvred *Upholder* clear. As all torpedoes had been expended, course was set for Malta where the submarine arrived on 1 February during an air raid.

Second Patrol

Morale was high when *Upholder* sailed on 12 February for another patrol in the same area. When only a few hours from Malta and just after dark, the lookout sighted a small object to the south. Wanklyn soon identified it as a submarine and hopes ran high through the *Upholder* at the prospect of

HMS Utmost *securing alongside the depot ship, HMS* Forth (*IWM*)

sinking this valuable target. However, Wanklyn being a master of his job, identified it as one of our *'T'* class; but, as he had no information about one of our submarines being in the area, he ordered the challenge signal to be made. The signal was repeated three times but no reply received. Nevertheless Wanklyn was so sure of his identification that he withheld fire. It transpired that the submarine was *Truant* returning early from patrol with her wireless out of action.

This patrol provided experience of glassy calm seas and the clarity of the Mediterranean water. The

The Control Room of HMS Utmost, *showing the Captain, Lieutenant-Commander R. D. Cayley, at the periscope. To the left, the Torpedo Officer operating the Torpedo calculator. On the right, the First Lieutenant supervising the hydroplane operators and adjusting the trim as necessary* (*IWM*)

An officer checking the Search periscope before sailing for patrol. Note the steering wheel and above it the bottom half of the Torpedo calculator (*IWM*)

forward casing, some 25ft below the surface could be clearly seen through the periscope and it was realised how visible the submarine must be to an aircraft, particularly when its attention had been drawn to the area by the disturbance on the surface made by the periscope when it was raised. This was one of the major problems the submarines had to face when operating in these conditions and, for this reason, the 10th S/M Flotilla adopted a 'Mediterranean Blue' paint to reduce visual detection below the surface. Fortunately only a slight breeze was needed to disturb the surface and restore the advantage of invisibility to the submarine.

Little was seen during this patrol and only one attack was made on a convoy of three ships escorted by three destroyers, obviously an important convoy. Although Wanklyn was able to fire from a favourable position no hit resulted.

Two further patrols were carried out in March. During the first only a small northbound convoy was sighted and in view of the shortage of torpedoes this was allowed to pass. The second patrol was a reconnaissance of the east coast of Sicily and although useful information was gathered no targets presented themselves.

The fifth patrol in early April provided three good opportunities of striking at the enemy supply lines and eight torpedoes were fired, but all missed.

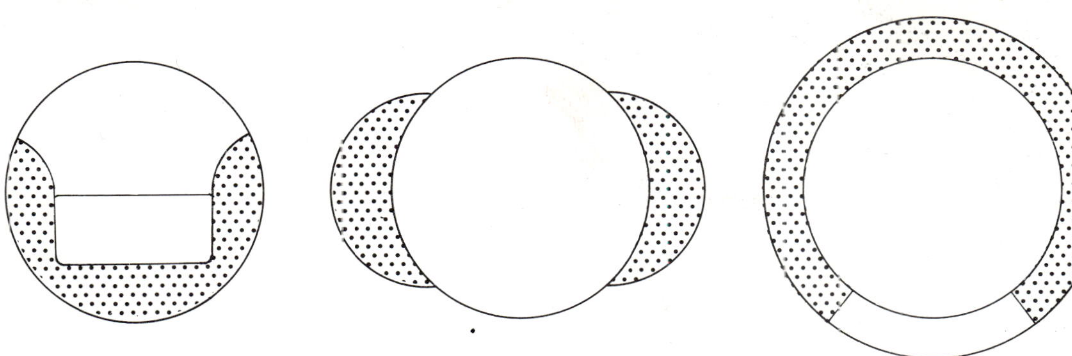

Types of hull (shaded portions indicate ballast tanks)

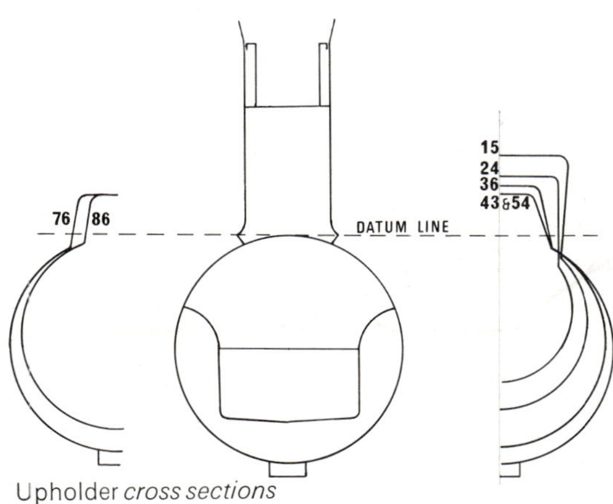

Upholder *cross sections*

Another view of the instruments used by the hydroplane operators who are seen in position (*IWM*)

A close up of the instruments in front of each hydroplane operator (*IWM*)

While returning to Malta yet another southbound convoy was sighted during the night. Knowing that there was a surface force operating from Malta, Wanklyn ordered gun action stations and fired starshell into the sky ahead of the convoy. As hoped, the convoy, thinking that an attack by a surface force was imminent, turned back on its tracks, while *Upholder* signalled an enemy report to Malta.

Wanklyn: Leader of Men

Upholder had now carried out four patrols with no success and had fired a number of valuable torpedoes. The three recent unsuccessful attacks following on the earlier miss raised doubts as to Wanklyn's competence. Even Commander Simpson, who commanded the submarine base in Malta, and who had such a high opinion of Wanklyn's capabilities, was beginning to wonder whether he could afford to retain a Commanding Officer who was using up valuable torpedoes with no result.

One might have thought that the morale of the ship's company would have suffered from the lack of success during the past three months, particularly as other submarines from Malta were scoring successes. The fact that this was not the case was entirely due to Wanklyn's personality and leadership. The ship's company still had every confidence in him and they went all out to give him the best support they could. It was a measure of the man that he was able to maintain that spirit under those conditions, particularly as he must have been undergoing considerable mental strain at the time. Being a perfectionist he must have spent many worried hours pondering over the run of unsuccessful attacks. However, he remained outwardly calm, concentrating on the preparations for the next patrol during which he was determined to break the run of bad luck.

A Crucial Patrol: The Fifth

It was in this light that Wanklyn set off on 21 April for what must have been for him a vital patrol. Three days later, in the well known area off the Tunisian coast, a convoy was sighted. Determined

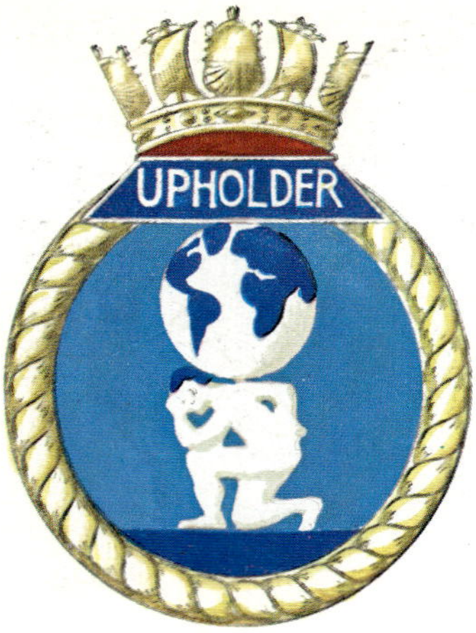

HM S/M *Upholder* is depicted in the 'Mediterranean blue' colour adopted by all boats of the Tenth Submarine Flotilla which operated from Lazaretto, Malta, during the three critical years from the last half of 1940 until the end of 1943.

In glassy calm conditions, the shape of a patrolling submarine could be sighted at depths of up to one hundred feet by enemy reconnaissance aircraft.

T. Brittain © Profile Publications Ltd

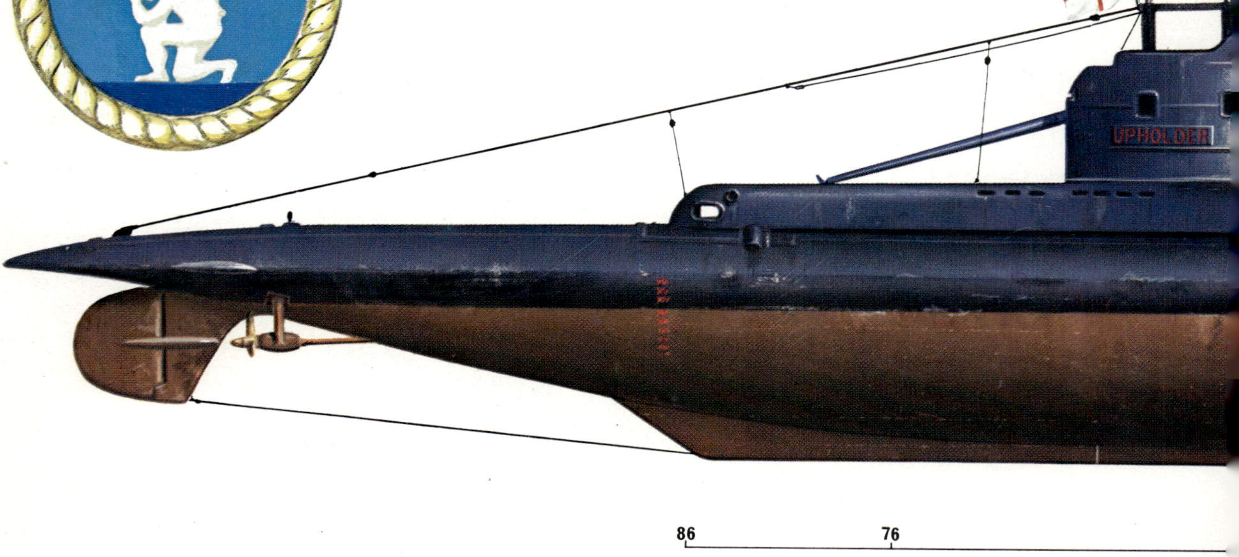

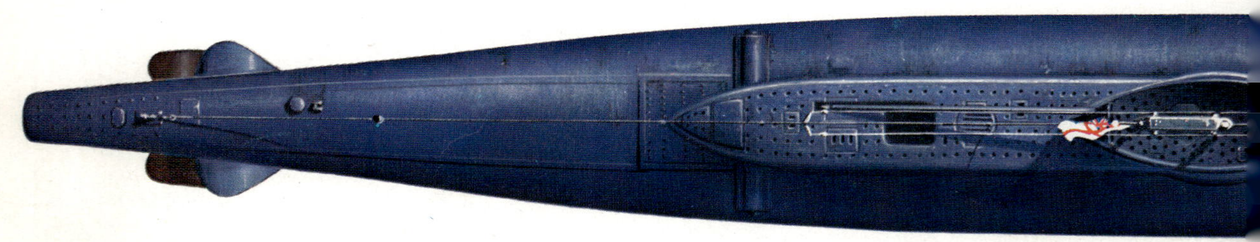

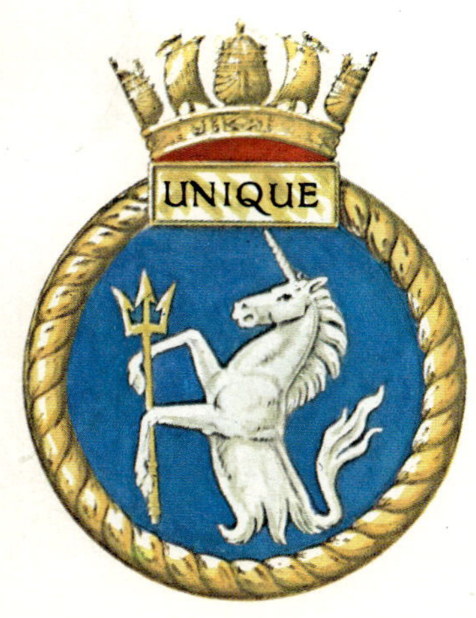

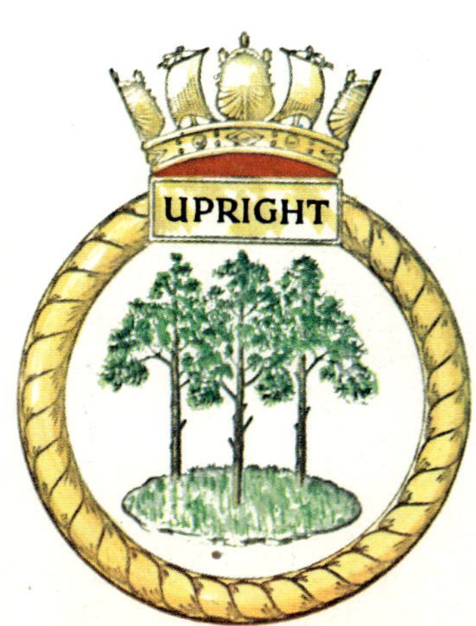

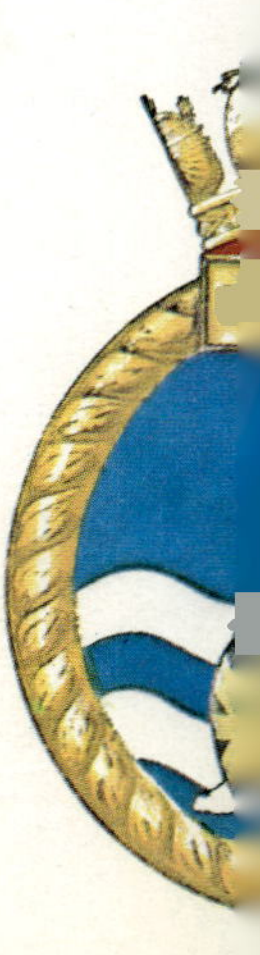

e Jolly Roger : key to symbols

vhite bar	=Supply ship sunk or probably sunk
ed bar	=A warship sunk or probably sunk
plit bar of her colour	=Target damaged but not sunk
ed bar with 'U'	=A U-Boat sunk (German or Italian)
ɔssed guns	=A successful gun action. Subsequent gun actions were shown adding stars round the guns
ggers	=Special operations such as landing agents, blowing up railways by landing demolition teams (*Cloak-and-dagger*)

he case of *Upholder's* Jolly Roger the split bar, ninth from the top, and the two s, fourth and fifth from the bottom, and the three U-Boat symbols are Red ; the : are white.

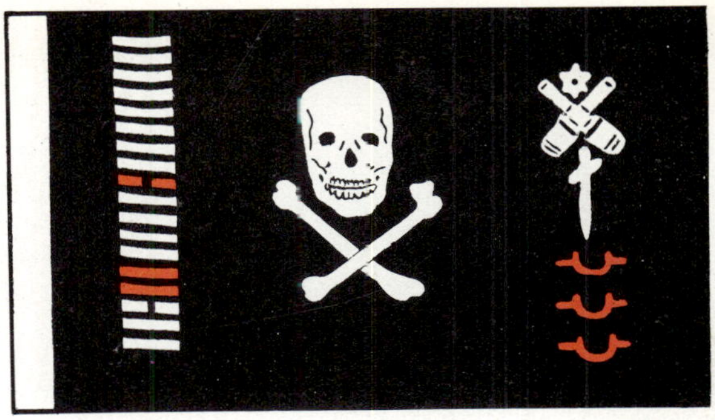

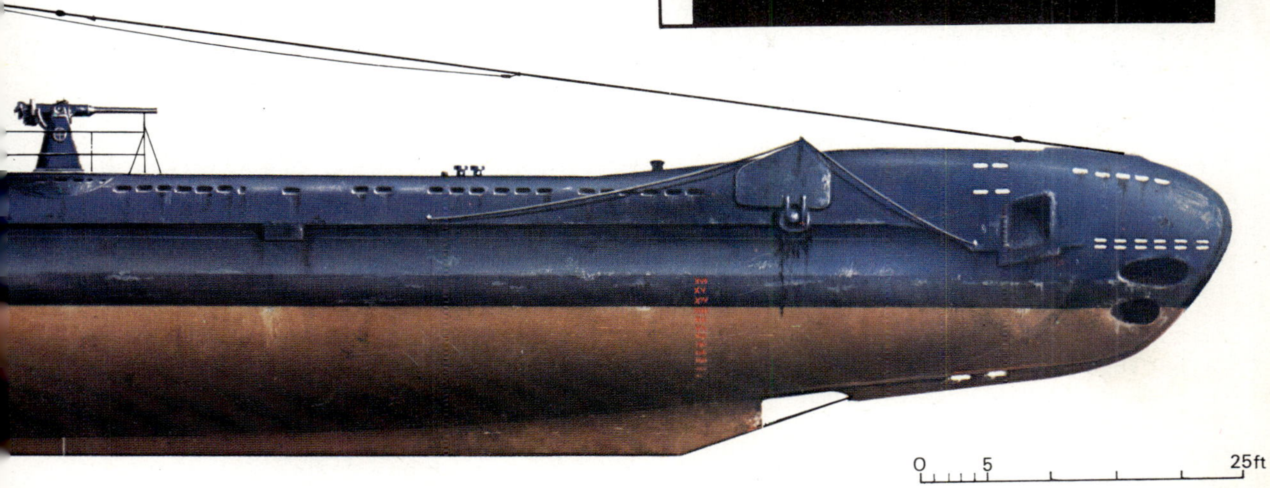

0
5
25ft

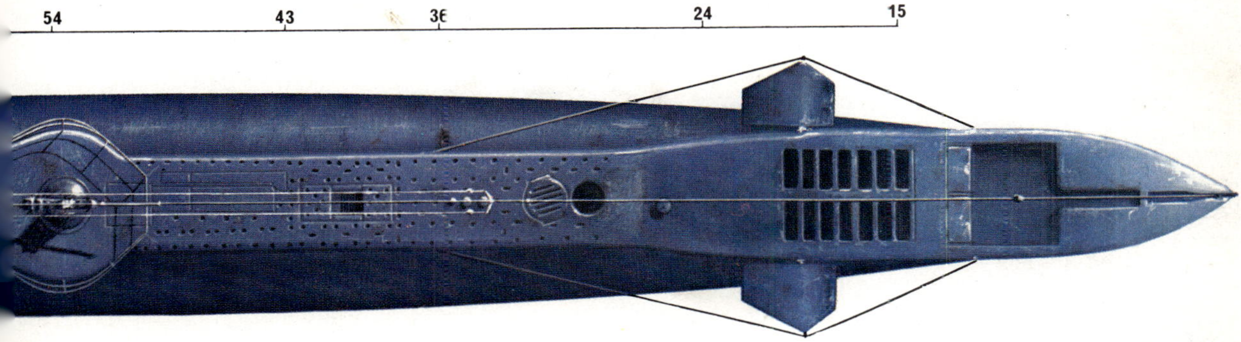

54
43
36
24
15

USK

UTMOST
N
E
W
S

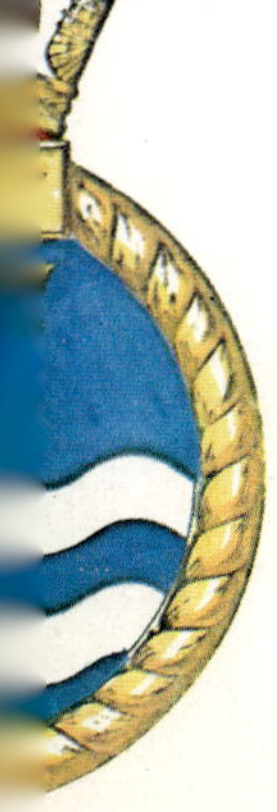

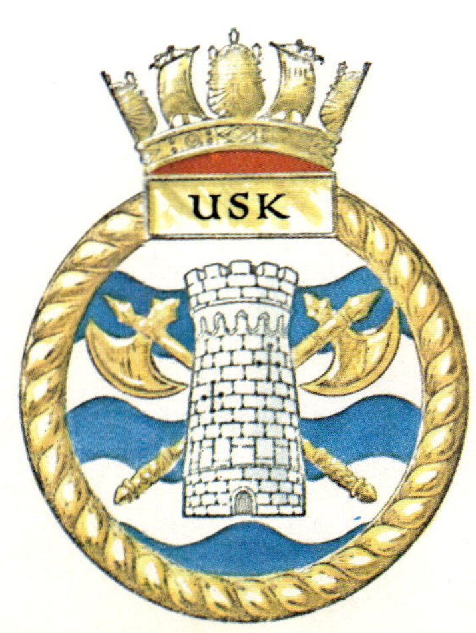

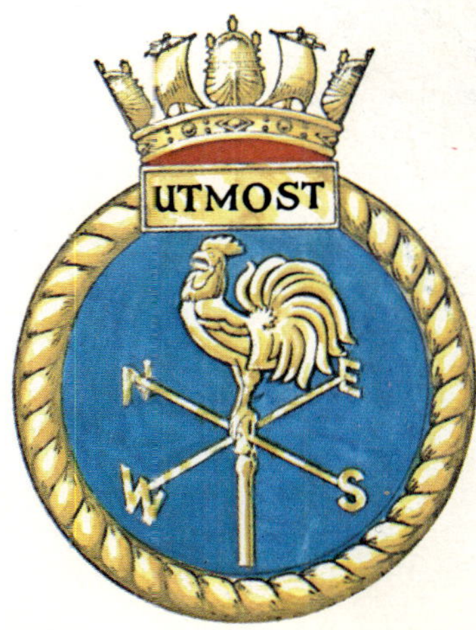

A spare submarine battery in a storage shed ashore. Note the size of an individual cell being lifted at left (IWM)

Provisions arriving by boat and being stacked on the casing (IWM)

Provisions being taken below for stowing. Note the free flood holes all over the top of the casing (IWM)

to succeed, but in no sense of desperation, the range was closed to 700 yards before firing at and sinking the *Antonietta Laura* of 5428 tons. Wanklyn must have felt with great relief that the spell had been broken.

The next day *Upholder* was ordered to close Kerkenah Bank and try to finish off a destroyer and a supply ship who were aground, and probably abandoned, on the Bank, the result of a successful surface force sweep. This meant entering water in which it was not possible to dive should enemy ships or aircraft appear, a situation which no submariner relishes.

The approach was left until the late afternoon so that the withdrawal could be carried out under cover of darkness. It was hoped to be able to put a torpedo into each of the ships but when *Upholder* grounded as she approached the destroyer, it was felt that there might be other shallow patches which could cause valuable torpedoes to be wasted. Wanklyn therefore decided to go alongside the supply ship and set her on fire.

A boarding party was put on board the ship, the *Arta*, who was loaded with transport and munitions and who had obviously been carrying a number of troops. After searching the ship and blowing the Master's safe, demolition charges were placed with the object of setting the ship on fire. The boarding party re-embarked together with their souvenirs, German tin hats and the like, and *Upholder* thankfully set course for deeper water. The demolition charges did their work satisfactorily and the ship could be seen burning late into the night.

A few days later, in very rough weather a convoy of five ships with four escorting destroyers was sighted. Depth keeping and periscope observations were difficult but Wanklyn fired a salvo of four torpedoes. Three hits were obtained resulting in the German ship, *Leverkusen,* 7386 tons, being sunk and the *Arcturus,* 2597 tons, being stopped. A moderate counter attack followed but, when the destroyers left to rejoin the convoy, Wanklyn finished off the damaged ship with his last torpedo.

Seventh Patrol

On 15 May *Upholder* was off again this time to the east coast of Sicily to intercept southbound traffic from the Straits of Messina. This patrol had an inauspicious start as, soon after sailing, one of the loaded torpedoes developed a leak and had to be exchanged with one of the re-loads. This involved a major upheaval in the Crew Space and a certain amount of juggling in this confined area. Three days later a more serious defect occurred in the Asdic set which robbed Wanklyn, not only of a means of detecting the enemy, but also of a valuable aid in taking avoiding action during a counter attack.

On 22 and 23 May escorted convoys were sighted and three torpedoes were fired at each. One hit was obtained on each occasion and a 4000 ton and a 5000 ton ship were considered sunk. The latter ship was thought to be the Vichy French ship, *Capitaine Damiani.* After the second attack, the escorts delivered a very heavy counter-attack and

Lieutenant-Commander Wanklyn being congratulated by Lieutenant R. Drummond on the award of the VC. December 1941 (*IWM*)

Lieutenant-Commander Wanklyn and the officers of HMS Upholder, *December 1941* (*IWM*)

Upholder suffered some minor damage including the bow cap of a torpedo tube.

The Sinking of 'Conte Rosse'

Just after sunset on 24 May a southbound convoy was sighted. There was a heavy swell running which made periscope observations difficult and only two torpedoes remained. This attack was to earn Wanklyn the award of the Victoria Cross, the first awarded to a submariner in World War II. The attack can best be described in the words of the citation for the VC:

On the evening of the 24 May 1941, while on patrol off the coast of Sicily, Lieutenant-Commander Wanklyn in command of His Majesty's Submarine, *Upholder*, sighted a southbound enemy troop convoy, strongly escorted by destroyers.
The failing light was such that observation by periscope could not be relied on, but a surface attack would have been easily seen. *Upholder*'s listening gear was out of action.
In spite of these handicaps, Lieutenant-Commander Wanklyn decided to press home his attack at short range. He quickly steered his craft into a favourable position and closed in so as to make sure of his target. By this time the whereabouts of the escorting destroyers could not be made out. Lieutenant-Commander Wanklyn, while fully aware of the risk of being rammed by one of the escort, continued to press on towards the enemy troopships. As he was about to fire, one of the enemy destroyers suddenly appeared out of the darkness at high speed and he only just avoided being rammed. As soon as he was clear he brought his periscope sights on and fired torpedoes, which sank a large troopship. The enemy destroyers at once made a strong counter-attack and during the next 20 minutes dropped thirty-seven depth charges near *Upholder*.
The failure of his listening device made it much harder for him to get away, but with the greatest courage, coolness and skill he brought *Upholder* clear of the enemy and safe back to harbour.'

The troopship which Wanklyn sank on that day was the 18,000 ton liner, *Conte Rosse*, cruising at an estimated speed of 20 knots. This was the sort of attack at which Wanklyn excelled. A quick thinker, with a very clear and mathematical brain, he soon had a clear picture of the main target and his quick reactions enabled him to deal with the sudden appearance of the escorts.

During the counter-attack nobody could assist the Captain other than those responsible for controlling the course and depth of the submarine. There was complete silence apart from a few inspired quiet orders from Wanklyn as he stood in the Control Room characteristically stroking his beard from time to time. These orders directed alterations of course, speed and depth in an attempt to throw off the destroyers, whose propellers could be clearly heard in the submarine as they passed over the top.

Photographs taken through the periscope of a 'U' class submarine showing salvage operations in progress on a sunken ship close to an enemy port and a torpedo exploding under the salvage craft (*Author's collection*)

As this happened most of the crew involuntarily bent their knees and crouched in anticipation of the next deluge of depth charges.

At one stage a peculiar noise such as might be made by a wire scraping along the hull caused all eyes to be turned towards the Captain who quickly dispelled all anxiety by confidently stating that it was the noise of the sinking ship breaking up. It was at moments like this that Wanklyn showed his greatness for, whatever doubts he himself might

A 'U' class submarine sailing from Malta for a patrol (*IWM*)

A 'U' class submarine sailing for patrol passing another submarine recently returned from patrol. Note the free flood holes around the torpedo tube apertures (*Author's collection*)

have had, he always exuded confidence and this, of course, had an effect on every member of the crew.

Torpedo Accident
It was on return from this patrol that another unfortunate accident occurred. While embarking torpedoes ready for the next patrol, one of the torpedoes started to run whilst being loaded into the tube, giving off large quantities of exhaust carbon-monoxide. Petty Officer Carter, a first class, experienced rating in charge of the Torpedo department, tried vainly to shut off the torpedo and collapsed in the Tube Space. The Torpedo Officer, Lieutenant Read, tried to assist Carter and was also overcome. By the time they were both brought up to the casing artificial respiration was of no avail to Carter, and Read was admitted to hospital suffering from severe carbon-monoxide poisoning.

Rest Periods
Normally there was a period of about ten days between patrols during which the submarine was re-stored, defects made good and the crew rested as far as possible. Facilities for relaxation and recreation were limited in Malta during 1941/42 with the frequent air raids; food and drink became increasingly scarce to the point of being unobtainable.
Occasionally part of the crew spent a few days at a rest camp in a remote part of the island but at the height of the bombing the crew was required to dive the submarine and sit on the bottom during the day raids. This put a great strain on personnel and it was almost a relief to sail on patrol.

Sicily-North Africa Mine Barrier
It was known that many enemy mines had been laid in the narrow waters between Sicily and the North African coast. It was necessary to find a route through these minefields to widen the area of operations for the Malta based submarines and to allow reinforcements from UK to join the submarine squadrons at

A harmless looking Italian Schooner typical of many which were fitted with hydrophones, asdics and A/S weapons (*Author's collection*)

Malta and Alexandria. It fell to the lot of *Utmost* to blaze the trail in June and her safe passage was communicated in a manner typical of the submarine commanding officers serving in Malta by the brief signal, *'Next please'.*

Twelfth Patrol

Wanklyn was rested in the first half of June and Lieutenant Hezlet commanded *Upholder* for the eighth patrol, during which only a hospital ship was sighted. Patrol followed patrol and in mid-August *Upholder* sailed for her 12th patrol. By this time Wanklyn had added two 6000 ton supply ships to his bag and had severely damaged the Italian cruiser, *Garibaldi* but, unfortunately, when the cruiser was sighted only two torpedoes remained. The target was proceeding at high speed (28 knots) and was passing at long range. Wanklyn once again demonstrated his quick thinking as the whole attack only took a few minutes from sighting to firing the torpedoes and he obtained two hits. The number of depth charges dropped on *Upholder* had also risen considerably.

Something new was in store for *Upholder* on this twelfth patrol as an Army Officer and a Corporal, together with a canoe, had been embarked. The area of operations was the north coast of Sicily near Palermo.

However, before the Army could carry out their operation, *Upholder* had run across three targets

The Torpedo Stowage compartment of a 'T' class submarine immediately prior to sailing for patrol. In a 'U' class submarine the junior ratings lived and slept in this compartment (*IWM*)

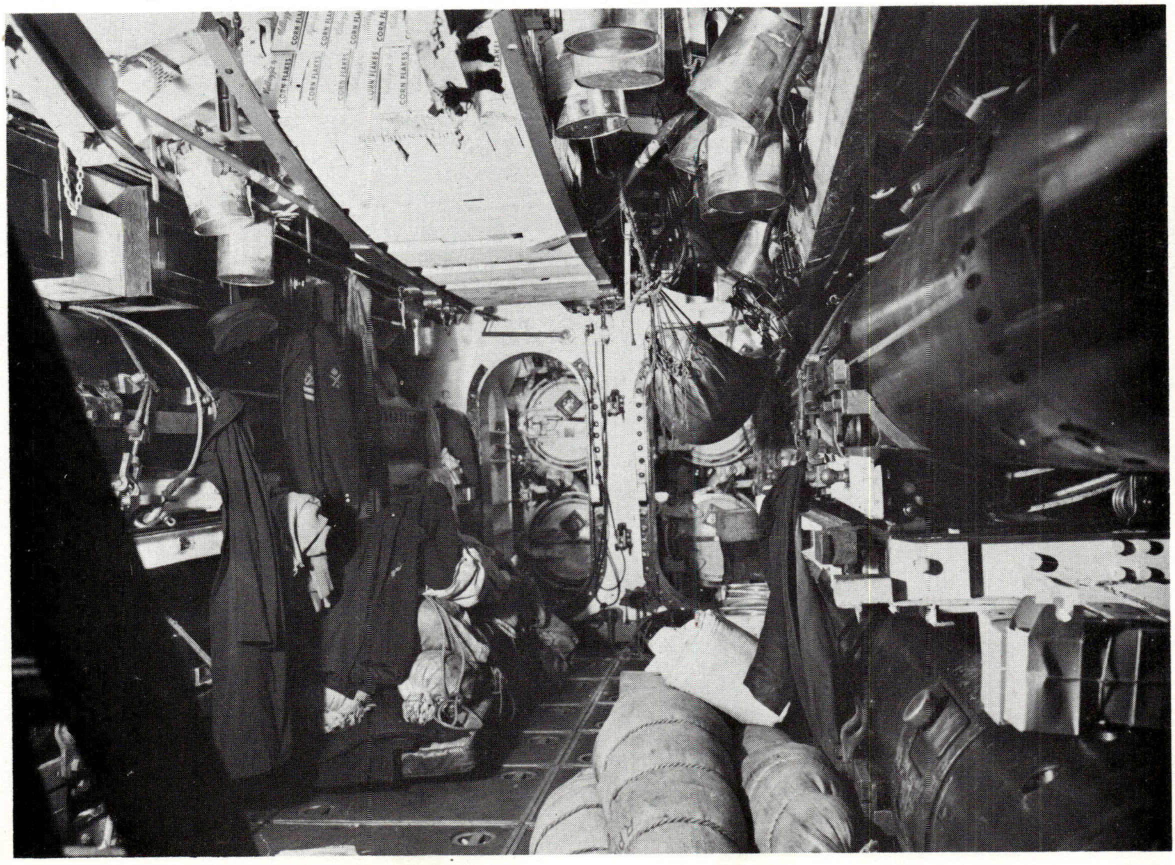

and expended all her torpedoes. First Wanklyn sank a trawler *Enotria,* 852 tons with two torpedoes. A few days later, four torpedoes were fired at a valuable convoy of three supply ships escorted by three destroyers and two hits accounted for a 4500 ton tanker. Finally, a naval force of one battleship, two cruisers and six destroyers were sighted and the remaining two torpedoes were fired. It was thought that one torpedo might have hit a cruiser but this has never been confirmed. The last two attacks were followed by very heavy counter-attacks.

On the night of 25 August the coast was closed and the soldiers paddled ashore in their canoe with the object of blowing up a railway line. Soon after they should have landed, a considerable disturbance, with shots being fired, was clearly heard in *Upholder* and it was felt that, at best, the soldiers must have been taken prisoner. Time passed and, in the submarine, anxiety grew but just as hope of recovering the soldiers was being given up the blue flicker of their torch was seen. They were soon embarked and the canoe stowed below. Wanklyn thankfully withdrew from the coast and set course for Malta arriving on 27 August.

It transpired that the alarm had been raised ashore but the soldiers had managed to hide up with their canoe. Later they made their way towards the railway line but were faced with a very steep climb carrying the explosives. By the time they had to turn back they were nowhere near the railway.

Sinking of Troopships

Two days after returning from patrol, *Upholder* was ordered to sea to intercept a large convoy reported by reconnaissance. The convoy, consisting of three liners escorted by six destroyers, was sighted on 31 August and four torpedoes were fired at it but with no success.

Upholder then had two weeks in Malta before being ordered to sea on 16 September in company with three other submarines to intercept an important southbound troop convoy.

Late on 17 September a sighting report from the submarine to the eastward (*Unbeaten*) was intercepted and *Upholder* was on the surface closing the reported track of the convoy when, at 0300 on 18 September, three large 2-funnel liners escorted by five or six destroyers were sighted.

The gyro compass was out of action and there was a moderate sea running which made it difficult to steer a steady course. By skilful manoeuvring Wanklyn was able to fire his torpedoes as two of these ships overlapped making a continuous target. The yawing of the submarine caused him to vary the normal sequence of firing. The first torpedo was fired at the bow of the leading ship but the second torpedo was fired at the stern of the rear ship. The third and fourth torpedoes were spread across the centre of this large target as the submarine swung back. The range at the time was about 5000 yards. *Upholder* then dived and after what seemed like hours at least two, and possibly three, torpedoes were heard to explode.

As no counter-attack developed, presumably because the escorting ships were busy recovering survivors, Wanklyn surfaced 45 minutes later to survey the situation. One liner was lying stopped with destroyers fussing around her, one was presumed to have sunk. The third had been heard steaming away to the westward and it was hoped that she would be attacked by the other submarines on the patrol line.

It was now a question of finishing off the crippled ship and so the submarine was dived to re-load torpedoes and as daylight broke *Upholder* was closing the liner to deliver the *coup de grace*. Three of the destroyers were circling the ship and, just as Wanklyn was about to fire, one of them forced him to go deep. At this stage *Upholder* was so close to the target that the only solution was to dive under the ship and open out on the other side, turn and fire. This was successfully done and two torpedoes sent her to the bottom. Woodward (*Unbeaten*), who was closing from the other side, was amazed to see his target disappear just as he was going to fire. The two liners sunk were the *Neptunia* and *Oceania* of 19,500 tons each.

Losses

Although Wanklyn continued with his run of successes, the submarines at Malta had not escaped without losses. *Usk* had been sunk in April, *Undaunted* in May, *Union* in July and *P32* and *P33* in August. These last two were *'U'* class submarines but the war programme ships were not given names until 1943.

The aim had been to keep the flotilla at Malta up to a strength of ten submarines but by the end of 1941 only three of the original ten were still operating from Malta; these were *Upholder*, *Urge* and *Unbeaten*.

The submarines at Malta formed into an independent flotilla, The Tenth, in June when Commander Simpson was promoted to Captain.

Seventeenth Patrol

Sailing on 7 November, *Upholder* was forced to dive that night when illuminated by an aircraft flare, but this was only a temporary delay. Just before dawn on 8 November, Wanklyn was called to the bridge and soon identified an Italian U-boat of the *Perla* class. By the time Wanklyn had closed the target it was getting light and so he dived to complete the attack, firing four torpedoes to sink the U-boat.

A signal was received that day informing Wanklyn that Force K, consisting of the cruisers *Penelope* and *Aurora* and two destroyers, would be passing through the area that night. The force was sighted and they laid on a magnificent firework display while demolishing an enemy convoy. Wanklyn decided to close the scene of the battle the next morning and picked off a destroyer (*Libeccio*) with one torpedo.

Later that forenoon, a force of two cruisers and four destroyers were sighted. They had probably been sent to see what they could salvage from the previous night's scrap. Wanklyn managed to get in an attack with his three remaining torpedoes but the centre torpedo ran wild. The other two torpedoes just missed ahead and astern of the cruiser but one torpedo damaged one of the escorting destroyers.

Preparing to reload the torpedo tubes in a 'T' class submarine. Portable rails being shipped between the stowage racks on which the torpedoes were moved into line with the torpedo tubes for loading (IWM)

A 'U' class submarine recovering survivors from one of its victims. Note the forward hydroplanes turned out ready for operating (Author's collection)

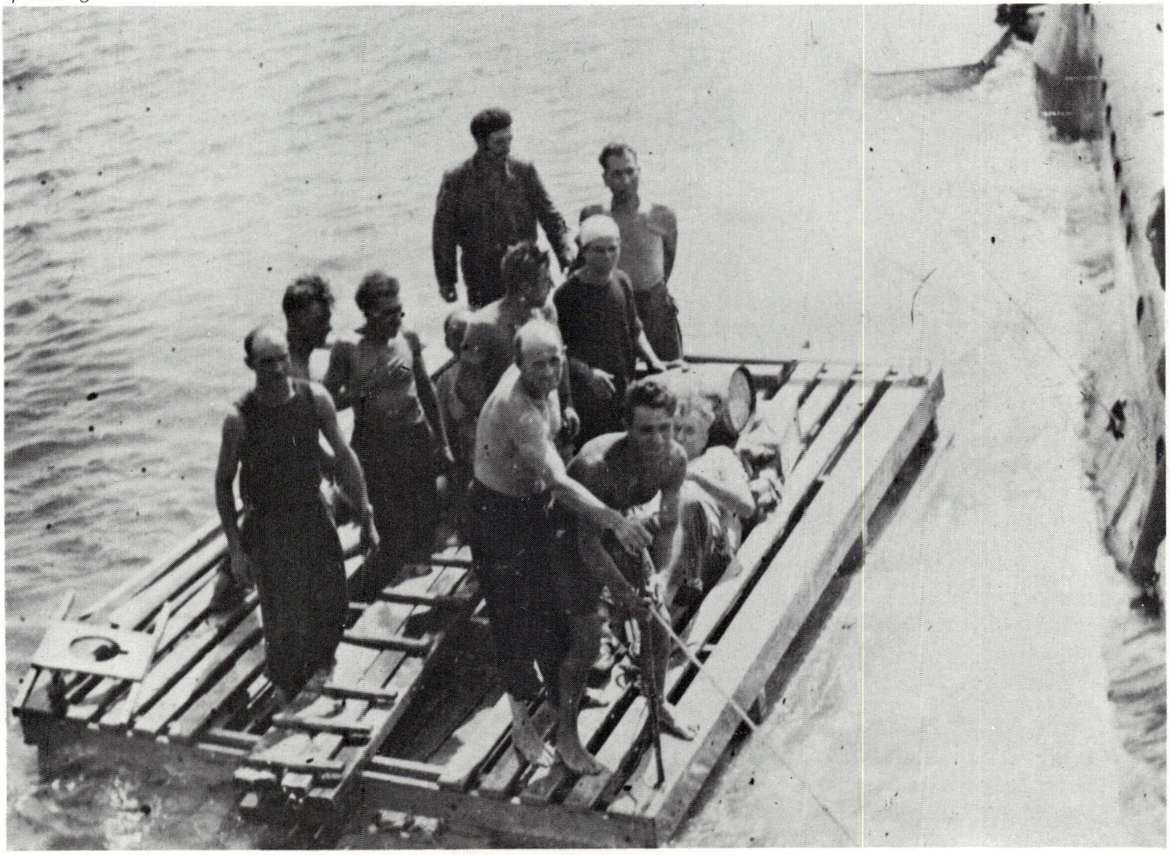

HMS Unseen *sailing for patrol. Note that the W/T mast has been omitted in the later 'U' class* (*Author's collection*)

The Captain of HMS Umbra, *Lieutenant-Commander S. L. C. Maydon, at the periscope* (*IWM*)

Upholder was back in Malta less than four days after sailing having sunk a U-boat and a destroyer and damaged another destroyer.

18th and 19th Patrols: Calabrian Coast

The next two patrols, at the end of November and in the middle of December were carried out off the south coast of the toe of Italy. During the earlier patrol two attacks took place but with no success. A tanker, escorted by two destroyers, was missed with four torpedoes and a force of cruisers and destroyers was missed in an attack using Asdic bearings to fire the torpedoes. In the second patrol there was intense activity throughout and *Upholder* had a hectic time avoiding numerous small A/S ships and aircraft, but no worthwhile targets were seen.

Air Attack

On 29 December *Upholder,* on this occasion under the command of Lieutenant C. P. Norman, carried out a day's exercises off Malta and, while returning to harbour on the surface, was forced to dive by German Messerschmitt aircraft. Cannon shots hit the water all round the bridge and some hit the conning tower as the submarine dived. Norman was hit by shrapnel in the head, arms and body and fell down the tower before he could shut the upper hatch. Realising the submarine was heading for disaster unless the hatch was shut he managed to drag himself up the tower and just managed to shut the hatch as the water reached the bridge level.

20th Patrol: Second U-boat

The twentieth patrol started on New Year's Eve and proved to be a very successful start to 1942. On 4 January two torpedoes were fired at *Sirio,* 5222 tons, one of which exploded on the bottom almost under the submarine but caused little damage to *Upholder*. Two further torpedoes were fired and one hit but the ship did not sink. Wanklyn surfaced to try and finish her off with his 12pdr gun but fierce

A torpedo being loaded into a 'U' class submarine. Note all the seat lockers on the casing which have been removed from the Torpedo Stowage compartment to make room for handling the torpedoes (*IWM*)

The Diving and Blowing panel of a submarine. The horizontal levers control the hydraulically operated vents of the Main Ballast Tanks. Rating on right operates the levers for raising and lowering the periscopes. Other rating has his hand on a HP Blow valve *(IWM)*

return fire from two Breda guns in the damaged ship forced him to dive and withdraw from the area.

On 5 January just before dawn, Wanklyn was on the bridge when a large Italian U-boat was sighted. Only one torpedo remained and Wanklyn, having seen that the forward gun in the U-boat was manned, decided to dive, hoping that he could fire his torpedo before the U-boat could dive. This he managed to do and scored a hit. On surfacing three survivors were recovered and they stated that the submarine was the *Ammiraglio St Bon* and they were just about to open fire on *Upholder.*

21st Patrol: Iron Ring

The next patrol had a special objective, namely, forming part of a ring of submarines round Taranto to intercept any of the Italian Fleet that might sail to attack a convoy which it was hoped to force through to the beleagured Malta. However, nothing was seen other than a hospital ship and a small supply ship which passed out of range.

Air Raids

The air offensive against Malta was stepped up during the first four months of 1942 and January was a very bad month for the submarines based there. Apart from *P 38* lost on patrol, five *'U'* class were damaged by air attack, two beyond repair. A Greek submarine under repair was sunk and *Pandora*, who was being used to run stores into Malta, was sunk before she had been completely unloaded: her torpedoes were later extracted for use by the Tenth Flotilla.

22nd Patrol

At the end of January, Captain Simpson ordered Wanklyn to take a rest and Norman was again put in command of *Upholder*, this time for a patrol off the north coast of Sicily. On 4 February three torpedoes were fired at a destroyer but with no result. Air and surface activity increased and *Upholder* was sighted by an aircraft while attacking a small convoy and was thwarted by a long and heavy depth charge attack.

On 7 February a successful attack resulted in a 2500 ton ship being sunk. The escorting destroyer delivered a counter-attack.

23rd Patrol: Tripoli

Wanklyn was back in command when *Upholder* sailed on 21 February to join a concentration of submarines around Tripoli where an important convoy was expected to arrive. Very bad weather caused the submarine to arrive a few hours late at her position but hopes soon rose when an aircraft was seen patrolling to the eastward, often the sign of an approaching convoy. Nothing was seen of this convoy and orders were received to shift patrol position to the west of Tripoli.

For the next few days there was intense destroyer activity in the area but no suitable target was seen until 27 February when two hits were obtained on *Tembien*. 5584 tons.

Italian Torpedo Boat, Pegaso, *manoeuvring to come alongside an Italian battleship*
(*Bibliothek Für Zeitgeschichte*)

24th Patrol: Adriatic

Wanklyn had always been asking for a patrol in the Adriatic and on 14 March he sailec for this area. He closed Brindisi and, observing that traffic did not appear to be following swept-channels, he felt it was safe to go really close in to the coast. He was justified in this decision by sighting a *Perla* class U-boat but this passed out of range. Later another U-boat was seen and, although four small fishing vessels in the area complicated the attack, he managed to get off four torpedoes, two of which sunk the *Tricheco.*

A chance to use the gun came when a small trawler and three small fishing vessels were sighted close in-shore. Wanklyn surfaced very close by the trawler and ordered the crew to leave before sinking her with a very small expenditure of ammunition. The Italians equipped many such vessels with A/S equipment and small guns and they could be a menace to submarines.

Upholder was then ordered to shift patrol to an area off Taranto to watch for movement of the Italian Fleet and so course was set to pass through the Otranto Straits. On 23 March in very rough weather and in poor visibility the Asdic operator reported the noise of enemy propellers and Wanklyn was just able to make out the top of a battleship. It was almost impossible to control the depth of the submarine at periscope depth but an attack was made firing four torpedoes, but with no success.

Having fired all her torpedoes, *Upholder* returned to Malta arriving on 26 March and all the crew had a few days break in a rest camp.

Last Patrol

Upholder sailed on 6 April for what was planned to be her last patrol before returning to the UK. Her first mission was to land some agents on the African coast and this was completed satisfactorily. Wanklyn then made a rendezvous with *Unbeaten* in order to transfer an Army officer, who had been in charge of landing the agents.

Upholder was then ordered to join a patrol line with two other submarines off Tripoli to intercept a convoy expected to arrive shortly. Nothing was heard from *Upholder* again.

Urge reported later that on 14 April she had heard heavy depth charging and as no other submarine was lost at this time it was presumed that this must have been a successful attack on *Upholder*. It is thought possible that the Italian Torpedo Boat, *Pegaso* may have unknowingly been responsible for the sinking. Her log for the afternoon of the 14 April reads:

> Day 14.4.42, 1615 hours—as a result of white smoke (*from*) escort seaplane and distant reading on echo-direction-finder, I carry out the prescribed alarm signals for submarine and begin the attack by dropping a pattern of depth charges.
>
> Day 14.4.42, 1630 hours—receiving no further echo on echo-direction-finder, I call off the attack and rejoin the convoy, resuming escort duties.

However the *Upholder* was sunk, the Navy lost not only an outstanding submarine commander but an officer who had all the qualities necessary for the highest appointments in the service. One must not forget that the Navy also lost a very highly trained and experienced team of officers and ratings, for of those that were lost all but a handful had been with Wanklyn throughout the life of *Upholder*.

SUMMARY OF SUCCESSES

In the 16 months that *Upholder* had operated in the Mediterranean Wanklyn had:

a. Sunk three U-boats and one destroyer.
b. Damaged one cruiser and one destroyer.
c. Sunk or damaged 19 supply ships totalling 119,000 tons.

Summary of Patrols

1941

1.	24/1 to 1/2	West of Tripoli
2.	12/2 to 23/2	West of Tripoli
3.	3/3 to 10/3	West of Tripoli
4.	19/3 to 25/3	East Coast of Sicily
5.	3/4 to 14/4	Off Cape Bon
6.	21/4 to 3/5	Lampedusa Channel
7.	18/5 to 28/5	East Coast of Sicily
8.	6/6 to 17/6	North East of Tripoli
9.	24/6 to 27/6	Off Tunisian Coast
10.	28/6 to 8/7	South of Straits of Messina
11.	20/7 to 31/7	North West Coast Sicily
12.	15/8 to 27/8	North West Coast Sicily
13.	29/8 to 2/9	Lampedusa Channel
14.	16/9 to 20/9	North East of Tripoli
15.	23/9 to 2/10	North Coast of Sicily and off Naples
16.	18/10 to 27/10	Tunisian Coast
17.	7/11 to 11/11	East of Malta on Italy/N. Africa route
18.	25/11 to 1/12	Calabrian Coast
19.	12/12 to 23/12	Calabrian Coast

1942

20.	31/12 to 8/1	North West Coast Sicily
21.	14/1 to 23/1	Gulf of Taranto
22.	1/2 to 13/2	North Coast Sicily
23.	21/2 to 2/3	Libyan Coast
24.	14/3 to 26/3	Adriatic and Taranto
25.	6/4 —	North of Tripoli

HM SUBMARINE 'UPHOLDER'—SPECIFICATIONS

Builder:	Messrs Vickers Armstrong Ltd, Barrow-in-Furness
Displacement:	Surface 630 tons Submerged 720 tons
Dimensions	Length 191 ft overall Beam 16 ft maximum Height 44 ft from keel to top of periscope when fully raised Draught (mean) 14 ft $4\frac{3}{4}$ in
Armament:	4-21 in bow torpedo tubes 4-21 in reload torpedoes 1-12 pdr HA/LA gun 2 Lewis machine guns
Machinery:	2-400 hp Paxman Diesel generators 2 pairs of electric motors, each pair on a single shaft and coupled direct to a propeller shaft
Speed:	12 knots surfaced 8 knots submerged
Fuel:	38 tons Diesel oil
Endurance:	Surface 3800 miles at 10 knots Submerged—Between 60 hours at $2\frac{1}{2}$ knots and $2\frac{1}{2}$ hours at 8 knots, depending on speed
Complement:	Peace—4 officers, 23 ratings War—4 officers, 27 ratings

'U' CLASS SUBMARINES
Built by Messrs Vickers Armstrong Ltd, at Barrow-in-Furness

Ship	Launched	First C.O.	Disposal
UNDINE	5/10/37	Lt-Cdr A. S. Jackson	Missing January 1940
UNITY	16/2/38	Lieut F. J. Brookes	Lost in collision April 1940
URSULA	16/2/38	Lt-Cdr G. C. Phillips	Transferred to USSR in 1944. Returned to UK and scrapped 1950
UTMOST	20/4/40	Lt-Cdr R. D. Cayley	Missing November 1942
UPRIGHT	21/4/40	Lt-Cdr F. J. Brookes	Scrapped 1946
UNIQUE	6/6/40	Lieut A. F. Collett	Missing November 1942
USK	7/6/40	Lt-Cdr P. R. Ward	Missing May 1941
UPHOLDER	8/7/40	Lt-Cdr M. D. Wanklyn	Missing April 1942
UNBEATEN	9/7/40	Lt-Cdr E. A. Woodward	Missing November 1942
URGE	19/8/40	Lieut E. P. Tomkinson	Missing May 1942
UNDAUNTED	20/8/40	Lieut G. L. Livesey	Missing May 1941
SOKOL (ex-URCHIN) (Poland)	30/9/40	Lt-Cdr B. Karnicki, Polish Navy	Scrapped 1949
UNION	1/10/40	Lieut R. M. Galloway	Missing July 1941
P 31 (UPROAR)	27/11/40	Lieut J. B. Kershaw	Scrapped 1946
P 32	15/12/40	Lieut D. A. B. Abdy	Missing August 1941
P 33	28/1/41	Lieut R. D. Whiteway-Wilkinson	Missing August 1941
P 34 (ULTIMATUM)	11/2/41	Lieut P. J. R. Harrison	Scrapped 1949
P 35 (UMBRA)	15/3/41	Lieut S. L. C. Maydon	Scrapped 1945/46
P 36	28/4/41	Lieut H. N. Edmonds	Sunk by bombs, Malta March 1942
P 37 (UNBENDING)	12/5/41	Lieut H. Winter	Scrapped 1950
P 38	9/7/41	Lieut R. J. Hemingway	Missing February 1942
P 39	23/8/41	Lieut N. Marriott	Sunk by bombs, Malta March 1942
P 41 (UREDD) (Norway)	24/8/41	Lieut R. O. Roren, R. Nor. N.	Missing February 1943
P 42 (UNBROKEN)	4/11/41	Lieut A. C. C. Mars	Transferred to USSR in 1944. Returned to UK and scrapped 1950
P 43 (UNISON)	5/11/41	Lieut A. C. Halliday	(as above)
P 44 (UNITED)	18/12/41	Lieut T. E. Barlow	Scrapped 1945/46
P 45 (UNRIVALLED)	16/2/42	Lieut H. B. Turner	Scrapped 1945/46
P 46 (UNRUFFLED)	19/12/41	Lieut J. S. Stevens	Scrapped 1945/46
P 54 (UNSHAKEN)	17/2/42	Lieut C. E. Oxborrow	Scrapped 1945/46
P 48	15/4/42	Lieut M. E. Faber	Missing January 1943
P 51 (UNSEEN)	16/4/42	Lieut M. L. C. Crawford	Scrapped 1949
P 47 (DOLFIJN)	27/7/42	Lt-Cdr H. van Oestrom Soede R.Neth.N	Scrapped 1947
P 49 (UNRULY)	28/7/42	Lieut J. P. Fyfe	Scrapped 1945/46
P 52 (DZIK) (Poland)	11/10/42	Lt-Cdr B. S. Romanowski Polish Navy	Transferred to R. Danish Navy 1946-57. Scrapped 1958
P 53 (ULTOR)	12/10/42	Lieut G. E. Hunt	Scrapped 1945/46
P 65 (UPSTART)	24/11/42	Lieut P. C. Chapman	Transferred to Greece

At Newcastle-on-Tyne

Ship	Launched	First C.O.	Disposal
P 55 (UNSPARING)	28/7/42	Lieut A. D. Piper RNR	Scrapped 1946
P 56 (USURPER)	24/9/42	Lieut D. R. O. Mott	Missing October 1943
P 57 (UNIVERSAL)	10/11/42	Lieut C. Gordon	Scrapped 1946
P 58 (UNTAMED)	8/12/42	Lieut G. M. Noll	Sunk on trials May 1943. Salvaged and commissioned as *Vitality*. Used as submarine target
P 59 (UNTIRING)	20/1/43	Lieut R. Boyd	Transferred to Greece
P 63 (UNSWERVING)	2/6/43	Lieut M. D. Tattersall RNVR	Scrapped July 1949

Built in Royal Naval Dockyard, Chatham

Ship	Launched	First C.O.	Disposal
UMPIRE	20/12/40	Lieut M. R. G. Wingfield	Missing July 1941
UNA	10/6/41	Lieut D. S. R. Martin	Scrapped 1949

NOTE: The first 15 submarines were given names. From P 31 onwards, numbers were allocated. In 1943, at Winston Churchill's instigation, all submarines were given names and these are shown in brackets.

BIBLIOGRAPHY

THE SUBMARINE AND SEA POWER Vice-Admiral Sir Arthur Hezlet KBE CB DSO DSC *Peter Davies: London.*

THE BRITISH SUBMARINE Commander F. W. Lipscombe OBE RN *Adam and Charles Black: London.*

SUBMARINERS VC Rear-Admiral Sir William S. Jameson KBE CB *Peter Davies: London.*

SUBMARINE *UPHOLDER* Sydney Hart *Oldbourne: London.*

Acknowledgements:

The author wishes to express his gratitude to the following for their assistance in the preparation of this *Profile*:
The Admiralty Librarian; The Museum Curator, HMS *Dolphin;* The Keeper of Photographs, Imperial War Museum; Doctor Jürgen Rohwer, Bibliothek Für Zeitgeschichte; Lieutenant-Commander Aldo Fraccaroli.

Series Editor: JOHN WINGATE DSC

Zara as she appeared on 6 August 1933 *(Photograph, Marius Bar)*

RN Zara

by Aldo Fraccaroli
Lt.-Commander (Pay), INR

An Evocative Name

The Italian cruiser *Zara,* keel number 219 of the Odero-Terni yards of Muggiano (La Spezia), was laid down on 4 July 1929.

A former *Zara* belonged to the Austrain Navy; she was the *Torpedoschiff* (torpedo ship) *Zara* of 840 metric tons, laid down in 1878 in the Pola Navy Yard and launched on 13 November 1879 (for other particulars see below[1]). Taken over by the Italian Navy after the First World War, she was broken up in 1920.

On 4 November 1918, as the 1914-18 War was coming to its end, the Italian torpedo boat, *55 OS,* with two infantry platoons aboard, took possession of the old Venetian town in Dalmatia—Zara—which was later given to Italy through the Treaty of Rapallo (12 November 1920).

In the following years *Zara* was one of the seven 'Washington Treaty' cruisers of the Italian Navy, and she also gave her name to the series of cruisers more heavily armoured than the first 10,000 tonners —*Trento, Trieste* and later *Bolzano.* These were very fast but only very lightly armoured. It is interesting to note that the seven Italian heavy cruisers had been named after the seven 'redeemed' provinces, i.e. the seven towns of Italian speaking people which, until the Italian victory of November 1918, were part of the Austro-Hungarian Empire.

Pre-First World War and War Programmes

Immediately after the end of the First World War, the Italian Navy completed one light scout, four destroyers and two large submarines, and laid down one class of light scouts and two classes of destroyers. These were part of the pre-war building programme which had been held up during the war because of the shortage of materials, steel in particular. The Italian Navy cancelled the completion of the four *Caracciolo* class fast battleships—similar to the British *Queen Elizabeth*'s in several particulars, including the main armament—and also cancelled the rebuilding of the *Leonardo da Vinci,* a battleship completed in 1914. She had been blown up by Austrian saboteurs at Taranto in 1916, and refloated in 1919. War had exhausted the Italian treasury and in the Adriatic Sea, the Italian battleship squadrons had been only a fleet in being. With the destruction of Austria as a naval power, Italy had nothing to fear in the Adriatic. Moreover, from wartime experience and the new conceptions in naval warfare, light ships seemed to be adequate for the Italian post-war fleet.

[1] She had a power rating of 1000ihp and a speed of 14 knots, her dimensions were 55×8·0×4·0 metres, and she was armed with five torpedo tubes and five light guns. When she became obsolete for fleet service, she was classed as a *Torpedoschultender* (ship for torpedo craft training), armed with 2-90mm, 1-66mm, 4-47mm guns and 3 machine guns.

New Naval Programmes

The Italian naval programmes of these years, as regards cruisers, consisted of:

Financial years	**1923-4**	**1924-5**	**1925-6**	**1926-7**	**1927-8**	**1928-9**	**1929-30**	**1930-31**
8in gunned cruisers (Washington Treaty 'A' cruisers)	2 20,320 tons (*Trento, Trieste*)	—	—	—	—	2 20,320 tons (*Zara, Fiume*)	2 20,320 tons (*Bolzano, Gorizia*)	1 10,160 tons (*Pola*)
6in gunned cruisers (Washington Treaty 'B' cruisers)	—	—	—	—	4 20,600 tons (*Alberico da Barbiano, Alberto di Giussano, Bartolomeo Colleoni, Giovanni delle Bande Nere*)	—	2 10,178 tons (*Luigi Cadorna, Armando Diaz*)	2 11,900 tons (*Muzio Attendolo Raimondo Montecuccoli*)

The yards and dates of construction of the seven 10,000 tonners were as follows:

	Yard	**ordered**	**laid down**	**launched**	**completed**
Trento class, 1st group					
Trento	Orlando, Leghorn	18 April 1924	8 Feb 1925	4 Oct 1927	3 April 1929
Trieste	Stabilimento Tecnico Triestino, Trieste	11 April 1924	22 June 1925	24 Oct 1926	21 Dec 1928
Zara class					
Fiume	Stabilimento Tecnico Triestino, Trieste	15 Sept 1928	29 April 1929	27 April 1930	23 Nov 1931
Gorizia	Orlando, Leghorn	16 Oct 1929	17 March 1930	28 Dec 1930	23 Dec 1931
Pola	Odero-Terni-Orlando, Leghorn	1930	17 March 1931	5 Dec 1931	21 Dec 1932
Zara	Odero-Terni, La Spezia	27 Sept 1928	4 July 1929	27 April 1930	20 Oct 1931
Trento class, 2nd group					
Bolzano	Ansaldo, Genoa	25 Oct 1929	11 June 1930	31 Aug 1932	19 Aug 1933

The Policy of Speed

The first two cruisers, and later *Bolzano* too, were a tribute paid to the fetish of speed. Indeed, Italian vessels had been remarkable for their speed for nearly 70 years (from the launch of the first *Duilio,* 1876)[1] and they were nearly always several knots faster than similar foreign warships.

For instance, *Italia* (launched in 1880) and her sister-ship *Lepanto* (1883), were not only very large warships compared with other ships of their era (about 15,000 tons), but, with speeds of 17·8 and 18·4 knots respectively, they were the fastest battleships in the world for more than 15 years. In addition, the three battleships of *Re Umberto* class, the two *Regina Margheritas* and, in particular, the four battleships of *Regina Elena* class had speeds at least 10 per cent higher than contemporary foreign battleships.

As Fred T. Jane rightly wrote in the 1909 issue of his *Fighting Ships,* 'The Italian naval construction is based upon the peculiar strategical conditions imposed by the Italian coast line, and there is no building of "ships of the line" and "cruisers" as in other navies. All armoured ships are a species of "Intermediate", and they are not officially classed as battleships and cruisers.' Indeed all Italian combatant vessels were, in those years, classed as *navi da battaglia* (battle, or fighting, ships), from those of 1st class (corresponding to all the large capital ships and the armoured cruisers of other fleets) down to those of 6th class. The latter consisted of small scouts or torpedo-cruisers of 800-1300 tons, apart from destroyers, torpedo-boats, submarines, and the *navi sussidiarie* (auxiliaries).

The first Italian dreadnought, *Dante Alighieri,* reached a speed of 22·83 knots in days when existing capital ships had a maximum speed of 19-21 knots. The four projected super-dreadnoughts of the *Caracciolo* class were also to be faster than the *Queen Elizabeths*. In fact *Caracciolo* class turbines were to be of 105,000shp in comparison with *Queen Elizabeth*'s 75,000, and the respective speeds were 28 knots (as designed) and 24 knots (as designed, 24½ actually reached).

Zara ready for launching in the Odero-Terni yard. The Princes of Piedmont were present at the ceremony
(Aldo Fraccaroli Collection)

1 ... 'I have just had a letter from Spezia from "our Mr Dacres" giving me an account of the trials of the *Dandolo,* the sister-ship of *Duilio.* Speed on the measured mile exceeded 15½ knots. ... We certainly cannot do more than 12½ knots at present for that time. It is difficult to exaggerate the importance of this excess of speed possessed by the *Dandolo.*' (From a letter written from Port Said on 12 September 1882 to Adm. Sir Beauchamp Seymour. Fisher was at that time the captain of HMS *Inflexible.*) Quoted by Arthur J. Marder: *Fear God and Dread Nought, The Correspondence of Admiral of the Fleet Lord Fisher of Kilverstone,* vol I, Jonathan Cape, London, 1952.

Muggiano (La Spezia), 27 April 1930: Another view of Zara *ready for launching. On the left, a slipway is ready for the laying down of the light cruiser,* Armando Diaz, *whose construction was begun three months later, on 28 July*
(Aldo Fraccaroli Collection)

It was not only in capital ships that the Italian Navy sought qualitative superiority (quantitative superiority being out of the question), but also in lesser categories. For instance, the four *Aquila* class flotilla leaders (officially 'esploratori') had a designed speed of 36·5 knots and actual of 35·52 (for the slowest boat) and up to 38·04 knots (for the fastest). These were for some years among the fastest ships in the world. This policy of speed was continued in post-First World War construction, but, in order to obtain higher figures, the Italian Navy often ran sea trials under unrealistic conditions. For example, there was only sufficient fuel aboard for the trials; no ammunition, no torpedoes, and sometimes, neither guns or torpedo-tubes! Consequently, under war conditions, British cruisers of 32·5 knots were as fast as their Italian counterparts of 35 knots.

Comparisons

The first post-war Italian heavy cruisers, *Trento* and *Trieste,* were among the fastest 10,000 tonners of all navies. Their machinery had a contractual power rating of 150,000hp and a projected maximum speed of 35 knots, while the fastest foreign *Washington 'A'* cruisers were less fast: 32-33 knots for British cruisers, 33·8-34·3 for the Japanese, 32-33 for U.S. cruisers. Only the French *Duquesne* class cruisers could compete with the *Trentos*:

Duquesne max 35·30 knots (under 4hr trials) with 131,770shp

Tourville max 36·13 knots (under 6hr trials) with 126,919shp

Trento max 35·6 knots (under 8hr trials) with 146,975shp with a maximum attained of 36·05 knots.

Trieste max 35·04 knots (under 8hr trials) with 124,761shp but 35·65 knots taking into account wind and sea.

(Some years later, in 1932, *Bolzano* reached 36·81 knots with 173,772shp.)

These speeds were paid for at the price of light armour, because within the limits of a standard displacement of 10,000 tons it was not possible to build ships which were, at the same time, well armed (most of these cruisers had eight 8in guns), very fast and heavily armoured. A salutary reaction to the *Trento* class resulted in the building of the *Zara* class which were better balanced in their features.

The chiefs of the Italian Navy recognised that the large light cruisers of 10,000 tons of the *Trento* type were not able to form the backbone of their fleet, particularly in view of the obsolescence and the poor efficiency of the existing battleships. Indeed, *Dante Alighieri,* the older Italian Dreadnought, was near to her end, and was in fact laid up on 1 July 1928. The two *Cavours* and the two *Dorias* had never been technically successful ships and in 1933-37 and, in 1937-49 respectively, were completely reconstructed.

Rear-Admiral Romeo Bernotti, the Deputy Chief of Naval Staff[1] had a resolute character supported by a world-wide reputation as a practical and theoretical naval expert. He proposed the building of 15,000-ton cruisers for the Italian Navy, asserting that three of them would knock out six 10,000-ton cruisers. However, displacements of this magnitude were forbidden by treaties, and the Italian Navy therefore

[1] Born in 1877, Adm. Bernotti is the author of fundamental books on naval strategy and tactics, and on the history of naval operations in the First and Second World Wars. He was the Deputy Chief of the Italian Naval Staff, 21 Dec 1927—5 Oct 1929, and the Chief of the Test Commission for new cruisers, 17 July 1931—5 February 1932. He is still writing, and his most recent work is a book of memoirs.

decided to build a new type of 10,000 ton cruiser, having three knots less than the *Trento* type but with improved armour. From this principle the *Zara* type was born.

The ships of this class constituted the first step to meet the Italian Navy's requirement to have ships whose qualities would give them superiority in a naval action. This had been the aim of the *navi da battaglia* at the end of the nineteenth and the beginning of the twentieth centuries. Thus the 1928-29 Naval Programme consisted of two 10,000 ton cruisers of the new type (*Fiume* and *Zara*), four destroyers of 1225 standard tons, and four submarines of 823 standard tons.

Possible Plans for Zara Class

The planning of the new type, however, was not an easy job. The Italian Staff wished to have sturdy cruisers, protected with an extensive armour 200mm thick, a good horizontal protection, eight 8in guns and an actual sea speed of 32 knots. A displacement of 10,000 standard tons was nevertheless insufficient to meet these requirements. Either the number of 8in guns had to be cut by two or the armour decreased. The reduction in the main armament would have been acceptable only if a third cruiser were built simultaneously. This was financially impossible. Accordingly the armour thickness was reduced to 150mm, giving a standard displacement of 11,500-12,000 tons, even after taking further measures to diminish the weight of the ship. For example, the four *Zara*s did not have a flush deck, but a forecastle 81½ metres long, which extended from the bow to the base of the bridge.

The project was the result of team work by the naval engineer officers of the *Comitato progetti navi* (Committee for projecting naval vessels). At that time, the Chief of Naval Construction was Eng. Lt-General (Eng. Rear-Admiral) Fabio Mibelli.

The displacements of the four *Zara*s, were, in tons:

	standard	normal	at full load
Fiume	11,508	13,260	14,168
Gorizia	11,900	13,660	14,560
Pola	11,730	13,531	14,360
Zara	11,870	13,580	14,530

PARTICULARS OF ZARA

Dimensions:

Length: 182·70m (overall), 179·6 (between perpendiculars)
Beam: 20·624m
Draught: 5·9m (standard), 7·2m (full load)
Length/beam ratio was therefore 8·86, and beam/draught ratio was 2·86, and the coefficient of fineness was 0·496.

Armament:

Eight 8in guns, 53 calibre long (called in Italy: 203/53 Ans.—viz Ansaldo built—model 1929), mounted in four twin axial turrets (B and X superimposed) formed *Zara*'s main armament. Their barrels were composed of two self-hooped elements, separable when cold, and had Welin type breech screw blocks.
Weight of gun: 25·0 metric tons
Weight of twin gun turret: 270 metric tons
Max pressure: 3200 atmospheres
Muzzle velocity: 940m/sec
Max elevation: +45°
Max depression: −5°
Max range: 31,566m
Weight of armour piercing projectile: 125kg
Weight of HE shell: 111kg
Weight of cordite (in canvas bags): 52kg
Rounds per minute: 3·8

Launching of Zara O.T.O., Muggiano yard. Note the bulbous shape of the bow, typical of Italian naval construction (Aldo Fraccaroli Collection)

These guns were suitable only for daylight engagements as flashless charges had not been provided by the Italian Navy for some mysterious tactical reason (night action was considered not possible for these ships!) During 1940-1 only 15in, 6in, 4·7in and 3·9in guns were provided with flashless cordite in the Italian Navy. Sixteen 3·9in guns, 47 calibre long, mounted in eight twin mountings, served for naval and AA use. These were the old so-called 10cm L50 built by Skoda for the Austrian Navy before the 1914-18 war, in fact, the 1910 model. Adapted by the Italians, they were known as 100/47. When mounted in special mountings designed by Eng. General Eugenio Minisini, these guns had a maximum elevation of 85° (depression—5°), and could therefore also be used as an AA weapon. These old barrels were later replaced by new Italian built (OTO, model 1931) 3·9in guns.

3·9" Guns	Old Skoda	New OTO
Weight of a barrel:	2020kg	2195kg
Muzzle velocity:	850m/sec	840m/sec
Max range in metres:	15,240 (as a naval gun)	
Max ordinate metres:	8500 (as an AA gun)	
Weight of a projectile (HE shell):	13·75kg	
Weight of a complete cartridge:	25·77kg	
Weight of cordite only:	4·7kg	
Rounds per minute:	10	

(In Autumn 1937, the two stern 3·9in twin mountings—one, to starboard, the other, to port—were replaced by two Breda 37mm 54 cal twin mountings.)

Originally *Zara* had four 40mm 39cal Vickers-Terni model 1915 machine guns, in single mountings, and eight 13·2mm Breda machine guns in twin mountings. But in 1940 she no longer had the old 40mm machine guns, and her light AA armament consisted of eight 37mm 54cal Breda model 1932 and eight 13·2mm machine guns.

Their particulars were:

	40mm 39cal Vickers-Terni	37mm 54cal Breda mod 1932	13·2mm Breda
Weight of barrel, in kg:	239	275	95
Weight of mounting, in kg:	711·2	1400 (twin)	..
Max elevation:	+80°	+80°	+80°
Max depression:	−5°	−10°	..
Muzzle velocity, in m/sec:	610	830	800
Max range (as a naval weapon) in metres:	7160	..	6480
Max ordinate (as an AA weapon) in metres:	4425	..	3200
Weight of shell, in g:	900	..	52
Weight of complete cartridge in g:	1290	..	..
Rounds per minute (each barrel):	200	120-150	400

Zara's magazines had a capacity of 1256 8in projectiles, i.e. 157 rounds for each barrel; about 6000 rounds for 3·9in guns; about 4000 rounds for 40mm machine guns; about 12,000 rounds for 13·2mm machine guns.

No torpedo tubes were mounted nor was the ship fitted for minelaying.

Protection:

The side armour of *Zara* was 150mm thick for the area comprising all the central part of the ship, including the turrets, machinery and magazines. This extended up to the 70mm thick armoured deck, but, under the waterline, it was reduced to a minimum of 100mm. Above the side armour, the bulwarks were protected with 30mm plates. The final bow and stern transverse bulkheads plates, holding the central armoured citadel, were 120mm thick, down to a minimum of 90mm under the waterline. Above the plates they extended to the main deck. Plates forming the main deck were of chrome-nickel steel fixed to the transverse beams and having a thickness of 70mm for the citadel area, reduced to 65mm along the waterway course. The cover deck had 20mm thick horizontal plates to absorb the initial shock of the nose caps of the enemy shells. The turrets and barbettes were formed with special steel plates, 140-120mm thick, from the main deck to the upper deck, and of 150-130mm on the upper deck.

The conning tower, of circular shape with an internal diameter of 3·30m, had vertical walls made of 150mm thick cemented steel plates. The roof was of 80mm armour and the bottom 70mm. Overhanging the bridge, there was the director, which also had a circular shape, with an internal diameter of 3·50m. The vertical walls had 130mm thick steel plates, the roof was 100mm thick and the mobile bottom was 15mm thick. The vertical armoured tube, connecting the conning tower with the underlying secondary fighting station (placed between the armoured deck and the middle deck) was 120-100mm thick.

Finally, the steering gear compartment was protected by means of a 30mm thick deck and by plates of 20mm at the bottom and sides.

It may be of interest to compare the thickness of armour of the 8in gunned cruisers of the principal navies during that period:

	max side armour in mm	**max deck armour in mm**
FRANCE		
Tourville class	30 (only for magazines and steering gear)	30
Suffren class	60	51-60 (according to ships)
Algerie	110	80
GREAT BRITAIN		
York/Exeter	76	38-51 (according to ships)
Kent class	76	76
ITALY		
Trento class	70	50
Zara class	150	70+20
JAPAN		
Nachi class	102	76
Atago class	102	127
U.S.A.		
Pensacola class	76	51+25
Northampton class	76	51+25
Astoria class	127 (only for boilers and engines) -37	76+51

The relatively good armour of the *Zara* class cruisers, compared with the very light armour of the *Trentos,* caused *Fiume, Gorizia, Pola* and *Zara* to be considered by the Italian Navy as 'armoured cruisers'. This was after an initial period when all the seven 8in gun cruisers had been classed as 'light cruisers'. Later, both the *Zaras* and the *Trentos* were all classed as 'heavy cruisers', in order

Zara *off the town of Zara (Dalmatia), from which she took her name. Photograph taken on 4 June 1932*
(Photograph, Aldo Fraccaroli)

Zara *as completed, Autumn, 1931*
(Photograph by Ansaldo, S.p.A.)

to distinguish them from the cruisers of the *Condottieri* types, which, being armed with 6in guns, were classed as light cruisers. The armour of the *Zaras* had, however, not been designed to resist 15in shells fired from less than 4000 yards as happened at Matapan.

Machinery:

The designed power of the *Zara* class was of 95,000hp, with a contractual speed of 32 knots and 270rpm. Unlike the two *Trentos* and the *Bolzano,* which had four shafts, the *Zaras* had only two shafts, like the *Condottieri* class cruisers whose first group (the four *da Barbianos*) and second group (the two *Cadornas*) had the same engine power. The concentration of nearly 100,000hp in only two power plants was regarded as a remarkable achievement by the Royal Italian Navy. As a comparison, the machinery of each of *Zara* class cruiser weighed about 1400 metric tons, and her armour weighed about 2700 metric tons, while for the *Trentos* the corresponding weights were about 2330 and 900 metric tons.

Zara had eight boilers of Thornycroft 3-drum type, which had a heating surface of 7558 square metres and produced 650,000kg of superheated steam per hour at a pressure of 25kg per square centimetre. Total fuel consumption was 53,906 kg per hour.

Two groups of Parsons type, OTO-built, geared turbines moved two three-blade propellers of Scaglia type. The entry diameters of the turbines were 1088mm for high pressure, 1796 for low pressure, and 1512 for the astern turbines.

Speed:

During the eight hour trials, run in 1931 without the turrets and their eight guns, and without the eight 3·9in twin mountings, *Zara* reached a maximum speed of 34·2 knots developing nearly 118,000shp, with a displacement of almost 10,800 tons.

Oil fuel capacity was normally 2150 metric tons, and her endurance was 1817 miles at full speed (about 32 knots), 3400 miles at the cruising speed of 25 knots, and 5360 miles at economical speed (16 knots).

Aviation facilities:
In the bows of the cruiser there was a hangar, initially containing two 'Piaggio P6 bis' reconnaissance seaplanes, which could be raised by a special derrick and placed on the rail of the Gagnotto[1] catapult. This was operated by compressed air and sighted along the ship's centreline. Later, the P.6 bis seaplanes were replaced by M41s, by Cant 25 ARs, by M.F.6s, and finally (1938) by Ro. 43s. Particulars of these aircraft were:

[1] So-called after Eng.-Major (Eng.-Lt-Commander) Luigi Gagnotto who designed it.

Motto:
Like nearly all the vessels of the Italian Navy, *Zara* had a motto, which was *Tenacemente* (Tenaciously), inscribed in several parts of the ship and in particular in large brass letters on Y turret (No. 4 turret).

Price:
The contractual cost of *Zara* was 106,000,000 Italian lire.

Complement:
Her established complement was of 31 officers and 810 petty officers and ratings.

The Commissioning
Until the outbreak of the Second World War, *Zara*'s history was not particularly eventful and her life was the normal one of an Italian cruiser in the Mediterranean. For several years she served as the flagship of what was, at that time, the backbone of

	Piaggio 'P.6 biş'	**Macchi** 'M.41'	**C.R.D.A.** 'Cant 25 AR'	**C.M.A.S.A.** 'M.F. 6'	**I.M.A.M.** 'Ro. 43'
Wingspan in metres:	13·50	10·82	10·40	11·05	11·57
Total weight (including crew, armament, fuel), in kg:	1850	1530	1700	2300	2285
Armament: number and calibre of machine guns (in mm):	2-7·7	2-7·7	2-7·7	1-7·7	2-7·7(+1)
Power plant in bhp:	500	400	410	575	700
Maximum speed in km/h:	180	260	245	265	290
Endurance in nautical miles:	240	470	680	600	620

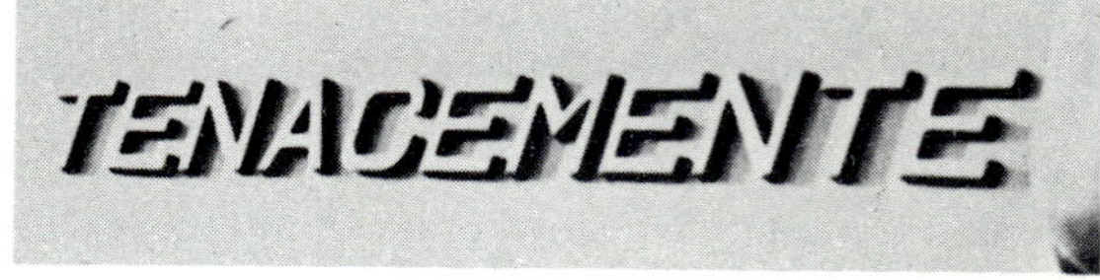

Right: *'Y' 8in gun turret ('203mm no. 4 turret' in the Italian terminology) and the ship's motto 'Tenacemente'. (Tenaciously)* (LUCE, Aldo Fraccaroli Collection)

Below left and right: Zara *photographed at about 1932-33, from an old 12in gun Italian battleship* (LUCE, Aldo Fraccaroli Collection)

A view of Zara *during her first years. Note the band on the funnels and the admiral's flag at her main mast. For several years (from 1 September 1933 until 15 September 1937)* Zara *was flagship of the 1st Squadron*
(LUCE, Aldo Fraccaroli Collection)

the fleet. In fact, when she entered service, the battleships *Conte di Cavour, Giulio Cesare, Andrea Doria* and *Duilio* were too obsolete and slow for a modern fleet; moreover, from 1933 till 1937 *Cavour* and *Cesare* were being rebuilt. Therefore the 1st Cruiser Division (*Zara, Fiume, Gorizia, Pola*) formed the more important squadron of Italian fighting ships (the two *Trentos* and *Bolzano* formed the 3rd Division, although it was realised that these fast cruisers were not sufficiently armoured).
Delivered by her yard to the Royal Italian Navy on 20 October 1931, *Zara* had in Captain Count Giuseppe Raineri Biscia her first commanding officer.

Zara's Captains:
Captain Count Giuseppe Raineri Biscia, 20 October 1931—27 September 1933;
Captain Luigi Spalice, 20 October 1933—14 Sept 1934;
Captain Enrico Accorretti, 15 September 1934—14 August 1935;
Captain Pellegrino Matteucci, 15 August 1935—26 September 1937;
Captain Emilio Ferreri, 27 September 1937—26 October 1938;
Captain Antonio Muffone, 27 October 1938—1 March 1940;
Captain Luigi Corsi, 2 March 1940 until the sinking of the ship (29 March 1941).

Zara's Admirals:
Zara was also the flagship of the following flag officers:
Squadron Admiral (Vice-Admiral) Ernesto Burzagli, C-in-C, 1st Squadron, 1 September 1933—31 October 1933;
Squadron Admiral Giuseppe Cantú, C-in-C, 1st Squadron and 1st Cruiser Division, 1 November 1933—30 April 1935;
Squadron Admiral Umberto Bucci, C-in-C, 1st Squadron, 1 May 1935—15 September 1937;
Division Admiral (Rear-Admiral) Count Alberto Marenco di Moriondo, Commander, 1st Cruiser Division, 1 September 1938—15 November 1938;
(from 16 November 1938 until 12 January 1940, *Zara* served as a private ship, *Fiume* being the divisional leader);
Division Admiral Pellegrino Matteucci, Commander, 1st Cruiser Division, 13 January 1940—12 December 1940;
Division Admiral Carlo Cattaneo, Commander, 1st Cruiser Division, 13 December 1940 until the sinking of the ship.

Short Pre-War History
After entering service on 20 October 1931, the cruiser required some months before becoming operational. On 5 June 1932, in the harbour of Zara, the cruiser received her battle flag. This was a traditional ceremony of the Italian Navy, consisting of the gift of a silk naval ensign by a town, an association of veterans, or a patriotic society. This ensign, preserved in a valuable wood or metal coffer, was to be hoisted when action was imminent, and when all hands were called to their battle stations. At that time, the hoisting of the battle flag was still possible. *Zara's* battle flag (2·40×3·70m) was presented by a committee of ladies from Zara, on behalf of the people of the town. HRH Admiral Fernando di Savoia, Duke of Genoa, was present and the torpedo boats *Grado* with four craft of the *Generale Papa* division also came to the Dalmatian harbour for this ceremony.
Some months later, summer exercises were carried out in mid-Mediterranean between the Libyan and South Italian coasts. All the available new 10,000 ton cruisers (and other major and minor warships) took part, and *Zara* acted as the direction ship of the manoeuvres (8-11 August 1932).

Naval Reviews
In addition to the regular fleet activity and training, *Zara* took part in the naval review carried out for Admiral Horthy, Regent of Hungary, on 26 November 1936, off Gaeta. The cruiser *Zara*, having on board the King, Horthy, Prince Royal Humbert, and Mussolini (Prime Minister and Armed Forces Minister) was the leading ship of the 1st Squadron, and altogether 16 cruisers, 25 destroyers, 14 torpedo boats, and 51 submarines were engaged in the

3·9in AA guns and one 40mm/39cal Vickers machine gun. These old 40mm machine guns were removed in 1939-40
(LUCE, Aldo Fraccaroli Collection)

Zara at the end of a summer exercise, about 1933
(LUCE, Aldo Fraccaroli Collection)

Zara in Naples bay, on 26 November 1936, with King Victor Emmanuel III of Italy and the Hungarian Admiral Horthy aboard. Note the removal of the range-finder tower abaft the second funnel. In the background on the left, the destroyer Nembo; on the right, the destroyer Lampo
(Priore, Aldo Fraccaroli Collection)

Zara entering the Taranto ship-canal in 1938. Note that her stern 3·9in AA mountings had been removed and replaced by 37mm/54cal AA Breda machine guns (double mountings)
(Photograph, Campese; Aldo Fraccaroli Collection)

exercise. Another review took place in honour of the German General von Blomberg (7 June 1937), and on 5 May 1938 *Zara* was one of the 161 naval vessels involved in the great 'Rivista H', the review carried out for Hitler off Naples. At this spectacle, the cruisers *Fiume* and *Zara* fired their main guns against the radio-controlled ship *San Marco*.

In April 1939, *Zara* was one of the ships of the second group (under the command of Division Admiral Sportiello) charged with the task of occupying Durazzo (Albania). The following months, saw the last naval review of the Italian Navy before the outbreak of war. This was in honour of the Prince Regent of Yugoslavia, off Naples, 11 May 1939.

Armament modifications

Some technical alterations were made to the ship, apart from the changes in the type of aircraft already mentioned. In 1936 *Zara*'s stern 5m rangefinder (placed between the second funnel and X turret) was removed. Towards the end of the following year, the two stern 3·9in (100mm/47cal) twin mountings were removed, and two twin 37mm/54cal Breda machine guns were mounted in their place. A shorter (base 4m) rangefinder was mounted in 1939 in the same position as the 5m instrument removed in 1936. The two side small rangefinders (base 3m), mounted on the mainmast's crow's nest, were taken away, together with the old 40mm Vickers-Terni machine guns. These were replaced by the same number of 37mm Bredas.

On 11 June 1940, when Italy entered the war, *Zara*'s armament was as follows:

8-8in 53cal guns (8-203/53)
12-3·9in 47cal AA guns (12-100/47 AA)
8-37mm 54cal Breda machine guns
8-13·2mm Breda machine guns.

The Second World War

When Italy entered the war, RN *Zara* was the flagship of the 1st Cruiser Division, including *Fiume* and *Gorizia*. Her more recent sister-ship, *Pola*, was the flagship of the 2nd Squadron.

At 0020 on 12 June 1940, the 1st and the 8th Cruiser Divisions (the latter including the light cruisers *Garibaldi* and *Duca degli Abruzzi*) sailed from Taranto in the company of their destroyer divisions (9th: *Alfieri, Carducci, Gioberti, Oriani;* 16th: *da Recco, Usodimare, Pessagno*). This force was intended as a support to *Pola* and the heavy cruisers of the 3rd Cruiser Division with their eight destroyers of the 11th and 12th Destroyer Divisions (11th: *Artigliere, Camicia Nera, Aviere, Geniere;* 12th: *Lanciere, Carabiniere, Corazziere, Ascari*). These ships were searching for the British light cruisers HMS *Caledon* and *Calypso*. The latter were not alone, being part of the Mediterranean Fleet which had sailed from Alexandria (HMS *Warspite, Malaya, Eagle,* the 7th Cruiser Squadron and nine destroyers). Both the British sweep and the Italian search were unsuccessful, but 'the cruiser *Calypso* was torpedoed south of the western end of Crete at 2am on 12 June; she sank at 3.30 with a loss of one officer and 38 ratings. It was a good performance

A view of Zara *during her Summer cruise in the Adriatic Sea, with several visiting tourists aboard*
(*Aldo Fraccaroli Collection*)

by the submarine, as the cruisers were close astern of a destroyer screen.'[1]

The Italian ships of the 1st and 8th Cruiser Divisions were attacked by five submarines whose torpedoes missed their targets. Three anti-submarine sweeps, carried out by five divisions of destroyers and by one of the torpedo boats, resulted in the sinking of HM S/M *Odin* by the Italian destroyers *Strale* and *Baleno.*

In another operation on 22-24 June, *Zara* and her Division gave support to a raid by the 7th Cruiser Division and the 13th Destroyer Division against French shipping and convoys in the Western Mediterranean.

Action off Calabria

The Action off Calabria, 9 July 1940, is known in Italy as *Battaglia di Punta Stilo* (Battle of Point Stilo). This title is not universally accepted as, in spite of the fact that many scores of warships were involved, not a single ship was sunk.[2] Taking part were *Pola,* the flagship of Vice-Admiral Riccardo Paladini, commander of the 2nd Squadron, which included the 1st Cruiser Division (*Zara,* flag of Rear-Admiral Matteucci, *Fiume, Gorizia*), and the 3rd Cruiser Division (*Trento,* flag of Rear-Admiral Carlo Cattaneo, and *Bolzano*). These six heavy cruisers, with the 12 destroyers of the 12th, 9th and 11th Destroyer Divisions, and with the four light cruisers of the 7th Cruiser Division (*Eugenio di Savoia,* flag of Rear-Admiral Luigi Sansonetti, *Duca d'Aosta, Attendolo, Montecuccoli*) and the four destroyers of the 13th Division, formed the outer escort to a convoy of merchantmen *Esperia, Calitea, Marco Foscarini* and *Vettor Pisani,* which sailed from Naples southbound for Benghazi.

The four transports, which were joined by a fifth (M/S *Francesco Barbaro*) from Catania, carried in total 2190 officers and soldiers, 232 lorries, 5720 metric tons of fuel and lubricants, 10,445 metric tons of miscellaneous materials. The close escort consisted of the 2nd Cruiser Division (light cruisers *Bande Nere,* flag of Rear-Admiral Fernando Casardi, and *Colleoni*), the 10th Destroyer Division, the 4th Torpedo boat division and a sub-division of old torpedo boats. Finally, the supporting force consisted of the 5th Battleship Division (*Giulio Cesare,* flag of Vice-Admiral Inigo Campioni, C-in-C, and *Conte di Cavour*), of the 4th Cruiser Division (light cruisers *da Barbiano,* flag of Rear-Admiral Alberto Marenco di Moriondo, *di Giussano, Cadorna, Diaz*). However, *Cadorna* and *Diaz* suffered from mechanical failure and were compelled to return home. The other forces were 8th Cruiser Division (light cruisers *Duca degli Abruzzi,* flag of Rear-Admiral Antonio Legnani, and *Garibaldi*), and the 7th, 8th, 15th and 16th Destroyer Divisions (13 destroyers, reduced to 10 by mechanical failure).

The Enemy

Ranged against them was Admiral Andrew Browne Cunningham's Mediterranean Fleet, in three groups. *Force A:* 7th Cruiser Squadron, under Vice-Admiral John Cronyn Tovey's command (five light cruisers and one destroyer); *Force B:* battleship HMS *Warspite* (with the C-in-C) and five destroyers;

[1] Admiral of the Fleet Viscount Cunningham of Hyndhope: *A Sailor's Odyssey,* Hutchinson & Co Ltd, London, 1951. The submarine was the Italian *Bagnolini.*

[2] Admiral Alberto Da Zara: *Pelle d'Ammiraglio,* **Mondadori,** Milano, 1949, at page 332.

At Naples, 7 May 1938, two days after the 'Review H'. The complete Italian 1st Naval Division (left to right): Gorizia (*partially visible*), Pola, Zara, Fiume (*flagship at that time*) (*Photograph, Li Virghi; Aldo Fraccaroli Collection*)

Force C: 1st Battle Squadron, under Rear-Admiral Henry Daniel Pridham-Wippell's command (two battleships, one aircraft carrier, 11 destroyers).

It would not be possible to describe here the whole action. It will be sufficient to say that *Zara* and her two sister-ships, together with the *Pola* (squadron flagship), sailing from Augusta, joined the two heavy cruisers of the 3rd Cruiser Division, from Messina at 0640 on 9 July.

Four of the 10,000 tonners were attacked by two torpedo-aircraft, and *Zara,* target of one of the torpedoes, avoided it by altering course.

Action is joined

From 1550-1601 the Italian 10,000 tonners (forming a line ahead: *Bolzano* leading, *Trento, Fiume, Gorizia, Zara, Pola*) opened fire. *Zara* in particular commenced firing at 1600, aiming three salvoes at the British light cruisers (who were outnumbered and outgunned) and her last six salvoes at the enemy battleships. *Zara* ceased firing at 1616. At 1609 HMS *Warspite* opened fire on a cruiser at the range of 24,600 yards, but no hit was scored. The only hits registered in the cruiser engagement by both sides were three AP projectiles, fired from the British light cruisers, which struck *Bolzano* at 1605, damaging her steering gear, one 8in barrel of her B turret, and her torpedo tube compartment.

Wrong Identification

After the action between the opposing fleets, 126 Italian aircraft, operating from the mainland, attacked the British Fleet and, in error, also the Italians (in particular the battleship *Cesare* and the cruisers *Bolzano* and *Fiume,* the latter being straddled by four 250kg bombs), in spite of the fact that the aircraft observers were naval officers and the Italian ships' forecastles were painted white.[1] Following this, Vice-Admiral Campioni ordered national ensigns to be spread on the turret roofs and red smoke to be made from his ships' after funnels. This was the practice in peacetime exercises, in order to distinguish the national party. Fortunately no bombs hit the Italian vessels. On the other hand, 'There were no hits (on the Mediterranean Fleet) and the fleet suffered no damage but there were numerous near misses and a few minor casualties from splinters'.[2] Only one Italian aircraft was shot down, an 'S.79', apparently hit by Italian AA fire.

Zara *in Mar Grande, Taranto. The fourth 3·9in AA double mountings and the after range-finder tower (abaft the after funnel) have been removed* (*Photograph, Priore; Aldo Fraccaroli Collection*)

[1] Later, the white painting of the forward part of the deck or forecastle was replaced by diagonal white and red stripes, a practice in use for the rest of the war.

[2] REPORT OF AN ACTION WITH THE ITALIAN FLEET OFF CALABRIA, 9TH JULY 1940, Supplement to *The London Gazette* of Tuesday, 27 April 1948.

Zara in Genoa harbour, May 1938, with practically all the Italian fleet. In the background on the right, the conning tower of Pola. *The photograph was taken from aboard* Fiume, *whose 37mm Breda machine gun is in the foreground on the left (Photograph, Aldo Fraccaroli)*

Operations from August till December 1940

On 31st August 1940 Supermarina, the Italian Naval High Command in Rome, with the knowledge that British naval forces had sailed from Gibraltar eastbound and, from Alexandria, westbound, sent out 5 battleships, 13 cruisers and 39 destroyers. The battleships included the brand-new *Littorio* and *Vittorio Veneto.* The cruisers included *Zara, Fiume* and *Gorizia* forming the 1st Cruiser Division, and the three *'Trentos'* forming the 3rd Cruiser Division. All these cruisers were under the command of Vice-Admiral Angelo Iachino who had replaced the former Squadron commander, Vice-Admiral Paladini on 25 July. The Squadron flagship *Pola* was also present. The Italian forces however failed to find the enemy and returned to their bases. On 29 September—1 October 1940 the Italian forces again sailed without success against a British convoy under a strong escort.

During the night air attack on Taranto (11-12 November 1940), *Zara* was moored in 'Mar Grande' (Great Sea), between *Fiume* and *Gorizia,* where she opened machine-gun fire against the torpedo-bombers. On the following day, *Zara,* her Division and the Squadron flagship *Pola* left Taranto, escorted by the 9th and 11th Destroyer Divisions, and in company with the three undamaged battleships and their 10th and 13th Destroyer Divisions, arrived at Naples.

Zara was not present at the action off Cape Spartivento on 27 November 1940. This was known as *'Scontro* (fight) *di Capo Teulada'* by the Italians. She was then under repairs, and meanwhile *Fiume* had become the flagship of the 1st Cruiser Division. On 15 December, *Zara* and *Gorizia* reached La Maddalena (Sardinia), having left the harbour of Naples after an air attack on the previous night. During this raid *Pola* was hit by a bomb which

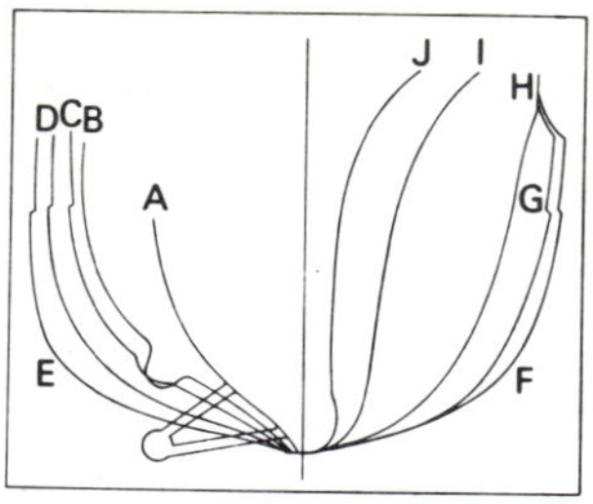

The flag of the *Ammiraglio di Divisione* (Rear-Admiral) which was flown at *Zara*'s foremast when she put to sea in March 1941 for her last operation.

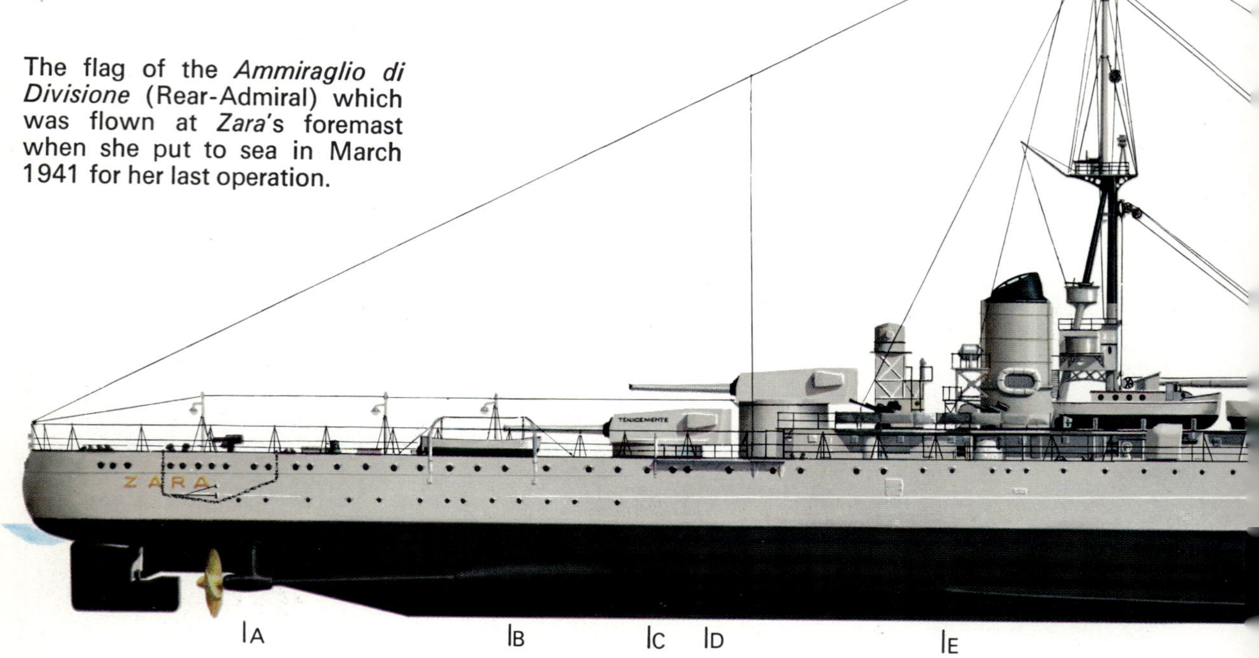

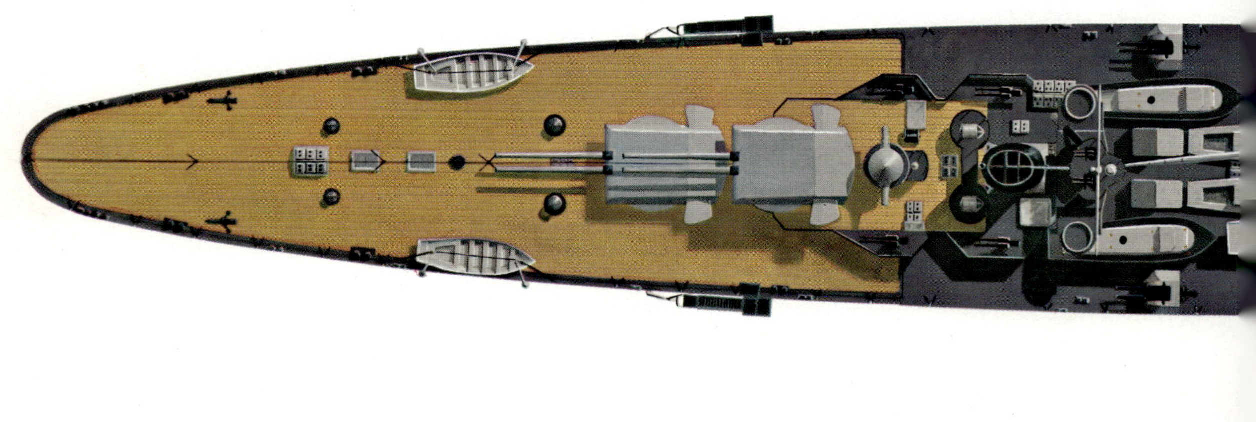

RN *Gorizia,* port side, as camouflaged at the end of 1942.

The heavy cruiser, RN *Zara,* is depicted as she appeared at The Battle of Matapan on 28 March 1941. Italian cruisers were not camouflaged at this time, with the exception of *Fiume.*
The diagonal stripes on the fo'c'sle and on the RO43 reconnaissance aircraft were for identification purposes.

D Johnson

The Italian Jack

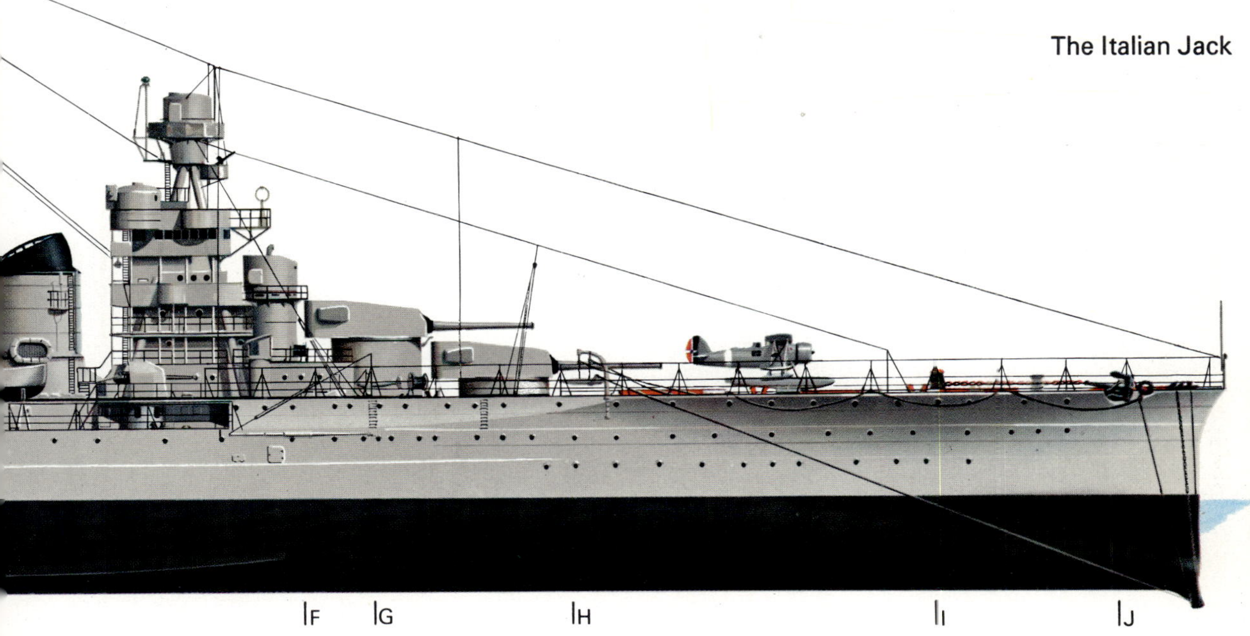

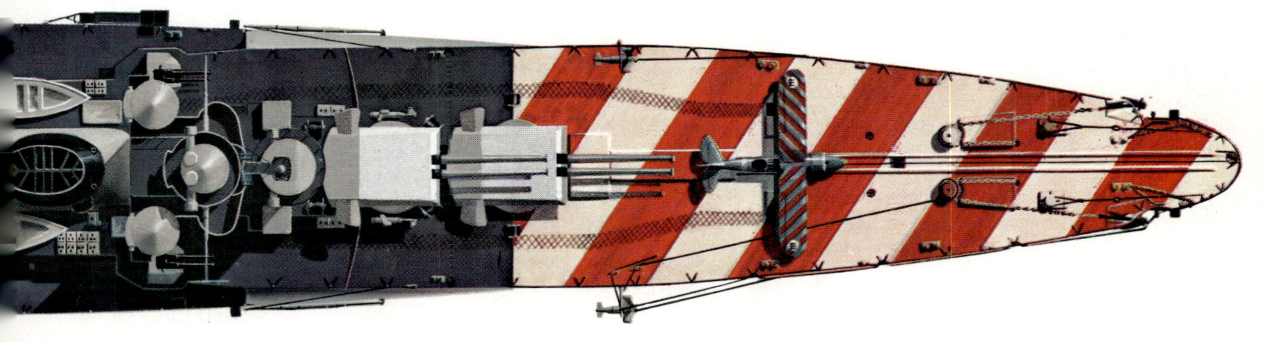

RN *Gorizia,* starboard side, as camouflaged at the end of 1942.

One of *Fiume's* three 'Ro.43' aircraft on the bow catapult, and the forward 8in turrets. Genoa harbour, May 1938
(Photograph, Aldo Fraccaroli)

Zara leaving Genoa harbour in 1938. Note the chains at her bow for protective minesweeping
(Photograph, F. Cali; Aldo Fraccaroli Collection)

A wartime photograph taken from aboard *Zara*: on the left in foreground, her forward 8in guns, in background, 3·9in AA guns; then left to right, *Fiume*, *Gorizia*, *Pola*. The forward part of *Zara's* deck is painted with diagonal red and white stripes, for aircraft recognition
(Aldo Fraccaroli Collection)

exploded in the compartment of No. 3 boiler. *Pola* listed to port, three compartments having been flooded. Thirteen officers and men were killed and 33 wounded. On 20 December both *Zara* and *Gorizia* returned to Naples from where they sailed on 22 December, arriving at 'Mar Piccolo' (Small Sea), Taranto, on 23 December.

Gavdo and Matapan

Following the heavy damage inflicted on the Italian battle forces by the air attacks on Taranto[1] and Naples,[2] only one battleship, *Andrea Doria,* remained operational after 9 January 1941. Even when *Vittorio Veneto* had been repaired, shortage of fuel prevented any extensive operations.[3] This put the Italian Navy at a great disadvantage, which was not helped by the lack of naval aviation and aircraft carriers, and the general unreadiness for night fighting which derived from lack of radar.

Genesis of the Operation

By the end of February, Vice-Admiral Iachino, the new C-in-C of the Italian Fleet,[4] had prepared a plan for an offensive sweep in the Eastern Mediterranean, employing only one of the faster and more recent battleships of *'Littorio'* class[5] and three of the faster cruisers. This proposal, sent by Iachino to the Chief of the Naval Staff, was similar to a plan already prepared by Supermarina. It was decided to carry out the raid against enemy shipping in the Eastern Mediterranean and the Aegean Sea on 28 March.

The Plan

The plan of the operation called for a greater number of warships than that planned by Iachino, and a double sweep was proposed: one to the North of Crete, in the Aegean Sea, as far as the Karavi Reefs; the other to the South of Crete as far as Gavdo Island. The forces which would take part were to be:

—the battleship *Vittorio Veneto* (flag of the C-in-C), from Naples,

—her attendant destroyer division, the 13th:

[1] Of the three battleships damaged during the air attack on the night of 11-12 November 1940, *Littorio* was under repair from 11 December 1940 until 9 March 1941; *Duilio,* after some repairs in Taranto, was transferred to Genoa, where she remained under repairs from 26 January 1941, returning to Taranto on 16 May 1941. *Cavour* was towed to Trieste on 22 December 1941, but could not be repaired in time for her to play any further part in the war.

[2] On 8 January 1941, *Vittorio, Veneto* and *Cesare* were damaged by bombs at Naples, and were transferred to La Spezia and Genoa, respectively, for repairs.

[3] In August 1942, in contrast to the British Operation 'Pedestal', the Italian Navy could only put to sea cruisers, destroyers, MAS and MS boats, and submarines, not having sufficient fuel for the battleships.

[4] Vice-Admiral Iachino had replaced Vice-Admiral Campioni on 9 December 1940, when the two Italian Squadrons were combined to form only one. Campioni was called to Rome as Vice-Chief of Naval Staff.

[5] *Littorio* and *Vittorio Veneto,* both launched in 1937 and operational since August 1940, had a maximum practical speed of about 28 knots (more than 31 at sea trials), were armed with 9-15in, 12-6in and 12-3·5in AA guns, and about 50 machine guns. Their standard displacement was about 41,000 tons, max almost 46,000 tons.

Granatiere (Captain Vittorio De Pace), *Fuciliere, Bersagliere, Alpino,* from Messina;

—the 3rd Cruiser Division: *Trieste* (flag of Rear-Admiral Luigi Sansonetti), *Trento, Bolzano,* from Messina;

—its attendant destroyer division, the 12th: *Corazziere* (Captain Carmine D'Arienzo), *Carabiniere, Ascari,* from Messina.

The above ships formed the so-called 'Iachino Group' and were all charged with the Southern sweep.

The second force consisted of:

—the 1st Cruiser Division: *Zara* (flag of Rear-Admiral Carlo Cattaneo), *Pola, Fiume,*[1] from Taranto;

—its attendant destroyer division, the 9th: *Alfieri* (Captain Salvatore Toscano), *Gioberti, Carducci, Oriani,* from Taranto;

—the 8th Cruiser Division: *Duca degli Abruzzi* (flag of Rear-Admiral Antonio Legnani) and *Garibaldi,* from Brindisi;

—its attendant destroyer division (in fact only a sub-division): *da Recco* (Captain Ugo Salvadori) and *Pessagno,* from Brindisi.

These two cruiser divisions (1st and 8th), with their six destroyers, formed the so-called 'Cattaneo (or *Zara*) Group', under Rear-Admiral Cattaneo's command, and were charged with the sweep North of Crete, into the Aegean Sea.

In addition, the Italian Navy prepared some submarine patrols, and five boats were ordered to reach positions between Crete and Alexandria.

Another wartime view of Zara *(right) in company with (right to left)* Fiume, *and* Gorizia *(plus another heavy cruiser behid* Fiume*—possibly* Pola *or* Trento*). Observe the after range-finder tower once again mounted aboard* Zara *(since 1939)* *(Aldo Fraccaroli Collection)*

The 1st Naval Division at sea, in 1940-41. Left to right: Fiume, Gorizia, Zara *(Aldo Fraccaroli Collection)*

Deficiency in Co-operation and Information

It was agreed with Regia Aeronautica (Italian Royal Air Force) and with the German X. Flieger-Korps (10th Air Korps, known in Italy as 'X CAT', viz. 10° Corpo Aereo Tedesco) to carry out reconnaissance over Alexandria harbour and the sea areas relevant to the operation. Offensive action would also be taken against enemy ships.

Co-operation between naval forces and aircraft requires very considerable experience to be effective: it failed on this occasion because of excessive improvisation. Moreover, the Italian C-in-C was not kept fully informed of some very important facts. For example, he received the signal on 17 March from some German aircraft of the 'X CAT' that they had torpedoed and damaged two British battleships, out of the three of the Mediterranean Fleet. But he was not told that—a week later—the same 'X CAT' had informed Supermarina that all the three British battleships (with one carrier and about 14 destroyers) had been observed under way off Mersa Matruh, on 24 March.

Vice-Admiral Iachino had several telephone conversations with Naples, where his flagship was moored, and with Rome until 2030 on 26 March, but neither Vice-Admiral Riccardi, Chief of Naval Staff, nor Vice-Admiral Campioni informed him that the former German signal was a mistake. In the same way, Iachino heard nothing of some important changes regarding the air reconnaissance and operations arranged between Supermarina, the Italian General High Command, and the Command of the Italian Islands in the Aegean Sea.

Lack of Surprise

It would not be possible to give here a full account of the Italian raid. The element of surprise, however, failed from the beginning because:

1) 'It had already been decided (by Admiral Cunningham) to take the battlefleet to sea under cover of night on the evening of the 27th . . .';[2]

2) '. . . when air reconnaissance from Malta reported enemy cruisers steaming eastward p.m./27th . . .'[3]

The latter was contained in the report, from a 'Sunderland' flying boat, that three Italian cruisers and one destroyer steaming eastward had been seen in position 36° 30' N, 16° 40' E (a position later amended). This was also decrypted by Supermarina (except for the position) but no counter-order was sent to the C-in-C afloat. This reassured him, as it was well known that the Italian Naval High Command in Rome did not confine its activities to keeping the Commander afloat informed. Unlike the British Admiralty, the Italian High Command would also interfere with the strategic and tactical conduct of operations. The only change ordered by Rome was radioed in the evening of 27 March. It cancelled the northern sweep planned for the '*Zara* Group' for the

[1] *Gorizia* was under repairs at the Taranto Navy Yard.

[2] DESPATCH SUBMITTED TO THE LORDS COMMISSIONERS OF THE ADMIRALTY BY ADMIRAL SIR ANDREW B. CUNNINGHAM, C-IN-C, MEDITERRANEAN FLEET (published in the Third Supplement to *The London Gazette* of 29 July 1947).

[3] Ditto.

An 'Ro.43' taking off from an Italian heavy cruiser. Note white and red diagonal stripes on deck (*LUCE, Aldo Fraccaroli Collection*)

One of Zara's reconnaissance aircraft (*Aldo Fraccaroli Collection*)

Two Ro.43's (not Zara's) flying over Italian cruisers, in 1943 (*Photograph, Aldo Fraccaroli*)

following day, ordering Cattaneo to join the 'Iachino Group' after the dawn of 28 March.

At the rendezvous, the '*Zara* Group' was slightly late, being sighted by the 'Iachino Group' at about 0635. At about the same time a 'Ro.43' aircraft from *Vittorio Veneto* signalled it had sighted four enemy cruisers and four destroyers.[1]

The Two Engagements off Gavdo Is.

The '*Zara* Group' took little part in the following events until the later afternoon of the 27th. In the morning there were two separate actions between the Italian and British vessels. In the first, steaming up to 32 knots,[2] the 3rd Italian Cruiser Division gave chase to the British Light Forces.[3] In the second, Iachino tried to cut off the Light Forces by attacking them with his flagship and the two heavy cruiser divisions. However, only *Vittorio Veneto* was able to fire at the British cruisers,[4] and after twenty minutes even this proved impossible, because, in taking evasive action to avoid air strikes, she had lost contact with the enemy.

Vittorio Veneto had been hit at 1519 by a torpedo from an Albacore during an air strike in the afternoon. Iachino therefore ordered his ships to form five columns, with three heavy cruisers (*Zara, Pola, Fiume*) to starboard of *Vittorio Veneto,* and the other three (the '*Trentos*') to port.[5] In the centre column there were two destroyers leading *Vittorio Veneto* and two others astern. The remaining seven

[1] Light cruisers *Orion* (Vice-Admiral Pridham-Wippell's flag), *Ajax, Perth, Gloucester;* destroyers *Ilex, Hasty, Hereward, Vendetta.*

An approach to the Action off Calabria, (known by the Italians as Battaglia di Punta Stilo), 9 July 1940. The cruisers in the photograph are beginning from the rear ship: Fiume, Gorizia, Trento, Bolzano. *Not visible abaft* Fiume *are* Zara *and* Pola

(LUCE, Aldo Fraccaroli Collection)

destroyers formed the two outer columns. In this way the damaged flagship[6] was protected from further aircraft attack.

Throughout the day no friendly aircraft was seen covering the Italian squadron from British striking forces, with the exception of two German 'Ju 88s', one of which was shot down by Fulmars when attempting to counter the attacks.

Meanwhile, Iachino had been informed that, besides Pridham-Wippell's Light Forces, there was only one enemy group at sea, consisting of a single battleship, one carrier and minor escorting vessels, 170 miles from his own force.[7] Warships of the remaining Mediterranean Fleet were said to be at Alexandria. This message proved vital in the light of later events.

From 1515 to 1645, '*Zara* Group, was repeatedly attacked by bombers, but without result.

Air Strike at Dusk

Warned by his Intelligence that air attacks would be carried out at sunset, with his battleship as target, and that the enemy was correctly informed of the composition, speed and course of the Italian ships, Vice-Admiral Iachino completed his counter measures. After having sighted 10 enemy aircraft since 1823, twenty-four minutes after sunset (1851), he ordered the whole squadron to alter course, steering 270°.[8] The destroyers were instructed to make smoke, and the outer warships to switch on their searchlights in order to dazzle the pilots. When

One of Zara's 37mm/54cal Breda AA double mounting, during the Action off Calabria, 9 July 1940

(LUCE, Aldo Fraccaroli Collection)

Crews of starboard 3·9in AA guns of a heavy cruiser, possibly Zara *(Aldo Fraccaroli Collection)*

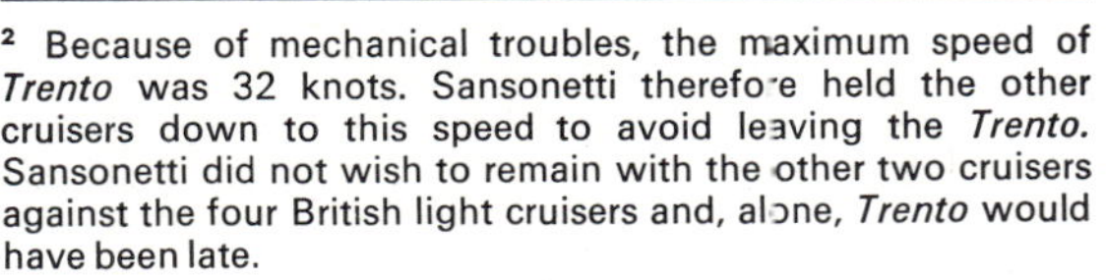

[2] Because of mechanical troubles, the maximum speed of *Trento* was 32 knots. Sansonetti therefore held the other cruisers down to this speed to avoid leaving the *Trento*. Sansonetti did not wish to remain with the other two cruisers against the four British light cruisers and, alone, *Trento* would have been late.

[3] It appears that *Trieste* fired 132 8in shots; *Trento,* 214; *Bolzano,* 190. No direct hit was scored.

[4] Twenty-nine 15in salvoes were fired, and of the 94 projectiles a number straddled HMS *Orion* (who suffered slight damage from a near miss) and HMS *Gloucester* (who became the rear ship after Pridham-Wippell's immediate alteration of course eastward under Italian fire). No direct hits were scored in this attack.

[5] The 8th Cruiser Division with its two destroyers was detached to return to Brindisi.

[6] About 4000 tons of water flooded *Vittorio Veneto,* who listed to port, her rudder pumps being put out of action and her engines stopped at 1530. Six minutes later the engines and the rudder were partially repaired and she was able to steam again, up to nearly 20 knots, but not regularly.

[7] In reality, Cunningham with all his Battle Force was 65 miles away, steaming at 22 knots towards Iachino's squadron.

[8] The ships thus offered the smallest target to the enemy, as at the end of March the sun sets due west.

Between about 1620 and 1930 on 9 July 1940 (Action off Calabria) the Italian cruisers were bombed by Italian aircraft, resulting in near misses, as in this view of Zara *(Aldo Fraccaroli Collection)*

One of the last photographs of Zara. *The two small side range-finders (for directing the fire of the 3·9in AA guns), mounted on tripod mainmast, have been removed (in 1939) (LUCE, Aldo Fraccaroli Collection)*

the aircraft approached, the Italians opened a very heavy fire with all their AA guns and machine guns, at the same time altering course, steering 30° to starboard. The six Fulmars and the four Albacores released their torpedoes. At 1945 *Vittorio Veneto* was able to increase speed from 15 to 19 knots, enabling the whole force to proceed faster. At 1950 the AA fire ended, the searchlights were switched off and twenty-one minutes later the smoke screen also ceased.

Pola torpedoed

Of the 10 torpedoes only one reached a target; this was *Pola,* hit amidships at 1950. She had three compartments flooded—her forward engine room and boilers 4-5 and 6-7. Temporary failure of electricity at first prevented her from signalling, by radio or flashing, that she had been hit. She lost speed, fell back, and finally stopped. The C-in-C later received the news, partly from *Fiume,* and partly from *Pola,* when able to radio. At 2018 he ordered Rear-Admiral Cattaneo to turn back with his 1st Cruiser Division to assist *Pola.* His signal crossed that from Cattaneo (sent at 2015 and received at 2025 aboard *Vittorio Veneto*) in which the Rear-Admiral proposed to send two destroyers to stand by *Pola.*

Fatal Night Sailing

On receiving Cattaneo's signal, Iachino decided that two destroyers would be insufficient assistance for the damaged cruiser. He therefore confirmed (at 2038) his original signal, ordering Cattaneo to turn back with *Zara, Fiume* and their attendant destroyers. In the meanwhile *Pola* was requesting a tow. This second order reached *Zara* at 2045, and the

Only one ship of the three cruisers sunk off Matapan was camouflaged: Fiume, *whose experimental camouflage was painted in March 1941, a few weeks before her loss. This is probably the only existing photograph of* Fiume *dazzle painted—a 'mondial first' photograph* (*Copyright photograph by Aldo Fraccaroli*)
Note: *The plan of this experimental camouflage does not exist*

A view of Zara *taken in about 1940* (*LUCE, Aldo Fraccaroli Collection*)

six ships turned back at 2106, in line ahead: *Zara* (flagship; Captain Luigi Corsi), *Fiume* (Captain Giorgio Giorgis), *Alfieri* (leader of the 9th Destroyer Division, Captain Salvatore Toscano), *Gioberti, Carducci, Oriani.*

Surprisingly, Cattaneo proceeded with his major units ahead, and the four destroyers in line, astern.[1] He also proceeded at slow speed,[2] which increased his delay in reaching *Pola.*

Cattaneo, leading the formation, ordered *Fiume* (2157) to make ready to tow *Pola.* The operation was hardly under way, when the 1st Italian Division was sighted by the British Mediterranean Fleet Battle Squadron—a surprise for both sides. The

[1] This was contrary to standard night cruising regulations. It might have been excusable if anything seen forward could be considered to be an enemy ship and therefore to be fired on. It must also be remembered that, as had already been stated, *Zara's* class main guns were not fitted for night engagements.

[2] Rear-Admiral Cattaneo ordered the following speeds: from 2107 till 2125: 16 knots, from 2125 till 2203: 22 knots, from 2203 till 2220: again 16 knots.

The first camouflage of Gorizia, (*the only survivor of the* Zara *class cruisers after the night action off Cape Matapan*), *was ordered by the C-in-C of the Italian Fleet on 15 February 1942. This was carried out at the end of February. The initial areas of white paintwork were later (in Summer 1942) replaced by light grey. This photograph shows* Gorizia *steaming at 30 knots towards the enemy, at about 1030 on 22 March 1942, just before the Second Battle of Sirte*

(*Aldo Fraccaroli Collection*)

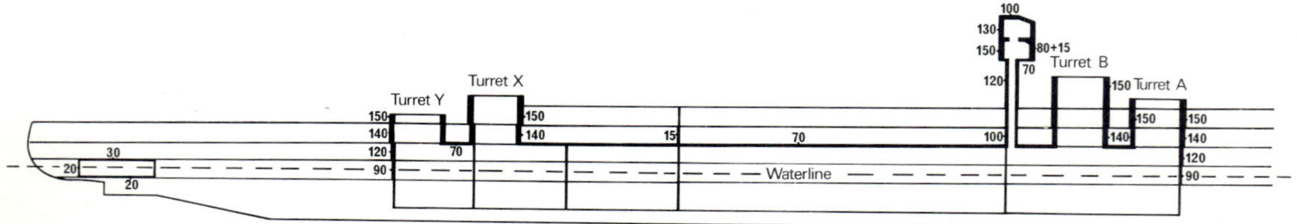

Zara *thickness of armour—figures are in mm* (*Profile Publications Ltd*)

latter was already on the alert, because the immobile *Pola* had been plotted, at 2015, by *Orion*'s radar, and at 2210 by *Valiant*'s. HMS *Warspite* (flag of the C-in-C, Admiral A. B. Cunningham), *Valiant* and *Barham* altered course and trained their 15in guns on the stationary vessel. At this moment Commodore Edelsten saw in the darkness the silhouettes of two more large ships[1] moving in the darkness. Admiral Cunningham at once ordered his battleships to turn to starboard, and turrets were swung round to the new target.

Surprise

Suddenly *Zara* was illuminated by HMS *Greyhound*'s searchlight, and at the same moment HMS *Warspite* opened fire at about 3800 yards—a point-blank range for her main armament. *Fiume* was hit by five out of six 15in shots of her first broadside. A few seconds later the searchlights of the other British vessels were switched on, star-shells were fired and Cunningham's flagship began firing also with her 6in guns at *Fiume*. At the same time *Fiume* was hit by *Valiant*'s first salvo of four 15in shells; *Valiant* then shifted target (as her X and Y turrets did not bear on *Fiume*), and, training her turrets on *Zara*, in about three minutes fired five full broadsides on the Italian ship. Meanwhile, *Warspite*, having fired two broadsides on *Fiume*, also turned her attention to *Zara*, who was hit at 3000 yards. 'The plight of the Italian cruisers was indescribable. One saw whole turrets and masses of other heavy debris whirling through the air and splashing into the sea, and in a short time the ships themselves were nothing but glowing torches and on fire from stem to stern.'[2]

The four Italian destroyers, whilst attempting to close on the enemy battleships to fire their torpedoes, were fired upon. *Alfieri*, was sunk after firing four salvoes with her 4·7in forward mounting and three torpedoes (none of which scored a hit), whilst *Carducci*, repeatedly hit and damaged, was scuttled.

Zara's Last Moments

Regia Nave (His Italian Majesty's Ship) *Zara*, with her turrets trained fore and aft, tried to reply with her

[1] Visibility was, evidently, asymmetrical. British sources state that a smaller Italian ship was ahead of the two heavy cruisers. At first (Cunningham's Narrative and others) this smaller vessel was described as a 6in gun ship; later it became the destroyer *Alfieri*. But all the Italian survivors' accounts agree on the fact that the leading ship of the line was *Zara*, followed by *Fiume* and then the four destroyers. Obviously, this discrepancy between British and Italian accounts may give rise to differences regarding the position of the Italian ships involved in the night engagement, and thus affect their names. The author has made every endeavour to obtain the maximum accuracy.

[2] Viscount Cunningham of Hyndhope: *A Sailor's Odyssey*, cit.

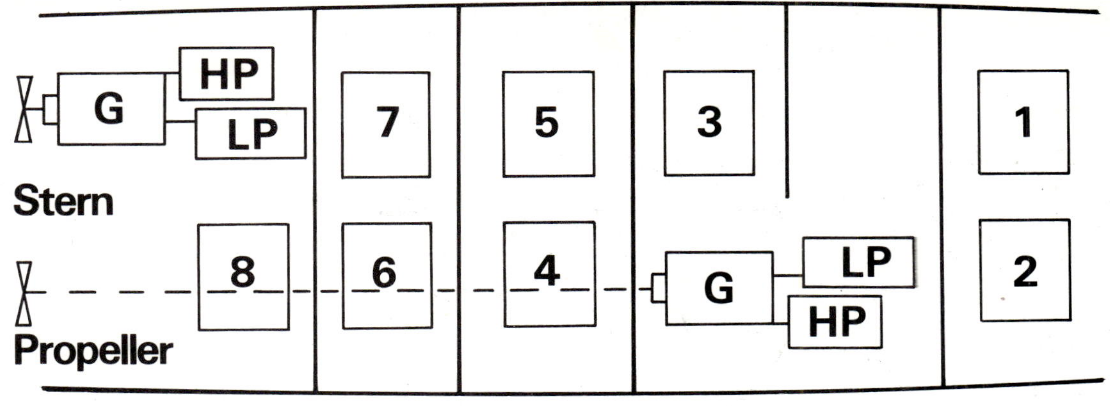

Machinery disposition aboard the Italian cruiser Zara. *G=geared reduction; HP=high pressure; LP=low pressure. 1=number of the boiler (4, 6, 8=small boilers)* (*Profile Publications Ltd*)

Zara *as she appeared on 6 August 1933* (*Photograph, Marius Bar*)

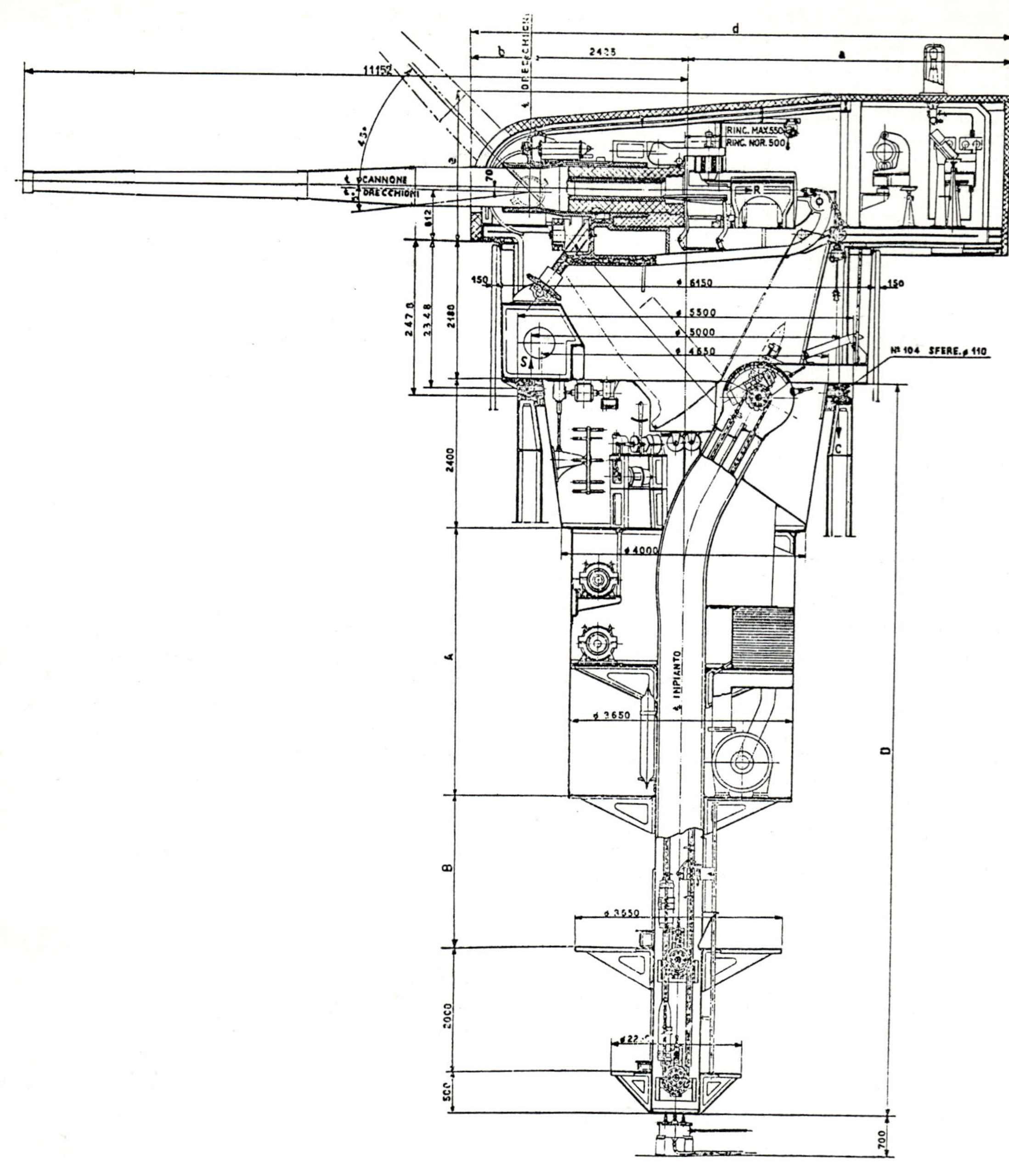

Zara *type 8in turret* (*203/53 Ans. mod 1929*)

3·9in guns, but even this was impossible. The tremendous damage to her installations prevented her from retaliation. Her helm no longer answered and at least five boilers had been put out of action. A-turret, hit by a shell, had been annihilated and the intercoms and the directors were also out of action. Only a machine gun fired.

For some hours *Zara's* surviving officers and crew, maintaining perfect discipline, tried to put out the fires. The ship still remained afloat although further hit by torpedoes and gunfire from HMS *Stuart* and *Havock.* At last, however, Captain Corsi realised that it would be impossible to save the vessel. In order to prevent her falling into the hands of the enemy, he ordered her to be scuttled by flooding her hull. Rear-Admiral Cattaneo agreed.

Before abandoning ship, about 200-250 officers and men gathered at the stern, and together with their admiral and their captain gave the traditional Italian cheer: *'Viva il Re!'* The executive officer, Commander

Giannattasio, then led a party of volunteers to sink the ship by blowing up the stern magazines.
Many men died as the sea was very cold, rafts and carley floats being damaged by gunfire. Among the dead were Rear-Admiral Cattaneo and Captain Corsi. Finally *Zara* received three torpedoes out of five fired by HMS *Jervis,* and sank—her battleflag still flying—in 35° 20′ N, 20° 57′ E, at 0240 of 29 March 1941. Losses were: 30 officers and 752 men.

Sister-ships' Fate

R.N. *Fiume* was the first cruiser to sink at about 2315 of the 28th, in 35° 21′ N, 20° 57′ E, with the loss of her commanding officer, Captain Giorgis, 32 officers and 780 men.
R.N. *Pola,* who had not received the fire of any enemy warships, had no prospect of escaping. Accordingly her commanding officer, Captain Manlio De Pisa, ordered the valves to be opened to scuttle her. However, eight British destroyers surrounded her and HMS *Jervis* boarded *Pola,* taking off 258 men. Losses were 328. Then one torpedo from *Jervis* and another from *Nubian* struck *Pola,* who blew up, sinking at 0403 of 29, in 35° 15′ N, 21° 00′ E.
On the morning of the 29th, 1015 men were picked up by British destroyers, a further 110 on the night of 29th by Greek destroyers, and 161 by the Italian hospital-ship *Gradisca* between 31 March and 3 April.
The fourth ship of the *Zara*-class, RN *Gorizia,* was sunk in shallow waters, at La Spezia on 26 June 1944, by British 'chariots' and Italian frogmen, brought in by the destroyer *Grecale* and *MS 74.* She had been there at the time of the Italian armistice (8 September 1943) and had been captured by the Germans. After the war, in 1946, her hull was dismantled.

War Operations

During the war, from 11 June 1940 to 8 September 1943, the four *Zaras* carried out the following operations:

	War operations, numbers	miles covered	hours under way	fuel burnt, metric tons	inactive for repairs, days
Fiume	9 (+12 various)	10,939	558	8578	76
Gorizia	36 (+20 various)	27,672	1471	20,929	207
Pola	12 (+8 various)	13,174	611	8813	57
Zara	10 (+16 various)	11,498	584	7843	25

ACKNOWLEDGEMENTS
The author would like to express his thanks for their assistance to: Ammiraglio di Squadra Carlo Paladini, Director of the Ufficio Storico della Marina Militare, Rome; and Generale del Genio Navale Gino Galuppini, of the same Ufficio Storico; Dr Franco Bargoni, Rome: Signor Mauro de Pinto, President of the 'Associazione Marinara Aldebaran', Trieste.

Warship Series Editor: JOHN WINGATE, DSC

Zara *armour thickening amidships—figures are in mm* (*Profile Publications Ltd*)

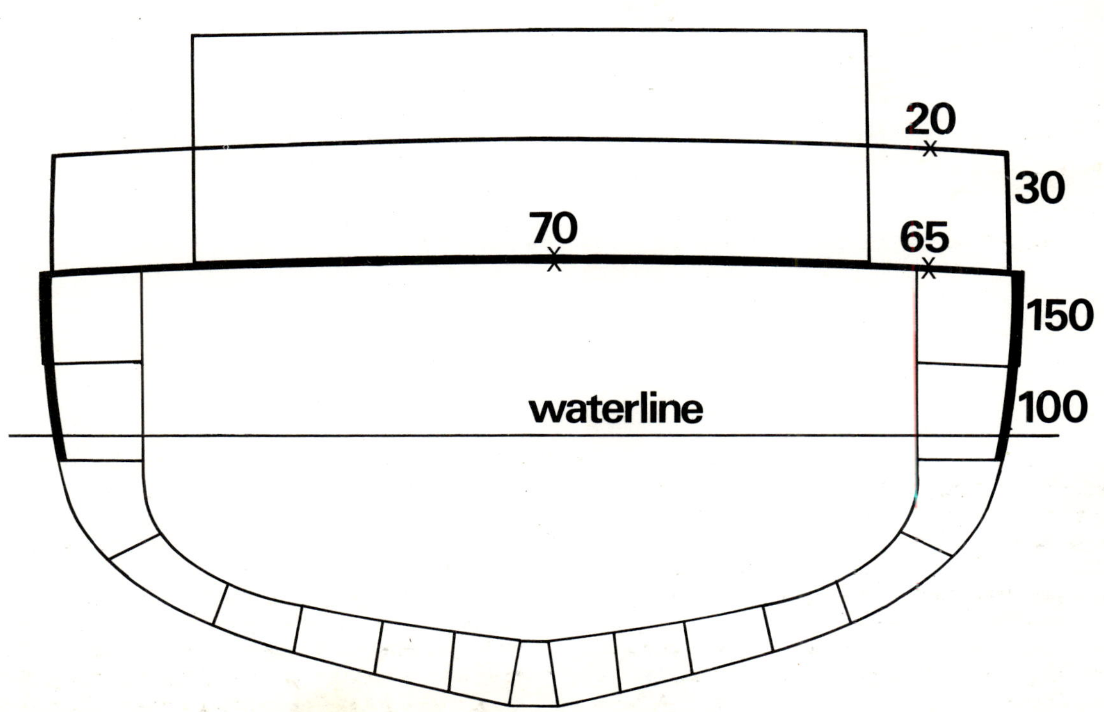

Zara as completed, Autumn 1931 (Photograph by Ansaldo, S.p.A.)

Bismarck *on commissioning* (*Author*)

Kriegsmarine Bismarck

by Paul Schmalenbach *Fregattenkapitän a.D.*

Historical Background to the German 35,000 ton Battleships

On 6 February 1922 the Washington Agreement was signed between the USA, Great Britain, France, Italy and Japan which limited naval armament. The definitions of types of ships, maximum displacement and maximum gun calibre laid down in the Agreement were one day to apply to the German Navy, a possibility no-one could foresee at the time of the signing of the Washington Agreement.

The Agreement limited future building of battleships to 35,000 tons (1016kg to the-ts.-ton), whereby the nature of the ship was for the first time exactly determined at the outset. The maximum calibre of gun was not to exceed 16in or 40·6cm—the Treaty of Versailles allowed Germany possession of only six ships of 10,000 tons having a maximum gun calibre of not more than 28cm. Two similar ships were allowed as an additional reserve.

With a few exceptions favouring Great Britain, France and Italy, the Washington Treaty stipulated a pause in ship building which was to last until the end of 1930. In the final year of the stipulated period the pause in ship building was extended by Great Britain, the USA and Japan for a further six years, i.e. until 31.12.36. Again, taking its name from the city where the conference was held, the 'London Agreement' on 30 June 1938 generally ratified, but amended in one very important point, the displacement of future battleships under standard (i.e. Washington Agreement) conditions was increased to 45,000 tons.

The negotiations and agreements of the great sea powers were now out of step with the endeavours of Germany and the German Navy to build up a minimum of modern naval armament within the limits of the conditions of the Versailles Peace Treaty. (See Warship *Profile* No. 6, pp. 121-122.)

The Three Panzerschiffe

The first results were the three Panzerschiffe *Deutschland, Admiral Scheer* and *Admiral Graf Spee* (see Warship *Profile* No. 4), proven in action and known universally as 'pocket battleships'. They were faster than all stronger, and stronger than all faster ships—the only exceptions to this being the British battle-cruisers. The situation changed overnight when France decided to build the two battleships permitted to her under the Washington Agreement. Both ships (the *Dunkerque* laid down in 1931, the *Strasbourg* in 1934) were, at 26,500 tons,

Launching day: the guard rails are manned as she slides down the ways. Note the mine boom at her forefoot (*Author*)

Fitting-out (*Author*)

to be the answer to the German pocket battleships. This shift in power in the Mediterranean in favour of France caused Italy to react by building the first battleships to make the most of the limitations of the Agreement. The Deutsche Reich acted with reserve in order not to destroy the negotiations already in progress with Great Britain over establishing a ratio of the relative strength of the two navies.

Gun Development

Only in 1934 was there talk of 'improved Panzerschiffe', with 28cm triple turrets, as before; these were the later, faster *Scharnhorst* and *Gneisenau* with a planned displacement of 26,000 tons. However, this gun calibre still seemed inadequate when compared with the French ships, as these had 8×33cm guns in two four-gun turrets. So in that same year there began construction of a 38cm double turret at Krupp's in Essen. This double turret was one day to replace the 28cm triple turret of the *Scharnhorst* class, but it was not available for delivery until approximately 1938, whereas four 28cm triple turrets were in the process of being manufactured for the fourth and fifth pocket battleships. Because of this situation in the production of heavier guns, the guns for both the battleships *Scharnhorst* and *Gneisenau* remained 28cm calibre. The two ships respectively received the construction designation 'Battleship D' as the replacement for the ship of the line, the *Elsass*, dating from 1903; and 'E' for the replacement of the *Hessen* of the same year.

18 June 1935 saw the signing in London of the Anglo-German naval agreement which laid down that—excluding the U-boats—the German naval strength could be 35% of that of the Royal Navy. The standard displacement in accordance with the Washington and London Agreements served as the criterion. Thus qualitative limitation of ships came into operation for the Germany Navy. This gave the Deutsche Reich the facility of possessing battleship tonnage of up to 183,750 tons. After allowing for the pocket battleships (3×10,000 tons) and the new battleships (2×26,000 tons) totalling 82,000 tons, 101,750 tons remained as capacity for building. This figure would thus allow the construction of three ships each of a maximum of 35,000 tons. The German Government decided in the first

The fitting-out proceeds apace. The turret range-finder housings are clearly shown (*Author*)

In the fitting-out basin. Note the armour belt (*Author*)

instance to build two ships, each of 35,000 tons. They were to incorporate findings of certain theoretical studies which had started in 1933, but most important of all they were to be suitable to take the 38cm double turret, already under construction.

The two new ships were respectively designated 'F' to replace the ship of the line *Hannover* dating from 1905, and 'G' to replace the ship of the line *Schleswig-Holstein* dating from 1906. These two vessels later became the battleships *Bismarck* and *Tirpitz*.

It was more difficult to distribute the remaining weight allowance on the defence equipment (armour plating, watertight compartments) and the superstructure with the manifold demands of the weapon command, ship's command and the ship's aircraft. Several plans were drawn up leaving the two shipyards freedom to adopt their own solutions for relatively minor sections. This was particularly the case amidships with regard to the arrangement of aircraft hangars, catapults and the large cranes. The 1936/37 plan showed two overlapping catapults, one behind the other, between the funnel and the after mast, an arrangement similar to that found in the *Scharnhorst* Class and in Heavy Cruisers (see Warship *Profile* No. 6, p 135).

One aircraft hangar was, however, excluded. Both of the stabilised anti-aircraft command positions aft stood on either side and to the rear of the funnel. The total superstructure forward with the command position, ship's command position and fighting mast was longer, but flatter therefore, and ended as shown in the final plans—very narrow at the second 38cm turret. The funnel cap appeared for the first time in the 1938/39 plans which differed even less from the final ones.

Notable features here were the first appearance of a catapult fixture athwartships, operational on both sides; and the arrangement of the two forward anti-aircraft command posts adjacent to one another, whereas these posts were later installed one abaft the other. Because of many uniform constructional concepts it is not surprising that the ships of this time, the heavy cruisers and battleships from the *Scharnhorst* to the *Tirpitz*, should resemble one another so strongly. On 24 May 1941, this similarity led to the *Hood* firing on the *Prinz Eugen* under the impression that she was the *Bismarck*.

The Building of the Battleship 'F'

At the beginning of 1936, the plans were sufficiently advanced for the contracts for battleships 'F' and 'G' to be allocated: 'F' went to the Blohm & Voss yard, Hamburg, and 'G' to the Naval Yard at Wilhelmshaven. Construction in Hamburg began on 1 July 1936

Adolf Hitler on board Bismarck. *Admiral Lütjens gives the naval salute. Cdr. Düwell, second in command, stands immediately at right.* *(Author)*

Bismarck *leaves the basin* *(Drüppel)*

with the laying of the keel. But in Wilhelmshaven it was not possible to start until the end of October, as the one slipway that was suitable was only vacated, on 3 October, by the launching of the *Scharnhorst.* For Blohm & Voss the new ship was the 509th to be laid down there.

Each day, in two shifts, about 5 to 6000 workers streamed to the dockyards. Work proceeded according to plan until it came to welding together medium thickness armour plating with the usual shipbuilding steel. Test pieces did not hold. Only a welding rod developed by the Friedrich Krupp AG for gun turret armour plating fulfilled all the requirements. The heavy side armour and the longitudinal torpedo bulkheads were not welded, however, but joined and riveted in the usual way.

The Launching

The launching took place on 14 February 1939. The ceremony was declared a state occasion by the German Government. The fact that Hitler was not only present for the occasion but also personally delivered the christening speech stressed the political importance of this first modern battleship. Everyone who had any pretension to name and rank at that time put in an appearance: beside the highest Admirals stood Reichmarshall Göring, Hitler's deputy, Hess, the Chief of the Armed Forces Supreme Command, Generaloberst Keitel and, on the platform of honour, the Federal Ministers Ribbentrop, Goebbels, Frank and Rust, as well as the various heads of other organisations like Himmler, Rosenberg, Borman and v. Schirach.

In his speech, Hitler expounded the importance of maritime armament for the Deutsche Reich, and charged the future crew that they should perform their duty in the spirit of the 'Iron Chancellor', in peacetime as in war. Hitler concluded his oration with the wish of the German people that Bismarck's spirit would uplift the crew in the most difficult hours of fulfilment of their duty.

The Naval Commander-in-Chief, Admiral Dr h. c. Raeder (who was promoted to Admiral of the Fleet on 1 April on the occasion of the launching of the *Tirpitz*) thanked the German Government for the energy with which they had pressed forward naval armament and this new ship, and promised that no effort would be spared to make the ship ready for action, a powerful weapon to secure peace. Frau Dorothea von Loewenfeld, née Countess of Bismarck (widow of Vice-Admiral a.D. von Loewenfeld, Leader of the Volunteer Corps in the post-war period and co-founder of the German Navy) gave the new ship the name of *Bismarck*; the name could be seen on either side of the bow while the Bismarck family coat of arms was revealed on the stem. The launching went off without a hitch.

Fitting out began the next day. Naturally at the outbreak of war at the beginning of September, it was necessary to gauge whether and, if appropriate, how urgently construction should continue. Great Britain's entry into the war considerably affected the crucial issues, and the U-boat had come strongly to the forefront of all plans. The German Government decided that both the battleships should be completed as well as the heavy cruiser, *Prinz Eugen,* and the aircraft carrier *Graf Zeppelin.* The work that then remained to complete *Bismarck* still amounted to 5·6 million working hours and the toil continued without interruption. In the full flush of enthusiasm during the first years of the war, the ship was even finished earlier than intended, enabling her to be commissioned as early as 24 August 1940. Kapitän zur See Ernst Lindemann commanded the vessel throughout her life.

Dimensions and Water Displacement

The shallow water in German river mouths and in the North Sea, as well as in the Kaiser-Wilhelm Canal (nowadays officially designated the Kiel Canal) limited the draught of projected battleships from the planning stage. The previously tested and established ratios of length, beam and draught resulted in an extraordinarily wide beam of 36m. This was welcome information for it enabled the intermediate space between the outer shell and the longitudinal torpedo bulkheads to be made both larger than was usual and also greater than adopted by other Navies. This had the effect of considerably reducing the adverse effect of underwater explosions.

The *draught* of the ship was 9·33m at standard displacement, the *length* at the designed waterline was 241·50m, the overall length being 251m. The *freeboard* was a notable 15·00m. These dimensions stemmed from the fulfilment of many staff requirements, which had now gradually forced an infringement of the then still valid standard displacement of 35,000 tons up to 41,700 tons. As mentioned earlier, this limit was increased in 1938 to 45,000 tons. This point should be stressed as, after the war, the admirals responsible at the time were reproached for failure to keep to the Agreement. The 41,700 tons standard (1016kg to the ton) corresponds approximately to the frequently quoted 42,343·5 tons at 1000kg to the ton. As these two units of measurement are also confused in official circles, there have occasionally been previous contradictory statements about the battleship's displacement.

Weights

A precise classification of the weights and division of weight are shown in the following tables in the then current standard of the Kriegsmarine.

WEIGHT SHEET (EXTRACT)
FOR THE BATTLESHIP 'BISMARCK'
Date of calculation 16.3.1940

			1000kg to the ton	*1016kg to the ton*
S	Hull		11,691·0	=11,507·0
	Armour plating, excl. revolving turret armour		17,540·0	
MI	Main engines	with instru-ments	2,800·0	
MII	Auxiliary engines		1,428·0	
A	Gunnery armament and armour		5,973·0	
T	Torpedo armament		———	
F	Aircraft equipment		83·0	
Spr	Barrage weapons		8·0	
I	General equipment etc		369·4	
N	Nautical instruments		8·6	
Ta	Rigging		30·0	
	Empty ship with instruments with oil and water in MI, MII etc		39,931·2	=39,302·0
A	Gunnery ammunition		1,501·4	
Spr	Barrage weapon ammunition		2·5	
	Consumables		155·4	
	Crew		243·6	
	Supplies		194·2	
	Drinking water		139·2	
	Washing water		167·0	
	Type displacement		42,343·5	=41,676·0
	Feed water (combat cells)		187·5	
	Oil		3,226·0	
	Fuel oil		96·5	
	Lubricating oil		80·0	
	Aircraft—working reserve 1 filling		17·0	
	Designed displacement		45,950·5	=45,226·0
	Feed water		187·5	
	Oil		3,226·0	
	Fuel oil		96·5	
	Lubricating oil		80·0	
	Aircraft—working reserve 1 filling		17·0	
	Freshwater—reserve		389·2	
	Ship fully equipped		49,946·7	=49,160·0
	Useful oil load		1,009·0	
	Ship with useful load		50,995·7	=50,153·0

PROPORTIONAL WEIGHTS
(SITUATION ON 19.10.40 IN ROUND FIGURES)

		tons	*% of weight*
Hull weight	SI-IV	12,700	27·0
Engine installations	MI	3,000	6·4
Auxiliary engines	MII	1,400	3·0
Armour	P	18,700	40·0
Gunnery	A	5,550	11·8
Armaments	Au	920	2·0
Fuel	Br	4,000	8·4
Water	W	530	1·0
Barrage weapon installations	—	100	0·2
Aircraft installations	—	100	0·2
Designed displacement		about 47,000	100

It is interesting to compare the preceding data with the results of the weighing carried out by the Blohm & Voss yard as each item was taken on board.

		1000kg to the ton
SI	Steelwork	10,150
SII	Fitters' work, pipelines	960
SIII	Sheetmetal work	335
SIV	Paint	220
		11,665
HoP	Horizontal armour, deck and torpedo bulkhead	8,910
S	Side armour	5,019
Z	Armoured transverse bulkheads	363
Ba	Barbettes	2,285
KoT	Fire command posts	466
		17,043
MI	Engines: turbines, auxiliary engines	3,370
MII	Engines: apparatus and auxiliary engines	1,430
		4,800
Guns	Total gunnery	6,180
TO	Torpedo tubes	40
		6,220
	TOTAL	**39,728**

In addition there was the water in the boilers and pipelines; the gunnery ammunition, all the aircraft and barrage weapon installations as well as the navigational instruments; the signalling and broadcasting apparatus; the weapon control instruments including range-finding equipment and the radar apparatus, not to mention the weight of the crew and their belongings, both professional and private. Finally there was drinking and washing water and the consumables as, for example, lubricants, cleansers and anti-freezing agents.

There were, however, some notable differences:

Group	*calculated by designers tons*	*weighed at the yard (see above) tons*
SI-IV	11,691	11,665
MI	3,370	2,800
MII	1,430	1,428
Armour (without gunnery)	17,540	17,043
Total gunnery	5,973	6,180
Torpedo weapons	—	40

Admiral Lütjens inspects Prinz Eugen's *company 11.00 at Gdynia, 18 May 1941. Note the Swastika aircraft recognition marking on the quarter-deck.* (*Author*)

Just how fluid the limits were is shown by the last entry, for example, for *Bismarck* never had any torpedo weapons. Nevertheless, equipment, which on other ships was classed with torpedo weapons, were attributable as, for example, pneumatic pumps and the ship's anti-mine devices such as the extendible spar for the paravane.

The following summary gives some indication of the weights included in what was termed the 'useful load'.

	1000kg to the ton
Gunnery ammunition	1,510·4
Barrage ammunition (primer cartridges for high explosive shells etc)	2·5
Consumables (cleansing, maintenance etc)	155·4
Crew	234·6
Supplies	194·2
Drinking water	139·2
Washing water	167·0
Total Useful Load	**2,412·3**

The Hull

The hull was a transverse and longitudinally framed steel structure, of which more than 90% was welded. The double bottom extended over 83% of the ship's length. 17 bulkheads divided the ship into 18 watertight compartments. The ship had a bow blister which housed the hydrophone. From the ship's foremost lower section, extended the previously mentioned spar for the paravane. When docking, the ship could be set down on four keels. The outershell was perforated in many places for the intake of seawater or the discharge of sea- or waste-water. Biggest of these openings were the outlets for the cooling water used in the condensers. The upper deck ran through from the bow to the after deck. Under it lay the battery deck, the armoured deck and the upper and middle platform decks. The lower platform deck ran parallel with the stowage almost everywhere i.e. with the upper boundary of the double bottom. The space on the sloping surfaces or 'pockets' of the armoured deck are included as armoured deck.

The material used was the newly developed shipbuilding steel St 52 which had an elastic limit of 36kg/mm^2 and a fatigue limit of 26kg/mm^2. This was superior to the St II material previously used, particularly with respect to its elastic strength. Considerable weight savings were made by the exclusive use of St 52.

The Armour Protection

The upper deck had armour of 50mm thickness, extending from approximately 4m forward of the foremost 38cm gun turret (turret A) to about 6m abaft the after turret D. At each of these positions an armoured bulkhead was installed. These bulkheads were of different thicknesses in the various decks: 145mm in the battery deck, 220mm in the armoured deck forward and 110mm aft. This 180mm transverse bulkhead forward descended to the upper platform deck and formed the boundary of the turtle-shaped section of the armoured deck, which ran from this bulkhead a further 16m forward and indeed formed a horizontal surface (30mm). The foremost nine metres of the forecastle, approximately, were without an armoured deck. Similarly the aft transverse bulkhead formed the after boundary of that armoured deck with a thickness of 145, 110 or 220mm. The armoured deck continued aft from here as a horizontal surface for about 10m and there rose obliquely about 50cm to protect the steering gear. Immediately abaft it, a third armoured transverse bulkhead closed off the armoured deck. Where it began under the battery deck, this bulkhead had a thickness of 45mm, which became 150mm thick around the armoured deck and 45mm thick underneath it. The armoured deck ran between both the previously mentioned main armoured transverse bulkheads and had a thickness of 80mm, increasing to 100 or 120mm in the area of the 38cm turrets.

The side armour was attached to the sides of those same main armoured transverse bulkheads. It was extremely thick, considered from top to bottom, being 145mm thick in the battery deck region and, under this in the region of the armoured deck, it increased from 270 to 320mm and then decreased again to 170mm. This was its thickness on the slopes of the armoured deck. 50mm teak provided the foundation for all the side armour.

The maximum thickness of the two-storey fire command posts (in the upper floor of which was housed the gunnery control post) was 350mm, on the front face and 220mm on the top. The revolving dome on top of it, which held the range finders, was reinforced to a thickness of 200 or 100mm. The aft command post was less thick (150 or 30mm) as was the revolving dome aft (100 or 50mm). Both posts were linked to the corresponding room under the armoured deck (control room and reserve control room in the middle engine room) by circular shafts (forward 220mm, aft 50mm armoured material). The main gunnery control post in the foretop had a protection of 60mm (20mm on the top) and a revolving dome (30 or 20mm). The command post stood on a two-deck high cylinder with 60mm armour thickness. This cylinder and the command post on top of it afforded protection for the combat communication control room.

As these ships were essentially gun platforms, it was natural for considerable weight to be allocated for protection of the guns. The turrets revolved within barbettes which had 220mm thick armour. The front faces were 360mm thick; the top, made up of three parts, 180, 130 and 180mm thick respectively; the back 320mm; the turret side walls 220mm and those connecting side and top 150mm.

The 15cm double turrets had 100mm thick barbettes, which also stood on the armoured deck. The forward face of the turntable was 100mm thick; the roof for'd was 35mm thick, and aft 20mm. The back and the side walls were 40mm thick.

For the rest, the vital connections outside the armour protection were laid in splinter-proof trunking in the *Bismarck* and the *Tirpitz,* similar to the arrangement in the heavy cruisers. The armoured material used was—as previously in the *Scharnhorst* and the *Gneisenau*—the material just developed in that year, which went under the name of 'Wotan'. There was 'Wotan-hard' (Wh) and 'Wotan-soft' (Ww) with the following characteristic properties:

tensile strength Wh 85 to 95kg/mm^2; Ww 65 to 75kg/mm^2. Elongation Wh 20%, Ww 25%; elastic limit: Wh 50 to 55kg/mm^2; Ww 38 to 40kg/mm^2. According to the particular problem to be solved, the more suitable material was used: Wh for the upperdeck and armoured deck, Ww for the torpedo bulkhead. Both sorts of material could be worked with the Krupp's special electrode Nichrotherm (Nickel-Chromium-Therm), though not the side armour or the armour used for the control posts or gunnery which was KC-material (=Krupp cemented). This was a modernised (chrome-nickel-molybdenum alloy) material, of which the resistance to shells exceeded material of usual manufacture by about 50%.

New Technology

The welding properties of the Wh and the Ww material allowed its use in places where previously only shipbuilding material could be used, for example in parts of the outer shell and the upperdeck. After consideration of the available materials, it was decided to use Ww material for the longitudinal bulkhead. This bulkhead was to protect, at a distance of about 6m from the hull, the vital parts from underwater hits. This torpedo bulkhead was extended upwards to the upper deck by a splinter-proof wall and downwards to the outershell by a strengthened longitudinal rib. The design of this bulkhead relative to the rest of the ship was selected because of the possibility of heavy stress on the torpedo bulkhead through an underwater hit. For the same reason, this bulkhead was not welded, but riveted with foil and one-sided coverplates.

The Superstructure

The original plan strongly resembled the *Scharnhorst* in the distribution of the superstructure; the final arrangement resembled that of the heavy cruisers, especially after the experiences of the *Admiral Hipper* had been evaluated for the two cruisers *Blücher* and *Prinz Eugen.* The forward bridge superstructure was four decks high, the after, three decks. The fighting mast stood on the forward superstructure with five sealed rooms, one on top of the other; on top came the open main anti-aircraft operational post, the main fire control tower and the foretop rotating cupola. The rooms were in essence divided and used as in *Prinz Eugen* (See Warship *Profile* No. 6, p. 136): the anchors, booms and accessories, masts and rigging, the radio and reconnaissance equipment, aircraft information centre, the bridges, the forward superstructure, the sick bay, accommodation, magnetic mine protection (de-gaussing), gyro compass, flag deck and smoke apparatus were all similarly sited.

The Propulsion Installation

The installation in the *Bismarck* consisted of three sets of geared turbines supplied by the shipyard (in the *Tirpitz* by Brown, Boveri & Co); these were three groups of boilers, each group being made up of four boilers of the Wagner type, as well as the necessary auxiliary engines. Each group of boilers

The after-superstructure, showing the sliding hangar door, the boat stowage and the signalling projector on the mast. Early 1940 (*Author*)

A and B turrets, the bridge and fighting top, port side: Hamburg 1940 *(Author)*

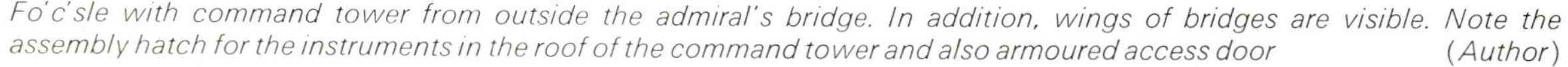

Fo'c'sle with command tower from outside the admiral's bridge. In addition, wings of bridges are visible. Note the assembly hatch for the instruments in the roof of the command tower and also armoured access door *(Author)*

Port night action range-finder sponson with access from below via climbing rungs. Above can be seen the port for'd anti-aircraft director enclosed by bullet-proof shield. Below left are the twin barrels of the 10·5cm anti-aircraft gun (Author)

consisted of two boilers each in the for'd and aft compartment (IX and XI). Both these compartments were divided twice by longitudinal bulkheads so that only two boilers were in one room. Each set of turbines comprised a high, medium and low pressure, as well as a cruising turbine, which had differing speeds of rotation (at max. load 2825 for high and medium pressure, 2390 for low pressure and 4130 for cruising turbines) which were reduced by a gearing to 265 rpm.

The installation of the four turbines was arranged around the gearing which allowed a considerable shortening in the length of the engines. The three propellers were three-bladed and had a diameter of 4·85m. The 12 boilers delivered steam of 58 atmospheres at 450°C. The steam used at full speed amounted to 20·5kg for each HP per hour. The engine installation weighed 20·5kg for each HP. Initially the projected efficiency amounted to 3×46,000HP=138,000HP, but in practice, thanks to a very careful approach by the builders to the measurement of efficiency and a stronger method of construction, amounted to 150,170HP, with a speed of 30·1 knots. The fuel used in various stages is given in the following chart:

Calculation of the total efficiency of the three shaft turbine installation with 12 boilers based on a test run displacement of 43,000 tons:

SHP	No. of boilers	Revs	Knots	Fuel used
3×46,000	12	265	29	325g/hp
3×38,350	12	250	—	320g/hp
3×23,300	9	214	—	335g/hp
Ahead				
3×13,000	6	176	—	370g/hp
3× 8,300	3	151	—	415g/hp
3× 5,000	3	128	—	500g/hp
Astern				
3×12,000	12	—	—	—

Fuel Supply The oil fuel carried amounted at designed waterline displacement to 3300cu.m, the max. supply 7900cu.m.

Operational Range The maximum fuel reserve allowed the ship an operational range of 8900 nautical miles at a speed of 17 knots or 9280 nautical miles at 16 knots.

Steering gear The steering gear comprised two balanced rudders connected in parallel, each with a surface of 24m², the steering gear being electrically driven. On the mainmast at the level of the foretop was a black, box-shaped rudder indicator which extended to the side and the back.

Mine protection MES (autoprotection-against-mines) equipment decreased the electro-magnetic field of the ship to such an extent that magnetic detonators would not explode when the ship came near. The cables for this ran along the outside of the hull and were protected from both the ravages of the sea and mechanical damage by semi-circular covers. These cableways lay supposedly on the underside of the side armour, and consequently under water.

Electrical supply Because of the need for high gunnery performance in battle, great demands were imposed for a constant and reliable supply of electrical energy. Accordingly, four electrical plants, each with two 500kW diesel generators, were variously sited about the ship. In addition, there were 5×690kW turbo-generators and one 460kW turbo-generator with a 400kVA AC generator attached, specifically for the radio and fire control installations. This generator was supported by a 550kVA AC diesel generator. The total output in electrical energy amounted to 7910kW at 220V. An extensive supply provided both fresh and sea water, heating and ventilation as well as all the crew's requirements.

Building costs: Bismarck, 196·8 million Reichsmark; *Tirpitz,* 181·6 million Reichsmark.

ARMAMENT

The following data applies to the *Bismarck.* Any differences are denoted in brackets, with *BS* for *Bismarck* and *TP* for *Tirpitz.*

Main Armament

Eight 38cm quick-firing guns, calibre L/47, C/1934 in turn-table mountings C/34. Maximum elevation 35°, maximum depression 8°. Maximum range 362hm. 840 normal, 960 maximum rounds, thus allowing 105 or 120 per barrel, consisting of shell primers and cordite charges. Because of the considerable weight of the shells, only a mechanical hoist could convey them from the magazines to the turret substructure. The magazines were situated

Midship section showing control tower with mattress radar aerial and range-finder trained on starboard beam (*Drüppel*)

Radar antennae mounted on the after-side of the revolving range-finder cupola. Hamburg 1940 (Author)

C turret: the covered hatchway to the battery deck is visible, as is also the 2cm machine gun. 1940, Hamburg (Author)

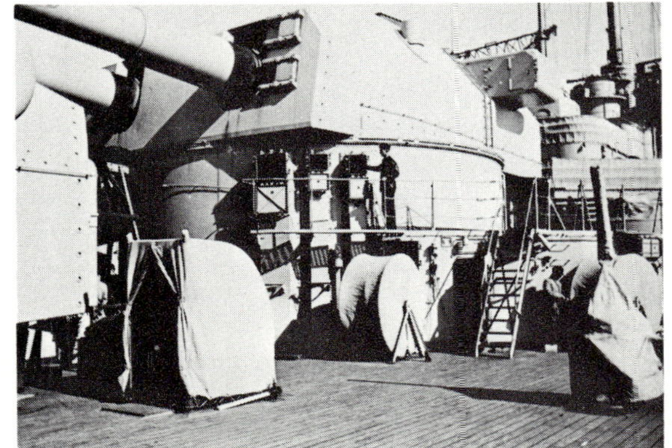

Anti-aircraft Gunnery and Fire Control

The anti-aircraft armament and instruments, as well as the whole combat organisation with target selection and co-ordination of the guns in the command posts, were the same as those in the *Prinz Eugen* (see Warship *Profile* No. 6, p. 130), as far as the major anti-aircraft operational control was concerned. The only difference was in that *Bismarck* and *Tirpitz* had 16, not 12, 10·5cm calibre guns. Similarly, in the *Prinz Eugen,* where both the forward spherical anti-aircraft command posts were missing, so in the *Bismarck* the two after command posts, plus the associated computer Reg VI were missing. The instruments were not installed so that the terms of delivery to the USSR could be kept at all costs, whereas in the *Prinz Eugen* the missing instruments (also including the equipment for the after target-directors for the 20·3cm guns) were installed immediately following the outbreak of war with the USSR: it was too late to carry out the corresponding measure for the *Bismarck.* The question must be asked today, whether the risk was justified in installing, in open control positions, the inferior replacement equipment which was stabilised only in height, in view of the fact that the aircraft torpedo hits so fateful to the *Bismarck* were scored by an attack from the stern. (*TP* was equipped in 1943 with radar on the third anti-aircraft control post, abaft, the mainmast.)

Below: *D turret showing the uncovered hatchway between the guns, top of ventilator and loud-speaker on the turret barbette. Hamburg 1940* (Author)

Funnel with surrounding platform. Underneath is the drive to the gear-wheel of the boat crane and overhead gantry. Note the rear side of the searchlight, which is remotely controlled three dimensionally: elevation and depression—training and tilt. Hamburg 1940 (*Author*)

The after anti-aircraft emergency control position protected by bullet-proof shield. Hamburg 1940 (*Author*)

The Ship's Aircraft
Changing views about the most favourable arrangement of the aircraft catapults were evidenced even in the plans. After originally relinquishing the aircraft hangars, whereby two catapults could have been installed with aircraft ready for take off, a decision was subsequently made in favour of a double catapult which could be used from both sides. In all, there were six aircraft of the Arado 196 type, of which one could be accommodated on either side of the funnel in one hangar, the other four in a hangar below the mainmast. As previously noted, there were differences between *Bismarck* and *Tirpitz,* namely in the details of the ships' cranes (balanced cranes and catheads) to lift the aircraft out of the water and to place them in the hangars or on the catapult. Because of this requirement, there were also slight differences in the siting of the two 10·5cm guns and the position of the boats.

The Ship's Boats
The *Bismarck* possessed three captain's gigs, four service boats, one motor launch, two motor pinnaces, two cutters, two dinghies and two lighters for outboard work. In addition there were the life-rafts.

Ship's Company
The crew totalled 1962 men of all ranks. The ship was fitted out for a further 27 men and was equipped to accommodate a Naval Staff of 103. The crew of the *Tirpitz* increased during the course of the war to almost 2500 men because of the strengthened anti-aircraft defences.

Ship's Colouring
During the work-up period in the Baltic from April 1941 until leaving the Grimstad-Fjord on 22 May 1941, the *Bismarck* carried three black and white zig-zagged camouflage stripes designed to make it harder for the ship's position to be estimated but during the subsequent sortie the ship was again painted normally. The funnel top was always silver in colour, whereas in *Tirpitz* it was black initially, before adopting normal camouflage later in Norway.

Manoeuvrability
Both ships manoeuvred excellently and rode well, despite their beam. This was because of the damping effect of the weight (side armour) far removed from the rolling axis. Pitching movements were slight and the ship heeled very little when the rudder was hard over because of her great beam. Consequently both ships were ideal weapon platforms. During trials, the ships were very hard to steer with the propellers, which was not surprising as the lever arm of the external propellers was small relative to the ship's beam.

The Life of the Battleship 'Bismarck'
The ship's real life began when she was commissioned on 24 August 1940. The first months followed the usual course of events for all new ships. After a

Front view of the three axes searchlight. Note the box-like structure on the mainmast with the pointer of the rudder indicator showing hard-a-starboard (side sketch). Hamburg 1940 (*Author*)

Admiral Lütjens (*Author*)

short training period, which principally served to accustom the crew with their new ship, there was a very extensive trials period; very extensive, because *BS* was the type-ship of a new Class.

The ship trials command and the various trials commands for gunnery, torpedoes and the communications systems, put the ship through rigorous tests in order to determine the technical quality and fulfilment of all delivery conditions and to give instructions on the best tactical application of the ship and her equipment.

After this, from about the middle of March 1941, the real training started and continued, for some days in April, with the *Prinz Eugen*; the training was then stepped up from the beginning of May. The two ships went on joint training exercises for the commanders and officers of the watch, as well as for the W/T communications personnel. The ships took turns to represent the enemy in exercises and also practised towing and fuelling at sea.

Offensive Staff Planning

In the meantime, the Naval Command prepared the sortie, which was code-named *'Rheinübung'*, and planned the offensive sweep of the battle group, comprising *Bismarck* and *Prinz Eugen*, into the Atlantic against the convoy routes to Great Britain. To this end, a network of supply ships and reconnaissance craft was set up in the North Atlantic and the European Arctic Sea. At a predetermined time, the battleship *Gneisenau* was to strike out from Brest to join the battle group but the ship was damaged by bombs. The sortie was deferred by magnetic mine damage to the *Prinz Eugen*. In May, the Naval Staff, under the leadership of the Commander-in-Chief of the Fleet, Admiral Lütjens, embarked on *BS* and joined in the last part of the battle training. On 16 May the C-in-C announced the future battle group ready for the *'Rheinübung'*.

Leaving Harbour

On Sunday 18 May, both ships left Gotenhafen, the Polish Gdynia, which in German times had earlier been called Gdingen, and had borne the German name Gotenhafen since 1939. The afternoon served once more as training for the ship's Command in station-keeping. *Prinz Eugen* then cruised to the west, while *BS* did not leave the waters of Gotenhafen until nightfall. Next day, off Cape Arkona, she was to rendezvous with three destroyers and her comrade-in-arms, so very similar and often to be referred to as *little brother*. The cruise continued to the west and north, led up the Great Belt and the Kattegat, and always covered during the day by barrier-breaking vessels and aircraft. At 1600 on 20 May, the gap in the minefield east of Cape Skagen was cleared, and in the night that of Kristiansand-Süd. Depending on the air situation and submarine danger, both watches were at action stations or else the anti-aircraft team were closed up. Early on Wednesday 21 May, the formation entered the Norwegian fjords and *BS* anchored in Grimstadt fjord south of Bergen. There the aerial photographic reconnaissances taken in the morning over Scapa Flow were shown to the C-in-C. At 1315 a Spitfire flew over the whole Bergen area and photo-

Bismarck *seen from* Prinz Eugen *during the training period, May 1941* *(Author)*

graphed the ships, without the aircraft itself being spotted. At 2000 the formation gathered outside Kalvenesbucht in order to leave the fjords to the north, while Bergen and the surrounding area was lit up by incendiaries and under attack from high explosive bombs.

Break Out

On the next day, the destroyers left the formation as planned while the two big ships steered a northerly course at high speed to rendezvous with a tanker. The C-in-C broke the monotony of the day with an air and submarine alarm practice. Because of the reconnaissance reports and the weather conditions, the C-in-C abandoned his intention to refuel and continually altered his course in the Denmark Straits, the straits between Greenland and Iceland which were half-closed by ice on the northern side. Visibility was at times very poor so that *Prinz Eugen* found it difficult not to lose her *big brother.* In the dusk of the short night *BS* showed a searchlight to help the following ship.

At midday, the battle group was about 75 nautical miles to the north of Iceland's northern coast which was invisible, not because of the distance but principally because of the thick mist hanging over the open water. The stretches of good visibility between pack ice and mist were only a few miles wide. In the mist to the south, the two heavy British cruisers which were to report on and follow the German formation were now on patrol; the first sighting was by HMS *Suffolk* at 1911. The *Suffolk* could be glimpsed only as a shadow but she was identified as a cruiser of the County class before she was again swallowed up by the mist.

At 2010 *BS* opened fire on a second heavy cruiser who could be identified with moderate certainty as HMS *Norfolk.* The five salvoes were ineffectual though in *BS* the radar on the foretop broke down: *PE* was ordered to take the lead so as to be able to reconnoitre with her radar.

For a long time, each alteration of course of the German ships was clearly known by the two cruisers and reported home by radio. However, one can be sure that the British Admiralty did not receive the decoded messages before the German Commanders, for the German radio observation service operated almost perfectly. It was known also by the German Command that the cruisers had lost contact for over two hours, because during that time the contact signal stopped. When the radar contact was re-established, it caused no surprise on the German side because the course could not really be altered.

Bismarck, *protected by a mine-sweeper, crossing the German mine barrage east of Skagen* *(Author)*

Bismarck *from aft: preparing to fuel from* Prinz Eugen *(Author)*

Off Bismarck's *port quarter. The Norwegian fjords loom up ahead* *(Author)*

Making a landfall off Norway *(Author)*

Below : *In foggy weather. The officer of the watch is in the background, while a merchant captain, as a possible prize captain, is looking out* (Prinz Eugen) *(Author)*

Off Bergen: Bismarck *passes* Prinz Eugen (*Author*)

An Historic Day

At 0535 hours on that memorable day—24 May 1941—the listening post in the *PE* reported the *'sound of two fast running turbine ships'*, a report that was immediately passed on to *BS*—the first report of the newly appeared enemy, which later transpired to be HMS *Hood* and a ship of the *King George V* class. At 0553 *Hood* opened fire on *Prinz Eugen* under the mistaken impression that she was the German flagship that lay ahead. The *Prince of Wales* fired at *BS*, which action divided the German battleship's battery. The main armament fired at *Hood*, the port 15cm battery at *PoW*. *PE* scored the first hit on the *Hood*, who was also hit in the stern by the fifth salvo from the *BS*, and at 0601 the *Hood* exploded. With her bows high out of the water, she sank in a remarkably short time, taking with her all but three of the crew.

The *Prince of Wales* suffered heavily under the now concentrated fire of 8×38cm, 8×20·3cm, 6×15cm and at times 6×10·5cm guns. It was clear that the ship's Command no longer had control, and that the heavy guns were to a great extent out of action. Yet mindful of his orders, Admiral Lütjens did not pursue his stricken enemy, but continued his southerly course, though not without his own problems for the *Bismarck* had suffered three hits, all from the *Prince of Wales*.

Early Damage

One hit was far in the bows which rendered inaccessible approximately 1000 tons of fuel and later caused difficulties because of the bows cutting deeper into the water; another hit on the side armour against the torpedo bulkhead which sprang a leak and in the course of the day put a generator out of commission, with a corresponding loss of electrical power, in addition to flooding a boiler room which subsequently reduced her top speed by two knots. The third hit destroyed a boat. Under the pressure of this damage to his flagship, Lütjens decided to release *Prinz Eugen* to continue the war on the convoy routes, but he himself would proceed to St Nazaire for repairs.

This decision was preceded by the intention to shake off the pursuers by drawing them south-west over a line of U-boats, the codeword for this separation being *'Hood'*. The oil slick left by the *Bismarck* was easy both to see and to smell. So it was evident

Bismarck *dips into the Atlantic swell* (*Author*)

to those in *Bismarck* that it would be very difficult to shake off their pursuers. The Naval Staff was also obviously surprised at the British radar. So the sorely troubled *Bismarck* continued the cruise and attempted to disengage from the *Prinz Eugen* for the first time at about 1540. In doing so, *Bismarck* encountered a heavy cruiser. There was a short exchange, after which the first attempt was abandoned, to be repeated at about 1814.

Break-away

Prinz Eugen was in the meantime instructed, on receipt of the codeword, to maintain course and speed for at least three hours, in order to facilitate the *Bismarck*'s separation. Whilst contact with *Prinz Eugen* was soon broken, *Norfolk, Suffolk* and *Prince of Wales* maintained contact with *Bismarck* almost uninterruptedly, and so brought up the aircraft-carrier *Victorious*, whose nine Swordfish torpedo aircraft, accompanied by six covering Fulmar aircraft, three times attacked the *Bismarck* and with 18 torpedoes scored one hit. This explosion did not however, have any serious repercussions.

Fatal Errors

In the hours following and, to some extent, during Sunday 25 May, *Bismarck* succeeded in shaking off her followers. Presumably, because the ship described a great curve to the west and then continued north, she could cross the course of her pursuers, but *behind* them. Yet, for some inexplicable reason, *Bismarck* was not aware of her success: at 0942 *Bismarck* transmitted a long radio message about the action on the previous day. The bearings of this W/T transmission enabled the enemy to fix the *Bismarck*'s position precisely. Yet the British Admiralty did not signal the bearings themselves, but the direction of the radio beams. Through an error in *King George V*, one of these radio beams was incorrectly evaluated. The false bearing thus obtained was given to all ships and served as a basis for the continuation of the hunt for the *Bismarck*.

The Hunt

In consequence, the majority of the ships steamed in the wrong direction, until the mistake was discovered in the afternoon and the courses corrected from 1810. In the meantime, further efforts were made in *Bismarck* to overcome the damage resulting from the hit in the bows.

On the next day, Monday 26 May, at about 1030, a Catalina seaplane which had started from Northern Ireland sighted *Bismarck* through a gap in the clouds. After this, from 1154, aircraft from the carrier *Ark Royal* maintained contact with the *Bismarck* until nightfall. It was thus an easy task

Hood*'s shell splashes on port-side, forward, of* Prinz Eugen, *as observed also by* Prinz Eugen*'s Second Gunnery Officer, Kapitän leutnant Paul Schmalenbach (author of this Profile)* *(Author)*

Another photograph taken from Prinz Eugen *of* Bismarck*'s broadside: her for'd turrets are trained well abaft the port beam* *(Author)*

Bismarck *opens fire on* Hood, *as seen astern of* Prinz Eugen *(Author)*

Action photograph of Prince of Wales *and* Hood *making smoke. Note the fall of shot at right* *(Author)*

Action photograph of the battle against HMS Hood *and HMS* Prince of Wales *(Author)*

Bismarck*'s broadside* *(Author)*

Bismarck *opens fire, as seen from* Prinz Eugen. *Note* Hood*'s shell splash at right of photograph* *(Author)*

One of Prince of Wales' *shells splashes between* Bismarck *and* Prinz Eugen *(Author)*

Another broadside from Bismarck (*Author*)

Bismarck *opens fire with her main armament. Photograph taken from* Prinz Eugen (*Author*)

HMS Hood *and HMS* Prince of Wales *on the horizon* (*Author*)

The flash from Bismarck*'s broadside* (*Author*)

Another view of the enemy (*Author*)

HMS Hood *blows up*

for the British Commander-in-Chief, Admiral Tovey, to concentrate his forces but the heavy units could not reach the position until the next morning. There was therefore the danger that *Bismarck* could steam sufficiently near to the French west coast to come under the protection of the German Luftwaffe. It was therefore vital to slow down the *Bismarck.*

Last Chance of Escape

Two possibilities were open to the British and both were used to advantage: first, the torpedo bombers of the *Ark Royal,* and, second, the four British, and one Polish, destroyers force, under the command of Captain Vian in *Cossack* (see Warship *Profile* No. 2). The first attack by the Swordfish was a failure, for it was directed mistakenly at HMS *Sheffield* who was also fired on by the *Bismarck.* The second attack, when the aircraft were directed by the *Sheffield,* had the desired effect, but in a manner hardly expected.

Lethal Damage

At 2103 a torpedo hit *Bismarck*'s stern and damaged her steering gear to such an extent that both rudders were jammed at 15° to port and could not be moved. Shortly afterwards, Admiral Lütjens reported in a radio message that the *Bismarck* was unmanoeuvrable. Despite the gale and the heavy seas, everything imaginable was done aboard *Bismarck* to restore the steering. Yet, more serious than any other factor was the weather that thwarted progress. The struggle was continued during the dusk and throughout the destroyer attacks, which produced no effect on the *Bismarck* and left the destroyers barely touched. What is noteworthy is that the *Bismarck*'s action against the destroyers was supported by radar, the first action of its kind.

The Trap Closes

Tuesday 27 May was to see the end of the hunt. At 0625 the *Bismarck* reported the situation unchanged and the wind strength eight to nine. At 0710 Lütjens requested a U-boat for the security of his war-diary. The German Naval Chief was therefore aware of the approaching end. For the sake of historical truth, he felt he had to preserve his decisions and their motivation for posterity: it was inevitable that the end of the hunt would come soon after.

At 0815 the *Norfolk* sighted *Bismarck* and led the *Rodney* and *King George V* to her, when they opened fire at 0847. *Bismarck* fired with the third salvo straddling the *Rodney,* but, because she was out of control, she could only occasionally co-ordinate her guns against one or other adversary.

Overwhelmed

One of the first hits on *Bismarck* destroyed her foretop. Thus the command of the main, secondary and anti-aircraft armament, as well as the most important officers, were wiped out. At about 0902 direct hits destroyed both the forward 38cm turrets, A and B. At 0912 the forward post was knocked out, at 0918 the after revolving cupola. At 0940, *Dorsetshire* joined in the action and *Norfolk* five minutes later.

A direct hit put the aftermost heavy turret out of action, so that now only C turret and some 15cm turrets returned the fire. Towards 1000 the main armament and, at about 1015, the secondary armament also petered out, all ammunition being used up. At the end, the range amounted to only about 6000 metres. Contrary to British public announcements, American reports told of severe damage to the *Rodney* who subsequently had to go to the shipyard in Boston, Mass.

The End

At about 1000, orders were given in *Bismarck* to prepare to scuttle the ship. A little later the command was given to lay the explosive charges (with a burning time of 9 minutes) and to open the Kingston valves, as well as to abandon ship, orders, which despite the chaotic conditions on board, appeared to have been carried out in an exemplary fashion. At 1020 *Dorsetshire* fired two torpedoes and, at about 1030, another torpedo into the already sinking ship who at 1036 heeled over. The *Dorsetshire* saved 85 of the *Bismarck's* crew, the destroyer, *Maori,* 25; the German U-boat, *U-74,* brought five survivors home and the weathership, *Sachsenwald,* three.

Track diagram of the action between the Bismarck *and* Hood *squadrons, 24 May 1941* *(Author)*

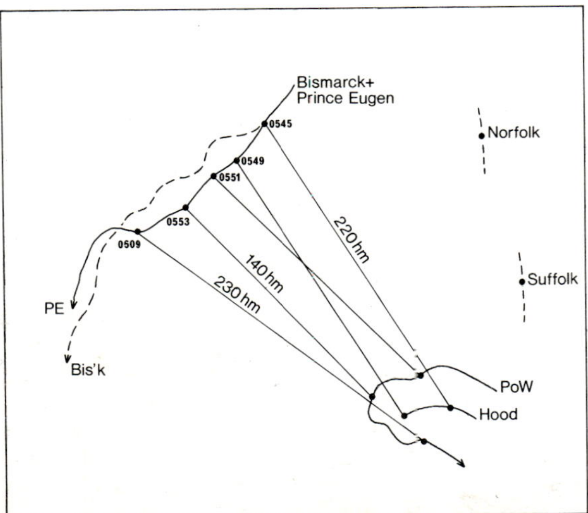

British Adversaries

Active participants in *Bismarck's* destruction were the battleships *Prince of Wales, King George V* and *Rodney,* in addition to the battle cruiser *Renown,* the aircraft-carriers *Victorious* and *Ark Royal,* the heavy cruisers *Suffolk, Norfolk* and *Dorsetshire,* the light cruiser *Sheffield,* as well as the destroyers *Maori, Cossack, Zulu, Sikh* and the Polish destroyer, *Piorun.* Three other battleships, five light cruisers and 14 destroyers also participated in the hunt.

The Effects of the Sinking of the Bismarck

When considering the effects that the sinking of the battleship produced on the German Naval Command, the consequences fall into two distinct groups:

a first group with immediate consequences of a more tactical nature

and

a second group of strategic character.

The immediate consequence for the Royal Navy was the clearing of the whole North Atlantic of German back-up and supply ships. Within a few days—partly aided by betrayal—the whole organisation, which had been set up with heavy ships for the trade war and which had been proved in collaboration with the *Scharnhorst, Gneisenau* and *Admiral Hipper,* was wiped out. However, as these supply ships were regarded by the British as the absolute pre-requisite for further German activity, they were destroyed by every possible means.

Thus the supplies for battleships and cruisers were eliminated, not just for a matter of weeks or months, but for the rest of the war. The German Naval Command took some time to recognise the basically changed position in the Atlantic. Further plans were still being made and more work was still being carried out to build up a similar supply organisation, in case it proved possible to send the battleships *Scharnhorst* and *Gneisenau* and the heavy cruiser *Prinz Eugen,* who were lying in Brest, into the Atlantic. There they would join up with the *Bismarck's* sister ship *Tirpitz* and the pocket battleships *Admiral Scheer* and *Lützow* (ex *Deutschland*), circumstances permitting.

Catastrophic Effect on German Sea Power

Yet the German Naval Command could not resign itself to the bitter realisation that, with the increasing air-threat over all parts of the North and Middle Atlantic, attacks by surface forces against allied convoys could no longer be carried out with any hope of success. Logically, the conclusion was to move the ships from Brest to elsewhere where they could be better used. The removal to Norway was the result and this was the strategic consequence of the sinking of the *Bismarck,* a conclusion which should have been drawn a year earlier, before the loss of the *Bismarck.*

The Home Fleet, stationed in Scapa Flow, lay at the focus of a semi-circle along which every German ship from Southern Norway to Northern Iceland had to pass to reach the Atlantic. Consequently, each German ship had to steam about three times as far, if this semi-circle was compared with the radius determined by the distance from Scapa Flow to the position where the *Hood* sank.

In the last analysis, through the eventual tracking down of the German ships, the venture must end with the destruction of all German units. That the Royal Navy had to 'pay' first with the *Hood,* and that the cruiser *Prinz Eugen* survived, are circumstances which are not discussed further here. *Hood*'s death throes only lasted perhaps as many minutes as the *Bismarck*'s did hours. Both ships were the pride of their navies. Both ships fought bravely.

The battle on 24 May 1941 was the last battle between heavy units in which the Luftwaffe had not been directly involved. Yet the torpedo hits on *Bismarck,* scored by an aircraft, may have served as the indication that the character of naval warfare had changed and that the role of the omnipotent battleship was played out.

Fleet Staff
Commander-in-Chief of the Fleet
Admiral Günther Lütjens
Chief of Staff
Naval Captain Harald Netzbandt
1st Officer of the Naval Staff (Operation)
Naval Captain Paul Ascher
2nd Officer of the Naval Staff (Gunnery)
Naval Captain Emil Melms
(3rd Officer of the Naval Staff (Torpedoes)
Commander Gerhard Böhmig (did not take part in the sortie)
4th Officer of the Naval Staff (Communications)
Lieut. Comm. Hans Nitzschke
Fleet Engineer
Commander (Eng) Dipl.Ing Karl Thannemann
Fleet Medical Officer
Surgeon Admiral Dr Hans-Roleff Riege (med)
Fleet Judge
Naval Chief Justice Langer
Luftwaffe Liaison Officer
Major Grohé (entered navy 1927)

Staff of the battleship Bismarck
Commander
Naval Captain Ernst Lindemann
First Officer
Commander Hans Oels
Navigation Officer
Comm. Wolf Neuendorff
1st Gunnery Officer
Comm. Adalbert Schneider
1st AA Gunnery Officer
Captain Lieut. Karl Gellert
Chief Engineer
Comm. (Eng) DipEng Walter Lehmann

Warship Series Editor: John Wingate, DSC

Side elevation of 38cm turret

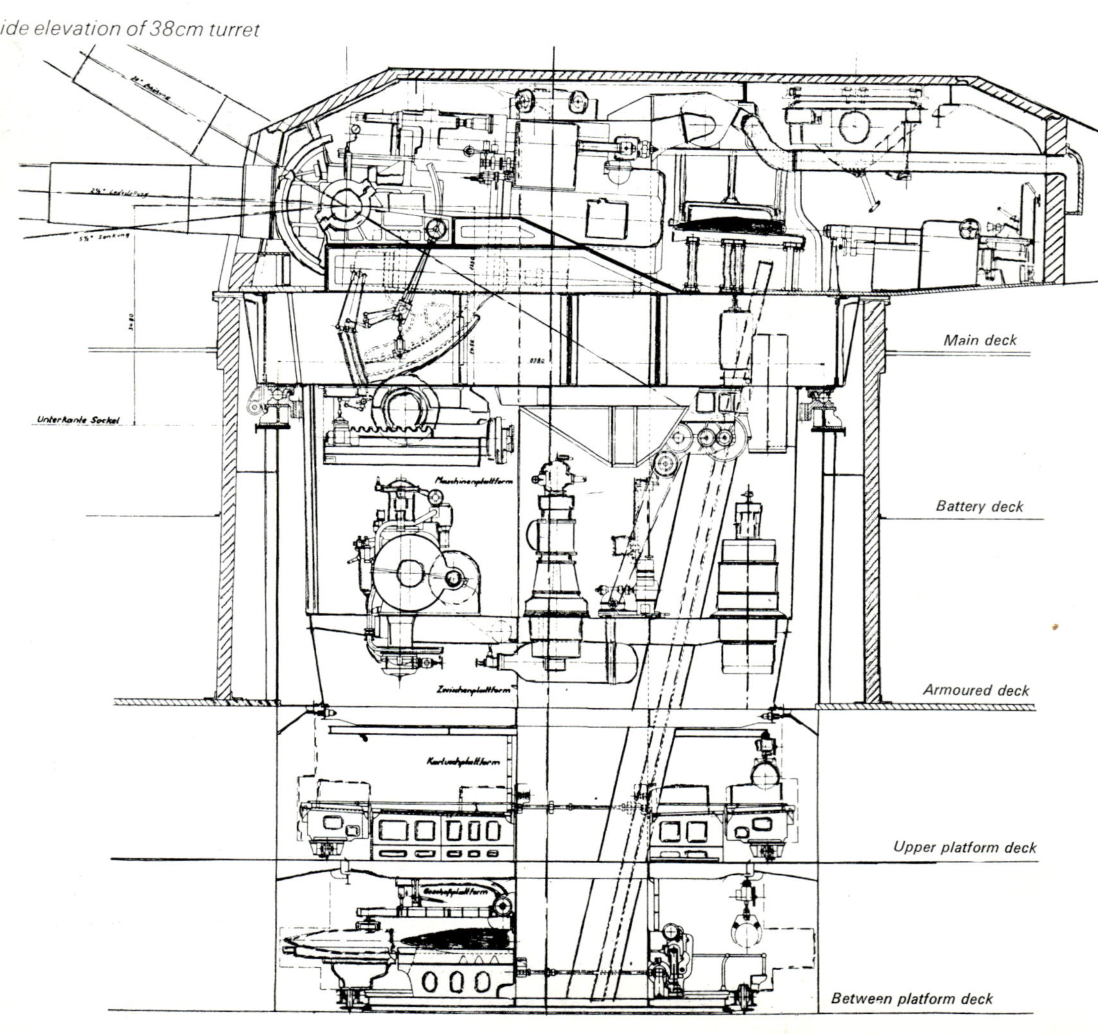

The Hood *fitting out at John Brown's Yard, Clydebank, 9 January 1920.*

HMS HOOD/Battle-Cruiser 1916-1941

by R. G. Robertson, CA

Operational History

For almost 20 years she was the largest warship in the world. Few, if any, of the others could match the beauty of her lines, none could match her speed of 30 knots, combined with a main armament of eight 15in guns. In the navies of the world she was in a class by herself and her formidable appearance excited the admiration of all who set eyes upon her. Such a ship was the *Hood.* When she was sunk by a few shells from the German battleship *Bismarck* in the early hours of Empire Day 1941 it seemed to many in Britain and the Commonwealth that they had lost a part of their naval heritage.

As it would be impossible to do justice to such a ship in one Profile it was decided to publish the story of the last 10 years of her life now, leaving a later Warship Profile to tell of her design, her building and her early years in service.

Design Changes

As a result of Jutland very extensive investigations were carried out on the design of the *Hood* and it was found that considerable protection could be added by accepting a deeper draught and a slightly reduced speed.

On account of the design changes an additional 5000 tons of armour were worked into her hull and although the total weight of the armour and protection at 13,800 tons was almost equal to one-third of her load displacement and was nearly as heavy as that of a contemporary battleship, the *Hood* remained a battle-cruiser in conception.

There is no doubt that she could have withstood severe punishment from torpedoes, mines or shell-fire directed against her sides. The tragedy of her otherwise superb design was her lack of sufficient deck armour. Had this been provided when she was

The Hood *on trials in the Clyde, 5 March 1920.*

built, the result of her action with the *Prince of Wales* against the *Bismarck* might well have been very different.

THE SHIP AS COMPLETED IN 1920

Laid down: 31 May 1916 (original design)
Design modified: 1 September 1916
Launched: 22 August 1918
Trials completed: 5 March 1920
Commissioned: 15 May 1920
Displacement: 41,200 tons at 28ft 6in draught
45,200 tons at 31ft 6in draught
Length (overall): 860ft 7in
Length (waterline): 850ft
Length (B.P.): 810ft
Breadth (waterline): 95ft at 28ft 6in draught
Breadth (outside bulges): 105ft $2\frac{1}{2}$in
Complement (1923): 1169

Armament

8 15in Mark I (1913)
12 5·5in Mark I (spare guns from *Chester* and *Birkenhead* who were taken over from Greece)
4 4in Mark V AA
4 3-pounders
2 21in submerged torpedo-tubes
4 21in above water torpedo-tubes

Protection

Side midships: 12in, 7in, 5in
Side forward: 6in, 5in
Side aft: 6in
Side submerged: 3in
Barbettes: 12in
Turrets: Face 15in
Side 12in, 11in
Conning Tower: Outer shell 12in
Inner shell 6in
Crown 5in
Director Tower: 6in
After Torpedo Control Tower: 4in, 3in
Decks: Fo'c'sle $1\frac{1}{2}$in
Upper 1in, $\frac{3}{4}$in
Main 2in, $1\frac{1}{2}$in
Main (over magazines) 3in
Lower, forward $1\frac{1}{2}$-1in
Lower, aft 2in 1in

Machinery

Brown Curtis geared turbine
SHP: 144,000
Propellers: 4
Designed speed: 31 knots
Trial speed (maximum): 32·07 knots
Oil fuel (maximum): 4000 tons

Searchlights

4 36in on platform between funnels
2 36in on After Control Position
2 36in on foremast
4 24in signalling (on admiral's bridge)

Boats carried

2 50ft steam picket boats
1 45ft admiral's barge
1 35ft motor boat
1 42ft sailing launch with auxiliary motor
1 36ft pinnace
4 32ft cutters
1 32ft galley
2 30ft captain's gigs
227ft whalers
2 16ft dinghies
7 large and 2 small Carley floats

Her Early Years

After reaching a mean speed of 32·07 knots on her trials held in the Clyde during February and March 1920 in stormy weather, the *Hood* commissioned on 15 May 1920. Two visits to Scandinavia and a world cruise were the most notable events of her early years in service.

On 17 May 1929 she paid off into Dockyard control at Portsmouth to undergo the most extensive refit since her completion, a reconstruction which lasted two years, until 12 May 1931.

Proposed Reconstruction

In the years immediately preceding the war, plans had been drawn up for a reconstruction of the *Hood.* It had been intended that the work would begin when the *Renown*'s major refit was completed in 1939. From 'B' 15in turret forward to 'X' 15in turret aft, the *Hood* would have been completely refitted. The changes would have included:

The complete removal of the conning tower and bridge structure.

The removal of all the 5·5in guns and the above-water torpedo tubes.

The removal of the 4in AA guns.

Hood's seaplane and catapult July 1931.

June 1931.

In their place would have been fitted a modern bridge structure incorporating aircraft hangars as in the *King George V* class; eight twin 5·25in dual-purpose guns in four twin mountings, to port and starboard midships. (These guns were to prove extremely successful in the *Dido* class of cruiser.)
A point of particular interest was the intention greatly to increase her deck armour. Modifications would also have been made to her under-water protection. It was also intended to fit new machinery with high-pressure boilers.
It was not expected that these alterations would have greatly increased her tonnage. About 4000 tons of unnecessary weight—the conning tower alone weighed over 900 tons—would have been removed and this would have allowed for the necessary increase in her protection, just where it was most needed.
Had it been possible for the *Hood* to have been modernised along the lines planned she would indeed have been a match for any of her adversaries, German, Italian or Japanese. With the international situation as it was in 1939 there was, of course, no possibility of allowing her to be out of commission for the time necessary to complete such a refit. All that could be done when she returned to Portsmouth in February 1939 was to increase her AA armament and fit other supplementary equipment.

Portsmouth Refit: February-August 1939

The four 4in single AA mountings were removed and replaced by four twin 4in mountings on the boat deck between the after funnel and mainmast.
Two High-Angle Directors were fitted on either side of the signal platform on the bridge structure. Two High-Angle Calculating Positions with the latest High-Angle calculating tables served the new 4in mountings.

June 1931.

Portsmouth Navy Week 1931.

27 June 1931.

Passing under the Forth Bridge 1934.

Passing under the Forth Bridge 1934.

Four 40in searchlights were added, one on either side of the After Control Platform and one on either side of the after funnel.
The former searchlight and control tower between the funnels was replaced by a small structure with a large wireless trunk on top and aerial spreaders at the side.
One eight-barrelled pom-pom was added on a platform on the boat deck in front of the ACP. The pom-pom director was placed at the fore end of the ACP.
Ready-use ammunition lockers were added in the vicinity of the gun mountings on the boat deck. The two 21in submerged torpedo tubes were removed.
The direction-finding equipment was improved with a DF aerial fitted at the top of the main topmast.
A wireless trunk was added between the ACP and the after pom-pom platform.
The Admiral's signal platform was extended at the after end to carry the repositioned signal searchlights and semaphore arms.
The sides of the Admiral's bridge were extended completely round the forward side of the forebridge. Plating was added between the wings of the forebridge and the compass platform extensions.
A deckhouse was added between the searchlights abaft the second funnel.
A wireless cabin was added at the rear of the Admiral's bridge.

Last Peace-time Recommissioning

On 2 June 1939 the *Hood* was due to recommission but in view of the developments in Europe, it was decided to retain most of the key ratings. After dry-docking, engine trials followed in the English Channel. The new members of her crew were impressed by her power and speed.
Final adjustments were made on her return to the dockyard and ammunition and stores were taken on board. When the compass trials were completed the *Hood* anchored in St Helen's Bay, Isle of Wight.
On 13 August 1939, flying the flag of Vice-Admiral W. J. Whitworth, she sailed north to join the Home Fleet.

First North Sea Patrol

By the end of August 1939 all the ships in the Home Fleet were moving to their war stations or were actually on patrol. From 20 to 28 August, the *Hood* was at sea, on patrol between the North of Scotland and Norway to watch for German warships trying to break out of the North Sea and raid our Atlantic commerce. The weather was poor and war conditions were observed on board. This was to be the first of many such patrols, patrols which did not

In dry dock following a collision with the Renown *February 1935. Note damaged propellers.*

Silver Jubilee Review 1935.

The Hood *during the Spanish Civil War, 1937. Note anti-torpedo bulge.*

1937. (Photo: P. A. Vicary)

Midship section 1937. Note her two steam picket boats (Photo: P. A. Vicary)

Hood *photographed from the French battleship* Dunkerque

The Hood *was always wet aft in a heavy sea. This photograph was taken during a Northern Patrol in 1940.*

hit the newspaper headlines but which were carried out by the Home Fleet, year in, year out, for the remainder of the war.

The *Hood* now carried her wartime complement of close on 1400 men and there was little room to spare below decks with hammocks slung in every available space and passage-way.

After refuelling at Rosyth the *Hood* sailed for Invergordon on 30 August 1939.

September 1939

The *Hood* was at sea when Germany invaded Poland on 1 September 1939. Then came Sunday 3 September. At sea all loudspeakers were tuned in for Mr Chamberlain's speech at 1100. Signals were exchanged between Admiral Whitworth and the Captain of the Destroyer Flotilla: Admiral to Captain Destroyers: 'Good luck and good hunting'. From Captain Destroyers to Admiral: 'Yoicks, Tally-ho'.

That Sunday afternoon men crowded on to the upper deck to watch the destroyers dropping depth charges. The alarm was a false one and the *Hood* resumed her zig-zag course.

On 8 September she left Scapa Flow, accompanied by *Renown,* for the patrol grounds between Iceland and the Faroes. For the following weeks she was similarly employed on these unknown, unreported missions and escort duties with brief intervals at Scapa for refuelling and taking on stores and ammunition.

The 'Hood' is Bombed

While providing heavy cover for the 2nd Cruiser Squadron, which was escorting the damaged submarine *Spearfish** across the North Sea, the *Hood* and *Ark Royal* were bombed by several German Heinkels on 26 September 1939. One bomb caught the *Hood* a glancing blow on her quarter but fell harmlessly into the sea. It was on this raid that the Germans first 'sank' the *Ark Royal.*

*See Warship Profile 29, *HMS Belfast*

Hood *after her 1939 refit.*

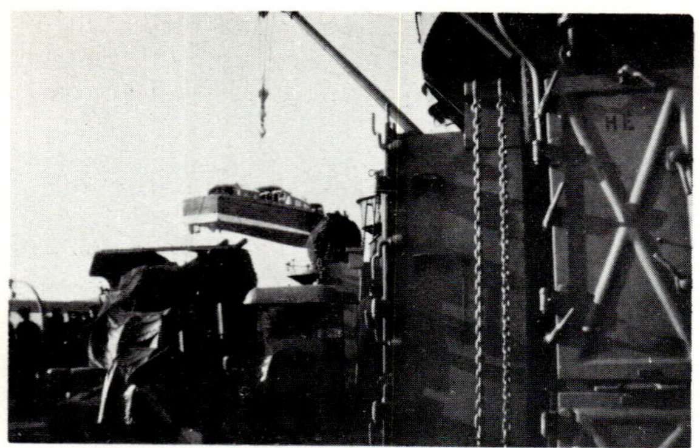

Hoisting out Admiral Somerville's barge, July 1940. Note ready-use ammunition lockers. These lockers caused a fire on the boat deck when the Prinz Eugen *hit the* Hood *during the action in the Denmark Straits.*

Wartime Routine

By the end of September the crew were settling down to the wartime routine. Generally speaking it was 'watch-on, watch-off', with action stations at dawn and dusk. The Captain gave periodic broadcasts on the progress of the war. The Chaplain had the unenviable task of being the chief censor for all the letters written by some 1300 men.

German Battleship Reported at Sea

On 8 October Coastal Command aircraft reported that the *Gneisenau,* with the heavy cruiser *Köln* and a destroyer escort were steaming out of the Skagerrak into the North Sea. The *Hood* and *Repulse,* with a destroyer escort, immediately left Scapa to patrol off the Norwegian Coast. Unfortunately the German warships turned back on reaching the south of Norway.

'Royal Oak' is Sunk

Shortly after returning to Scapa Flow the *Hood* was at sea again. Then came the news of the sinking of the *Royal Oak* on 14 October. Until the defences of Scapa could be improved, the main units of the Home Fleet moved to Loch Ewe on the North West Coast of Scotland. On 23 October the *Hood* was at sea again. With the *Nelson* and *Rodney,* and escorted by six destroyers, she sailed as far north as the Lofoten Islands, west of Narvik, to cover a Norwegian iron ore convoy. She returned to the Clyde on 30 October.

Churchill Visits the 'Hood'

On 31 October, Winston Churchill, then First Lord of the Admiralty, and the First Sea Lord, visited the *Hood* in the Clyde. On the following day she sailed to Plymouth and arrived at 0900 on a Saturday morning in Plymouth Sound. She berthed alongside at 1800 the same day.

First Wartime Leave

The minor repairs were completed by 24 November. The first watch had already been on seven days leave but those on the second leave were unlucky as, after four days, telegrams were sent out recalling them. This was at the time of the sinking of the *Rawalpindi* by the *Scharnhorst* and *Gneisenau.*

Hood*'s boat-deck during the action at Mers-el-Kebir in July 1940.*

Re-ammunitioning at Gibraltar after the action at Oran.

'Hood' Under Orders of a French Admiral

The Home Fleet had sailed to cover every escape route by which the German battleships might break out into the Atlantic. On 25 November the *Hood* left Plymouth and rendezvoused with the French battleship *Dunkerque,* accompanied by the cruisers *Georges-Leygues* and *Montcalm.* As Vice-Admiral Gensoul was senior to Vice-Admiral Whitworth, the French Admiral took over the command of the combined force. It must have been a strange experience for those in the *Hood* to be keeping station on the French battleship! Little could it have been imagined that some seven months later the *Hood* and *Dunkerque* were destined to meet again —in very different circumstances.

Unfortunately the German warships had come out only to create a diversion and, after sailing north, they doubled back on their tracks and returned

The Hood *under aerial attack by Italian bombers in the Mediterranean in August 1940.*

Recreation at Gibraltar August 1940.

Hood's *Captain presents prizes after swimming races at Gibraltar, August 1940.*

home. The *Hood* arrived back at Loch Ewe on 3 December.

'Hood's' Increased Displacement

During the operation with the *Dunkerque* very heavy weather was encountered and the French Admiral took photographs of the *Hood* as she almost disappeared in the heavy seas.

The wartime additions had increased her displacement and at somewhat less than deep load she was now showing a displacement of 48,360 tons. She had always been wet aft but now, even in a moderate sea, tons of water crashed over her quarterdeck. The strain was beginning to make itself felt, not only in her superstructure but also in her hull. Her top speed was also down to 26½ knots. She was badly in need of a refit, but could not be spared. The *Nelson*, flagship of the Home Fleet, had been damaged by a magnetic mine on entering Loch Ewe on 4 December, and the *Rodney* had developed certain defects which had temporarily put her out of commission.

Covering the First Canadian Troop Convoy

On 13 December 1939 the *Hood* sailed from the Clyde with the *Barham* and six destroyers to provide an escort for the first Canadian troop convoy. She returned to the Clyde on 15 December. On shore leave at Greenock some of the ship's company were entertained by Gracie Fields.

Christmas 1939

The *Hood* was again on patrol. There were, of course, no festivities but the cooks and caterers managed to provide an excellent menu. Admiral Whitworth went the rounds of the Mess Decks and wished everyone the compliments of the season.

The heavy seas running caused much leakage of water throughout the fan shafts etc. This kept the 'Emergency Party' busy mopping up. Huge waves swept over the boat deck causing considerable damage to the picket and motor boats.

Based at Greenock

During January and February 1940 the *Hood* was based at Greenock, but spent most of her time on patrol. On 7 February 1940 she covered the Third Canadian Troop Convoy.

Return to Scapa Flow

When the defences at Scapa Flow had been strengthened the *Hood* returned on 7 March, in company with the battleship *Valiant*. She left again on 27 March and arrived at Devonport two days later for a long overdue refit. When Norway was invaded she sent an expeditionary force of 250 men, mostly Royal Marines. All but three returned to the ship one month later.

Devonport Refit 29/3/40—27/5/40

The 5·5in guns were removed and the two forward open batteries were plated over.

Three twin Mark XVI 4in guns were added, one at the end of the boat deck in front of the after pom-pom platform and one on either side of the ACP near the deck edge. All the 4in guns could be sighted and trained manually, but were, of course, usually controlled by the three HADTs, which were stabilised for roll and fitted with steel blast covers.

With the removal of the 5·5in secondary armament the seven twin 4in mountings could also be used against surface targets. The old 5·5in Gun Control Towers (or Tops) were converted to the 4in GCTs. Each GCT was found on the flag deck forward of the Directors and could be used if the Directors were put out of action. In each one were the Dumaresq, a Vickers double-dial range clock and binoculars. They were in communication with the guns, the Directors and the Calculating Positions. The starboard GCT was in communication with the three starboard and the after 4in mountings, the port GCT being in communication with the three port mountings.

The old and the new 4in guns were grouped for control as follows:

Forward groups: Nos 1 and 2 guns each side

After group: Nos 3 and 4 guns

Two low-angle fire-control tables were fitted beside the high-angle tables in the Calculating Positions.

Each 4in gun weighed 1 ton $4\frac{1}{4}$cwt, a mounting 7 tons and a shell and cartridge 63lb. The maximum rate of fire was 20 rounds per minute. After firing, the breech opened and the empty cartridge case was automatically ejected. Loading was by hand.

Five Unrifled Projectors (UPs) were fitted, four on the boat deck and one on top of 'B' turret. UPs were designed as a protection against bombing attacks. The mounting fired 20 small bombs into the air; attached to each was a parachute, the idea being that the attacking aircraft would hit some of the parachute wires which would then explode the bomb and destroy the plane. UPs were not particularly successful as they could be blown off course so easily—in one of *Hood*'s UP practice firings one landed on the quarter-deck! Fortunately the bomb did not explode so no damage was done. The UP mountings were protected by plating four feet high.

Ready use ammunition lockers were fitted around the 4in and UP mountings. A sound power telephone system was fitted.

A de-gaussing strip for protection against the magnetic mine was fitted round the hull.

Machinery repairs were carried out including the replacement of defective condenser tubes.

Her refit at Devonport completed, the *Hood*, escorted by the *Witch, Escort* and *Wolverine*, headed north for Liverpool and Gladstone Dock where she arrived on 28 May.

The Resolution *following the* Hood *during a Mediterranean operation, August 1940.*

Deck hockey on the quarterdeck.

'There has never been such a Convoy before'

The underwater repairs and painting completed, the *Hood* left Gladstone Dock on 12 June and put to sea with a screen of Canadian destroyers, the *Skeena, Restigouche* and *St Laurent*. Two days later the aircraft carrier *Argus* was sighted, along with a mighty convoy of liners, the *Queen Mary, Empress of Britain, Aquitania, Mauretania, Andes* and *Empress of Canada*. The liners were bringing the first contingent of New Zealand and Australian troops to Britain. The *Hood* provided the heavy cover back to the Clyde. The Captain of one of the liners reported, 'In this convoy we had probably the best ships in the Mercantile Marine. I do not think there has ever been such a convoy before'. After several submarine scares the convoy arrived safely in the Clyde on Sunday 16 June.

France Falls

France fell on 17 June and the following day the *Hood* left the Clyde for Gibraltar, rendezvousing with the *Ark Royal* on 19 June. Four days later both ships arrived at 'The Rock'.

On 26 June it was reported that the French battleship *Richelieu* had left Dakar and was sailing north. The *Hood* left 'with all despatch' under orders to escort the French ship back to Gibraltar. Later the same day the *Ark Royal* reported that the *Richelieu* had returned to Dakar. A few days later there was another report that the *Richelieu* was at sea but after putting out from Gibraltar once again the report was confirmed as being a false one and the *Hood* returned to Gibraltar.

Force 'H' is Formed

On 30 June Vice-Admiral Sir James Somerville hoisted his flag in the *Hood* and on the following day Force 'H' was formed. With the *Hood, Resolution, Valiant* and *Ark Royal* were the cruisers *Arethusa* and *Enterprise* and 11 destroyers. On 2 July all the Flag and Commanding Officers attended a conference in *Hood* and in the afternoon the whole fleet put to sea and turned East into the Mediterranean.

Mers-el-Kebir

Early on 3 July, when Force 'H' was off Oran, the Commander of the *Hood* broadcast to the ship's company and told them four alternatives were to be put to Admiral Gensoul and the French fleet at Mers-el-Kebir:

1 Sail with Force 'H' and continue the fight.
2 Sail to a British port with reduced crews.
3 Sail to a French West Indian port with reduced crews.
4 Scuttle your ship within six hours.

Failing the acceptance of one of these alternatives Force 'H' was under orders to prevent the French fleet from falling into German or Italian hands. In the harbour at Mers-el-Kebir were the battleships *Dunkerque, Strasbourg, Bretagne* and *Provence*, the seaplane carrier *Commandante Teste* and six destroyers. This fleet, although sheltered by a large breakwater and cliffs on either side, were moored closely together and so presented an easy target.

Junior Officer's cabin.

The 'Hood' in Action

All through the morning and afternoon of 3 July Force 'H' patrolled off the Oran area. Tension was rising as the French Fleet were seen to be raising steam with all despatch. In the late afternoon Admiral Somerville received a signal from the Admiralty stating that a French signal had been intercepted ordering all French ships in the area to proceed to Oran and render assistance to Admiral Gensoul. The Admiralty impressed on Admiral Somerville the necessity of reaching a solution without more delay.

A further signal was sent to Admiral Gensoul in the *Dunkerque* informing him that the British ships would open fire if no reply was received by 1730. By 1754 when no satisfactory reply had been received the British ships opened fire. To quote Winston Churchill, 'We had hoped that one or other of the alternatives would be accepted without the necessity of using the terrible force of a British battle squadron'.

At 1758 the French ships returned the British fire and gained two straddles on the *Hood*. At 1809 the British ships engaged the shore batteries. At 1812 they ceased firing. Apart from the *Strasbourg* and five destroyers the entire French fleet had been destroyed or beached.

An aircraft from the *Ark Royal* spotted the escape of the *Strasbourg*. The *Hood* gave chase and although she reached a speed of over 28 knots the French ships were fifteen miles ahead and there was little chance of catching them. Two torpedoes were fired at the *Hood* and, making an emergency turn of 180° to port, they passed just astern. At 1952 two planes were sighted. The *Hood* opened fire but no bombs were dropped. When there was no hope of catching the *Strasbourg*, the *Hood* turned eastwards towards Oran to join the remainder of Force 'H'.

In the action she had fired 56 15in shells and about 120 4in. Although her funnels were holed in many places her only casualties had been a lieutenant struck by shrapnel and one rating who received an eye injury.

So ended the *Hood*'s first large scale action of the war. She returned to Gibraltar on 4 July. The following day Force 'H' were ordered back to Oran to bombard the French fleet again but the order was rescinded and instead there was a torpedo-bombing attack on the *Dunkerque* by aircraft of the *Ark Royal*. Four hits were scored.

Escorting the 'Ark Royal'

On 8 July the *Hood* and *Resolution* left Gibraltar to escort the *Ark Royal* near enough to Sardinia for her aircraft to bomb the submarine and air bases on the island and so create a diversion for a naval operation being carried out at the same time in the Eastern Mediterranean. Those in *Hood* had their first taste of high-level bombing during this operation. Although several concentrated attacks by Italian aircraft were made against the British ships no damage was done. The *Hood* had been firing almost continuously for three hours. One plane was claimed by her gunfire. The scale of the air attacks, however, combined with the nature of the operation, led to its being cancelled, and the ships returned to Gibraltar on 11 July.

A UP mishap

When the UP control was being tested at Gibraltar on 27 July, the mounting on 'B' turret went off by mistake and twenty of the charges floated down

'Painting ship' in the Forth, September 1940. The shutters in the Admiral's quarters are closed. The scuttles are those of the Captain's harbour cabin.

Hood*'s quarterdeck.*

The Hood *at Scapa Flow, 9 October 1940.*

pack-ice which skirts the northern side of the Denmark Strait could be seen. Several icebergs were spotted and it was difficult to appreciate the intense cold until the spray was seen to freeze immediately it landed on the fo'c'sle. When the minelayers had completed their operations the *Hood* altered course and arrived back at Scapa on 29 November.

Christmas 1940—at Sea

The *Hood* was again at sea for the second Christmas of the war. The cruiser *Berwick* was giving chase to an 8in German cruiser and it was hoped that the *Hood,* accompanied by the cruiser *Edinburgh,* would make an interception. Once again she was denied the opportunity; the German warship had escaped to the West.

New Year 1941

The chimes of Big Ben were broadcast throughout the ship at midnight. The Junior Midshipman rang 'sixteen bells' on the quarterdeck. Thus began 1941. 2 January saw the *Hood* at sea again. She covered another minelaying operation which was being carried out to the north and the south of the Faroes. The operation successfully completed, the *Hood* returned to the Flow on 5 January.

Rosyth Refit 16/1/41—18/3/41

On 10 January the Boatswain's party struck the pole-masts on both the fore and mainmast. The ship's company now knew that the refit at Rosyth was very near. At 1800, however, the whole fleet at Scapa went to two hours' notice and just after midnight the *Hood* sailed into the Pentland Firth, accompanied by the *Repulse, Edinburgh* and *Birmingham* and six destroyers. Altering course westwards, the object of this operation was to investigate some unidentified wireless signals. Once again nothing transpired. On 12 January the Admiral announced the *Hood* was proceeding to Rosyth for a refit. She passed under the Forth Bridge at 1540 on 13 January and after de-ammunitioning arrived in Rosyth dockyard on 16 January.

Major machinery repairs were carried out and the blades in the starboard inner turbine, which were stripped when the *Hood* was chasing the *Strasbourg,* were replaced. Engineers from John Brown & Co, Clydebank, builders of the *Hood,* assisted the dockyard with this work.

Radar

Extensive improvements were effected in the Gunnery Control with the provision of Type 284 Radar for the main armament. Air Warning Radar—Type 279—was also fitted.

Many other minor repairs and improvements were carried out including the fitting of new screens in the after ends of the port and starboard batteries, the removal of the fore-topmast and the replacement of the two steam-picket boats by two 35ft motor boats. The propellers, rudder and the underwater hull were inspected in dry dock.

King George VI visits 'Hood'

During the first leave Mr Churchill visited the *Hood.* He addressed the ship's company and said how sorry he was to see her in dock and hoped that after her 'insides' had been put right they would continue to uphold the traditions and maintain the reputation of the famous ship. On 6 March 1941, King George VI, on a visit to Rosyth dockyard, inspected the ship's company.

The *Hood* left the dockyard basin on 17 March. The following day she completed ammunitioning while lying in mid-stream just above the Forth Bridge. At 1650 hours she left her anchorage and, passing under the Forth Bridge, sailed down the estuary into the North Sea.

Sailing to intercept the 'Scharnhorst' and 'Gniesenau'

During the night of 19 March the *Queen Elizabeth* and the cruiser *London* joined the *Hood* from Scapa Flow: on the following day it was learned that the ships were sailing to intercept the *Scharnhorst* and *Gniesenau,* a signal having been received from the *Renown* and *Ark Royal,* a thousand miles to the southward, that they had contacted the German battlecruisers. As zero hour approached and no news was received, the *Hood* set course for Scapa Flow arriving at her anchorage on 23 March. The next few days were spent exercising in the Flow.

Full Power Speed Trials

At full power speed trials off the North coast of

Hoisting inboard a practice torpedo.

Scotland on 25 March the *Hood* worked up to a maximum speed of 28·8 knots with paravanes streamed. This was one knot faster than the *Prince of Wales* had attained the previous week.

Patrolling off Brest

On 28 March the *Hood* was at sea again. Admiral Whitworth made a general signal stating that the *Scharnhorst* and *Gneisenau* were at Brest and the *Hood* was to carry out a patrol off this area. On 4 April *King George V* was sighted on her way to relieve the *Hood* with the patrol off Brest. After spending only ten hours at Scapa on 6 April, the *Hood* sailed south once more to patrol off the Brest area.

While on this patrol she received her first radar report of an aircraft approaching. The plane was a Whitley bomber and the 279 radar had picked it up at a distance of fifteen miles.

After spending Easter at sea the *Hood* returned to Scapa on 14 April.

'Bismarck'* reported to have left Kiel

After a few days exercising in the Flow, the *Hood* passed through Hoxa Gate at 1615 on 18 April. On reaching the Pentland Firth she turned westwards and the ship's company were informed that, once more, the ship was to patrol off Brest.

During the middle watch on 19 April the plans were suddenly changed and the ship altered course to 060°. A signal had been received that the *Bismarck* and two *Leipzig* class cruisers had left Kiel and were sailing in a north-westerly direction. The *Hood* patrolled in northern waters.

If the 'Hood' encounters the 'Bismarck'

On 20 April Admiral Whitworth made known his intentions if an *'enemy in sight'* report was received: the *Hood* would close the enemy at speed so as to bring her guns within effective range. If possible the approach would be 'end-on' so as to present the minimum target. (The weakness of the *Hood*'s deck armour made it imperative that any action be fought at as close a range as possible. The closer the range the flatter the trajectory of the shell and the less likely it would be to penetrate through her decks and reach the magazines.)

As no further news of the *Bismarck* was received and, so as to be more conveniently placed should she attempt to break out into the Atlantic, the *Hood* sailed to Hvalfiord in Iceland.

At Hvalfiord, Iceland

She remained in Icelandic waters, awaiting for news of the *Bismarck* until 28 April when she left Hvalfiord and steered a south-westerly course. She escorted two convoys and covered them against a possible surface attack. Five days later, when both convoys were past the danger zone, she returned to Hvalfiord.

Vice-Admiral Whitworth leaves the 'Hood'

On Sunday morning, 4 May, the *Hood* left Hvalfiord and returned to Scapa Flow. On 8 May Vice-Admiral

Scapa Flow, October 1940.

* See Warship Profile No. 18, KM *Bismarck*

October 1940. Note the U.P. mounting.

Scapa Flow: Pom-pom, 4in and U.P. mountings are visible. The funnel of the picket-boat can be seen hinged back in its stowage position. October 1940

The Hood's *ships company, November 1940. The Midshipman at the extreme right hand of the second row is Midshipman Dundas, one of the* Hood's *three survivors.*

Whitworth left the ship. Vice-Admiral L. E. Holland joined her on 12 May and assumed command of the Battlecruiser Squadron and second-in-command of the Home Fleet.

Exercising in Scapa Flow

Apart from carrying out a Range and Inclination Exercise with the *King George V* in the Pentland Firth on 13 May, the *Hood* remained in Scapa Flow, exercising, until 16 May when she was ordered to 'raise steam and proceed to sea with all despatch'. A report had been received that the *Bismarck* had left Bergen. This report was later corrected and the *Hood* reverted to four hours' notice for steam.

On 19 May Admiral Holland confirmed the tactics that would be used should the *Hood* meet the *Bismarck,* stressing the necessity of closing the range.

21May 1941—'Hood' and 'Prince of Wales' sail for Hvalfiord

On 21 May 1941 Admiral Tovey, C. in C. Home Fleet, decided to sail the *Hood* and *Prince of Wales* to Hvalfiord. With two heavy units in Iceland, the Home Fleet would be better placed to intercept the *Bismarck* if she attempted to leave Norwegian waters and break out into the Atlantic.

Little was it known that only a few hours before Admiral Holland's ships had left Scapa Flow, the *Bismarck,* in company with the heavy cruiser *Prinz Eugen,** had slipped out of the Norwegian fjord past Bergen to sail on a course that would take them through the Denmark Strait by 0600 on 24 May.

'Hood's' Armament—May 1941

8 15in in 4 twin turrets
14 4in in 7 twin turrets

* See Warship Profile No. 6, KM *Prinz Eugen*

Scapa Flow: Hood's *boat deck. The* Repulse *is in the background.*

Boat Deck.

Looking aft from the spotting-top.

3 8-barrelled pom-poms
5 UP mountings
2 quadruple machine guns
4 above-water 21in torpedo tubes
Radar—Type 284 for the main armament
—Type 279—air warning.

'Battleship and Cruiser have left Bergen'

At 1939 on 22 May Hatston Air Station in the Orkneys reported to the Commander-in-Chief of the Home Fleet, 'Following received from Hatston reconnaissance aircraft over Bergen. Battleship and cruiser have left.' Three minutes later Admiral Tovey took the following action:

The remaining units of the Home Fleet in Scapa were ordered to be ready for sea by 2300.

The cruiser *Suffolk* to join the *Norfolk* in the Denmark Strait.

The cruiser *Arethusa* to join the *Birmingham* and *Manchester* in the Iceland-Faroes channel.

The *Hood* and *Prince of Wales* were told to cover the area to the south-west of Iceland so as to be in a position to intercept the *Bismarck* should she attempt to break out into the Atlantic via the Denmark Strait or the Iceland-Faroes Channel.

'Ship bearing Green 140. Two Ships bearing Green 140.'

With these, now historic, words reported at 1922 on 23 May by Able Seaman Newell, the starboard after lookout in the *Suffolk*, one of the most memorable naval actions of the Second War was about to commence. The *Bismarck* and *Prinz Eugen* had been found.

The *Norfolk* and *Suffolk* took up their shadowing positions and at 1939 Admiral Holland received one of the *Suffolk*'s reports. The *Hood, Prince of Wales* with the destroyers *Antelope, Achates, Anthony, Electra, Echo* and *Icarus* were only 300 miles to the south. If the enemy remained on its present course there was little doubt that battle would be joined early the next morning.

'Hood' alters course and increases speed to intercept

At 1945 Admiral Holland signalled his force to increase speed to 27 knots and steer a course of 295°, With the deteriorating weather the escorting destroyers were having difficulty in keeping up with *Hood* and *Prince of Wales.*

Although Admiral Holland gave them the alternative to 'follow at your best speed' they elected to hold on and accept some superficial damage to their boats and gear.

At 0015 on the morning of 24 May 1941 Admiral Holland ordered his ships to 'Prepare for action'. Battle ensigns were hoisted.

Meanwhile, in the Denmark Strait the *Suffolk* had lost radar contact with the *Bismarck* during a snow storm. The fact of receiving no signals from the *Suffolk* presented Admiral Holland with an extremely difficult decision. Had the *Bismarck* turned back or had she made a major alteration of course to elude the shadowing cruisers or had she even sunk them? If it was still her intention to break out into the Atlantic then her alteration of course could only be to port—that is to due south or slightly east of south—owing to the Greenland pack-ice to starboard.

Admiral Holland decided—wrongly as it transpired—that the *Bismarck* and *Prinz Eugen* had turned south and he altered course to due north and reduced speed to 25 knots. This, it was hoped, would have put the *Hood* and *Prince of Wales* in a good interception course to bring the enemy to action in the shortest possible time. In fact, no alteration of course had been made by the German ships.

At 0210 Admiral Holland, wishing to maintain his position and not put his ships too far ahead of their adversaries, made a further alteration of course—to south-east and ordered his escorting destroyers to continue searching to the north.

At 0247 the welcome news was received in the *Hood* that the *Suffolk* had regained contact with the *Bismarck* who was still on a course to bring her out into the North Atlantic by 0600 on 24 May. The *Hood* and *Prince of Wales* altered course back to due north and increased speed to 28 knots. (It is difficult to understand why Admiral Holland did not recall his destroyers when this news was received).

'Bismarck' Twenty Miles to the North-East of 'Hood'

At 0400 the plotting officers in the *Hood* estimated that the *Bismarck* was some twenty miles to the north-east and at 0500 Admiral Holland made the signal, 'Instant readiness for action'.

The 'Hood' and 'Prince of Wales'; The 'Bismarck' and 'Prinz Eugen'

On paper Admiral Holland would seem to have had superiority but it must be remembered that the *Hood* was over 21 years old and had inherited that inborn weakness of all British battle-cruisers: inadequate deck armour. (This weakness in her design was one of the principal reasons for the tactics adopted by Admiral Holland in the ensuing engagement). With regard to the *Prince of Wales* she was a brand new ship, nowhere near being properly worked-up. Indeed, when she went into action workmen from her contractors were still on board. In addition, a defect had been discovered in one of her four guns in 'A' turret. It would only be able to fire in the first salvo before becoming unserviceable.

On the other side of the coin, we have the *Bismarck,* constructed with complete disregard for Naval Agreements, and modern in every respect. She had spent months working-up in the Baltic carrying out every manoeuvre and exercising against all eventualities. Being nearer 50,000 tons than the 35,000 tons allowed by the Washington Agreement she had been given an armoured hull of almost impenetrable nickel-chrome steel, 14 inches thick over two-thirds of her length.

The *Prinz Eugen,* although classed as a heavy cruiser, was of some 18,400 tons displacement, again far in excess of the figure allowed under the Washington Treaty.

These were the ships which Admiral Holland faced when action was joined on Empire Day 1941.

The following sonnet was written by Lieutenant Steegman RNVR, formerly an ordinary seaman in the

Hood, while he was on patrol, 500 miles north-east of Cape Farewell—over the spot where the *Hood* blew-up:

'We pass, alert and cautious, o'er your grave
Now three years old. A thousand friends and more
A thousand fathoms deep. I humbly crave
Forgiveness for my tears; my heart is sore.
What blessed hopes would I not now forswear,
Deny my faith, distort the desperate truth,
If, by some miracle, the sounding gear
Could echo up the voices of your youth.
Rage on, ensanquined seas; hurl on your heads
The ancient curse of sailors yet unborn.
Not all the storms in hell can rock the beds
of *Hood*'s great company. No more I'll mourn
For now I know no sailor ever dies.
We pass right on. "All's well", her echo cries.'

Air Defence Position.

'Plowing through a heavy sea'.

Taking it green.

The fo'c'sle from the Air Defence Position.

0537—24 May 1941—
'Enemy in Sight. Distance 17 Miles'.

When this report was made by the *Prince of Wales,* Admiral Holland realised that, owing to his alteration of course during the night, he had lost considerable bearing on the *Bismarck.*

Wishing to close the range as soon as possible, at 0546 the *Hood* and *Prince of Wales* altered course 40° towards the *Bismarck.* A few minutes later Admiral Holland turned his ships a further 20° towards the enemy. Even with this latest alteration the British ships were still approaching the enemy 30° to port of an end-on approach. This meant that, not only were they presenting a much greater target than would have been the case if an end-on run-in had been adopted, but the after turrets of both ships were no longer able to bear. Thus, in the early stages of the action the British ships were not able to take advantage of their superior fire-power.

'Hood' opens the firing

With the *Hood* and *Prince of Wales* continuing at 28 knots the range was closing rapidly and at 0549 the Admiral signalled for fire to be concentrated on the leading ship—the *Prinz Eugen* who had been mistaken for the *Bismarck.* Three minutes later, realising his mistake, he signalled to, 'Shift target right'—at the very moment the *Hood* had opened the firing. The *Prince of Wales* had already decided to ignore the Admiral's signal and had opened fire from the beginning on the *Bismarck.*

Seconds later the *Bismarck* and *Prinz Eugen* replied, both concentrating their fire on the *Hood* who was soon obscured in a forest of foam as the German salvoes fell all around her.

The *Norfolk* and *Suffolk,* who kept out of the action,

View from fo'c'sle looking aft, April 1941. Note 279 Radar on spotting top and forward U.P. mountings on boat deck.

could see that the *Hood*'s salvoes were falling close to the enemy and it is believed that her third salvo was a straddle.

At 0555 the *Hood* was hit on the boat deck near the mainmast and a huge fire broke out, caused it would seem, by the setting-off of the ammunition in the ready-use lockers. It is now known that this hit was scored by the *Prinz Eugen.*

At this time the Admiral made his last signal—a turn 20° to port, which would have brought the *Hood* and *Prince of Wales* on a course approximately parallel to their adversaries and thus would have opened up the arcs of the after turrets. The full weight of the combined salvoes of the British ships could then have been brought to bear.

The tragedy of the whole action is that, just as the *Hood* and *Prince of Wales* began to execute this turn to port, the *Hood* received her death blow.

'Hood' Blows-Up

The fourth salvo from the *Bismarck* fell very close to the *Hood.* 'X' turret had just fired its first salvo when the fifth salvo from the *Bismarck* hit the *Hood* and plunged down to her 4in magazine, about 65ft abaft the mainmast. The explosion in her 4in magazine set off the after two 15in magazines. At 16,500 yards the *Hood* had received a fatal hit. A pillar of fire soared a thousand feet into the air and in the huge explosion which followed, her back broke, her bows lifted high out of the water and within 90 seconds there was little to be seen other than a dense pall of smoke hovering over the foaming sea. The *Hood*'s grave is 63°20'N, 31°50'W. With her she took 1418 officers and men.

The fo'c'sle during full power speed trials on 25 March 1941.

Hood *at Scapa Flow, three days before she sailed to meet the* Bismarck.

The Hood *pictured from the* Prince of Wales *the day before meeting the* Bismarck. (*Central Press Photos Ltd.*)

Position 63° 20′ N. 30° 50′ W. The smoke on the left is from the Prince of Wales.

The Author

Empire Day 1941. The Hood *exploding.*

Acknowledgments
I am particularly indebted to the editor of *Ships Monthly* for permission to reproduce many of my photographs in this Profile.

My thanks also go to Mr. D. G. WELDON for his valued assistance with information on the *Hood* and also for his kindness in allowing me to use certain of his photographs.

Bibliography

Janes Fighting Ships 1939.
The Mighty Hood by ERNLE BRADFORD, *Hodder.*

Warship Series Editor: JOHN WINGATE, DSC

Havant, *the first of the class, as originally completed in December 1939 with tall funnels, three boats and minesweeping gear aft. Like* Hesperus, *she lacked her DCT but was fitted with eight depth-charge throwers and three traps* *(MOD)*

HMS Hesperus

by Captain Peter Dickens DSO, MBE, DSC

FOREWORD by Captain Donald G. F. W. Macintyre DSO DSC, Royal Navy who commanded 'HMS HESPERUS' from 15.1.40—13.3.41 and from 28.8.42—22.3.44.**

When the torpedoing and sinking of the liner *Athenia* without warning by a German U-boat on the first day of World War II led to the immediate institution of a convoy system, the Admiralty became a victim of its own lack of foresight as well as the nation's parsimony in the provision of money for defence and found itself woefully short of ships suitable for escort duties. Covetous eyes were turned on the six destroyers similar to the British 'H' Class which were being built, two of each by Thornycroft, Samuel White and Vickers, for the Brazilian Navy. They were quickly requisitioned and completed with equipment limited to what was essential for anti-submarine warfare.

One of these, launched by Thornycroft on 1 August 1939, was given the name *Hearty*. The phonetic risk of confusion with the flotilla leader *Hardy*, already in commission, caused this to be changed to *Hesperus* soon after commissioning under my command in January 1940.

Her debut was far from auspicious. Hurried to sea at Winston Churchill's insistence, her upper deck had been incompletely caulked and she leaked like a sieve in a seaway and had to be taken in hand for this to be remedied. She had no gun-director nor any form of gun-control. Her only anti-aircraft weapons were two four-barrelled 0·5 inch machine guns. Her gyro compass was a Brown's, designed for the gentle motion and absense of shock to be expected in a passenger liner; only in the calmest weather did it function under the rough treatment provided by a destroyer.

Nevertheless, as Captain Peter Dickens' narrative shows, the *Hesperus* was to be a credit to her builders, give great good service to the Royal Navy and follow a splendidly successful career throughout the Battle of the Atlantic.

THE SHIP AND HER VITAL ROLE

The Battle of the Atlantic was as critical for us as the Battle of Britain. On our ability to keep our merchant ships and their cargoes at sea depended our very survival and, having assured that, our ability to wage war.

The Flag-Officer U-boats, Admiral Doenitz, knew this perhaps better than we did ourselves; and he went even further by stating clearly that the *only* way Germany, despite her massive armies, could hope to defeat Britain was by cutting her sea lifelines. The drive, courage and persistence behind the U-boats' attack reflected this single-minded conviction and it very nearly succeeded.

Only *Hesperus* and her small, rust-streaked, storm-battered, much-modified and perhaps not very beautiful sisters, together with the aircraft of Coastal Command and the Fleet Air Arm, held the enemy at the eleventh hour and then routed him. It is important to recognize this stark, simple truth so as not to fall into the common error of assessing these ships as ancillary to the mighty battleships and carriers. They were the front line itself against the only menace that really frightened Winston Churchill. *Hesperus* is particularly interesting as representing in microcosm every stage of the Battle from initial unpreparedness, through frantic improvisation, to fully-specialised Anti-Submarine (A/S) Escort. She was always in action at the key phases and used every weapon and equipment with deadly effect.

The Launching

Senhora Heitor Galliez launched the Brazilian destroyer *Juruena* at Thornycroft's Yard on

Hurricane *as completed in the summer of 1940. She has her DCT* (MOD)

Right: *Asdic, showing dome, oscillator and housing arrangements*

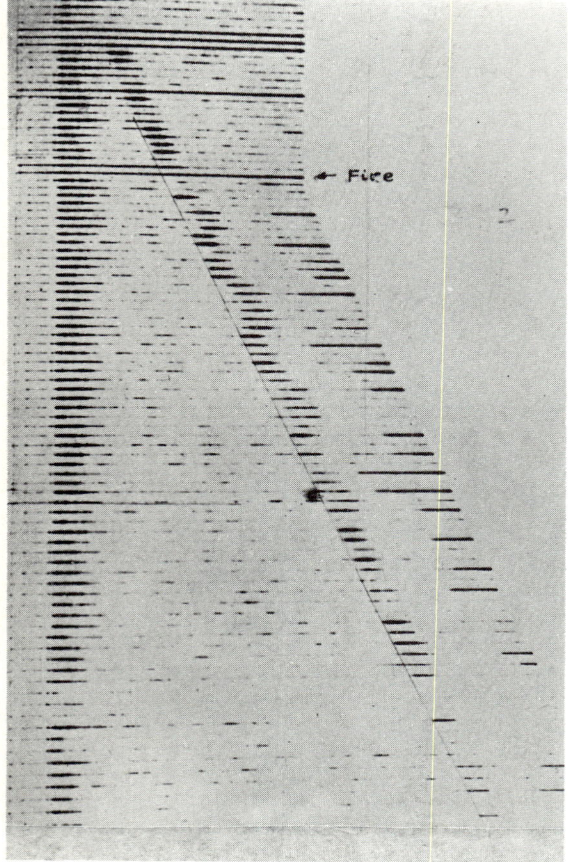

A typical range recorder trace of an attack on a submarine with an ahead-throwing weapon.
The iodised paper slowly descends. A 'stylus' at the top starts from the left simultaneously with each transmission and moves across, marking the paper with any signal detected by the receiving circuit. The transmission itself is not recorded as it would be too loud, but then are seen the sea-reverberations gradually diminishing in intensity until the echo stands out clearly.
The echo marks are firm when the oscillator points directly at the submarine but the operator deliberately steps across it to ensure that he always knows the centre bearing and is not misled into losing contact if the target's bearing changes rapidly. There are therefore faint echoes between the firm ones; on two occasions he has stepped off the submarine on to its wake, but the trace has perhaps helped him to see his error.
The slope of the line of echoes gives the rate of approach and the bar, adjusted for own ship's speed, estimated depth and weapon data, is aligned with it. When the moving paper brings the two together the weapon is fired. (MOD)

1 August 1939 but by 9 September her owners had submitted gracefully to the inevitable and she became one of His Majesty's Ships. The name *Hesperus,* the Greek's Evening Star, was the first of the name in the Royal Navy and unquestionably attractive; that it was also well-known as the Wreck of Longfellow's poem seems to have been overlooked by the Ships' Names Committee, usually so anxious not to upset the sailors' morale, in its search for anything beginning with 'H', but no harm was done for she was happy, lucky and very successful.

Built to the plans of the well-tried British 'H' Class with insignificant alterations she and her sisters, *Havelock, Havant, Hurricane, Highlander* and *Harvester,* were Fleet Destroyers designed as adjuncts to the battlefleet in attack and defence against a surface enemy. Four low-angle 4·7in guns and eight torpedoes were to be their main armament and although they would have asdic and a few depth-charges they had virtually no defence against aircraft. Except for their sturdy hulls and high speed they were thus thoroughly ill-adapted to modern war.

However, the first important improvement was ordered before completion. This was a massive depth-charge armament in place of 'Y' gun which was unique to the class and set it firmly on the A/S road. More innovations followed until the ships were fully equipped for the climax of the Battle in the spring of 1943 and it is important therefore to know what the modifications all were.

Asdic

This means of detecting a submerged submarine by emitting a sound beam into the water and hearing the echo was already generally fitted in small ships at the outbreak of war; much credit is due to the small band of dedicated scientists and naval officers who developed it with little official encouragement. The component parts were:

The Oscillator, a quartz crystal disc suspended beneath the ship which converted an electrical impulse into sound and, if an echo was returned, vice versa. The instrument could also hear other under-water noises which was most useful but all would be drowned by the rush of water past one's own ship were it not for:

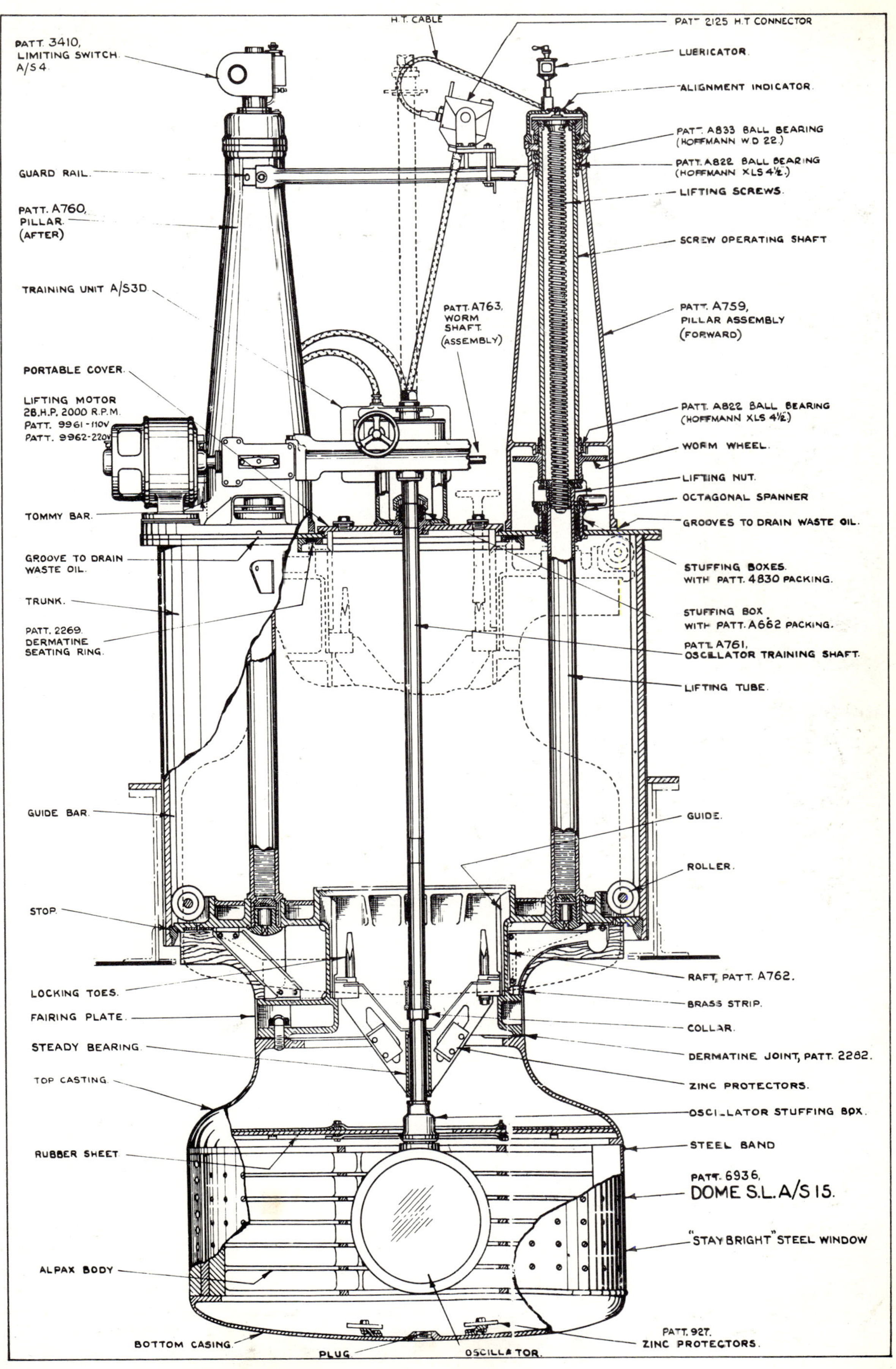
H.T. CABLE
PATT. 2125 H.T CONNECTOR
PATT. 3410,
LIMITING SWITCH.
A/S 4.
LUBRICATOR.
ALIGNMENT INDICATOR.
PATT. A833 BALL BEARING
(HOFFMANN W.D 22.)
PATT. A822 BALL BEARING
(HOFFMANN XLS 4½.)
GUARD RAIL.
LIFTING SCREWS.
PATT. A760,
PILLAR.
(AFTER)
SCREW OPERATING SHAFT
TRAINING UNIT A/S3D.
PATT. A763,
WORM
SHAFT.
(ASSEMBLY)
PATT. A759,
PILLAR ASSEMBLY
(FORWARD)
PORTABLE COVER.
LIFTING MOTOR
2.8.H.P. 2000 R.P.M.
PATT. 9961-110V
PATT. 9962-220V
PATT. A822 BALL BEARING
(HOFFMANN XLS 4½.)
WORM WHEEL.
LIFTING NUT.
OCTAGONAL SPANNER
TOMMY BAR.
GROOVES TO DRAIN WASTE OIL.
GROOVE TO DRAIN
WASTE OIL.
STUFFING BOXES.
WITH PATT. 4830 PACKING.
TRUNK.
STUFFING BOX
WITH PATT. A662 PACKING.
PATT. 2269.
DERMATINE
SEATING RING.
PATT. A761,
OSCILLATOR TRAINING SHAFT.
LIFTING TUBE.
GUIDE BAR.
GUIDE.
ROLLER.
STOP.
RAFT, PATT. A762.
LOCKING TOES.
BRASS STRIP.
FAIRING PLATE.
COLLAR.
STEADY BEARING.
DERMATINE JOINT, PATT. 2282.
TOP CASTING.
ZINC PROTECTORS.
OSCILLATOR STUFFING BOX.
STEEL BAND
RUBBER SHEET.
PATT. 6936,
DOME S.L. A/S 15.
"STAYBRIGHT" STEEL WINDOW
ALPAX BODY.
PATT. 927.
ZINC PROTECTORS.
BOTTOM CASING.
PLUG.
OSCILLATOR.

The Dome, a streamlined container which enclosed the oscillator in still water and allowed operation up to speeds of about 20kts in calm weather. At full speed or in heavy seas the dome could be housed snugly inside the hull to avoid damage.
The Controls were near the Captain in a tiny hut on the bridge and were operated by one man, directed and assisted by the A/S Control Officer. A knob at the centre of a gyro compass repeater rotated the oscillator; and the Range Recorder initiated the short, sharp transmissions, displayed visually any noise or answering echo, computed the relative approach speed and indicated the moment of weapon release.
The receiving circuit was also amplified aurally and this was essential to allow the greatest chance of hearing the first suspicion of an echo and then to classify it as wake, rock, wreck, tide-rip, fish or, when sharp and clear, a possible submarine. A difference in note between sea reverberations and echo indicated target movement and there were many other esoteric subtleties; operating skill was an art superimposed on science and *Hesperus*'s Petty Officer Coster was a master.

The Controls. *This exercise mock-up shows: Control Training Unit (bottom left) with which the operator directed the oscillator.* Range Recorder (*with sloping bar*) *which displayed all underwater noises visually.* Plotting table. *Own ship's track was drawn automatically and on to this was superimposed ranges and bearings of an echo which revealed any movement. An important use of the plot was to suggest a new direction of sweep when contact was lost. In* Hesperus *it was sited below the bridge and could be viewed through an aperture.*
Not shown are the operator's earphones and a loudspeaker. An echo was first detected almost invariably by ear, and much could be deduced by its sharpness and pitch
(*MOD*)

Depth Charge Mark VII

The first and, until 1942, the only weapon, this was a simple drum of high explosive which could be set to detonate at varying depths by hydrostatic pressure. The standard equipment for small ships in 1939 was a trap from which charges were rolled over the stern and two mortars, or Throwers, which projected them 120ft on either beam.
The Captain guessed the submarine's depth, for the asdic could not help him there, and steered to put the ship's stern over her future position. Contact would be lost in the final stages as the U-boat passed below the beam, but the recorder trace would give him the moment to fire and this was done in the sequence:
1. *Trap and throwers;* the trap charge would sink straight down but those from the throwers would carry forward through the air to splash abreast the
2. *Second trap charge,* which was followed at the same interval by the
3. *Third trap charge.*
The pattern thus produced was a centred diamond and allowed some margin for error but experience soon showed that this was rarely enough. In 1940 the ex-Brazilians were fitted with no fewer than three traps and eight throwers giving a pattern of 17; but even so, and although this terrifying series of explosions might well cover the submarine in plan, there could be no likelihood of a kill unless some latitude was also allowed in depth. The answer was to bolt heavy weights to half the charges which then sank faster and exploded deeper.
The final pattern to emerge after many trials and much experience consisted of 10 from two traps and four throwers of improved marks. This might be called the killer pattern for use against a probable or certain U-boat; for urgent attacks on newly detected and possibly unidentified targets it was usual to fire a five-charge pattern, while for the massive 'creep' attack on a slow, deep enemy as many as 26 would be sent down.

A Mark VII Depth-charge exploding at 50ft (*IWM*)

Depth Charge Mark X-One Ton

A logical addition to the Mark VII, but not a replacement, since a shallow burst could sink the firing ship, this contained as much explosive as a 10-charge normal pattern and was discharged from a torpedo tube. Little faith and a good deal of awe was evidently given to it, for each ship was allowed only one and even that was rarely used, but with *Hesperus* the aim of sinking U-boats took precedence over all else and she could have used more had she carried them.

Hedgehog

Even Coster's skill could not induce his asdic to keep contact with a submarine at close range when it had passed under the beam, and an ahead-throwing weapon was a clear need. *Hesperus*'s hedgehog replaced 'A' gun in early 1943 and fired an elliptical pattern of 24 bombs over the bow at a U-boat still in firm contact; detonation was triggered by impact and one hit was lethal. The only snag was, 'no hit, no bang' and consequently no secondary damage or morale effect; but it was a great advance and when teething and familiarity problems had been overcome, the percentage of successful attacks rose from six to thirty.

German Counter-Measures

Before 1943 there was little a U-boat could do to engage an escort. To fire a torpedo with only hydrophone data had small chance of success and would identify her for certain, wh le to surface and fight it out, though done, was a last ditch throw. Her main asset was the ability to lose herself and success in this depended on the courage, wit and patience of both her Captain and his opponent. Macintyre of the *Hesperus* had an uncanny gift of apparently looking into his unseen enemy's mind and divining his next move.

There was however one ingenious gadget available to a U-boat, the *Pillenwerfer,* a chemical discharged into the sea which effervesced like a monstrous Alka-Seltzer and returned a convincing echo to the asdic. Even Coster was misled when he first encountered one and temporarily ost contact with the submarine, gliding away silently and end-on,

Above: *The Hedgehog Ahead-Throwing Anti-Submarine Weapon.*

The spigot bombs are mounted in four rows, rising towards the rear. Each has its propellant charge in the stalk and an arming vane to allow detonation only when it is sinking. Firing was in a ripple (MOD)

Each spigot was angled differently to produce the elliptical pattern and the rows were mounted on spindles which could tilt to allow 20° of training either side of the bow and compensate for ship's roll (MOD)

Left: *The 24 bombs in the air* (MOD) and right: *The pattern fell 200 yards ahead of the ship in an ellipse 120ft by 140ft (wide). Each bomb contained 35lb of Torpex, sufficient by itself to hole and sink a U-Boat* (MOD)

beyond it. Once known however, this ruse was much less effective.

As allied fighting ability and strength increased and the U-boat casualty rate rose, a weapon became a vital need. The *Zaunkonig* (we called it 'Gnat'—and a nasty sting it inflicted) was the answer: an electric torpedo that could hear an escort's propellers and home towards them. From mid-1943 ships began, at first unaccountably, to have their sterns blown off and A/S action became a two-sided affair.

Our Intelligence however was not unprepared and counter-measures, material and tactical, were soon in operation. The 'Foxer' was a pair of towed noisemakers, each consisting of two, loosely fitting steel bars which 'chattered' at speeds over 10kts many times more loudly than the propellers and effectively decoyed the gnat. But they also made a hideous racket in the asdic which often drowned the echo; so we compromised with one, 'Unifoxer', whose noise it was found possible, after much training, to operate through, albeit still with reduced efficiency.

On approaching a U-boat, ships had to 'step aside' with 60° zig-zags so that a gnat would follow the unifoxer clear of the ship and not catch her 'down the throat'; or approach indirectly, faster than the gnat's 25kts. At close quarters, there was the option of slowing to silent speed of about seven knots if the unifoxer's noise made contact-holding difficult. More skill and courage were needed to sink a U-boat equipped with gnats and we suffered many casualties: even the ship commanded by the wily Macintyre after leaving *Hesperus*, *HMS Bickerton*, fell victim in 1944.

THE ELECTRONIC WAR

So much for close action, but how was the escort's asdic, with its range of little over a mile, to be brought into contact with a U-boat in the vast Atlantic? The secret lay in convoys which, being few in number, were hard to find, but when found, forced the attacker to brave the escorts. Two aims were thus achieved: protection was afforded to the merchant ships and U-boats could be sunk. Both were necessary since, although it might seem sufficient to protect a particular convoy passively, U-boat strength was growing as fast as Germany could build and would, if unchecked, eventually become overwhelming. It was often difficult for an Escort Commander to decide whether to leave the convoy to destroy a U-boat or to stay in close company.

The Wolf Packs

Doenitz's answer to the convoy was to mass as many U-boats as practicable and attack on the surface at night, thus retaining flexibility, speed and vision which were lost when dived. To bring this about, he would station lines of U-boats across likely routes and, when one sighted a convoy, she would surface and report by high frequency (H/F) radio; the rest would then close, moving on the surface except when necessary to avoid detection, until the 'Wolf pack' was formed and poised. On the next night the U-boats, trimmed down to their conning-towers and appallingly difficult to see, would dash in between the escorts to sink and burn, leaving pathetic groups of survivors to the coldly merciless ocean; and a steeper downward slope on the critical graph of available merchant shipping.

Until 1942 we could not detect the enemy during any of these phases but this we had to do or lose the war. Aircraft were the answer to the surfaced U-boat but that aspect, though vital, is not appropriate to this Profile. Sighting reports and surfaced U-boats at close quarters at night were however *Hesperus*'s direct concern and both these were mastered in the nick of time by devoted scientific effort at the Admiralty Signals Establishment.

High Frequency Direction Finding (H/F D/F)

Usually called 'Huff-Duff', the aerial did not revolve but achieved its directional sensitivity by measuring the signal strength received by each of the several loops. It was remarkably accurate and, like the asdic, could be induced to yield far more than just the bearing by an operator with a real flair: Lieutenant Harold Walker of the *Hesperus* could tell one U-boat from another, whether the aerial was wet or dry, and the range, often to within a mile.

Completely dedicated, Walker rarely left his set and sooner or later the bridge would be alerted by the report, '*B-Bar*', a German operating signal indicating that a U-boat had a sighting to report urgently. Then,

The purpose of it all, 'The safe and timely arrival of the convoy'. The box shape was standard, the leading edge being the longer, to give a U-Boat the most difficult interception problem. In this case the mean course of advance is to the right, with the Commodore's ship in the centre of the leading edge. He is probably exercising his ships in emergency turns which they may have to carry out to avoid wolf-packs at any time, at night or in foul weather (IWM)

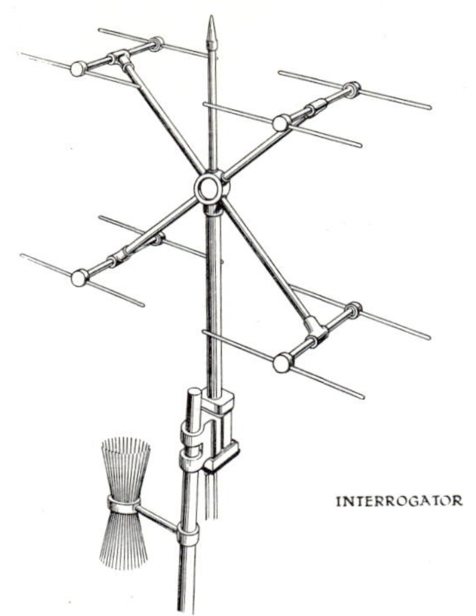

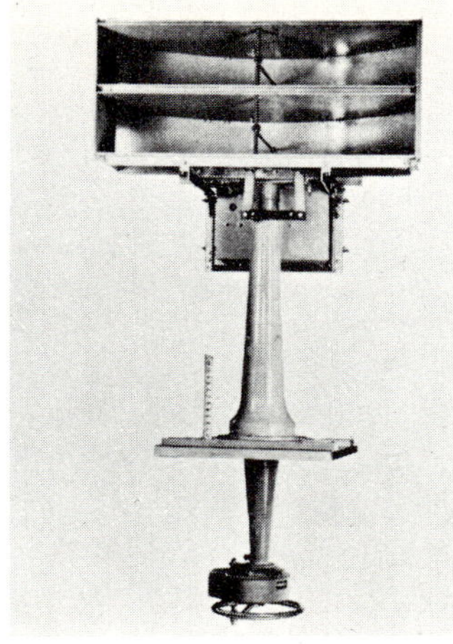

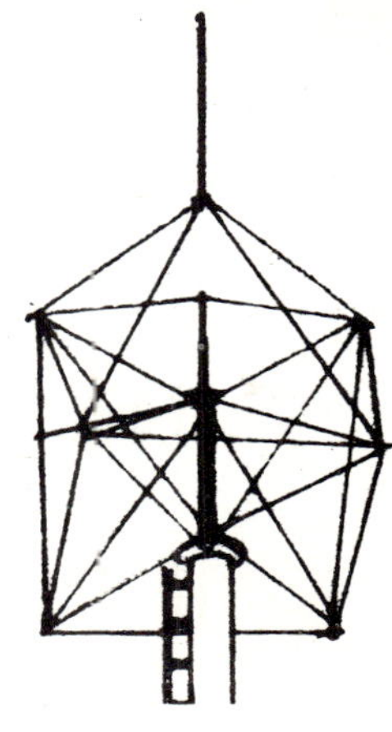

The aerials of some of the sets fitted in Hesperus *which started what subsequently became known as Electronic Warfare.*

Left: RDF Warning Combined, *first fitted in late 1941. Primarily for air warning, but with a surface capability (it detected* U93*), this set was a great advance in performance and flexibility over the earlier, fixed aerial, type. At first aerial rotation was by hand and echoes were displayed on an 'A' scan (a line of light displaced in a 'blip' at the scale distance of the echo) but, in about 1943, power rotation and Plan Position Indicator (PPI), as in modern radars, were fitted giving an all-round presentation of everything within range. Also at this time the term 'radar' was introduced.*

The interrogator was part of a device (IFF) for identifying a contact electronically as friend or foe in association with the radar *(MOD)*

Centre: RDF Warning Surface. *The battle-winning set evolved by the Naval Signal School and Admiralty Signals Establishment expressly to detect the trimmed-down, surfaced U-Boat; it was fitted in* Hesperus *in 1942.*

With a frequency of 3000mc/s and a $1\frac{1}{4}$ micro-second pulse, the aerial was designed to give a very directional beam in azimuth while being broad in elevation to allow for the roll of a small ship. This meant two dipole aerials with cheese-shaped reflectors, one transmitter and one receiver, mounted one on top of the other. The first magnetron only allowed a power output of 5kW and to avoid any losses through cables, part of the circuitry was mounted on the aerials and had to be protected from the weather by a perspex lantern. Like the warning combined set it developed from hand-rotation and 'A' scan to power and PPI *(MOD)*

Right: High Frequency Direction Finder *(H/F D/F or 'Huff-Duff'). Two aspects of the same aerial, showing how the strut arrangement altered the apparent shape when viewed from different angles. This was the set with which Harold Walker extracted detailed information about U-Boats without their knowing.*

A U-Boat's sighting report on H/F travelled in an approximately straight line at a tangent to the earth's curvature and achieved the long distance to base by being reflected by the ionosphere. This was the 'sky wave' but if the 'ground wave' were detected the U-Boat could not be more than 15-20 miles distant and the set could sense this vital difference *(MOD, Courtesy A. Raven)*

if the range was close, *Hesperus* would race down the bearing at 30kts with every sense alert, both human and scientific. Even if the U-boat was not heard or seen again, she was at least forced to dive and become blind, so that the convoy could be diverted away from the threat; but the team of Macintyre, Walker and Coster, supported by a supremely happy and efficient ship, was so formidable that *Hesperus* sank no fewer than three U-boats directly from H/F D/F reports. The Huff-Duff was at least as important as the more glamorised radar since, when that was called into play, the enemy was already dangerously close.

Radar

Developed initially for what turned out to be the Battle of Britain, in which it succeeded dramatically, radar was first fitted in ships primarily for air warning. *Hesperus*'s first set had fixed forward-looking aerials and was soon replaced by one whose aerial rotated; but these could not be relied upon to detect the surfaced U-boat at close range, for which it was realised that a much higher frequency in the 10cm band must be developed. The RAF's invention of the Resonant Cavity Magnetron permitted this, and a surface warning (SW) set was evolved and fitted in the first escorts in 1942. Its conspicuous hooded lantern evoked a sense of awe in the uninitiated beholder and also, no doubt, the enemy; as well indeed it might, for it could detect a trimmed-down submarine at $2\frac{1}{2}$ miles or more. Not much perhaps, but enough to tip the tactical balance and it is a measure of its importance that the Director Control Tower (DCT) was removed to make space for it, thus relegating the guns to a very secondary role.

Shore Support

By the spring of 1943 *Hesperus* had become wholly specialised for A/S warfare but improvements to asdic, weapons and electronics continued until the war's end.

From this regrettably over-simplified account of *Hesperus*'s development, it will be appreciated that the Battle was not waged only at sea. To compensate for our peacetime failure to understand where our real security lay, enormous effort had to be devoted: in the Admiralty (Staff, Intelligence and Technical departments), in drawing offices, on trial ranges, in Tactical Schools, the Anti-Submarine School, the Signal School, the Admiralty Signals Establishment, the Commander-in-Chief Western Approaches' Headquarters and many less likely places such as Gilbert's deserted garage at Waterlooville. The effort was applied and the Battle won.

'HESPERUS'S' STORY

She commissioned on 15 January 1940 under Commander Donald Macintyre into the 9th Destroyer Flotilla which comprised all six ships of the ex-Brazilian Class. By a long stretch of official imagination she was pronounced ready for sea in early April; but her DCT was not available so that her three 4·7s had to be controlled locally and their target indicated by the Captain waving his cap in its general direction; her torpedoes were a commercial type which could not be run for practice and were reputed to blow up if hit; and she was defenceless against air attack. Her engines were good, however, and she did possess her large A/S armament which proved in the end to be what mattered most. Indeed she seemed inexorably impelled towards this role through being, by chance, virtually useless for anything else and also by her bond of union with Macintyre whose dedicated ambition was to sink U-boats, a rare desire in a Navy dominated by thundering guns and gunnery officers.

Faroes Take-over

Hesperus and *Havant* were first assigned to the A/S defence of Scapa Flow, but soon after the Germans invaded Norway on 8 April, they were sent to the Faroes to advise the Danish Governor that we intended to occupy the islands and forestall the enemy doing so; a likely move which would have greatly facilitated the passage of German ships and submarines into the Atlantic. This was accomplished in an atmosphere of civilised courtesy. Then to Norway, and real war.

Norway

It was almost enjoyable at first, when she found herself patrolling Narvik Fiord with orders to fire on any enemy troops or vehicles that appeared, even though her gunnery, as might be expected, was not spectacular. Air attack started painlessly, too, with high level bombing which was not accurate against small ships who would use the long time of fall to get out of the way; and Macintyre, a former Fleet Air Arm pilot, achieved a reputation among his men as an artful dodger.

It was a different matter further south off Mo where *Hesperus* supported a troop landing on 15 May, hastily mounted to delay the enemy's advance on Narvik. Here she was within range of Stuka dive-bombers whose close approach, which could not be prevented by the wholly inadequate 0·5in machine-guns, allowed no time for manoeuvre. She twisted and turned at high speed—one technique was to steer towards an approaching enemy to force him into an uncomfortably steep dive. It was not long before those on the upper deck had to steel themselves to watch, first the end-on view of the aircraft with its menacingly crooked wings, then the bomb, perfectly circular and growing larger, shrieking in a crescendo as it fell, until the time came to hurl themselves to the deck and pray.

Hesperus was damaged aft by two near-misses and sent home with the next convoy. Perhaps she was lucky; to have survived Norway intact would have made her available for Dunkirk where, with her useless guns against even fiercer air attack, she might well have been sunk like the poor *Havant* after a very brief career.

Western Approaches

In addition to repairs at Dundee, the after torpedo-tubes were removed and a 3in high-angle gun of ancient vintage substituted. AA gunnery was a vastly complex technology which defied improvisa-

Depth-charge attack (lower right)

The ship has a firm echo, the characteristics of which imply that the contact is 'probable submarine'. As she approaches, the echo pitch is clearly lower than the reverberations, indicating movement away, which is further evidence that the contact is a submarine and which also provides useful attack data.

A 10-charge standard pattern is ordered and the ship's speed steadied at 15kts. As she nears her target, the echo is held almost to the time when they become instant with the transmission which indicates that the submarine has probably been surprised and is very shallow, since otherwise she would have passed below the asdic beam much earlier. A mean depth setting of 75ft is ordered.

The submarine now becomes aware of her danger having heard both the asdic and propellers and increases speed, turns to port and dives; the ship however cannot detect or allow for these alterations.

The range recorder, using information by now 30 seconds stale, initiates the firing sequence. First to go is one heavy charge, set to explode below the target's assessed depth at 100ft, from the midship trap; three seconds later (so that neither charge should damage the other) comes a light set to 50ft from the starboard trap and two heavies from the forward throwers which carry forward with the ship's speed while in the air. At eight seconds the after throwers fire two lights and the trap releases another heavy.

The 10-second point is depicted above and it can be seen that in theory the submarine has escaped damage, even though three more trap charges have yet to be dropped. The ship then strives to regain contact, but against the noise of exploding charges and her own wake it is improbable that she will do so until she has run out to about 1200 yards, turned, and started a new asdic sweep by which time the submarine will have moved considerably

---

Hedgehog attack (upper right)

The initial situation is the same but now the ship has been fitted with Hedgehog. The submarine takes similar avoiding action but since she is in firm contact right up to the moment of firing her movements are assessed and the weapon aimed accordingly. An indication of depth is important to the calculation of time to fire but extreme accuracy is unnecessary as the bombs explode only on impact. Immediately after firing the ship turns sharply to avoid running over the submarine and so maintains contact

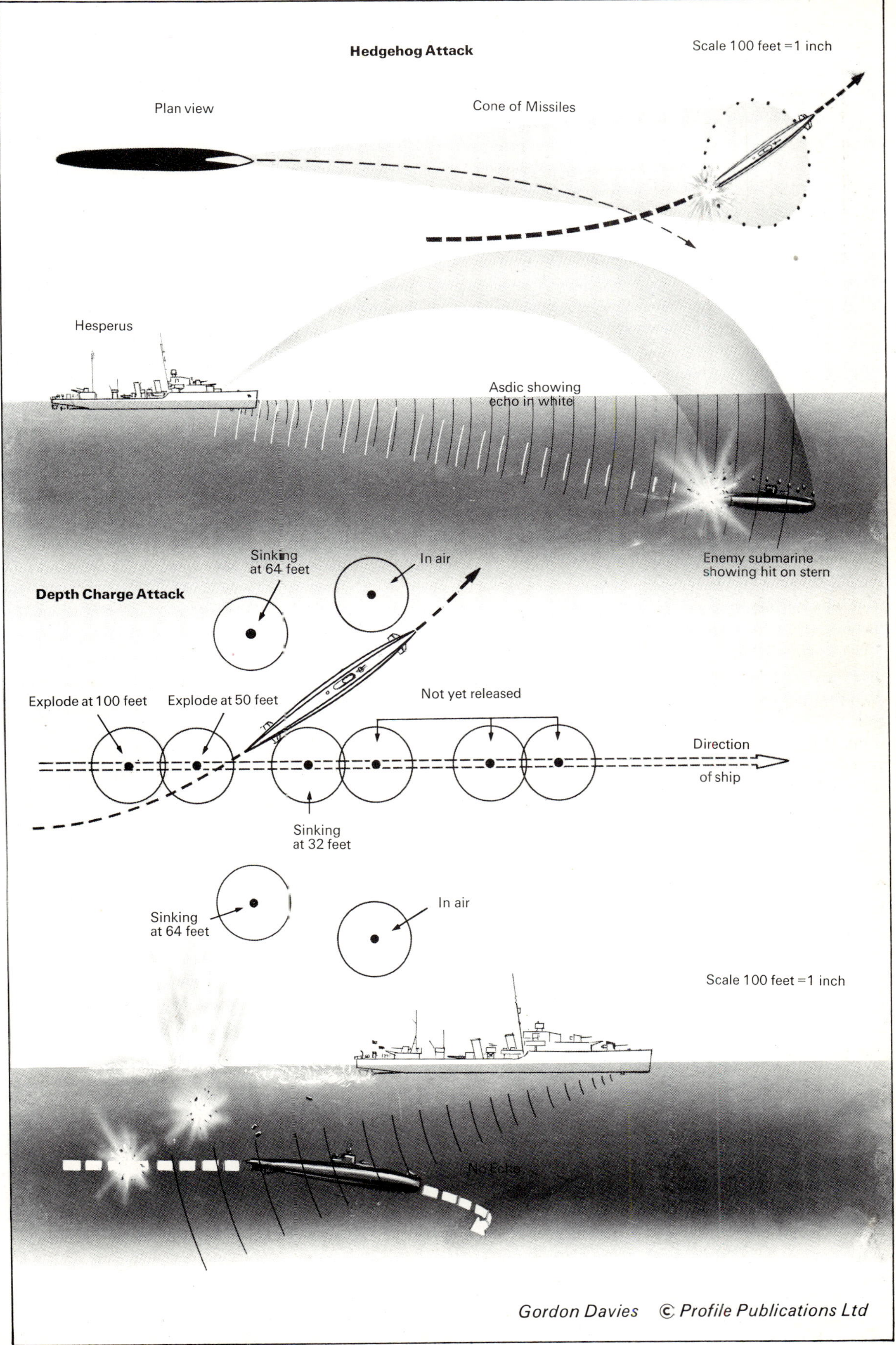

Gordon Davies © *Profile Publications Ltd*

tion, and the 3in gun without a control system or even a good field of fire was a waste of space; the obsolete weapon even failed to boost morale.

Towards the end of the year, the 9th Flotilla was transferred from the Home Fleet to Western Approaches Command and re-named the 9th Escort Group. Macintyre was delighted, for here were the U-boats he knew to be his destined foes; but first we had to re-learn an old lesson the hard way before the long, slow climb to victory was even started. True, our merchant ships sailed in convoy but an aggressive spirit, morally proper but tactically disastrous, led us to dispatch our A/S ships to the reported position of a U-boat, even though the evidence was uncertain and the position was many miles distant. High speed, combined with North Atlantic weather, put a severe strain on engines, hulls and men so that many of our small force became non-operational unnecessarily, the U-boats having more than enough time to lose themselves in the ocean wastes.

Havant *arriving at Dover with troops from Dunkirk on 31 May 1940. The next day she was crippled by bombing and had to be sunk by the minesweeper* Saltash. *Note her shortened funnels and the early Ninth Destroyer Flotilla markings* (*black/white/white*) (*IWM*)

Highlander *passing through a troop convoy in the summer of 1941. The 9th D.F. funnel marking has now become black-white/black/white. At her foremast head is the fixed aerial of the early RDF. The merchant ship carries a PAC anti-aircraft rocket* (*MOD*)

The Gale

Hesperus, who can always highlight any aspect of the Battle, rode out a freak storm of tropical force in company, appropriately, with *Hurricane* in January 1941. The war was forgotten and all efforts concentrated on staying afloat; mountainous breakers towered then crashed on board, carrying with them everything moveable: in *Hurricane*'s case what should have been immovable as well, for the whole of 'B' gundeck, with 'B' gun on it, was lifted upwards and pressed against the bridge. The mass of metal induced 30° of deviation in the magnetic compass, which was all she had to steer by, for the gyro had long since succumbed; and a gaping hole to the messdeck below was exposed. Even Macintyre was reduced to prayer if, at the approach of a mast-high comber, "*Climb you bitch, climb*!" can be so described.

Above: *Toll of the battle. Child survivors from SS* City of Benares *on board* Hurricane (*Courtesy Cdr C. Dickens*)

Left: *Weather damage to* Hurricane *and* Hesperus *in January 1941. The normal maximum elevation of* Hurricane's *'B' gun was 40°* (*Courtesy Cdr C. Dickens*)

Progress: Spring, 1941

Another period in dock therefore followed. Then the new Commander-in-Chief, Admiral Sir Percy Noble, saw clearly, and implemented the essential truth, that the only place in which a submarine was forced to reveal her presence, if she was to accomplish her mission, was near her target; so that, if our escorts were to be concentrated around the convoys, they would stand the greatest chance both of protecting the merchant ships and of sinking U-boats. From this time onwards, the Battle became really purposeful.

An important application of this principle was the formation of Escort Groups which, instead of being merely an administrative unit of the same class of ship, would comprise all types needed for a convoy's escort and remain together for training and operations. For some reason, the Brazilians were not yet absorbed into this organisation and, in March, Macintyre left *Hesperus* to form the 5th Escort Group which he immediately led to glory in the famous 'Three Aces' battle, our first major victory. Prien, Schepke and Kretschmer were all sunk which raised our morale as much as it depressed that of the enemy.

Force 'H'

Macintyre had exchanged ships with his Dartmouth term-mate, A. A. 'Harry' Tait of HMS *Walker*, who had not yet been promoted Commander but who was none-the-less of a fighter and leader for that. Gay and apparently extrovert, one nevertheless senses an underlying unrest: indeed he confessed to one of his officers that he knew he would be killed. A genuine premonition of death is rare, for most of us are illogically convinced that, 'it can't happen to me.' Tait was even more specific, predicting that he would go down with his ship after ramming a U-boat. If this remarkable presentiment affected his will to fight, his reaction was certainly not for the worse.

Fighters to Malta

Hesperus was not yet allowed to engage in the Atlantic Battle but was sent to Gibraltar in the spring of 1941 to join Admiral Somerville's Force 'H' of carriers and heavy ships. She was with him in an operation to fly Hurricanes to Malta from carriers and no doubt her A/S protection was welcome; but since the threat was mainly from the air, she was really more of a liability—Lieutenant David Seely, tongue in cheek, issued rifles to his gun's crew as being more effective than the uncontrolled, low angle 4·7s—and Somerville resolved never to take her on such an operation again.

Sent Home

In late May, Force 'H' hurried into the Atlantic to look for the *Bismarck* but the destroyers could not keep up in the heavy weather and were detached. *Hesperus* was sent home with a convoy and underwent a short refit at Liverpool whence she emerged, still with the 3in gun and without a DCT, but fitted with voice radio, H/F D/F and the early radar with fixed aerial. Although this radar proved less perceptive than the human eye on a dark night, the innovation was a start; it remained only for a few months and was then replaced by the far superior rotating aerial set.

In August she helped escort the Prime Minister in the *Prince of Wales* for his Atlantic Charter meeting with President Roosevelt, but here again the weather was too bad for the destroyers to maintain high speed and the battleship was judged to be safer on her own. On this occassion structural distortion had occurred which necessitated going alongside a repair ship in Iceland to patch up,

Hesperus *in late 1941 after repairing weather damage at Immingham and fitting RDF Warning Combined. She also has her DCT at last but will soon exchange it for RDF Warning Surface. Note: mainmast abaft the searchlight platform to extend the AA gun's field of fire; four depth-charge throwers a side, the forward pair angled aft, giving a 14-charge pattern; 'Charlie Noble' or galley funnel (IWM)*

before proceeding to Immingham for permanent repair. Here at last she was given her DCT.

The U-Boat War at Last

From November 1941 onwards *Hesperus* was properly employed in her destined role, starting with a convoy to Gibraltar and then a spell of A/S patrol in the Straits through which the enemy was sending U-boats to interfere with our North African operations. On the night of 14 December her hand-cranked radar made what must have been one of the first detections of a surfaced U-boat. Lieutenant Duncan Knight, the First Lieutenant, was on watch and gave her a full 14-charge pattern which it seemed could not miss; but she survived despite *Hesperus*'s and her consort's night-long efforts.

The question was asked, should she have rammed? Perhaps Tait's mystical fascination for ramming started then for he evidently thought so and resolved to do it next time and make sure. His chance came with a northbound convoy from Gibraltar.

Convoy HG 78, January 1942

Hesperus was not part of the close escort but, under the orders of Captain R. M. J. Hutton in the destroyer *Laforey*, was acting as striking force in the vicinity. On 14th the Admiralty signalled that a U-Boat had made a sighting report to the westward so the unit took station on that side, patrolling first to the south and then the north. Then, having drawn a blank, Hutton cleverly decided to go south again in the hope that the U-Boat having heard him apparently retire would surface and follow up the convoy.

RDF Contact

At 0110 on the 15th, a fine, calm, moonless night, *Hesperus* was stationed $1\frac{1}{2}$ miles on *Laforey*'s starboard beam when an exactly similar contact was reported bearing 205°, $1\frac{1}{4}$ miles. To complete the coincidence Knight was again on watch and, wasting not a second, rang down for 18kts and turned towards. Almost at once confirmation came

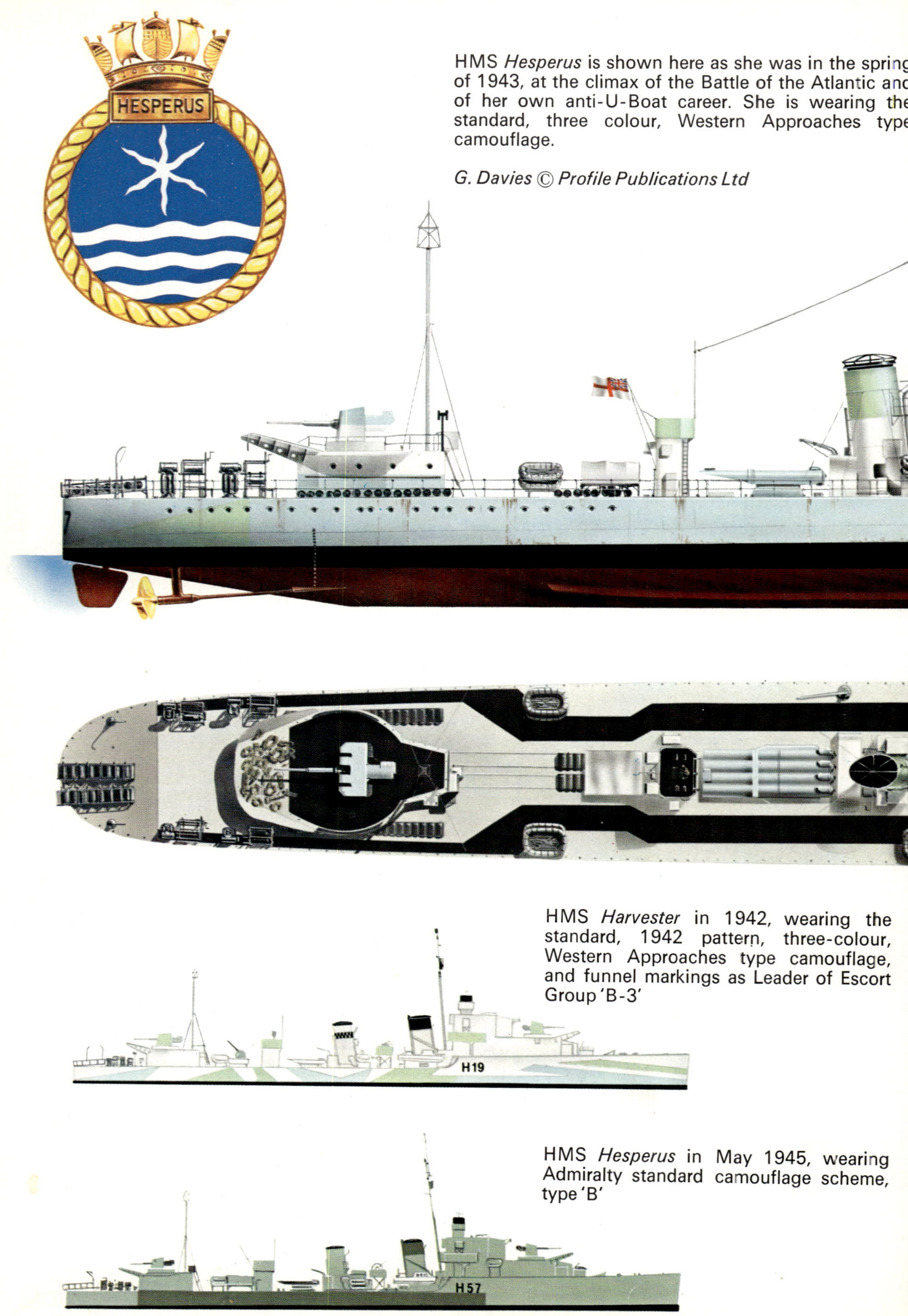

HMS *Hesperus* is shown here as she was in the spring of 1943, at the climax of the Battle of the Atlantic and of her own anti-U-Boat career. She is wearing the standard, three colour, Western Approaches type camouflage.

G. Davies © Profile Publications Ltd

HMS *Harvester* in 1942, wearing the standard, 1942 pattern, three-colour, Western Approaches type camouflage, and funnel markings as Leader of Escort Group 'B-3'

HMS *Hesperus* in May 1945, wearing Admiralty standard camouflage scheme, type 'B'

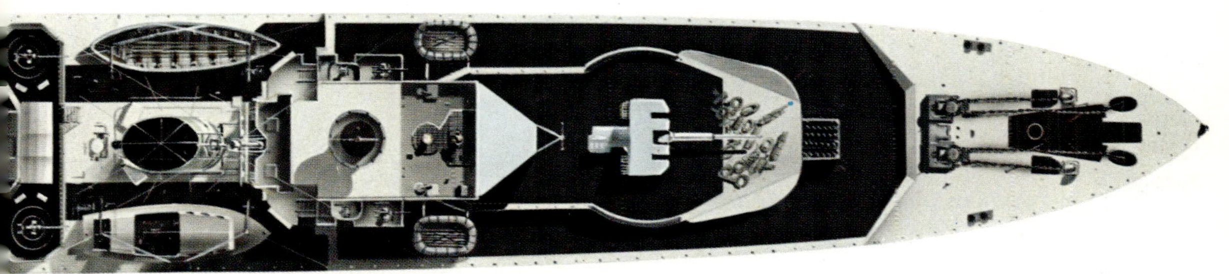

HMS *Havant,* the first of the class, in the winter of 1939/40

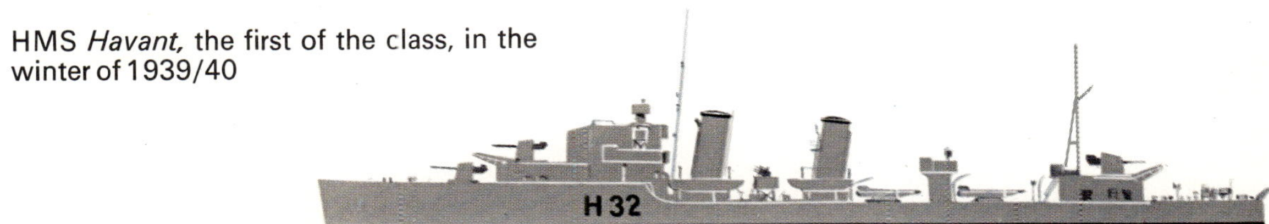

HMS *Hurricane* as she was completed in the summer of 1940, wearing the semi-official, dazzle-type camouflage, and funnel markings of the 9th Destroyer Flotilla

from the asdic and at 0113 a distinct wake was sighted; fire was opened with 'B' gun but unfortunately full-flash cordite was used, although flashless was embarked, and this was blinding so fire was soon checked.

Welcome Aboard

At 0120 the port 10in signalling projector illuminated a U-boat steering away at her full speed of 17kts and Tait, who had taken over, rammed instinctively. Because of the relative positions of the ships, the blow was glancing but the submarine nevertheless heeled violently away. Then, equally fiercely, she catapulted back at which precise moment the top of her conning tower and *Hesperus*'s motor boat came in contact: the U-boat's Captain and First Lieutenant were thrown, or flung, from one to the other.

When the conning tower was abreast the stern, the depth-charge team got away a five-charge pattern set to 50ft in what must have been a scene of wild confusion; the charge of the starboard thrower flew right over the target and one from the trap landed on her casing. As the ship drew ahead, 'X' gun opened fire and when Tait had swung her to starboard, 'A' gun was able to join in; both scored hits, two on the conning tower and one on the pressure hull, and at 0126, only 16mins after first contact, U93 abandoned ship.

Distinguished Service Order

David Seely in the whaler made a determined attempt to board, for the U-boat still seemed in good shape but, pull as the men might, they could not reach her. He discovered later that her Engineer Officer, a brave man but a thoroughly unpleasant, dedicated Nazi, had not only set the demolition charges and opened the seacocks, but left the engines running slowly astern. Forty prisoners were taken and *Hesperus* retired to Gibraltar to lick her honourable wounds. She was flooded from the bow to No 14 frame, the whole of her starboard side was buckled, including the bilge keel, and the tips of her starboard propeller were bent over. After temporary patching, she was sent home with a convoy for permanent repair at Falmouth, but not before Tait and his company had been enthusiastically congratulated and he had been recommended for a DSO. This was the normal reward for a U-boat kill and few would deny that in this case it was truly earned. Knight received the DSC.

To Ram or not to Ram?

Ramming, with which neither Tait nor *Hesperus* were finished, became the subject of official and unofficial controversy never to be wholly satisfactorily resolved. Clearly one could easily lose one's own ship by over-riding a submarine at speed and tearing the bottom out; but perhaps this was a fair exchange? Was there a compromise whereby one reversed engines before impact or would that reduce damage to the enemy to something less than lethal, observing that a pressure hull is very strong, whereas a lightly built destroyer is not? Or would not the very manoeuvrable U-boat wriggle out of trouble if one's speed was low? For the time being each Captain answered these questions in his own way.

After ramming U93 *and subsequently sinking her in January 1942,* Hesperus *enters Gibraltar listing to starboard in consequence of extensive damage. Note: RDF (rotating aerial) with which she detected the U-Boat; DCT, H/F D/F early type, 24in searchlight* (IWM)

Hesperus*'s Captain, Lt-Cdr A. A. 'Harry' Tait, is congratulated by Rear-Admiral Syfret and Captain William-Powlett. He will shortly be promoted and awarded the DSO* (IWM)

The Captain of U93 *leaves* Hesperus *as he joined her, dry shod* (IWM)

Hesperus *(not surprisingly sometimes known as* Heinz*) in April 1942. She has gained the battle-winning equipments, warning surface RDF (in place of the DCT) and H/F D/F improved type. Oerlikons have appeared on the bridge wings but she still has her 3in AA gun and ·5 machine guns* (MOD)

Escort Group B 2

In March 1942, it was decided that the five remaining Brazilians were ideally suited as leaders of escort groups. *Hesperus* was allotted 'B' (for British) 2, and Commander A. F. St G. Orpen appointed in command. Tait, now a commander, unaccountably became Senior Officer of 'B'3, but since his leader was the *Harvester* he remains within the orbit of this Profile.

Hesperus was herself again in early April and the newly formed Group took convoy after convoy across the Atlantic without incident; it was monotonous, rugged work but every merchant ship arrived safely and that, after all, was what the Battle was all about. In June, Orpen was promoted Captain and Macintyre, who was languishing ashore in the responsible but unexciting post of British Representative at the US Naval Base in Newfoundland, begged and was allowed to rejoin his old love.

His team now comprised the destroyers *Vanessa* and *Whitehall,* the corvettes *Campanula, Clematis, Gentian, Heather, Mignonette, Sweetbriar,* and, of course, *Hesperus*. She was an even finer instrument in the hands of her master for, on the back of the bridge in place of the only recently fitted DCT, had appeared the battle-winning SW radar. Her close range anti-aircraft capability had also been improved by two 20mm Oerlikons: not inappropriately, for convoys were occasionally subject to low-flying attacks by long-range, bomber/reconnaissance Condors.

'B-Bar'

The Group continued on the North Atlantic run for the rest of 1942 without a single U-boat approaching within torpedo range, but not for want of trying. Walker was nick-named *'B-Bar'* for the frequency with which he used the expression to report enemy transmissions. Macintyre would send a ship racing down the bearing, to attack the U-boat if possible or, at least, to force her to dive, after which the convoy could evade.

Only one indecisive action took place during this period, but once there were at least four U-boats trying to get at the convoy and all were given the slip. Macintyre used the time to train his ships to a high pitch of efficiency and, particularly in *Hesperus,* a relaxed gaiety was superimposed on the earnest professionalism of the war that was a strength in itself.

They sailed from Newfoundland laden with Christmas presents unobtainable in wartime Britain; in *Hesperus,* every man had a turkey and these were stowed in the fore peak, 'so as to be out of the way.'

'B-Bar—astern—10 to15 miles!' The convoy was past Rockall and about to disperse, when Walker made his report and *Vanessa,* closely followed by *Hesperus,* raced at full speed down the bearing and soon sighted the surfaced U-boat, seven miles distant.

Periscope!

She dived at once and there followed a period of anxiety when the two ships had closed the position, reduced to asdic operating speed and lowered their domes. Were they searching in the right place and would the enemy have a crack at them before they pin-pointed him?

Macintyre was astonished to see a full six feet of periscope rise out of the sea 50 yards on *Hesperus*'s beam and stare malevolently at *Vanessa*. Yelling for full speed, Macintyre turned *away,* so as to swing the stern as close as possible to the U-Boat, and dropped an urgent pattern of shallow charges. It was accurate enough to startle the enemy, save *Vanessa* and force the U-boat to evade at depth.

'Echo Bearing . . . !'

Asdic contact was obtained and deliberate attacks were delivered but, disappointingly, to no avail. *How deep was the target?* There was no way of telling. *Was she too deep for the charges?* While Macintyre pondered, both ships lost contact for a desperate half-hour, possibly misled by *Pillenwerfers;* but it was at moments like these that Macintyre revealed his mastery of the game in looking at the situation as his opponent saw it and heading straight for the right place.

'Stand by to Ram!'

'Contact!'

More attacks but, as before, no apparent results. However, this was not really so and, as Macintyre was still searching his mind for some more effective tactic, *Vanessa* signalled, 'U-boat on surface—am ramming.'

The destroyer struck a glancing blow; in the darkness the U-boat twisted and turned at full speed inside the turning circles of the two destroyers who hurled themselves at her, time and time again. Gunnery

Hesperus *in September 1942 as Leader of Escort Group B-Two. She still has eight throwers giving a 14-charge pattern* (*MOD*)

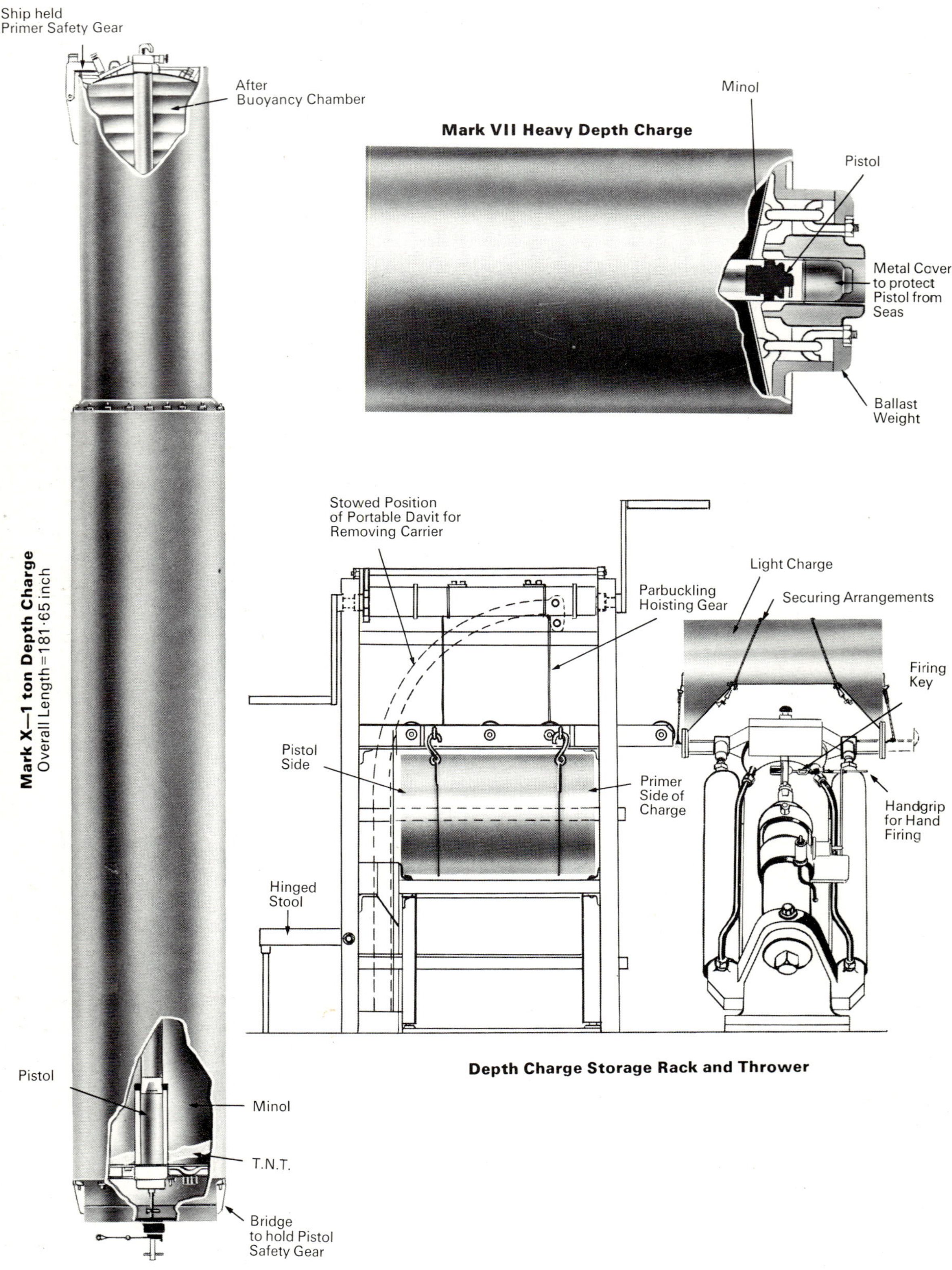

Gordon Davies © Profile Publications Ltd

1 *Mark 7 Heavy Depth Charge. The light charge was the same without the weight. Sinking rates 10ft/sec (light), 16ft/sec (heavy). Maximum depths 500ft (light), 900ft (heavy). Lethal range 25-40ft* (Gordon Davies)

2 *The Mark 4 Depth Charge Thrower and Loading Rack. With this improved system, charges were loaded and fired quicker and more safely as they did not have to be hoisted on swaying davits in a seaway, nor did the carriers have to be replaced each time, being sucked back into the mortar after imparting the necessary impetus. Small sized racks are shown for simplicity;* Hesperus's *were twice this size* (Gordon Davies)

3 *The Mark 10 Depth Charge, as carried in one of* Hesperus's *torpedo tubes in 1943. Depth settings 200, 600, 800ft. The buoyancy chamber slowed the sinking rate to allow the ship to get well clear but in later marks this was reduced to ensure that the charge would reach a deep submarine as quickly as possible. Main charge—1 ton Minol* (Gordon Davies)

became too dangerous at such close quarters and it was Macintyre's skill at ship-handling that finally told. He clawed *Hesperus* round, helmsman and engine-room crew sweating as they obeyed his violent, ever-changing orders. There was the enemy where he wanted him: right ahead and beam on. *U357* disappeared under the flare of the forecastle with 'a deeply satisfying crunch' and sank at once, cut neatly in half. *Hesperus* came to a standstill without vital damage because Macintyre had remembered in the excitement to stop engines before impact.

Crippled

The damage was serious enough, however, and, after the repair team had patched and shored, she managed only 15kts back to the convoy, which congratulated her noisily on their sirens. Then to Liverpool and more honour but alas no turkeys: these had been very much in the way and thoroughly and finally marinaded with sea water and diesel oil.

Docking down revealed an ugly wound, the ship's bottom having been ripped open for nearly a quarter of its length, the ship needing three months away from the Battle to repair. Inevitably the ramming argument was revived and then, while *Hesperus* was still in dock, Harry Tait tragically pursued it to the bitter end.

'HARVESTER'S' LAST FIGHT, MARCH 1943

Not all ships were lucky enough to have a Walker, and a pack of U-boats had been able to close *Harvester*'s convoy and sink four ships before midnight on 10 March. Then she ran down a radar contact, saw the U-boat dive, dropped a pattern, and turned. The submarine, blown to the surface, appeared right ahead and Tait rammed her fair and square, evidently at high speed; the U-boat rolled over, crashed aft under the destroyer and became jammed between her propellers for ten incredible minutes. An internal explosion finally threw her clear and she limped away on the surface, *Harvester* being immobile; however, the Free French corvette, *Aconit*, bustled up at her slower speed and rammed the submarine again, after which a final, shallow pattern put *U444* out of what must have been her truly desperate misery.

Hesperus *entering Liverpool in the last days of 1942 with a crumpled bow, honourably won by ramming and sinking* U357 (IWM)

Hesperus *is honoured by a visit from the Commander-in-Chief Western Approaches, Admiral Sir Max Horton, after sinking* U357. *He is accompanied by Captain 'Johnny' Walker; Commander Donald Macintyre is behind the Admiral; wearing glasses is Lieutenant Harold 'B-Bar' Walker RNVR (subsequently DSC); and Lieutenant the Hon David Seely is at the other end of the line* (IWM)

Harvester, *Commander Tait DSO, in May 1942 as Leader (black top to fore funnel) of Escort Group B-Three (pattern on after funnel). She already has her hedgehog in place of 'A' gun and the later pattern H/F D/F* (MOD)

Destiny?

Harvester's propellers and shafts were so badly buckled that she could only crawl on one engine, nevertheless Tait sent *Aconit* back to the convoy which was still under attack. During the night *Harvester* picked up 50 survivors from merchant ships but finally her remaining shaft fractured under the strain and she stopped, a one and terrifyingly vulnerable.

At daybreak, *Aconit* returned to look for her and was just in time to see her hit by two torpedoes, break in half, catch fire and sink. *Aconit* pressed on undaunted and immediately made contact with the submarine which was blown to the surface by her first pattern. The gallant little Frenchman turned, hitting the U-boat with shell-fire as she did so, rammed yet again and dropped a shallow pattern which finally sank her. She picked up 20 survivors from *U432* but very few from *Harvester:* Tait was not among them.

Ramming was then officially discouraged, though still not forbidden.

CONVOY ONS 4 APRIL 1943

Hesperus returned as good as new to the battle at the height of its crisis. Better indeed, since she now had a hedgehog instead of 'A' gun, a Mark X depth charge, four Mark IV throwers with loading racks, greater depth-charge stowage in place of the 3in gun, foxer against the gnat, and two more oerlikons.

Seventeen U-Boats

By 23 April the westbound convoy had reached mid-Atlantic where Doenitz had exploited our lack of shore-based air cover to achieve many of his devastating successes. This time however the advantage was nullified by a major innovation, the Escort Carrier, and HMS *Biter* was operating in support. Without knowing it, one of her Swordfish forced the first-sighting U-boat to dive and lose contact, but she had reported the convoy and Doenitz vectored a group of 17 U-boats to the attack. *U191* found herself in the convoy's track in daylight and fired four torpedoes which, had they found their marks, would have displeased Macintyre very much. As it was, she surfaced astern to raise the alarm—right into Walker's eager ear.

'Action Hedgehog!'

Away went *Hesperus*, with *Clematis* following, and almost at once they sighted momentarily the U-boat on the horizon before she dived; Macintyre divined her evading course and asdic contact was quickly obtained. Now to try out the hedgehog—conditions were good and it was an unaccustomed luxury to retain contact right until the order, 'Fire!' Alas, it must be recorded that *Hesperus,* like the rest of us, was not perfect; a vital mistake was made in the drill and nothing happened. Then the U-boat went deep.

This U-boat had to be killed or the shame would be intolerable. *Clematis* joined and attacked; then *Hesperus* ran in again, with both a pattern of 10 and a one-ton charge. Strange noises were heard, as the enemy was forced upwards and back to within the compass of the hedgehog. This time there was no mistake; 24 bombs sailed precisely through the air to splash in a perfect ellipse and, after an agony of suspense to the watchers as the projectiles sank, two sharp and final explosions thudded through the ship.

Sea/Air/Sea Co-operation

Walker was soon able to report that no other U-boats were in contact with the convoy whose safety, after *U191's* prompt dispatch, had been greatly enhanced. Two days later *U203* was heard transmitting and this time the information was signalled to *Biter,* one of whose Swordfish quickly sighted the diving U-boat before homing HMS *Pathfinder* (of *Biter*'s screen) to the spot. The submarine was sunk after as neat an example of professional teamwork as could be desired.

The gallant Free French corvette Aconit *after ramming and sinking both* U444 *and* U432 *and doing her best to save* Harvester *in March 1943* (*IWM*)

Crafty

U108, alone, was the last on the scene; in trying to close, she was constantly prevented by the escorts and, equally frustratingly, could not obtain an acknowledgement from any German station for her H/F reports. In fact, the only operator to hear her was Walker and, as she continued to transmit, it was clear that she did not relate her harassment to her breaking of radio silence. But she never could be brought to action, so Walker sought Macintyre's approval to 'pull the teutonic leg.' Knowing German wireless procedure intimately, he answered the U-boat and accepted her message for onward transmission to Headquarters. She then ceased signalling, no wolf pack materialised and the convoy sailed on to Halifax in uninterrupted peace.

CONVOY SC 129, MAY 1943—THE CLIMAX OF THE BATTLE

Massed U-Boats

Macintyre records a gay interlude in Newfoundland where officers and men relaxed, played schoolboy pranks and were serenely content with each other and their ship. On 5 May, the Group sailed for home and into a battlefield, for it was known that U-boats were at sea in unprecedented numbers and that the time to defeat them utterly was at hand. Confidence was high and only perhaps in the most secret recesses of War Headquarters was it fully understood that our ability to continue at war depended upon success being achieved.

Two Merchant Ships Lost

Doenitz too knew that it was now or never. His Intelligence had warned him of SC 129's approach and he disposed Group 'Elbe' of eighteen U-boats to meet it.* On 11 May the convoy passed through

*Warship Profile No. 8: *U107*, page 189

the line and *U402,* directly on track, torpedoed two ships in broad daylight and broke *Hesperus's* proud record of escorting all her charges safely for the first and only time.

The most thorough search was made without result and then of course the convoy was reported. Walker heard more and more U-boats transmitting from astern and Macintyre, vengeance in his heart, stationed *Hesperus* in that quarter for the night battle to come. No one slept.

SW Radar into Action

It started with a very small contact five miles on the quarter and *Hesperus* was quick off the mark as usual; Macintyre himself sighted the white line of the U-boat's wake through Kretschmer's captured binoculars. The water was phosphorescent and the swirl left by the diving submarine was clearly visible, enabling the first, shallow pattern to be dropped by eye on the precise spot.

U223 reeled to the shock with lights out, crew flung to the deck, broken glass everywhere, water spurting in through a dozen distorted glands and diving out of control. Levelling off at 180m, she was met by the next shattering pattern of 10, followed by another with a one-ton charge added.

Macintyre had judged the depth to perfection for the result was cataclysmic: nothing in the boat seemed undamaged—even the handwheels came off control valves and sea water rushed into a darkness made the more terrible by flames leaping from the starboard motor. At 220m, somehow, they held her and Oberleutnant zur See Wächter took the only decision still open to him: to surface if he could.

U223 Fights Back

She came up and lay still, so close ahead of *Hesperus* that the 4·7s would not bear, but the oerlikons swept her casing and prevented her own guns being manned. Then her diesels started and she moved ahead, increasing the range so that, by the light of the signal projectors, *Hesperus's* guns scored several hits. *Surely she was beaten?* But, incredibly, she had not yet begun to fight back. Driven off the bridge by the gunfire, Wächter fired a torpedo and subsequently three more, even trying to ram, until the U-boat was stopped at last.

The submarine lay sullen and still dangerous, Macintyre surveying her with respect. What should he do? Ramming and consequent damage was out of the question, because the convoy was under massive attack and needed every escort. Gently he nudged his bow into her flank and pushed: she rolled on to her beam ends and only sluggishly righted herself, lower in the water. The end *must* have been near and, anxious to hasten it, Macintyre ran out to gun range, only to be narrowly missed by yet another torpedo. This surely was the last fling, for then the crew came on deck and some jumped over the side. Macintyre was satisfied and, concerned for the convoy, left at high speed to rejoin.

Never say Die!

But *U223* was still not finished. Reprieved at the last moment, the indomitable but astonished Wächter rallied his men and, toiling with disciplined

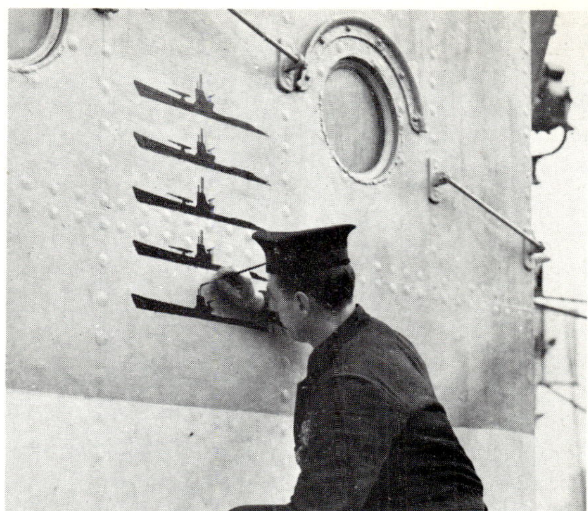

Hesperus's *presumed score at the end of May 1943*—U93, U357, U191, U223, U186. U223 *was not, in fact, sunk but* Hesperus *did complete her five with* U242 *in 1945* (*IWM*)

frenzy, they saved her. In twelve hours she was securely afloat, able to move and to dive to shallow depths; in twelve days she limped into St Nazaire and received a richly deserved commendation from Admiral Doenitz for her gallant fortitude.

Daylight Action

It was certainly time for *Hesperus* to be back with the convoy. At daylight on the 12th, H/F D/F reports showed that at least twelve U-boats were in touch, mostly abaft the beam, and striving to gain bearing for the next night's attack. Suddenly, however, one boat transmitted from close ahead, most ill-advisedly, because Walker was on to her at once. Such was his accuracy that, as soon as *Hesperus* slowed to asdic speed, there was the echo, confirmed seconds later by a sight of the periscope: *U186's* Captain was not in the same class as Wächter and retribution for his inexperience was swift and awful.

Fourth Kill

As before, the first urgent attack was by eye, and equally effective. By the time *Hesperus* had turned, the U-boat was already deep but that did not prevent the next, deliberate, pattern being very accurate. Escaping air and other unusual noises were heard and, after a third and final attack, the pressure hull crushed with an explosion that was felt throughout the ship; indisputable evidence of *Hesperus's* fourth kill then came welling to the surface.

U-Boats Everywhere

All that day the U-boats surrounded the convoy: no fewer than eight were sighted on the surface by the escorts and pinned down, several being severely damaged, though that fact could not be known at the time. At nightfall, Macintyre drastically altered the convoy's course in a bid to evade at least some of the enemy: everyone waited, alert in spite of near exhaustion, for what should have been from past experience a massive assault.

*Commander Donald G. F. W. Macintyre DSO** DSC, Senior Officer Escort Group B-Two and Commanding Officer HMS* Hesperus *on his bridge in May 1943* (*IWM*)

Anti-climax

Nothing happened for hour after hour; then *Whitehall* obtained a radar contact and rushed off, as did *Heather* on the other side of the convoy, but nothing came of either; were they phantoms, or U-boats whose fire had left them? Finally *Hesperus* had her chance against a certain enemy, probably *U107**, whose contact was soon transferred from radar to asdic and subjected to the usual treatment. The first shallow attack sent her deep, so deep that only heavy charges could have reached her, but none of these were left, constant action and high swell having made it impracticable to replenish from the merchant ship carrying stocks. Macintyre turned over the contact to *Clematis* who made two attacks and then lost it, most understandably, being all alone as she was.

Victory

Macintyre would have stayed had he known that the attack was to be the last engagement. The 'Elbe' Group had been beaten by B2 Group's aggressive dash and knew it; the convoy steamed serenely into the dawn and once again *Hesperus* had both typified and contributed to the outcome of the Atlantic Battle. Doenitz himself quoted SC129 as one of the five major convoy defeats which forced his decision to withdraw the U-boats from the North Atlantic on 24 May.

EUROPE INVADED—NARROW WATERS

Hesperus and her Group took convoy after convoy safely across the ocean during summer, autumn and winter. In March 1944 Macintyre left, sadly but with three DSOs, to command another Group and Commander G. V. Legassick DSC, RNVR took over. The same drearily triumphant progress continued, nor did a couple of convoys to Gibraltar provoke any noteworthy opposition.

Then, in the summer, the Allies, secure in their hard won command of the sea and air, deployed their enormous military strength across the Channel and our coastal waters had to be kept clear of U-boats at all costs.

Wreck Problems

Doenitz had prepared his boats to operate in narrow waters by fitting them with Schnorkel, a breathing tube which allowed the diesels to be run submerged and obviated the need ever to surface. The U-Boats soon learnt that the best evasive tactic was to lie on the bottom indistinguishable, except to a highly experienced A/S team, from the thousands of wrecks which litter our shores. They knew better than to transmit unnecessarily and all had gnats.

A great force of A/S aircraft and ships, including *Hesperus,* was allotted to the task of destroying the U-boats but it was still a painstaking, wearisome business which demanded constant alertness and allowed little sleep: every probable wreck had to be minutely investigated in the constant awareness that it might suddenly eject a deadly gnat. Many new techniques were evolved, including the use of the echo-sounder to draw a rough outline of the bottomed object; and a close watch was even kept for conger eels surfacing after an attack, for these made their homes in the crannies of wrecks though not, naturally, in submarines.

Not enough U-Boats

In the autumn, *Hesperus* was transferred to the 19th Escort Group and carried out endless but uneventful patrols which were tactically dull but strategically successful for our armies were unmolested. In January 1945, she joined the 14th—all destroyer—Group as leader, under Commander R. A. Currie DSC, RN. Several times she rushed to assist other Groups in contact with U-boats but she never got a look in; with so many ships in such a small area, each had figuratively to queue for the privilege of closing the enemy.

*Captain F. J. Walker CB DSO***, the greatest U-Boat killer of all, who died of overstrain in July 1944 and was buried at sea from* Hesperus. *The then CO Commander G. V. Legassick DSC RNR, is saluting to the left of the coffin* (*IWM*)

* See Profile No. 8, page 189.

Hesperus *in September 1944 as a fully specialised Anti-Submarine Destroyer; with two 4·7in, four Oerlikons, Hedgehog, four throwers, two traps, Radars, warning surface and warning combined; H/F D/F, four torpedo tubes carrying one Mark X depth charge and three torpedoes, large upper deck depth charge stowage* (MOD)

Hesperus *in September 1944. The H/F D/F mast is tall, straight and uncluttered to keep the aerial clear of hull currents* (MOD)

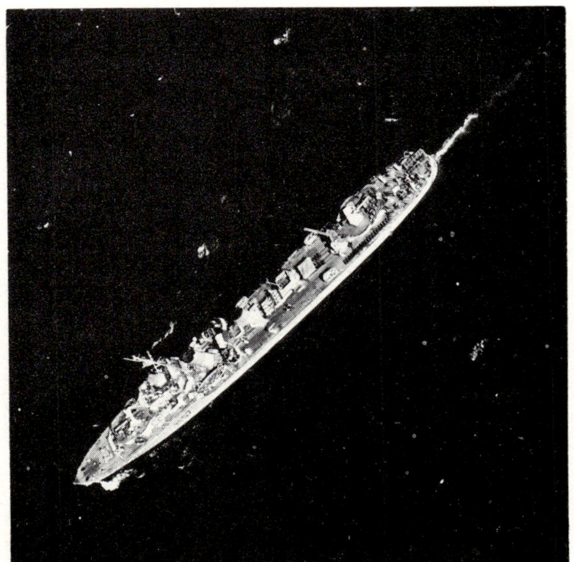

Hesperus *in September 1944. Note thrower loading racks* (MOD)

'HESPERUS'S' LAST U-BOAT

Co-operation with the RAF

Currie, with *Havelock* and *Hotspur** sailed from the Clyde during the morning of 30 April 1945 and immediately intercepted a U-boat report from Coastal Command Sunderland H/201. The aircraft had sighted a possible schnorkel and attacked, but the depth-charges had undershot and the surface was then obscured by an unseasonal snow squall. The first position received was on Mount Snowdon but the error was soon sorted out and the ships hastened to the right spot, northwest of Anglesea, where they reduced to 13kts with unifoxers streamed.

Wreck?

Currie decided to search a small 12 mile square on the assumption that the U-boat (if the contact was one and he was far from convinced) had bottomed. He was right, but wreck after misleading wreck had to be probed before a submarine-sized echo was

* British 'H' Class

Hesperus *at the end of the war as Leader of the 14th Escort Group* (*IWM*)

U-Boats at Lisahally, Co Londonderry. Hesperus *brought in the first eight to surrender ceremonially to the Commander-in-Chief on 14 May 1945* (*IWM*)

returned, slightly more promising than the rest. Two hedgehog attacks were delivered, probably very accurately, since the target was stopped and its exact depth known. There was no evidence of a hit because all the bombs exploded either on the bottom or on the target: a hit from one, though powerful enough to sink a submarine, might well not open her up enough to allow anything to escape.

U242

No eels appeared, however, and then an echo-sounder run produced an outline very like a submarine which encouraged the still sceptical though persistent Currie. *Hesperus* and *Havelock* made six more hedgehog attacks, followed by two with depth charges whose heavier explosions at last had the desired effect: air bubbles, oil and wreckage spouted to the surface and a German food tin marked with the date of filling, July 1944, was conclusive.

ENVOI

On 4 May, Doenitz ordered the U-boats to cease hostilities. The symbolic end of the Battle of the Atlantic came on 14th when eight were escorted up the River Foyle by a large group of allied warships, led proudly and fittingly by *Hesperus,* to make their surrender to the Commander-in-Chief in person.

Back to Norway

Her last operational task was to escort the exiled Norwegian Government home to Oslo, where she was given a triumphant reception. Hungry boys swarmed over the ship devouring the sailors' rations; and in the wardroom an old English lady drank her first tea for five years, from 1430 until 1830 without intermission. Was this anti-climax or did it symbolise what the war, and *Hesperus*'s part in it, was largely about: freedom and tea?

Ready, Aye, Ready?

A front-line warrior all her short life, *Hesperus* was spared the indignity of a lingering old age and she was sold for scrapping in December 1945; her ensign may still be seen in Yeovil Parish Church. She did us proud, and was certainly an excellent example of our national gift for improvisation; but she also typified our near-fatal unawareness of the vital importance of merchant shipping in war.

Why did we not have escorts designed for the task? And now, in 1972, do we have the proper, up-to-date weapons systems for it, and in sufficient numbers, against a threat on a scale the Germans never approached?

We have not.

When will we ever learn?

U-boat surrendering at Scapa

Above: *U-boats surrendered in Lisahally*

Below: *Surrendered U-boat crews, drying out*

THE 'H' CLASS (EX-BRAZILIAN) ESCORT DESTROYERS

War Complement: 7 officers. 145 men
Dimensions: 323(oa) 33 $12\frac{1}{2}$(dl)ft
Displacement: 1350(st), 1860(dl) tons
Boilers: 3-three drum, water tube, with superheaters
Engines: 2-shaft geared turbines
S.H.P.: 34,000=$31\frac{1}{2}$ knots (dl)
Fuel: 439 tons=5000/1200 miles at 14/30 knots

	1940	**1945**
Guns:	3-4·7in, 45cal semi-automatic, low angle 2-quad 0·5in M/Gs, anti-aircraft	2-4·7in with 2-2in illuminating rocket launchers on 'B' gunshield 4-20mm Oerlikon AA
Torpedo Tubes:	2-quad 21in	1-quad 21in
A/S Weapons:	8-Depth charge Throwers 3-Depth charge traps	4-Throwers, 2-Traps, 1-Mk X(1 ton) depth charge. Hedgehog Increased depth-charge stowage
Asdic:	Yes	Yes, improved type
Radar:	None	Warning Surface Warning Combined
H/F D/F:	Early type	Improved type
M/F D/F:	Yes	Yes
Radio:	W/T only, up to H/F	W/T and Voice, up to VH/F
Searchlights:	1-24in	2-20in Signalling Projectors

THE SHIPS

Name	**Builder**	**Leader of Escort Group, 1942/3**	**U-Boat Score**	**Fate**
Harvester (ex-*Handy*, ex-*Jurua*)	Vickers	B-Three	2-sunk, 2-damaged	Sunk by *U 432* 11/3/43
Havant (ex-*Javary*)	White			Sunk by bombing and own forces off Dunkirk 1/6/40
Havelock (ex-*Jutahy*)	White	B-Five	2-sunk, 5-damaged	Scrapped 1946
Hesperus (ex-*Hearty*, ex-*Juruena*)	Thornycroft	B-Two	5-sunk, 2-damaged	Scrapped 1946
Highlander (ex-*Jaguaribe*)	Thornycroft	B-Four	1-sunk, 1-damaged	Scrapped 1946
Hurricane (ex-*Japarua*)	Vickers	B-One	1-damaged	Sunk by *U 305* Christmas Eve 1943

Bibliography

U-Boat Killer (*Weidenfeld & Nicholson*) Donald Macintyre
The Battle of the Atlantic (*Batsford*) Donald Macintyre
The War at Sea (*HMSO*) S. W. Roskill
Admiral Doenitz Memoirs (*Weidenfeld & Nicholson*) Admiral Doenitz
Janes Fighting Ships (*Sampson Low, Marston*)
Warships of World War II (*Ian Allan*) Lenton & Colledge
The British Destroyer (*Putnam*) T. D. Manning
British Destroyers (*Seeley, Service*) Edgar J. March
Chronik des Seekrieges Dr Jürgen Rohwer

Warship Series Editor: John Wingate, DSC

Acknowledgements

While picking peoples' brains in order to put this short history together, I have stumbled on the previously unsuspected truth that those whose interest is in ships are invariably charming. I am immensely grateful to: Captain Donald Macintyre DSO**, DSC, Rear Admiral R. A. Currie, CB, DSC*, Lord Mottistone (Formerly Lt. David Seely) Anthony Preston Esq. (National Maritime Museum) Martin Brice Esq. (Imperial War Museum) J. D. Lawson Esq. (Naval Historical Section) Dr Jürgen Rohwer (Director, Bibliothek für Zeitgeschichte, Stuttgart) Alan Raven Esq. Miss M. E. Joll (Ship Dept. MOD) Captain Stuart Farquharson-Roberts OBE and Lt-Cdr Jack Calam (HMS Vernon) Captain Douglas Poynter (Director of Naval Signals) Mrs M. Esson (Admiralty Surface Weapons Establishment) John Wingate Esq. DSC. Gordon Davies Esq. The Naval and MOD Libraries Commodore Duncan Knight, DSC

Tennessee *from the port quarter. She had this general configuration from commissioning in 1922 until the attack on Pearl Harbor. The three aircraft shown are Curtiss SOC-3 scout-observation types. Circa 1938* *(Photo: US Navy)*

USS Tennessee (BB 43)

Battleship 1920-1959

by William H. Cracknell, Commander, USN

The Battleship in the US Navy

The US Navy from its beginning to modern times developed a number of innovations and designs that contributed to the evolution of the battleship—culminating in World War II when the ultimate designs of this type of warship appeared. These firsts included: the steam warship, the unique USS *Fulton* of 1815; the screw propelled warship, Ericsson's USS *Princeton* of 1843; the power-driven turret on the revolutionary USS *Monitor* of 1862*, the superimposed-centerlined turret arrangement on USS *Michigan* of 1910.

The US Navy entered the 'modern' battleship era in 1895 with the commissioning of USS *Texas* and USS *Maine*. It was the USS *Indiana* (BB-1), also commissioned in 1895, that is considered the first true battleship in the USN. At the beginning of the twentieth century several factors influenced the growth of the US Navy changing it from a relatively small coast defence force to a world-girdling multi-ocean navy.

In 1898, as a result of the Spanish-American War, the United States found itself the holder of a number of distant possessions, and there was an immediate need to protect the long lines of communications to these territories. The Navy had won total victory in all its engagements with the Spanish during the War and was riding a crest of immense popularity with the American people. The internal frontiers in the United States had been all but overcome and slowly the country turned its focus outward. The major European powers were just starting their great naval build-ups that were to challenge the almost 100 years of 'Pax Britannica.' Lastly, there came to the presidency in 1901, the aggressive and naval-orientated 'Teddy' Roosevelt (of 'Talk softly and carry a big stick' fame). All of these factors contributed to the accelerated naval expansion program which the United States pursued up through the end of World War I.

From the commissioning of USS *Indiana* (BB-1) through the commissioning of USS *Wisconsin* (BB-64) in 1944, the United States would build 57 battleships (seven BBs were cancelled after the end of World War I and an additional seven were cancelled prior to the end of World War II). The last authorised battleship in the US Navy was USS *Louisiana* (BB-71) of the stillborn *Montana* Class. USS *Tennessee* was commissioned approximately halfway through this period. She was one of the last of the pre-Washington Conference battleships and almost 20 years would pass before the United States would commission another battleship. But the Dreadnoughts built during and immediately after World War I would prove just as useful to the United States in World War II as the super Dreadnoughts built 20 years later.

* Civil War Monitor USS *Tecumseh* will be the subject of a future Profile.

Tennessee immediately after commissioning 10 August 1921. Note main battery directors, forward on top of bridge and aft on turret III. No aircraft were carried until 1924 (Photo: US Navy)

Battleship Names

From the outset, battleships in the US Navy have been named after the states of the Union (except USS *Kearsarge*). Down through the years this has brought a number of fringe benefits to the ships. The respective states furnished their ship namesakes with recruits, silver service, etc. It was from 1920 that ships in the US Navy received letter designations as well as numbers, such as BB for battleships, DD for destroyers, SS for submarines and so on.

Except for a short period from April 1968 to December 1969, when USS *New Jersey* was reactivated to give gunfire support in the Vietnam War, the battleship era for the US Navy ended on 8 March 1958 when the USS *Wisconsin* was decommissioned. The four BBs of the large *Iowa*-class (*Iowa, New Jersey, Missouri and Wisconsin*) are still held 'mothballed' in the Reserve Fleet and USS *Texas* (BB-35), USS *North Carolina* (BB-55), USS *Massachusetts* (BB-59), and USS *Alabama* (BB-60) were turned over to their respective states to be preserved as memorials. These eight ships are the last examples of what really was a philosophy of naval power for a period of more than four decades.

Since no battleships are now active in the US Navy it has been decided that future nuclear powered frigates will be named for states. USS *South Carolina* (DLGN-37) and USS *California* (DLGN-36) are now being built. As an interesting aside the turbines from the USS *Kentucky* (BB-66), (stricken after being three-quarters completed) were installed in the Fast Combat Support Ship USS *Sacramento* (AOE-1). This 53000-ton ship is designed to steam with a fast carrier force providing underway replenishment of aviation fuel, black oil, ammunition and general supplies.

Naval ships named Tennessee

1. Confederate side wheel steamer captured by Union forces 25 April 1862, commissioned in the USN and later renamed USS *Mobile*; sold 30 March 1865. 1275 tons, 210ft×33ft×19ft, two 32-pounder Parrott rifle, one 12-pounder rifle.
2. Confederate ironclad captured by Union forces in the Battle of Mobile Bay 5 August 1864, commissioned in the USN and scrapped in 1867. 1273 tons, 209ft×48ft×14ft, complement 133, armour 25in of wood and 5-6in of iron, two 7in and four 6in Brooke rifles.
3. First-rate frigate launched 8 July 1865 (originally named USS *Madawaska*)—in 1879 was the largest ship in the USN. Sold 15 September 1886. Cost $1,673,079, 4840 tons, 355ft×45ft×21ft, complement 480, speed 13·9kts, two 8in pivot rifles, two 100-pounder rifles, one 60-pounder rifle and eighteen 9in smooth bores.
4. Armoured Cruiser commissioned 17 July 1906. Name changed to USS *Memphis* and driven ashore during storm in 1917. 14,500 tons, 502ft×72ft×25ft, speed 22kts, four 10in rifles, sixteen 6in rapid fire and twenty-two 3in rapid fire.

USS TENNESSEE (BB-43)

Congressional Act of 3 March 1915, "... The President is hereby authorised to have constructed two first-class battleships carrying as heavy armor and as powerful armament as any vessel of their class, to have the highest practicable speed and greatest desirable radius of action, and the cost, exclusive of armor and armament, not to exceed $7,800,000 each ..."

This was the authorisation that lead to the construction of the two *Tennessee*-class battleships, USS *Tennessee* and USS *California*. *Tennessee* was named for the sixteenth state of the Union which was also one of the Confederate States during the Civil War. In basic design these ships were practically identical to the three ships in the earlier *New Mexico* class. The main differences were enlarged bridges and fire control tops, increased elevation of the main batteries and the elimination of secondary battery recesses in the hull (secondary battery removed to upper decks).

The keel for *Tennessee* was laid at the New York

Tennessee under construction at New York Naval Shipyard, Brooklyn, New York, 1 October 1918. In this view looking forward the shell plating can be seen rising in the stern area; the cylinders are the armored barbettes of the main battery: and forward of the second barbette, the slanting, side structures are the armored stack uptakes (Photo: US Navy)

One of Tennessee's *two main turbines on the test floor prior to installation. The turbines turned electro-generators which furnished the current to drive four electric motors, one turning each shaft* (Photo: US Navy)

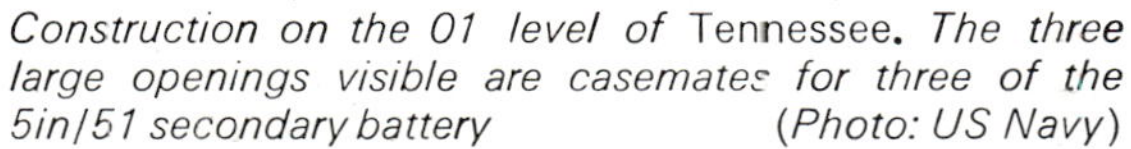

Construction on the 01 level of Tennessee. *The three large openings visible are casemates for three of the 5in/51 secondary battery* (Photo: US Navy)

One of Tennessee's *boat cranes. Sitting on the deck beyond is one of the 5in/51 secondary battery and behind that is a 3in anti-aircraft gun* (Photo: US Navy)

Tennessee *completing after launching at Brooklyn. Outline of armor belt can be seen below the lower line of ports. Battleship in background is probably* Nevada *(BB-36)* *(Photo: US Navy)*

Tennessee*'s flag locker aft 12 October 1920. There was storage furnished for 150 signal flags. The canvas covered objects around the mainmast are searchlights* *(Photo: US Navy)*

Control tower, bridge, forward main battery director and foremast on Tennessee, *12 October 1920. The three level observation and fire control tops on the foremast were first used by the US Navy on* Tennessee *(Photo: US Navy)*

Navy Yard, Brooklyn, New York 14 May 1917. She was launched 30 April 1919 being christened by Miss Helen Lenore Roberts, daughter of the Governor of Tennessee. The ship was commissioned 3 June 1920 with Captain Richard H. Leigh, USN, commanding. *California* followed closely behind, built at Mare Island Navy Yard, Vallejo, California with keel laid 25 October 1916, launched 20 November 1919, commissioned 10 August 1921. *California* was outfitted as a flagship.

Hull

The hull dimensions were: Length 624·5ft (600ft between perpendiculars), extreme beam 97ft 3in, mean draft 30ft 3in and normal displacement 32,300 tons. She had an extreme clipper bow and a somewhat pointed stern. A balanced rudder of approximately 200 square feet was hung at the extreme end of the center line, aft of the four screws.

The watertight integrity of the hull was of a most sophisticated design. The whole of the bilge area was of double bottom construction. From the turn of the bilge, which was girdled with a torpedo bulkhead, up to the main deck and running the whole length of the ship from the forward peak tank to the after peak tank there was built a system of multiple void compartments. In the vital center two-thirds of the ship, below the waterline, there were five rows of voids totalling 16ft of space between the outer shell plating and the inner shell; above the waterline there were two rows of voids approximately 10ft wide between the inner and outer sides. These voids were divided into many watertight compartments and many were used to store oil or fresh water.

Within the inner sides, the ship was also divided by a minimum of two (in some areas more) longitudinal watertight bulkheads running practically the full length of the ship (including the engineering spaces) and from the inner bottom to the main deck. Transverse watertight bulkheads bisected the longitudinals at irregular intervals the whole length of the hull, again extending from inner bottom up to the main deck.

The result of this extensive watertight compartmentation was a hull that contained an inner bottom with 40 watertight spaces plus approximately 768 watertight spaces in the area below the waterline and approximately 180 of the same in the area above the waterline.

Engineering

The *Tennessee*-class was equipped with turbo-electric drive. The only other battleships so equipped in the US Navy were the earlier *New Mexico* and the later three ships of the *Colorado*-class. The arrangement had eight boilers powering two turbo-electric generators (turbines) which in turn furnished electrical power to four motors turning four, three-bladed, 14ft diameter propellers. There were several advantages to turbo-electric drive. Because the motors could be placed well aft of the boilers and the turbines, the propeller shafts were shorter. This meant the shafts were less vulnerable, easier to maintain and the shorter shaft alleys contributed to watertight integrity. Because power was transmitted through an electric motor, full power reverse was possible by reversing the polarity of the motor.

Each of the eight Babcock & Wilcox, superheated, forced-draught boilers was located in a watertight fireroom. The two Westinghouse turbines were located on the centerline, each in a separate watertight engine room. Boilers #1, #2, #3, and #4 powered the forward turbine and boilers #5, #6, #7 and #8 powered the after turbine. The boilers were located outboard of their respective turbine, the odd number firerooms on the starboard side and the even number firerooms on the port.

The turbo-electric generators produced 3400 volts at 2130rpm. This electric power was fed aft to four Westinghouse 3400 volt alternating current electric motors which could produce 26,800shp capable of propelling *Tennessee* at better than 21kts. Two motors were located in the center motor room and one each in the port and starboard motor room.

The total weight of this machinery was estimated to be 2045 tons.

Superstructure

The *Tennessee*-class had the traditional cage masts installed on US battleships of the World War I era, but the tops had a more massive appearance than the previous classes because of the three-level control and observation structure that capped both the fore and mainmasts. Height was necessary to extend the visible horizon for look-out and fire spotting purposes. To gain height and to minimise topside weight the lattice construction was used, this being relatively light yet strong. Both masts carried a large yardarm and the mainmast was topped with a tall spar mast with crosstree.

Between the masts were two tall, relatively slim funnels. On each side of the fore stack was a boat crane. Four 3ft-diameter searchlights were located on platforms around the after funnel; an additional four searchlights were positioned halfway up the mainmast.

The 01 deck was the weather deck back to just forward of the mainmast; from there aft the main deck was the weather deck. A great portion of the covered main deck forward was crew berthing space.

Although not originally designed for aircraft, in 1928 *Tennessee* was fitted with a catapult and light aircraft crane on the fantail and two observation aircraft could be carried, one on the catapult and one on a cradle. In the early 1930s, an additional catapult was installed on top of turret III making provision for a third aircraft. At this time, a larger aircraft crane was added to the fantail and another one installed on the starboard side next to the mainmast. *Tennessee* would carry this aircraft fit, through her repair after Pearl Harbor. When she was completely rebuilt in 1943 her aircraft installation reverted to one catapult and two aircraft on the fantail.

Although originally planned to convert her to tripod masts in 1940-41, this was deferred and *Tennessee* kept this basic configuration until she was damaged during the Japanese attack on Pearl Harbor. After emergency repairs she steamed to Puget Sound Navy Yard, Bremerton, Washington and went through a quick overhaul and repairs, during which time her cage mainmast was removed.

From September 1942 to May 1943 *Tennessee* underwent a complete rebuild. Included in this reconstruction was practically a new superstructure (*California* was given the same treatment). The result was a ship that had the pyramid appearance of a modern battleship resembling the new *South Dakota*-class in silhouette. Although the main battery was kept intact, the cage mast and slim stacks were removed. In their place was a massive bridge and control spaces topped with a short armored fire control tower and a stick foremast. To the rear of this and almost an integral part was a massive single funnel. Behind the funnel was a short stick mainmast mounted on a small armored fire control tower and aft and slightly below was a secondary battery director.

Completely new and extensive secondary and anti-aircraft batteries were installed along with a multiplicity of radar antennas. These included surface search, air search, height finders, and fire control radars for the main, secondary and anti-aircraft batteries.

Armor

In true Dreadnought fashion, *Tennessee* had all her vital spaces well shrouded with armor plate. An armor belt 14in thick, averaging 18ft in height (approximately half above and half below the waterline) stretched down both sides of the ship from forward of the Number 1 barbette to aft of the Number IV barbette. This armor belt was layed on the shell plating in 10ft-long plates which were secured to each other by keys and keyways. One bolt was used for every five square feet of armor surface, (see diagram for method of securing armor).

An 8in thick armour belt about 12ft in height (most of this below the waterline) extended aft from the main belt to just short of the stern, protecting the steering-gear room. Athwartship armored bulkheads 14in thick ran between the ends of the port and starboard belts.

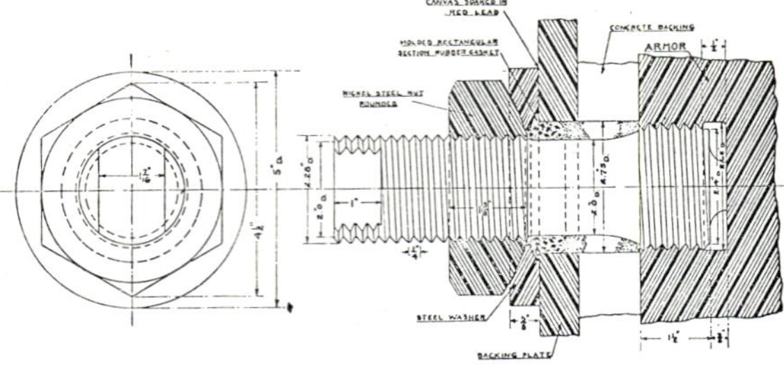

Method of securing armor

Fourteen-inch shells in one of Tennessee's *ammunition handling rooms, 30 August 1920* *(Photo: US Navy)*

Tennessee's *forward main battery, 14in/50 guns, during construction 30 August 1920. Gun bucklers are leather* *(Photo: US Navy)*

The upper armor deck of 3½in was the second deck, which capped the top of the belt armor. The lower armor deck of 2½in was the third deck (waterline). Where the lower armor deck extended aft beyond the upper armor deck and over the steering gear room, it was 5in thick. A 3in armor deck-end extended forward on the first platform deck from the forward athwartships armored bulkhead.

The funnel uptakes were surrounded with armor varying from 9 to 15in in thickness.

When *Tennessee* received her major rebuild in 1942-43 her extreme beam was extended from 97·5ft to 114ft ⅛in to increase stability and to provide space for the new 5in secondary guns and their handling rooms. This also provided two additional lines of protective void spaces from the waterline down. Essentially the same armor belt arrangement, removed from the original sides, was hung on these side blisters. Additional splinter shields were also added at this time around the anti-aircraft guns, bridge and directors.

Main Battery Armor

The barbettes extended from the first platform deck and, from the third deck up, were encased in 13in armor. The turret armor varied from 9 to 18in, the latter being on the face of the turret. Turret armor was supported against impact with a teak wood backing.

The control tower and control tower tube just forward of the bridge was enclosed in 16in armor.

ARMAMENT

Main Battery

The *Tennessee*-class was the last to be built with a 14in main battery; all succeeding battleship classes in the US Navy carried 16in guns. *Tennessee* carried twelve 14in 50 caliber (diameter×caliber=barrel length) Mk IV guns in four turrets on the center line. All four turrets were identical assemblies (see diagram for details) placed on protective cylindrical barbettes. The only difference in the barbettes was that number II and III were higher to support their turrets in the superimposed position above turrets I and IV.

One of Tennessee's *5in/51 guns in its casemate 30 August 1920, starboard side looking aft. Shutters for the gun port are secured to the bulkhead just forward of the gun* *(Photo: US Navy)*

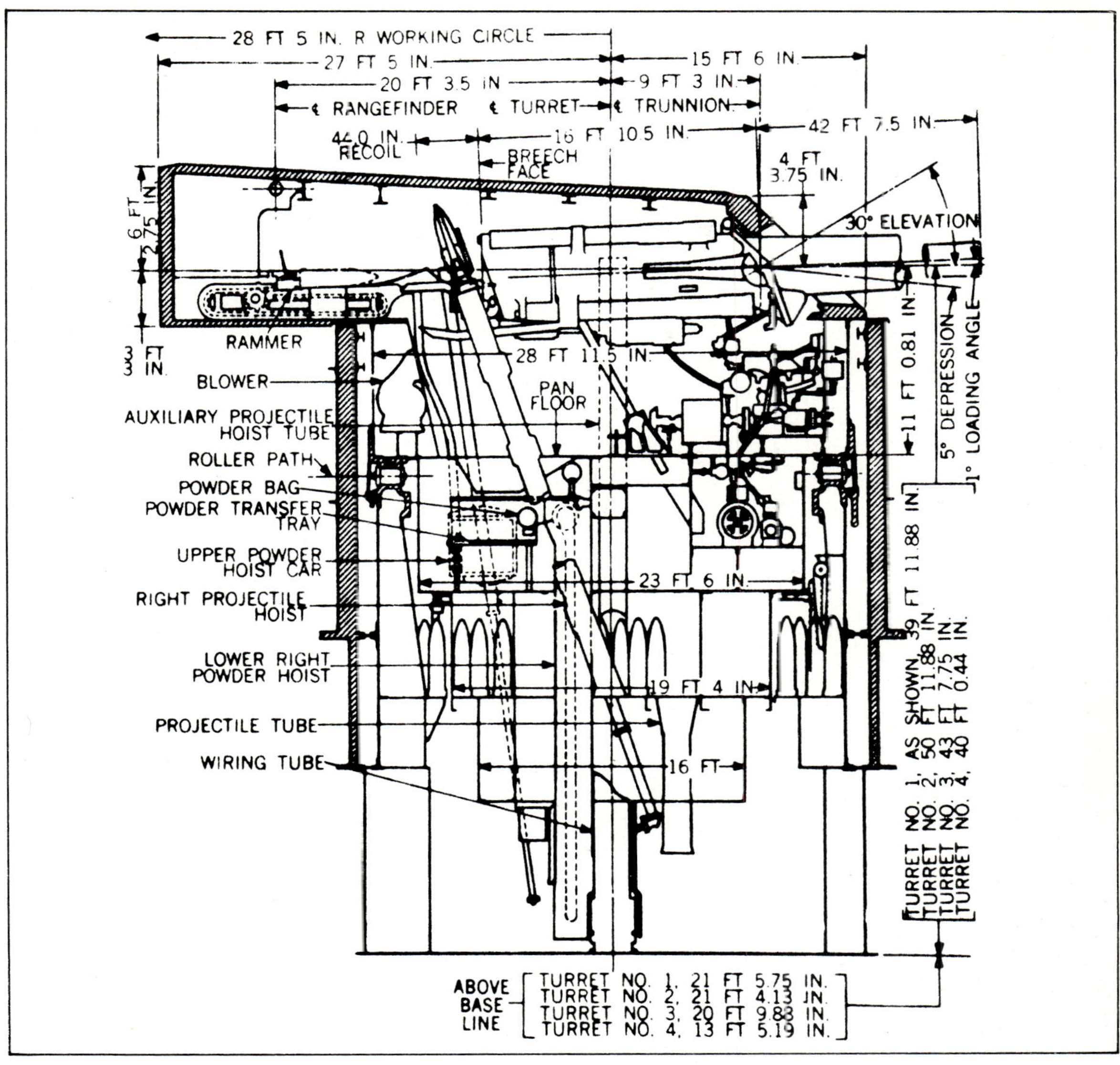

14-INCH GUN MARK II MOD O 50 CALIBER

The 14-inch Gun Mk II Mod O was a 50-caliber bag ammunition gun designed for use in 14-inch 3-gun turrets on battleships. It was a built-up gun consisting of a tube, jacket, liner, three hoops, two locking rings, and a screw-box liner which has a flange four inches thick and 48 inches in diameter. The gun was constructed of nickel steel and gun steel. It was mounted in the turret by means of a yoke and slide. The yoke stop was located 42·50in from the face of the breech. The slide surface started 120in from the breech, had a diameter of 44in, and was 132in long, with one key set in on top of the gun. The bore was chromium plated for a distance of 613·0in from the muzzle. The 14in Breech Mechanism Mk 4 Mod 5, used with this gun, was of the down-swing carrier type with a Welin breech plug, De Bange gas check system, and Smith-Asbury operating mechanism.

The 14in Gun Mk II Mod O is the 14in Gun Mk 4 Mod 8, Mk C Mod O, or Mk 7 Mod O relined, having an alloy-steel liner with a small chamber, shell centering cone, single slope band seat, uniform twist rifling, a chromium plated bore, and a tube locking ring.

Tabular data

Gun Dimensions	
Length	714·0in
Diameter over chamber	48·0in
Weights	
Gun	176,089lb
Gun with breech mechanism	178,263lb
Turret rotating weight without projectiles	958 long tons
Oscillating weight	244,000lb per gun
Recoil weight	291,000lb per gun
Brake load	780,000lb per gun
Trunnion pressure at 30° elevation fire	825,000lb per gun

Rifling	
Twist	Right hand, uniform, 1 turn in 25 calibers
Length	607·358in
Plating	Chromium
Thickness	0·0005in
Length	613·0in (measured from muzzle)
Ammunition	
Type	Bag
Classification	Ap Service, HC Service, T Target
Ballistics	
Volume of powder chamber	16,982cu in
*Muzzle velocity	2700fps
Maximum powder pressure	18 long tons per sq in
†Maximum range of 45° elevation	42,585yd

*Measured with 420lb charge and 1500lb projectile.
†Measured with a 1275lb projectile at 2825fps muzzle velocity.

The rotating structure of the turret and all ordnance components were supported on a carriage located below the pan floor; thus the machinery floor, projectile handling levels and powder handling floor were suspended from the carriage and structure above and all rotated with the turret.

The turret was further subdivided into separate flameproof compartments for the three guns, extending to the pan floor, the two sight stations and the rangefinder station.

Each gun had an interrupted screw, down-swing breech. Separate slide, rammer, powder hoist, and projectile hoist serviced each gun. The turret moved in train by a power driven training gear. Each gun had its own elevating gear. Both train and elevation drives were electric-hydraulic and could be controlled remotely, locally or even cranked by hand.

Tennessee *with guns in turret I rippled. Extensive radio antennas can barely be seen in this view. Circa early 1920s* *(Photo: US Navy)*

Tennessee *at San Pedro, California October 1922. The marking on turrets II and III were bearing marks by which the ships ahead and behind in the battle line could determine on which relative bearing the main battery was training. The black strip at the waterline is the 14in-thick armor belt* *(Photo: US Navy)*

Pilot house of Tennessee *12 October 1920, showing shaft revolution counters and telegraph. Binnacle is in shadows on left* *(Photo: US Navy)*

The limits of elevation were minus 5° to plus 30°; in train turrets I and IV could be rotated through 290° and turrets II and III through 280°. The maximum range of the 1500lb armor-piercing projectile was 35,100yd through a maximum altitude of 18,744ft—muzzle velocity 2,625ft/sec. The maximum range of the 1275lb high capacity projectile was 36,650yd through a maximum altitude of 20,500ft—muzzle velocity 2,825ft/sec.

The sight equipment on each turret was a duplicate arrangement, with right and left pointer's and trainer's gun sights and sight setter's instruments.

Secondary Battery

The *Tennessee*-class was the first US battleship built that had no gun ports on the main deck or below. As originally built *Tennessee*'s secondary battery consisted of fourteen single 5in/51 caliber Mk IV mounts. Ten of these mounts were enclosed casement type gun ports on the 01 deck, five to a side. These were arranged in a staggered fashion allowing six of the guns to fire directly forward and four directly aft. The arc of fire of these guns was restricted to approximately 135°. The remaining four 5in guns were open mounts located on the 02 deck, one on each side of the control tower and one on each side between the funnels. However, in 1922 the latter two guns were removed to make room for additional 3in anti-aircraft guns.

Secondary Battery: 1942

During her quick repairs and modernisation after her damage at Pearl Harbor *Tennessee* had the two 5in/5l cal guns removed from the 02 deck.

Secondary Battery: Post 1942

The major rebuild that *Tennessee* experienced from September 1942 to May 1943 gave her a completely new and more powerful suit of secondary armament. This consisted of sixteen 5in/38 cal guns in eight twin mounts, four to a side in the amidships area, with the forward and aft mounts located on the 01 deck and the four center mounts on the 02 level. The 5in/38 rapid fire, dual-purpose gun was one of the most widespread naval weapons used in the US Navy in World War II and is still widely used in the fleet today.

The 5in/38 used semi-fixed (projectile separate from powder case for ease of handling) ammunition consisting of a 54-pound projectile (weight varied somewhat with type of projectile) and a 28-pound powder case containing 15 pounds of powder. With a muzzle velocity of 2600 ft/sec, maximum horizontal range was 18,000yd and maximum vertical range was 37,300ft. An experienced crew could maintain a 15 round per minute per gun rate of fire for long periods.

The gun had a maximum depression of —15°, a maximum elevation of 85° and each mount could be trained through 360° but on *Tennessee*, because of restrictions incurred by the superstructure, the mounts had an effective radius of approximately 180°.

For a more detailed description of this gun see *Profile* No 9, USS *Charles Ausburne*—although a single mount version is therein depicted the same general characteristics apply to the double mount. Also included is additional information on the 40mm and 20mm guns.

Anti-aircraft Battery: Pre-1942

Originally *Tennessee* had four 3in Mk III anti-aircraft guns installed on the 02 deck, one each just forward of the two boat cranes and one each side of the mainmast. In 1922 four additional 3in anti-aircraft guns were installed on the 02 deck, one each behind the two forward 5in mounts and one each in place of the two after 5in mounts.

Tennessee *takes on a new draft of men dressed in 'undress blues'. Port side tubes of the individual turret range finders on turrets III and IV are visible* (Photo: US Navy)

In 1928 these eight 3in guns were replaced by eight 5in/25cal open mount anti-aircraft guns. These guns could elevate to 85°.

About 1940 two 3in/50cal open mounts were installed in tubs on the forward superstructure on each side just below the bridge wings. These were removed during the rebuild in 1942-43.

About 1935 splinter-shielded platforms were added to the roof of the middle level of the tops of both the foremast and the mainmast. Two 50 caliber machine guns, one forward and one aft, were installed on these platforms in the foretop and four 50 calibers installed, two on each side, on the platforms in the maintop. Two 50 calibers were also added on pedestals, one each side of the foremast.

Anti-aircraft Battery: 1942

During repairs at Bremerton after Pearl Harbor the eight 5in/25s had semi-enclosed splinter shields added. In addition fourteen single 20mm Oerlikon machine guns and four quad 1·1in caliber machine guns, nicknamed 'Chicago Pianos' or 'pom-poms', were installed. All of these were protected by light armored gun tubs.

The 20mm guns were arranged as follows: two on the control tower, one each side of turret II, one each side of the base of the mainmast, one each just aft and one level lower than the previous mentioned 20mm guns, one each side and just forward of the after funnel, one each side and just aft of the after funnel, one each side of turret III.

The quad 1·1in machine guns were located one mount each side of the after control tower and one mount each side of the lower bridge area in place of the 3in/50 cal.

Anti-aircraft Battery: Post 1942

The complete rebuild of *Tennessee* in 1942-43 included an extensive anti-aircraft battery reflecting the many lessons learned the hard way by the US Navy early in the war. Besides the sixteen 5in/38 guns of the secondary battery there were forty 40mm Bofors machine guns arranged in ten quad mounts and forty-three single 20mm mounts.

The 40mm quads in splinter-shielded tubs were arranged: one on the centerline just aft and above turret II, one on the centerline just forward and above turret III, one each side of the bridge superstructure, one each just aft and slightly above the mounts just previously mentioned, one each side and slightly aft of the funnel and one each side of turret III on the main deck.

The 20mm mounts in splinter-shielded tubs or with splinter-shield surrounds were located: three on the forecastle between the anchor chains, a nest of two each side of turret II on the 01 deck, a nest of four each side of turret II on the 02 deck, one each side and below the forward main battery director, a nest

Tennessee *getting underway in the late 1920s. An indication of the relative size of the foretops can be gained from the men on top of the observation level* (*Photo: US Navy*)

of four each side of the funnel on about the 03 level, a nest of two each side of the after control tower, two each just aft the after 5in/38 mounts on the main deck, a nest of two each side and below the after centerline 40mm quad mount, two on top of turret III, one each side of turret III on the main deck and one each side of the aircraft crane on the fantail.

Additional Armament

As originally built *Tennessee* carried four 6 pounder saluting guns; two underwater 21-in torpedo tubes, one on each side; and several machine guns and a 3-in field gun for her landing party (made up of her embarked marines and selected sailors). The torpedo tubes were removed about 1937.

Fire Control

When the *Tennessee* was commissioned in 1920 the provisions for optical gun fire control were dispersed in several areas. The masthead tops were used for control and spotting fire, the middle level for the main battery and the lower level for the secondary battery. In addition there was a forward main battery director on top of the bridge house and an after main battery director on top turret III. Each turret was also equipped with a range-finder and sighting equipment and therefore could be controlled locally.

The main battery plotting room was located deep in the hull on the first platform deck. There the mechanical computer solved the firing problem and fed the solution to the turrets. Information was received from the bridge, fire control stations, directors and turrets; this included own ship's course and speed, target ship's course and speed, range, powder temperature, air temperature, wind direction and velocity, humidity and spotting reports. A gyroscopic stable element provided corrections for pitch and roll of the ship.

In the early 1930s the after main battery director was removed to make room for the second aircraft catapult installed on the ship. During a period in the early 1930s she carried a second forward main battery director on top of turret II and for a shorter period a second after main battery director on a small tripod between the mainmast and turret III.

Secondary and Anti-aircraft Directors

During an overhaul period in 1940 a starboard and port secondary battery director was installed on each side of the foremast at the bridge level. Also a port and starboard anti-aircraft director were added on each side of the foremast just above the bridge level.

After her repairs in 1942, *Tennessee* retained essentially the same fire control arrangements she had prior to Pearl Harbor except now she had search and range-finding radar for the first time.

Fire Control: Post 1942

Upon the completion of her extensive rebuild in 1943, *Tennessee*'s fire control capabilities came up to the most modern battleships of the period. Included was an impressive array of radar as well as a total of 16 fire control directors.

The forward main battery director was located on the top of the armored forward control tower immediately above the bridge and had an FH type fire control radar fixed on its roof. The after main battery director was on top of the after armored control tower and had a smaller FH type fire control radar constructed on its roof.

There were four Mk 37 secondary battery directors for the eight 5in/38 twin mounts, each with an FD type fire control radar mounted on top. Both the optics and radar functions of these directors were dual-purpose, capable of furnishing both the surface and more complicated air fire control solutions. Two of these directors were located on the centerline, one forward just aft of turret II and one aft immediately aft of the after control tower. One each was located either side of the funnel at about the 04 level. With this arrangement there were three directors able to cover almost any bearing of the compass simultaneously.

Each 40mm quad mount had its own Mk 51 director located in a light armored tub immediately behind and above the mount. The Mk 51 was a hand-operated director. The operator tracked the target through his optical sight controlling the elevation and train of the sight with handle grips. The director automatically computed the lead angle by the rate and direction in which the operator moved the sight.

The 20mm mounts were controlled manually by the gunners. Of course, all of the larger guns could be controlled locally and operated manually if required.

USS TENNESSEE (BB-43)

After launching at New York Naval Shipyard, Brooklyn, New York, 30 April 1919, it took another year's completing and fitting out at the yard before *Tennessee* was commissioned 3 June 1920. At the time of the commissioning, in terms of armor, weight of broadside, performance, range and watertight integrity, *Tennessee* and sister ship *California* were probably the most formidable battleships of the day.

An extensive recruiting campaign was conducted in the state of Tennessee the results of which procured the great majority of the ship's crew from 'the Volunteer State.' The slogan was, 'A gun crew from each town.'

Tennessee made her shakedown cruise off the Atlantic Coast and finished her work-up and qualification exercises out of the US Naval Station, Guantanamo, Cuba. During her shakedown she was clocked from rest to full speed of 21·01 knots in a little less than three minutes. Her tactical turning diameter was recorded as 700 yards—full helm with all screws turning forward. On 31 May 1921 she departed New York for the West Coast and her new home port, San Pedro, California.

Pacific Bound

There she settled into the routine of the peacetime Navy carrying out drills and exercises and engaging in battle practice with the Pacific Fleet off San Pedro. In early 1922 she participated with the US Fleet in the winter maneuvres in the Caribbean area. Usually these maneuvres combined the elements of Atlantic

USS *TENNESSEE (BB-43)*

Depicted in her final configuration from 1943 until her disposal. The extent of this modernization can be realized by comparison with the small profiles below.

Gordon Davies *© Profile Publications Ltd*

1

1 *Tennessee* as she appeared when first commissioned in 1921.

2 *Tennessee* as she was modified in 1942 immediately after Pearl Harbor.

3 Sistership *California* after modernization and with 'crazy quilt' camouflage she carried in the last years of World War II.

Tennessee *in 1934, the 5in/25 high-angle guns can be seen lining the 02 level of the superstructure. The extreme clipper bow is obvious in this view.* Lexington *in the background* (*Photo: US Navy*)

and Pacific Fleets which exercised problems for the defence of the Panama Canal, Puerto Rico and Guantanamo. *Tennessee* returned to San Pedro in April 1922.

In 1924 *Tennessee*, now commanded by Captain Luke McNamee, USN, won the coveted Efficiency Pennant for the highest combined score in gunnery and engineering among battleships in the Pacific Fleet. As a prelude to winning this honor the crew had also registered the highest score in gunnery in 1923. *Tennessee* also received the Pacific Fleet's 'Iron Man' Award for outstanding ship in athletics for 1928, 1934, 1936, and 1938.

FLEET PROBLEMS

During the period 1923 to 1940 the US Navy conducted the famous Fleet Problems commencing with Fleet Problem I in 1923 and ending with Fleet Problem XXI in 1940. These war games concentrated on the Panama Canal area, the US west coast and Hawaiian waters. *Tennessee* participated in a number of these Problems either as a unit of the *Blue Force* (the good guys) or the *Black Force* (the bad guys). It was from these Problems that the attack carrier tactics evolved and which the US Navy applied so successfully in the Pacific in World War II. Fleet Problem XIX reads like a dress rehearsal of the Japanese Attack on Pearl Harbor.

As these exercises progressed over the years it became evident that the carrier was more than an addition to the scouting force—it was also an offensive weapon in its own right. Tying the 30-knot carriers to the 21-knot battleships of the Battle Force was often self-defeating; carrier advocates argued, and the exercises proved, that the carriers should never be allowed within range of an enemy's surface guns. It became more evident through the 1930s that *Tennessee* and her kind would have to be replaced by faster battleships to keep pace with the new carriers.

In March 1925 *Tennessee* took part in Fleet Problem V, the first phase taking place off the West Coast. The second phase took her to Hawaii in April where the joint Army-Navy maneuvres tested the defence of the territory. From there she steamed to Australia and New Zealand on a goodwill tour returning home to the West Coast in September 1925. In April 1927 she made a three month cruise to Hawaiian waters.

Tennessee passed through the Panama Canal in March 1930 on her way to Fleet Problems X and XI which were conducted in the Caribbean in March and April. She then visited New York departing again for the Pacific 19 May 1930. In June she left the West Coast for a 14 month tour in Hawaiian waters. In February 1932 she returned to the West Coast and operated in the eastern Pacific until October 1934 when she again transited the Panama Canal for operations in the Atlantic. Several months later she returned to Hawaii where she was based until late 1938. The next year she spent both in the Atlantic and the Pacific participating in several war games. On 31 December 1940, Captain Charles E. Reardan, USN, took command.

Pearl Harbor Based

It had been the practice to keep the bulk of the United States Fleet in the Pacific, based on the West Coast. But with the Japanese becoming more aggressive in the western Pacific it was decided as a deterrent to Japan to move the bulk of the Fleet to Pearl Harbor. Thus at the completion of Fleet Problem XXI, held in the Hawaiian area in the spring of 1940 the majority of the Fleet, including *Tennessee* remained at Pearl Harbor. On the fateful morning of 7 December 1941 *Tennessee* was moored off the east side of Ford Island in 'Battleship Row' with six other pre-1923 battleships.

PEARL HARBOR ATTACK

That Sunday morning on which the Japanese attacked, the *Tennessee* was flying the flag of Rear Admiral Bagley, Commander, Battleship Division TWO (BATDIV TWO). She was moored to mooring blocks at berth F-6 inboard of *West Virginia* (BB-48), with *Arizona* (BB-39) about 75 feet astern and *Maryland* (BB-46), nested inboard with *Oklahoma* (BB-37), immediately ahead.

The attack commenced at about 0755, 7 December 1941 and the primary targets of the Japanese carrier aircraft were the battleships. The following impression by Captain Reardan, Commanding Officer of

Tennessee summarises the events on and around the ship during the attack:

At about 0755, planes, observed to be Japanese by their markings, were seen dropping bombs on Ford Island. This ship went to General Quarters and started setting condition Zed. Immediately, after the bombing of Ford Island, planes began torpedoing and bombing the battleships and other ships in the Harbour. This ship opened fire with 5in 25 caliber, 3in ·50 caliber and ·50 caliber machine guns about five minutes after the first attack. Orders for sortie were received but later cancelled for battleships. This ship was ready to get underway with both plants and 6 boilers about 0930. Shortly after the attack began, the *Oklahoma, West Virginia* and *California* received torpedo hits. The *Oklahoma* listed over and in about 10 minutes capsized. The *West Virginia* listed heavily but was righted by counter flooding. The *California* listed. The *Arizona* received several large bomb hits at least one of which apparently penetrated the magazines. There was a large explosion forward. The foremast fell forward and burning powder, oil, and debris was thrown on the quarterdeck of the *Tennessee.* The *Arizona* settled rapidly by the bow. The *Nevada* got underway, but was struck by bombs and torpedoes and grounded in the channel. Large fires were raging around the *Arizona* and *West Virginia.* The *Arizona* was moored to quays about seventy-five feet astern of the *Tennessee* and the *West Virginia* was moored to the *Tennessee.* The burning powder, oil and debris from the *Arizona* explosion plus the intense heat from the fires started fires in the stern and port quarter of this ship. These fires and the subsequent wetting caused considerable damage to the wardroom and officers' quarters in this vicinity. The fires were brought under control about 1030...

...There are 21 blanked off ports in the area which was exposed to great heat. Of these blanked ports the welding pulled apart due to the distortion of the shell plating. The regular ports in this area had the lenses fused, rubber gaskets burned, and the canvas stopwater between the port frame and the side of the ship destroyed. Except in small isolated cases, there was no burning of linoleum. This was probably due to the fact that the heat was above all linoleum rather than under...

...The following ammunition was expended during the battle: 760 rounds 5in 25 AA common, 180 rounds 3in/50, 4000 rounds 50 caliber machine gun...

... The conduct of the officers and crew of the *Tennessee* was uniformly in accordance with the highest traditions of the Service. Not only did they fight the battle with calmness and deliberation but for the next twenty-four hours they fought the oil fires in the *Arizona* and *West Virginia* which threatened to destroy the *Tennessee.* The *Arizona* was eighty feet to windward and her burning oil was a real menace to this ship; the *West Virginia* was alongside with her forward magazines in danger of explosion; nevertheless, the crew carried out their gunnery and damage control duties as if at drill.

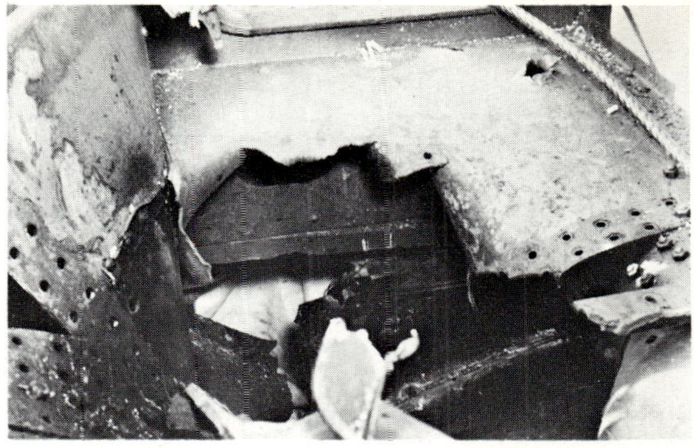

View showing where a Japanese 15 or 16in naval shell converted to a bomb penetrated the catapult and roof of turret III. Fortunately for Tennessee *the bomb had a very low order of detonation* *(Photo: US Navy)*

'Battleship Row' alongside Ford Island after the attack on Pearl Harbor. Reading from bottom up: The demolished Arizona, *sunken* West Virginia, *with* Tennessee *inboard of her, capsized* Oklahoma *with* Maryland *inboard of her, and, beyond the T-pier, sunken* California. *Dark streaks are oil leakage* *(Photo: US Navy)*

Tennessee *sits inboard of the sunken* West Virginia *after the Japanese attack on Pearl Harbor 7 December 1941. The two secondary battery directors added about a year earlier can be seen in their respective sponsons, just aft of the bridge; in the sponsons just above are the anti-aircraft directors. The barrels of the 50cal machine guns can be seen sticking out of their tubs in the fore and main tops. Note* Tennessee *has no radar at this time. Photo taken from the overturned hull of* Oklahoma *(Photo: US Navy)*

Fight for Survival
Tennessee was wedged between the forward mooring quay and the sunken *West Virginia.* After the attack the quay had to be blown with explosives in order to extricate *Tennessee*. Although unable to move, *Tennessee* turned her propellers at five knots in an effort to push the burning oil drifting down from *Arizona*'s hulk away from herself and *West Virginia*. *Tennessee*'s forward and after magazines were purposely flooded as a precaution against fire.

Besides the damage from fire and explosions close aboard, *Tennessee* received two bomb hits. Both of these bombs were converted from 15 or 16 inch naval shells and fortunately had a low order of detonation or perhaps did not explode at all. One struck the centerline gun of turret II, cracking the barrel and rendering all three guns inoperable. The second passed through the catapult and roof of turret III and damaged the structure as well as the rammer of the left gun. Seaman S. F. Bowen, who was in turret III, reported the bomb did not explode with a shattering crash but a ball of fire seemed to materialise overhead and melted down into the space. *Tennessee*'s inboard position saved her from any torpedo damage. The oil fires from *Arizona* were not completely extinguished until the evening of 9 December.

The ship's crew did an almost impossible task of damage control during the attack and also were credited with (or with assisting in) the shooting down of five enemy aircraft.

Tennessee was finally freed from her berth about 16 December and moved to the Navy Yard. Through the efforts of the crew, the repair ship *Medusa* and the Navy Yard she was repaired and ready for service 20 December.

Repairs on the West Coast
In late December 1941 *Tennessee* steamed to Puget Sound Navy Yard at Bremerton, Washington, where she underwent more extensive repairs and modernisation of the secondary battery and anti-aircraft armament. By early March 1942 this work was completed, which, as previously mentioned, included the removal of her mainmast, greatly altering her silhouette.

By mid-March she was in San Francisco and then sailed back to Hawaii. *Tennessee* became part of Vice-Admiral Pye's Task Force One which included seven old battleships. During the Battle of the Coral Sea (May 1942), the Battle of Midway (June 1942) and the invasion of the Solomons (August 1942) Task Force One patrolled in the Pacific west of the Hawaiian Islands protecting those islands and the lines of communications to the battle areas from possible attack. On 20 June 1942 Captain Robert S. Haggert relieved Captain Reardan.

Rebuild
In September *Tennessee* returned to Puget Sound Navy Yard at Bremerton and began a major conversion and rebuild in preparation for her participation in the march across the Pacific. During the nine month period of this rebuild *Tennessee* was fashioned into a modern looking battleship with up-to-date anti-aircraft armament, fire control, radar, communications and equipment of all description.

As previously described the remaining cage mast, the secondary battery, and a portion of the superstructure were removed. The side blisters were added to the hull, all old machinery was overhauled and updated, the superstructure completely rebuilt with armored control towers and a single large stack, a combat information center and modern flag spaces added, the new 5in/38, 40mm quads, 20mm singles, added, and a full range of radars and modern fire control equipment installed.

The crew that took the reborn *Tennessee* to sea in May 1943 consisted mostly of recently enlisted reservists. Since the battleships were too slow to be employed with the fast attack carriers, the primary role in which *Tennessee* and the rest of the old battleships (all of which were rebuilt by varying degrees early in the war) were to be used was that of fire support for amphibious landings. *Tennessee* was to prove herself one of the best of the lot.

The North
Upon completion of shakedown and work-up *Tennessee* was ordered north to Alaskan waters where she arrived in Adak in June 1943 when Rear-

Rush repairs were undertaken on Tennessee *in Puget Sound Naval Shipyard from December 1941 to March 1942. When completed her appearance was altered greatly by the removal of the main cage mast, greater anti-aircraft protective armament and the additions of radar and more splinter shielding. Note welded-over portholes (Photo: US Navy)*

Nearing completion of rebuild at Puget Sound Navy Yard, 1 May 1943. The inked identification point out the various radars on Tennessee's *new superstructure: FH=main battery fire control; FD=secondary fire control; SG=surface search; SC=air search. Also in this view are the tops of two 5in/38 mounts, four 40mm quads, seven 20mm singles, five 40mm directors* *(Photo: US Navy)*

Admiral Howard F. Kingman, USN, joined the ship as Commander Battleship Division Two.

During the Battle of Midway in June 1942 the Japanese had occupied two of the barren western islands, Kiska and Attu, in the Aleutian Chain, of the then Territory of Alaska. For over two months *Tennessee*'s task group patrolled in the fog shrouded waters of the north hoping to intercept Japanese supply missions to Kiska as Attu had been recaptured in May.

On 2 and 15 August Kiska was bombarded by the ships and on the fifteenth was seized by troops—the Japanese had already abandoned the island. *Tennessee* returned to San Francisco in September 1943 for rest and liberty.

Central Pacific Campaign

In late 1943 the United States' mobilization and defence production had accelerated to the point where plans for the march across the Central Pacific could be commenced. The islands that had to be occupied were for the most part heavily defended by well dug-in Japanese troops. Opposed amphibious landings, historically the most risky of military assaults, could only be successful if proper pre-invasion bombardments softened the landing areas. *Tennessee* would become one of the most successful ships in the US Navy at this mission and at supporting the troops after the landings. The initial trial of the planned island-hopping campaign was to be Tarawa Atoll in the Gilbert Islands: the US Marines and *Tennessee* were there.

Tarawa

Early on the morning of 20 November 1943 *Tennessee, Maryland, Pennsylvania* and lesser ships subjected Tarawa to two and one-half hours of pounding, pouring 3000 tons of naval projectiles on to little Betio Island, not nearly enough as events would prove; but most of the enemy's crew-served guns were knocked out. The marines took the island at a costly price but many lessons were learned that would improve future amphibious operations.

On 22 November an enemy submarine was driven to the surface and *Tennessee*'s 5in guns scored several hits before a destroyer rammed the sub and finished her off.

The Marshalls

Tennessee returned to the West Coast and after extensive rehearsals at San Clemente Island, California, steamed for Kwajalein Atoll in the Marshall Islands. On 31 January 1944, flying the flag of Rear-Admiral H. F. Kingman, USN, Commander Fire Support Unit 1, and hosting Secretary of the Navy, James V. Forrestal, *Tennessee*, the other fire support ships and aircraft commenced a three day bombardment of the islands of Roi-Namur. Reconnaissance had been more thorough than Tarawa: targets were individually assigned to each ship and

Another view as she appeared in 1942 (Photo: US Navy)

the fire carefully spotted. When the Marines landed they were met with meager resistance compared to Tarawa. *Tennessee* had approached closer than a mile to the beach during her fire support mission.

After a quick replenishment of ammunition and supplies, *Tennessee* proceeded to Eniwetok Atoll and conducted a fire support mission 17 February against Engebi Island on which the Marines conducted a successful assault the next day.

After the capture of Eniwetok Island, Parry Island in the atoll now received the attention of the ships and aircraft of the fire support force. *Tennessee* anchored in the lagoon 850 yards off shore and assisted in levelling all the trees and standing structures on one and one-half mile long Parry. The bombardment continued from the evening of 20 February until after the landings on the morning of the twenty-third. The conquest of Eniwetok Atoll cost 195 American dead and missing while some 3430 Japanese suffered the same fate. *Tennessee* headed south to the advance base at Efate in the New Hebrides Islands.

New Ireland

Tennessee, accompanying a force comprised of *New Mexico, Mississippi, Idaho,* two escort carriers (CVE) and fifteen destroyers (DD), moved into the Southern Pacific Area in support of General MacArthur's campaign in the Bismarck Archipelago. As a diversion the Navy force bombarded Kavieng, New Ireland 20 March 1944. *Tennessee* was straddled twice by an enemy shore battery but no damage resulted. On 25 March Captain Andrew Mayer, USN, relieved Captain Haggart as commanding officer and the ship headed back to Pearl Harbor for rest and firing practice on the Kahoolawe Range.

The Marianas Campaign

The next long hop across the Pacific was to be to the Marianas Islands with the main targets Saipan, Tinian and Guam. The capture of these islands would put the Japanese home islands within bomber range of the new B-29 superfortresses and also cut the transit time of marauding US submarines to their patrol areas by more than half.

Making a brief stop at Kwajalein en route from Pearl Harbor, *Tennessee*, in company with seven other old BBs, arrived off Saipan on the morning of 14 June 1944; the bombardment had commenced the day before by the new battleships of Task Force 58. The ship was assigned a position on the right flank of the landing beaches off Agingan Point. On the fifteenth, while firing close to the beach, *Tennessee* received a 6in round from a shore battery on a 5in mount killing 8 and wounding 26.

The troops landed on the fifteenth and were supported by naval gunfire until Saipan was secured on 21 June. During the action, a Japanese plane was shot down that had commenced its run on *Tennessee*.

After a short repair and replenishment period at Eniwetok *Tennessee* was back on the line providing support to the troops on Guam 20-21 July. On 22 July *Tennessee* was softening up Tinian for the landings on the twenty-fourth. During one fire

In Adak Harbor, Alaska August 1943. The additional blisters added to the side of the ship in 1942-43 are apparent. Note signal flags hung out to air, three 20mm singles on forecastle. *(Photo: US Navy)*

In 1943 Tennessee *showing her stern and broad beam. The single catapult can be seen just forward of the aircraft crane on the stern; two 20mm gun tubs overhang the stern* *(Photo: US Navy)*

This view from dead ahead shows how the additional blisters to Tennessee's *sides added during rebuild in 1942-43 were faired into the bows*

Tennessee *poses in her mid-1942 'garb'. She is carrying three Vought-Sikorsky OS2U 'Kingfisher' observation aircraft* *(Photo: US Navy)*

mission *Tennessee* and *California* levelled Tinian Town with 480 14in and 800 5in shells. One of *Tennessee*'s 'Kingfisher' observation planes was lost over Tinian killing both the observer and the pilot. From 2-9 August she returned to Guam to give inland support for the advancing troops.

Palau

The Marianas mission completed, *Tennessee* returned to Eniwetok, then south to Espiritu Santo, thence to the Solomons and on to the next operation, the Palau group of islands. The once great Japanese bastion at Truk was now far to the east, by-passed and no longer a threat. *Tennessee, Pennsylvania,* four cruisers, five destroyers and carrier aircraft pounded Anguar Island for five days. On 17 September the troops landed and occupied the island with little opposition. The airstrip constructed on Anguar brought the Philippines within bomber range.

Tennessee withdrew to Manus in the Admiralties to prepare for the invasion of the Philippines. At Manus Rear-Admiral T. E. Chandler, USN, relieved Rear-Admiral Kingman as COMBATDIV TWO and Captain John B. Heffernan, USN, relieved Captain Mayer as commanding officer.

Leyte

Departing Manus 12 October 1944 *Tennessee* joined the Seventh Fleet Leyte invasion force. After fighting a typhoon, the force entered Leyte Gulf on the twentieth. *Tennessee* assisted in the bombardment on the twentieth and the next day the troops landed under cover of naval gunfire. General MacArthur went ashore the same day fulfilling his promise to the Filipino people a little over two years earlier, 'I shall return.'

Enemy air reaction to the landings was heavy. *Tennessee* shot down one enemy plane and was credited with assists on three others.

The Battle for Leyte Gulf

The Japanese Imperial Fleet was committed to the defence of the Philippines. As soon as the landings were made on Leyte, Japanese naval units sortied from the home islands in the north and Lingga Roads near Singapore to the south. The resulting four day Battle of Leyte Gulf covered an area of nearly 30,000 square miles with four major engagements. Three separate Japanese groups moved toward Leyte.

(1) The Main Force with four carriers, two battleships and escorts steamed from Japan. Its mission was to decoy the covering force for the invasion, Admiral Halsey's Third Fleet (totalling 17 fast carriers, 6 new battleships, 17 cruisers and numerous destroyers), to the north. The Main Force accomplished its mission, but in the Battle off Cape Engano lost all four of its carriers.

(2) The First Striking Force, Vice-Admiral Kurita commanding, from Lingga Roads, was in three sections. The first and second sections, comprising five battleships (including 18in super battleships *Yamato* and *Musashi*), ten cruisers plus escorts fought the Battle of the Sibuyan Sea, and the Battle off Samar, north of Leyte. In the latter battle the

Another view showing Tennessee *as she appeared after 1943* (*Photo: US Navy*)

Tennessee *after her major rebuild. The modern lines and extensive anti-aircraft armament are apparent* (*Photo: US Navy*)

Japanese missed the chance of a lifetime when they decided to break off the surface engagement with the small escort carriers and their escorts of the Seventh Fleet, the only force between them and the helpless Leyte invasion force. The third section (Force C) under Vice-Admiral S. Nishimura, with two battleships, one cruiser and four destroyers, were to approach Leyte from the south and it was this force that would meet *Tennessee* and the other old battleships in the Battle of Surigao Strait.

(3) The Second Striking Force of three cruisers and seven destroyers, commanded by Vice-Admiral K. Shima, steamed from Japan and was to co-operate with Nishimura's section but never effectively got into battle.

THE BATTLE OF SURIGAO STRAIT
History's Last Battleship Engagement

In the afternoon of 24 October Rear Admiral Jesse Oldendorf, Commander Fire Support Force for the Seventh Fleet, organised his forces to meet Nishimura's force of battleships, *Yamashiro* and *Fuso*, heavy cruiser *Mogami* and four destroyers, approaching from the south. The Japanese force had to pass through Surigao Strait between Leyte and Dinagat Islands. Oldendorf positioned his torpedo boats (PT) at the southern entrance to the strait to harass the Japanese and furnish intelligence. The majority of the 28 destroyers were stationed on both sides of the strait to make torpedo attacks on the Japanese flanks as they passed.

To achieve that classic of surface battle tactics, 'crossing the T', Oldendorf steamed his old 14in and 16in battleships, *West Virginia*, *Maryland*, *Mississippi*, *Tennessee*, *California* and *Pennsylvania*, across the northern end of the strait. The light cruisers, including HMAS *Shropshire*, were in two lines south of and on each flank of the battleship line. The old battleships were low on ammunition and fuel after four days on the firing line but the great superiority in numbers and tactical position was overwhelming.

About 0100 25 October 1944 Nishimura entered Surigao Strait and steamed into the American trap.

Amphibious tractors head towards the Okinawa beaches on 'L' day, 1 April 1945, as Tennessee *provides close-in support fire within a few hundred yards off the beach* (Photo: US Navy)

This stern-on aerial view of Tennessee *in 1943 depicts the broad beam of 114ft she received after her major rebuild. The dark lines on the main deck curving back toward the stern outline her original sides* (Photo: US Navy)

Fighting their way successfully past the PT boats, the Japanese were hit by the destroyer torpedo attacks. *Fuso* was disabled, eventually split in two and sunk, one destroyer was sunk and most of the other destroyers put out of action.

The *Yamashiro, Mogami* and one destroyer continued determinedly north into the combined broadside of the battle line. *Tennessee*, with her Mk-8 fire control radar, had a firing solution before the enemy came within range. The Japanese were allowed to approach within 17,000 yards before the battleships opened up. At 0355 she commenced firing six gun salvos to conserve the armor-piercing ammunition. After taking a tremendous beating *Yamashiro* capsized and sunk at 0419, fighting to the last. *Mogami*, badly battered, managed to escape south but was finished off by aircraft at 0910. Destroyer *Shigure*, although badly damaged, was the only Japanese ship that escaped the Battle of Surigao Strait. *Tennessee* had fired 69 rounds of 14in AP ammunition and suffered no damage. She had fired for a total of only over 12 minutes. After this battle Oldendorf was promoted to Vice-Admiral as Commander Battleship Squadron

Tennessee *in Buckner Bay, Okinawa, in mid-1945. The large 'bedspring' radar is a Mk 8* (Photo: US Navy)

ONE—he flew his flag on *Tennessee*. It was on 25 October at Leyte that the Japanese *Kamikaze* (divine wind) Corps made its initial appearance.

Homeward Bound

Tennessee headed back to the States and Puget Sound for a well earned leave and overhaul. Stopping in Pearl Harbor en route Fleet Admiral Nimitz came aboard and gave her officers and crew a tremendous accolade for their numerous accomplishments.

By 27 January 1945 *Tennessee* had completed her overhaul, trials, and work-up and was heading west for her final combat tour.

Iwo Jima

The next campaign for the ship was the invasion of Iwo Jima, a small island in the Volcano Group, needed as a fighter base so that B-29s from the Marianas could be escorted all the way to Japan.

On 16 February 1945, Task Force 54 including 5 old BBs and 5 cruisers commenced the close-in bombardment of Iwo. *Tennessee* was assigned the preparation fire of the left flank of the landing beaches which included four large caliber guns on Mount Surabachi. The Marines launched their costly conquest of the island on the nineteenth. *Tennessee* remained close off-shore until 7 March providing fire support for the troops ashore and star shell illumination at night to frustrate Japanese infiltration tactics.

Tennessee steamed south to the large advance afloat base at Ulithi Atoll to join 600 US and British ships anchored in the lagoon preparing for the Okinawa assault.

Operation Iceberg

The invasion of Okinawa was by far the largest amphibious operation conducted in the Pacific during the War. It was planned to use this 70 by 15 mile island as the jumping off point for the invasion of Japan later in the year. With the island well within aircraft range of Japan, and approximately 100,000 Japanese ashore, the enemy was going to make the invaders pay dearly. From 26 March to the end of July, 30 naval vessels were sunk and 368 damaged, mostly by *kamikaze;* 4900 sailors, and 7613 soldiers and marines were killed in the conquest of Okinawa.

Tennessee, flying the flag of Rear-Admiral M. L. Deyo, USN, Commander Gunfire and Covering Force, led ten old battlewagons, including the thirty-three year old patriarch of the battleships, *Arkansas,* on the intial bombardment 26 March 1945. 'L' day was Easter morning, 1 April.

Tennessee remained off-shore almost daily until 3 May delivering fire support to the troops. At dawn 27 March, a *kamikaze* was splashed close on the port beam. The intensity of *kamikaze* attacks on the force increased markedly through April.

Kamikaze

Tennessee's relatively charmed life ended at 1450 12 April. Six *kamikazes* picked her for a target. Coming in from port, the first was shot down at 4000 yards, the next three approaching low on the port beam were splashed between 500 and 100 yards and the fifth, in a 45° dive on the port bow, plunged into the sea just missing the ship's bow.

The sixth, a Val, was not detected until it closed to 2500 yards. Heading directly for the bridge from ahead it was deflected slightly by 40mm hits. The Val's right wing clipped the stanchions on the starboard bridge wing, then crashed one of the 40mm mounts, continued aft over fire-directors and 20mm mounts, spewing burning gasoline all the way, with the wreckage finally coming to rest abreast turret III. Its 250lb bomb went through the deck and exploded in warrant officers' country.

Although the material damage was superficial, *Tennessee* had 25 officers and men killed and 104 wounded.

A strange experience befell Corporal W. H. Putnam, USMCR, when he dove for cover, tripped, and fell overboard, which probably saved his life. When he came to the surface he was surrounded by pieces of the burning aircraft but close to a big life raft. When he climbed aboard he found the headless

On 12 April, during the Okinawa campaign, Tennessee *fights off a* kamikaze *attack. In the top photo she is in the process of shooting down five Japanese aircraft; in the bottom photo she has been hit on the starboard side by a sixth* kamikaze *and is already fighting the resultant fires* (*Photo: US Navy*)

Tennessee *and* California *spent their last years in the Atlantic Reserve Fleet at Philadelphia Navy Yard. In this aerial is a portion of that fleet.* Tennessee *and* California *nest together in the large dry dock at the bottom of the photo* (*Photo: US Navy*)

body of the Japanese suicide ,pilot apparently thrown into the raft by the explosion.

The day was not yet over for *Tennesee*. At 2040 her formation was illuminated by star shell. An emergency turn was ordered and, immediately after it was executed, torpedoes exploded in *Tennessee*'s and *Idaho*'s turbulent wakes.

The War's Last Days

Tennessee steamed for Ulithi and permanent repairs 3 May. After three weeks alongside a repair ship, she was back on the line at Okinawa for three days of fire support ending 14 June.

During July *Tennessee* was flagship for the group covering the minesweeping operations in the East China Sea, ending with a sweep in the waters between Shanghai and Japan. *Tennessee* was at Okinawa preparing for further operations when the Japanese offer to surrender was announced.

Occupation

On 7 September 1945, in Buckner Bay, Okinawa, Captain H. F. Cope, USN, relieved Captain Heffernan as commanding officer. *Tennessee*'s last assignment before returning home was to cover the landing of occupation troops at Wakayama, Japan.

Mothballed and Scrapped

Tennessee joined the Philadelphia Group of the Sixteenth Fleet (Inactive) on 8 December 1945. Commander E. A. Abbot, USN, relieved Captain Cope and held command until *Tennessee* was decommissioned 14 February 1947.

Placed in 'mothballs' she remained in the reserve until 1 March 1959 when she was struck from the Navy List. *Tennessee* was sold to Bethlehem Steel Corporation 10 July 1959 and arrived under tow at Baltimore, Maryland for scrapping 26 July 1959—forty years after launching.

TENNESSEE SPECIFICATIONS

Authorised:	3 March 1915
Builder:	New York Naval Shipyard
Authorised Cost:	$7,800,000 less armour and armament
Laid down:	14 May 1917
Launched:	30 April 1919
Commissioned:	3 June 1920
Stricken:	1 March 1959
Dimensions:	Length 624·5ft Beam 97ft 3in (1943 114ft) Draft 33ft
Displacement:	33,300 tons (1943 40,500 tons)
Machinery:	Eight Babcock & Wilcox Superheated boilers driving two Westinghouse turbo-generators powering four Westinghouse motors. 26,800 shaft horsepower through four, three-bladed 14ft diameter propellers. Machinery weight 2,045 tons.
Speed:	21 knots
Fuel:	3328 tons maximum
Complement:	1920—57 officers, 1026 men 1943—90 officers, 2219 men
Armament:	1920—12-14in/50(4×3), 14-5in/51, 4-3in/AA, 2-21in torpedo tubes 1943—12-14in/50(4×3), 16-5in/38 (8×2), 40-40mm(10×4), 43-20mm
Aircraft:	1920 none 1943 Two (one catapult)
Armour:	Sides 8-14 in Ends 14 in 2nd deck $3\frac{1}{2}$ in 3rd deck $2\frac{1}{2}$ in Barbettes 13 in Turrets 9-18 in Uptakes 9-15 in Control tower 16 in

Warship Series Editor: JOHN WINGATE, DSC

SELECTED BIBLIOGRAPHY

Dictionary of American Naval Fighting Ships,
Naval History Division, Department of the Navy.

History of United States Naval Operations in World War II,
by Rear Admiral Samuel Elliot Morrison, USNR (Ret.), *Little Broan and Company.*

The Battleship in the United States Navy,
Naval History Division, Department of the Navy.

Pearl Harbor: Why, How, Fleet Salvage and Final Appraisal
by Vice Admiral Homer N. Wallin, USN (Ret.), *Naval History Division, Department of the Navy.*

Jane's Fighting Ships
(various editions) edited by Raymond V. B. Blackman, *Sampson Low, Marston & Co Ltd.*

The Ships and Aircraft of the US Fleet,
(various editions) by James C. Fahey, *United States Naval Institute.*

ACKNOWLEDGEMENTS

I wish to express my gratitude and thanks to the following without whose help this Profile *would never have been written:*

Miss Anna Urband, Magazine and Book Branch, Office of Information, Department of the Navy.

Mr Robert Carlisle, Still Photo Branch, Office of Information, Department of the Navy.

Mr John Riley, Naval History Division, Department of the Navy.

Mr Jim McGhee, Navy Records, The National Archives.

The Office of Information, Department of the Navy.

The Naval History Division, Department of the Navy.

The National Archives of the United States.

The Naval Photographic Center.

The Library of Congress.

The Library of the Royal United Services Institute, London.

Tennessee's *sister USS* California *(BB-44) in 'crazy-quilt' camouflage.* California *received a near identical conversion as her sistership in 1943* *(Photo: US Navy)*

The Mikazuki, *the tenth destroyer of the* Mutsuki-*class destroyer who was equipped for the first time with 61cm torpedo tubes among the Japanese destroyers. This picture was taken in 1932, five years after her commission.*

The Fubuki *in 1930, the first ship of the Special Type Mark I destroyers. This Special Type destroyer took a world lead, with her large size and heavy armament.*

IJN Yukikaze/Destroyer/1939-1970

by Masataka Chihaya and Yasuc Abe

There is a special reason why the destroyer *Yukikaze* was chosen as a typical and representative destroyer of the Imperial Japanese Navy. Built in 1940 as one of the large, heavily armoured destroyers of the *Kagero*-class, she took part in World War II from the very beginning, and was involved in almost every sea battle. She nevertheless survived the war without receiving a single hit from shell, bomb, torpedo or mine. During this time she logged well over 100,000 miles, all on combat missions. This was a brilliant record without precedent in the Japanese Navy.

Towards the end of the war, this magnificent performance gave her an almost legendary fame. She had three captains and several crews, but all who sailed in her, from skipper to stoker, felt her to be an invincible ship, immune from all enemy attack. In the Japanese Navy the *Yukikaze* had long been regarded as having a charmed life. Indeed, she survived the war unharmed, although her many sisters had been sunk or damaged.

This fame has been carried into the post-war world. When Japan's Maritime Defence Force began to stand on its feet by building its own ships, the first warship built in Japan was named after her—*Yukikaze.*

The name *Yukikaze* is Japanese for Snow Wind. This follows the traditional custom in the Japanese Navy of giving its first-class destroyers names associated with natural phenomena such as wind, cloud, snow, mist and rain.

DEVELOPMENT OF JAPANESE DESTROYERS

Pre-Washington Naval Treaty

In 1895, only two years after the British Royal Navy had built its first destroyer *Havock*, the Japanese Navy decided on a new policy of building a large number of these new warships. They rightly believed that such a force, armed with torpedoes, would constitute a powerful threat to the Russian Fleet.

Under the naval expansion plans for 1895 and 1896, the Japanese Navy ordered from British shipyards a total of sixteen destroyers, almost identical to the Royal Navy's 'Thirty-Knotters'. In 1902, thirty-nine similar destroyers were laid down in various Japanese yards. When the Russo-Japanese war broke out in 1904, a total of thirty had been commissioned. They soon had the opportunity of successfully displaying their merits in battle.

In 1907 the Japanese Navy commenced building two *Umikaze*-class destroyers, having displacements of 1150 tons. These followed the design of the Royal Navy's *Tribal*-class destroyers. In 1911 the construction of two *Sakura*-class destroyers of 600 tons displacement was also started. Both of these classes had heavier guns and torpedoes than the *Tribals*, thus paving the way for the Japanese policy of depending on heavier armaments for their destroyers.

Subsequently the Japanese Navy continued their destroyer programme by building the *Uranami* (907 tons), two *Tanikaze*-class (1300 tons), four *Isokaze*-class (1227 tons), ten *Kaba*-class (665 tons), four *Momi*-class (835 tons) and six *Nara*-class (850 tons).

From the early 1910s, the Japanese Navy began to attach increasing importance to the seaworthiness of their fighting ships. High regard was paid to this when the 15 destroyers of the *Minekaze*-class and the 21 *Momi*-class were built between 1919 to 1922. The former had a displacement of 1345 tons, a speed of 39 knots, and was armed with four 12cm guns and six 53cm torpedo tubes. The latter displaced 850 tons, had a speed of 36 knots and an armament of three 12cm guns and four 53cm torpedo tubes.

Between 1922 and 1927, nine destroyers of the *Kamikaze*-class (1400 tons, 37·25 knots), twelve of the *Mutsuki*-class (1445 tons, 37·25 knots), and eight of the *Wakatake*-class (900 tons, 35·5 knots) were all completed. The *Kamikaze*-class and the *Wakatake*-class were improved versions of the *Minekaze* and *Momi*-classes respectively. The *Mutsuki*-class was the first destroyer in the Japanese Navy to have 61cm torpedo tubes, and she also had a longer range than the *Kamikaze*-class.

The Birth of the 'Special Type' Destroyer

The Washington Naval Treaty of 1922 limited the capital ship and aircraft carrier strength of the world's major naval powers. The Japanese Navy accordingly made plans to ensure that its heavy cruisers, destroyers and submarines were more powerful than the corresponding vessels of other navies.

In 1925, with this policy in mind, the Naval General Staff requested a new destroyer programme based on the following specifications:

Displacement:	1650 tons
Maximum Speed:	38 knots
Range:	4000 miles at 14 knots
Armament:	3 twin mountings of 12·7cm guns 3 triple 61cm torpedo tubes with 18 torpedoes.

The armament of these new destroyers represented a 50% increase above that of the *Mutsuki*-class but the shape of the hull had to be as compact as possible. This was a difficult problem in such a heavily armoured vessel.

In spite of this, the naval architects of the Naval Construction Department were able to surmount all difficulties in designing a new destroyer of the following specifications:

Displacement:	1680 tons
Length:	378ft
Beam:	34ft
Draught:	10ft 6in
Main Machinery Output:	50,000hp
Maximum Speed:	37 knots
Range:	5000 miles at 14 knots
Armament:	As specified above

In this vessel the conflicting demands of heavy armament and a compact hull were successfully reconciled. This was achieved by using every opportunity to reduce weight in the construction of the hull. These methods had already been demonstrated in the light cruiser *Yubai.* This vessel had astonished the naval world by her revolutionary design in reducing weight without losing hull strength.

To provide better sea-keeping qualities, she was given a large fo'c'sle with an extensive sheer and higher freeboard; her hull sides were also considerably flared. The new destroyer was fitted with a roofed bridge in order to improve her performance in bad weather, a feature not previously seen in any of the world's destroyers. In order to avoid top-heaviness, duralumin was used as much as possible in the construction of the bridge. Her air intakes supplying the engines were also mounted higher, and were carefully designed so that her performance in rough weather would not be impaired.

Armament

The armament of this new destroyer was an outstanding feature. She was designed to have three twin mountings of 12·7cm guns in a turret-like structure: one forward and two aft in a superimposed position. This gun design subsequently became standard for all first-class destroyers in the Japanese Navy.

Her torpedo armament consisted of three triple 61cm torpedo tube mountings: one between her first and second funnels and two aft of the second funnel. Stowage for spare torpedoes was provided on both sides of the second funnel and

The Ayanami, *one of the Special Type Mark II destroyers. The installation of her main armament, air intake for the boiler rooms and the upper part of the bridge were different from those of the Special Type Mark Is.*

The Inazuma, *one of the Special Type Mark III destroyers. Her first funnel became slim and her bridge more complicated with various control installations which were added. In the background can be seen the* Hibiki (*left*) *and the* Ikazuchi (*right*), *both being sister ships of the* Inazuma.

also on the port side of the second gun turret. Reloading was made as easy as possible.

This epoch-making destroyer of the Japanese Navy became known as the 'Special Type' destroyer. It was to pave the way in the development of Japanese destroyer construction. These destroyers could be further divided into three types according to their completion dates. The first ten, classed as Mark I, were equipped with A-type twin mountings of 12·7cm guns, which were elevated together to a maximum angle of 55°. The fire control post was unenclosed and situated above the bridge. A single range-finder was provided.

The next ten, classified as Mark II, were equipped with B-type twin mountings of 12·7cm guns which could be independently elevated up to 75°. The fire control and tower-shaped DCT were situated above the bridge.

The last four, classified as Mark III, were provided with a torpedo fire control above the bridge in addition to the gunnery fire control, DCT and range-finder tower. The superstructure was accordingly more elaborate than in Marks I and II. Shields were fitted to the torpedo tubes to prevent the entry of sea water. As more powerful boilers were installed in this class the number was reduced to three, and the first funnel was therefore reduced in size.

Altogether 24 destroyers were completed between 1928 and 1933. The Naval General Staff originally requested 36, but the numbers were cut to 24 to avoid provoking competitive building of heavy destroyers among the world's naval powers.

Effect of the London Naval Treaty

As a result of the London Naval Treaty of 1930, the displacement of individual destroyers was limited to 1850 tons; the total Japanese destroyer tonnage was limited to 105,500 tons. This was 70·4% of that of the US Navy. Of the total permitted tonnage 16% was allowed to be above 1500 tons.

This limitation of destroyer strength put the Japanese Navy in a very awkward position, because no more of these heavy destroyers could now be built. The only construction possible would have to be of 1500 tons or less. This created the very difficult problem of designing a destroyer of equal fire power to the 'Special Type', but packed into a smaller hull. The tonnage proposed by the Naval General Staff to

The Nenohi, *the second ship of the* Hatsuharu-*class destroyers, when she was completed in 1933. For the first time among the Japanese destroyers, she had two superimposed gun turrets (No 2 turret being a single mounting) in her fore part and torpedo-reloading equipment installed for her torpedo tubes.*

the Naval Construction Department was 1400 tons. This was a formidable task for the naval architects.

The Naval Construction Department finally arrived at a compromise with the *Hatsuharu*-class destroyer, which had the following specifications:

Displacement:	1400 tons
Length:	354·9ft
Beam:	32·8ft
Draught:	9·9ft
Main Machinery Output:	42,000hp
Maximum Speed:	36·5 knots
Range:	4000 miles at 18 knots
Armament:	5×12·7cm guns (2 in twin mountings and 1 single mounting) 18 61cm torpedoes in three triple torpedo tube mountings.

Compared with the 'Special Type' destroyers, the *Hatsuharu*-class had only one gun less, the rest of the armament being similar. The 12·7cm guns were of an improved pattern, and were in fact heavier than those installed in the 'Special Type' destroyers. A new feature was the torpedo loading device which enabled the tubes to be reloaded even during action. All this was achieved within the limitation of 1400 tons displacement.

The heavy armament carried by this relatively small displacement was not obtained without some effect on the stability of the ship. In order to remedy this, the beam was increased in relation to the displacement and the draught was made shallower. Consequently the total area of the side above the water line was very large in comparison with that below the water line. This disadvantage would later lead to a serious problem.

Under the fleet expansion programme for 1931, the construction of 12 *Hatsuharu*-class was begun, and work was started during that year. By 1933 the first two, *Hatsuharu* and *Nenohi,* were completed and, after extensive trials, were deemed to have adequate stability. The capability of the Japanese Navy to overcome the severe handicap in building the light warships required by the London Naval Treaty was widely acclaimed.

This acclamation was short-lived. On 13 March 1934, the 'mini' destroyer *Tomozuru* capsized during manoeuvres in severe weather. She was one of a few 'mini' destroyers designed on the same principle as the *Hatsuharu*-class, with a maximum armament installed in a small hull. In fact, the weight of the *Tomozuru*'s armament was 22·7% of her displacement. During her trials it had been thought that she had a good margin of safety.

This disaster was a great shock to the Japanese Navy. The reputation of Japanese naval technology to be able to build the warships of tomorrow had been proved to be utterly without foundation. It was clear, even to a layman, that if the *Tomozuru* had insufficient stability, other ships of this design could also be expected to have this defect.

As a result of careful technical investigation, the *Hatsuharu*-class destroyers were subject to drastic modification. One triple mounting of the 61cm torpedo tubes together with its reloading equipment was removed, and the single mounting of the 12·7cm guns moved from for'd to aft. The superstructure, funnels and masts were lowered and additional ballast provided in the bottom. The stability was accordingly considerably improved, although her maximum speed was reduced to 34 knots.

Following the *Tomozuru* incident, further construction of *Hatsuharu*-class destroyers was discontinued after the completion of six vessels. The remaining six were completely re-designed under the name of the *Shiratsuyu*-class. These had the following specifications:

Displacement:	1685 tons
Length:	352·5ft
Beam:	32·5ft
Draught:	11·5ft
Main Machinery Output:	42,000hp
Maximum Speed:	34 knots
Range:	4000 miles at 18 knots
Armament:	5×12·7cm guns (2 twin mountings and 1 single mounting) 16×61cm torpedoes in two quadruple torpedo tube mountings

The torpedo tubes were newly developed for a torpedo salvo of eight, the minimum number deemed necessary to obtain at least one hit. The elevation of the 12·7cm guns was lowered to 55° in order to reduce weight. Four additional ships of the *Shiratsuyu*-class were built from 1936 to 1937, making a total of 10 ships of this class.

Fourth Fleet Incident

On 26 September 1935, while on manoeuvres, the 4th Fleet was hit by a severe typhoon off the east coast of Japan. The ships were relentlessly pounded by waves of a height without precedent, at times reaching a height of up to 15 metres. Serious damage was inflicted. The most severely hit were the 'Special Type' destroyers, and two of them, *Yugiri* and *Hatsuyuki* broke their backs just for'd of the bridge, the for'd parts sinking. Other destroyers of this type were also damaged.

The Japanese Navy thus suffered another severe blow; two of their prize destroyers were cut in two by nothing more formidable than heavy seas. Extensive investigations were commenced to analyse the cause of the disaster. The inquiry revealed that the typhoon produced waves of which the ratio of height to length reached a factor of 1:10. Previously ship designers had accepted a factor of 1:20.

It was also found that the 'Special Type' destroyers had insufficient hull strength to withstand the sagging moment caused by such mountainous seas. When the bows were thrust upwards the hull broke at its weakest point. In designing these ships, waves of this magnitude had never been contemplated.

Following this disaster, the Japanese Navy carried out an immediate review of all naval craft in service,

The Wakaba, *the third ship of the* Hatsuharu-*class destroyers, after she was drastically reconstructed to improve her stability after the disastrous sinking of the torpedo boat* Tomozuru. *Note that her No 2 turret was moved aft and one triple torpedo tube mounting removed. This picture was taken in 1937 while she was operating in the Yangtse River in the mainland of China.*

The Umikaze, *the seventh ship of the* Shiratsuyu-*class destroyers. This Class One was equipped with quadruple torpedo tube mountings for the first time among the Japanese destroyers.*

The midships section of the Nenohi *after the drastic modifications were made on her to improve her stability. Note that her No 2 funnel is offset slightly to starboard so that torpedo reloading equipment can be installed. The picture was taken in 1937.*

The Yamagumo, *the sixth ship of the* Asashio-*class of destroyers.*

those under construction and in the process of design. It was also revealed that, apart from capital ships and carriers, the 'Special Type' destroyers were not the only ships having insufficient hull strength to encounter waves of this height. All naval and civil shipyards were mobilised to strengthen these vessels to enable them to withstand the heaviest seas likely to be encountered in the Pacific. The design of the *Shiratsuyu*-class was also modified. The bitter lesson of the 4th Fleet incident eventually proved to be invaluable in the subsequent design of Japanese warships.

The Asashio-class Destroyer and its Design Problems

Just before Japan withdrew from the London Naval Treaty, the Japanese Navy decided to build new destroyers having a displacement of 1700 tons. Following this policy a total of 10 *Asashio*-class destroyers were built from 1937 to 1939. They had the following specifications:

Displacement:	1961 tons
Length:	377·5ft
Beam:	34·1ft
Draught:	12·1ft
Main Machinery Output:	50,000hp
Maximum Speed:	35 knots
Range:	3800 miles at 18 knots
Armament:	Three twin mountings of 12·7cm guns 16×61cm torpedoes in two quadruple torpedo tube mountings

In building the *Asashio*-class destroyers, care was taken to ensure sufficient stability and hull strength. Although satisfactory in these respects, these ships later developed two new faults during service.

The first of these faults arose from rudder design. The turning circle proved to be larger than had been expected. This was solved by providing a transom stern, which also resulted in a useful slight increase in speed.

The second problem first occurred in late 1937, and arose from faulty turbines. The blades on the rotor

The Asagumo, *the fifth ship of the* Asashio-*class, running at full power. Note her peculiar stern wave. This photograph was taken during her official trial run in 1939, when she registered 34·26 knots.*

of the Medium Pressure turbine were found to be stripped. The cause was not immediately understood, but investigation revealed that the trouble appeared to be due to the synchronisation of vibrations from the turbine rotor and its blades. Modifications on the turbines of all the *Asashio*-class destroyers were accordingly carried out. Later in 1943 it was discovered that the actual cause of the trouble was a synchronisation of the vibratory frequency between the turbine blades and the two-cycle circular vibration of the rotor.

Development of the Oxygen Torpedo

In 1926 the Japanese Navy started to study the feasibility of the oxygen torpedo. All experiments ended in failure because air-mixed oxygen was used as the source of power for the torpedo. In every case explosion occurred.

In late 1927 intelligence reported that the Royal Navy was testing this type of torpedo, and the Japanese renewed efforts in this direction. This time it was decided to employ pure oxygen, and the key to the successful development of the torpedo depended on the method used to fire the oxygen in the combustion chamber. Initial experiments always ended in explosions, until the Japanese Navy conceived the idea of starting ignition in the first place with air in the combustion chamber. This was then gradually changed over to pure oxygen by increasing the ratio of the latter. Success was thereby achieved.

The first oxygen torpedo in the Japanese Navy, and indeed in the whole world, was ready by 1930. This epoch-making torpedo had the following characteristics:

Diameter:	61cm
Length:	9m
Weight:	2·7 tons
Explosive:	490kg
Range:	22,000m at 48 knots 32,000m at 40 knots 40,000m at 36 knots

After long and extensive trials under actual conditions, the new torpedo was formally adopted in 1938 by the Japanese Navy under the name 'Type 93 Mark I Torpedo'. Heavy cruisers were the first to be supplied with this weapon in 1938 and destroyers in 1941. The *Hatsuharu* and the *Shiratsuyu*-class destroyers had to be slightly modified to carry the new torpedo, and the *Asashio*-class were modified during construction.

The Japanese Navy kept 'top secret' the oxygen torpedo. In order to conceal the invention, oxygen was known as 'second air', speeds were marked 10 knots less than actual, and ranges half those in fact obtained. In spite of this, the characteristics were still markedly superior to the world's conventional torpedoes.

The oxygen torpedo with its unrivalled characteristics was destined to play an important role in surface engagements during the war.

Development of Kagero and Yugumo-class Destroyers

Following the withdrawal from the Naval Treaty in 1937, the Japanese Navy was freed from the restrictions which had fettered the expansion of its budget and the armament of its vessels. The naval architects accordingly were free to design completely new ships using all their skill and the lessons of past experience. The *Kagero*-class were the first destroyers to be designed under these conditions. They were the final answer to the requirements of the Japanese Navy.

Basic Plan

Under the expansion programme for the fiscal year 1937, it was decided to commence construction of 15 *Kagero* destroyers. The specifications required were (1) *Maximum speed* to be greater than 36 knots, (2) *range*, 5000 miles at 18 knots, (3) *armament* as fitted to the 'Special Type' destroyers, (4) *hull* not to be larger than that of the 'Special Type'.

The Naval Construction Department found it impossible to satisfy all four conditions at the same time, and therefore offered two alternatives. Either the maximum speed would have to be limited to 35 knots, or the range reduced to 4500 miles at 18 knots.

The Naval General Staff preferred the first alternative, and on this basis the following specification was designed:

Displacement:	2000 tons
Length (bp):	363·9ft
Beam:	35·4ft
Draught:	12·3ft
Main Machinery Output:	52,000hp
Maximum Speed:	35 knots
Range:	5000 miles at 18 knots
Armament:	3 twin mountings of 12·7cm guns 2 twin mountings of 25mm AA machine guns 16×61cm torpedoes in two quadruple torpedo tube mountings

Hull Structure

In order to ensure stability, the so-called 'shabby' type hull form was adopted, giving a relatively shorter length and deeper draught in relation to its width. Its block coefficient was 10·74 compared with 11·2 for the 'Special Type' destroyers. A transom stern with flat bottom was used to reduce resistance to propulsion by a factor of 7%. A stern of this design is usually disadvantageous at cruising speed, but in this case the designers were able to overcome the problem by reducing propulsion resistance at cruising speed by 2%.

The maximum use of welding was employed in building these destroyers. Although the Japanese Navy had been somewhat reluctant to rely on welding after the 4th Fleet incident, the necessity to reduce weight made the use of this method essential.

Welding was accordingly applied to frames, web frames, weapon supports, water-tight compartments, parts of the secondary decks and subsidiary bulkheads. Welding was not applied to the outer shell, longitudinals and upper decks, with the exception of the ends of the bow and stern.

Main Machinery

The main machinery consisted of two reduction geared turbines of the Naval Construction Department type with a total output of 52,000hp. Steam was superheated to 30kg/cm° and 350°C. Each power plant consisted of four turbines: high pressure, medium pressure, low pressure and cruising. The last was connected to the medium pressure turbine through two-stage reduction gearing. The new method of using the cruising turbine enabled a reduction in weight to be achieved and gave improved fuel consumption at cruising speed.

Three boilers of the Naval Construction Department type were provided, each having a pre-heating system.

A feature of the main machinery plant was that the rate of fuel consumption was greatly improved. The rate at full power was 0·721/hp/hr, which was 21·5% less than that of the 'Special Type' destroyers destroyers and 12% less than the *Asashio*-class. The weight of the machinery (empty) was 667 tons.

Armament

The armament of the new destroyer was generally similar to that of the *Asashio*-class, but a number of improvements were incorporated. The main armament consisted of three twin mountings of 12·7cm guns, one for'd and two aft in superimposed positions. The maximum elevation was 55°, and the maximum range was 18,000m. A DCT was provided above the bridge for fire control.

The AA armament was originally not especially heavy, consisting of two twin mountings of 25mm machine guns installed on each side of the second funnel. This somewhat inadequate armament became a major issue when the ships were later engaged in actual combat.

As in the *Asashio*-class, the new destroyers were given two 61cm quadruple torpedo tube mountings, one between the first and second funnels and the other immediately aft of the second funnel.

The reloading equipment was also improved to ensure easy reloading during action. In addition, by re-arranging the air intakes into the boiler rooms, the first torpedo tube platform was substantially lower in comparison with other types, thus contributing to improved stability.

Although equipped with a sonar system, these ships were considerably inferior in this respect to those of other navies. Together with the lack of radar, this inferiority made the ships less effective than they should have been under wartime conditions.

The Yukikaze, *the eighth ship of the* Kagero-*class destroyers. This photograph was taken in January 1940 as she sailed from the port of Sasebo after being completed.*

Performance

A total of 15 *Kagero*-class destroyers were completed between 1939 and 1941. Three more were planned for the subsequent expansion programme, and these were also completed in 1941. Altogether a total of 18 destroyers of this class were built.

During the trials of the first few ships, two minor defects were revealed. The first was the failure of the destroyers to reach the designed speed of 35 knots. This failure was due to the incorrect shape of the propellers and, by changing the blade-section from aero-foil to ogival, the cavitation was reduced and the maximum speed was increased accordingly to 35·5 knots.

The second defect arose from the designers' faulty estimate of the fuel consumption. Trials on the *Isokaze,* one of the class, showed that the range was actually more than the required 5000 miles, being 6053 miles at 18·07 knots. If this performance had been foreseen, the hull of the destroyers could have been reduced in size.

The *Kagero*-class was highly acclaimed by the Fleet as the ideal solution to the destroyer question, and its appearance attracted the close attention of the major naval powers. The US Navy began the design of the *Fletcher*-class destroyer, and the British Navy shortly replied with the *Battle*-class.

Yugumo-class Destroyer

Following the brilliant achievement of the *Kagero*-class, the length of the new destroyers was increased by 1·65ft in order to reduce still further propulsion resistance. The elevation of the twin mountings of the 12·7cm guns was raised to 75° to allow for their use for AA. It may be noted that an AC electrical system was also used to reduce weight. As most of these destroyers were built after the outbreak of war, efforts were made to reinforce the AA armament and to install radar.

The specifications of this class were as follows:

Displacement:	2077 tons
Length (bp):	363·9ft
Beam:	35·4ft
Draught:	12·3ft
Main Machinery Output:	52,000hp
Maximum Speed:	35 knots
Range:	5000 miles at 18 knots
Armament:	As *Kagero*-class

The Life Story of the Yukikaze

The keel of *Yukikaze,* the eighth ship of the *Kagero*-class, was laid at the Sasebo Naval Yard on 2 August 1938. After being launched in the following year, she was completed and delivered to the Japanese Navy on 20 January 1940. She immediately joined the 16th Destroyer Division of the 2nd Destroyer Squadron.

At that time the 2nd Destroyer Squadron was the cream of the Japanese Navy's destroyer group, and it was fervently hoped that this force would be able to destroy the main enemy fleet, by engaging them in night actions with their powerful oxygen torpedoes. When war broke out in December 1941, the squadron consisted of 10 *Kagero* and six *Asashio*-class destroyers. Thanks to arduous training, the men of this Force were convinced at the end of 1941 of their second-to-none fighting ability.

The first assignment of *Yukikaze* was to participate in the landing operations on Legaspi in the Philippines. She then supported a series of landing operations on Manado in the Celebes from 9 to 14 January 1942, on Kendari (also in the Celebes) from 21 to 27 January, on Ambon from 28 January to 4 February, and on Kupang on Timor Island from 17 to 23 February. During the whole of this time she did not encounter any enemy surface forces.

The Battle of the Java Sea

It was not until the engagement off Surabaja on 27 February 1942 that *Yukikaze* took part in an actual battle. The Allied Fleet, consisting of two heavy cruisers,* three light cruisers and nine destroyers challenged the Japanese naval force of two heavy cruisers, two light cruisers and 14 destroyers, which were supporting landing operations on Java. One of the 14 destroyers was *Yukikaze.*

The battle opened with an exchange of fire between the heavy cruisers of both fleets. This was followed by the launching of torpedoes by the Japanese cruisers and destroyers. One of the torpedoes fired from a Japanese cruiser sank the Dutch destroyer *Kortenaer,* but none of the destroyer launchings were successful. The destroyers were too far from the target, and the fuses of the oxygen torpedoes were so sensitive that most of them exploded while still underwater.

In the night engagement which followed, the Japanese heavy cruiser group obtained excellent results with their long-distance oxygen torpedoes, sinking the Dutch cruisers *De Ruyter* and *Java.* The destroyer group, including *Yukikaze,* took no part in this engagement.

On 3 March 1942 *Yukikaze* encountered the US submarine *Perch* off northern Surabaja and sank her by gunfire. She then supported landing operations on western New Guinea, and finally made port in the homeland to prepare for her next operation.

The Battle of Midway Island

In this operation, in which four of its first-class aircraft carriers were sunk, the Japanese Combined Fleet suffered complete defeat. From this moment, it could be said that the tide of war had turned against the Japanese. During this battle *Yukikaze* played a minor role in supporting the landings on Midway Island from bases in Saipan in the Pacific.

The disaster to the fleet in the battle of Midway Island brought home to the Japanese only too bitterly the importance of aircraft carriers. On 13 July 1942 the carrier force, known as the 3rd Fleet, was reorganised to become the main striking force of the Combined Fleet. Fast battleships, heavy cruisers and destroyers were the supporting forces of the 3rd Fleet. Sixteen *Kagero* and *Yugumo*-class destroyers formed the destroyer group, which

* Warship Profile No. 13, HMS *Exeter*

The Isokaze, *the twelfth ship of the* Kagero-*class destroyers, undergoing official trial runs in November 1940.*

The Arashi, *the sixteenth ship of the* Kagero-*class destroyers, on trial runs in December 1940 with a top speed of 34·76 knots.*

became known as the 10th Destroyer Squadron. Among these destroyers was *Yukikaze*.

Guadalcanal and the Solomons

The scene of battle now shifted to the Solomon Islands, where the Allied Powers made a surprise landing on Guadalcanal during August 1942. The Japanese fought desperately against tremendous odds to stem the tide of war.

On 26 October 1942 a battle took place between the carriers of the Japanese and the US naval forces north-east of the Solomon Islands. In this battle the Japanese succeeded in sinking USS *Hornet** and the US destroyer *Porter,* and in damaging USS *Enterprise* and other warships. No Japanese ships were lost, although several were slightly damaged.

After the successful air attacks on the carriers, *Yukikaze* joined in the onslaught on the enemy fleet; a unique moment came for this fortunate destroyer when she witnessed the last of the USS *Hornet.*

Yukikaze now became deeply involved as the tempo of battle escalated in the Solomons' theatre. On the night of 13 November, the Japanese battleships *Hiei* and *Kirishima* attempted a heavy bombardment of Guadalcanal with their 36cm guns in order to neutralise the airstrip. A fierce night engagement developed near this notorious island between the attacking forces and the Allied defenders. *Yukikaze* was one of the eight destroyers taking part in this desperate endeavour.

As one of the van she fought valiantly with her 12·7cm guns. During the engagement she fired a total of 374 rounds from her armament, and she was given the credit for sinking the two American destroyers *Barton* and *Laffey.* During the same night *Hiei* was seriously damaged with her steering gear out of control, and two destroyers, *Yudachi* and *Akatsuki,* were sunk. Three other destroyers, *Ikazuchi, Murasame* and *Amatsukaze* were damaged. Casualties on the Allied side were considerably heavier: two cruisers, *Helena* and *Juno,* and four destroyers, *Barton, Cushing, Laffey* and *Honsen* were sunk, while two heavy cruisers, *Portland* and *San Francisco,* and three destroyers, *Aaron Ward, O'Bannon* and *Sterett* were seriously damaged.

All the following day *Yukikaze* and another destroyer stood by the damaged *Hiei,* now stopped and out of control in the face of continual air attack. When darkness fell, she took on board *Hiei's* survivors, before administering the *coup de grâce* to the crippled battleship.

As her main boiler had developed a crack due to a near-miss from a dive bomber, *Yukikaze* returned to the homeland for repairs on 10 December 1942.

Evacuation of Guadalcanal

The famous destroyer was unable to enjoy a much needed rest, because the Japanese Navy was forced to mobilise all operational destroyers to evacuate

* Warship Profile No. 3, USS *Hornet* (CV8)

The *Yukikaze* in 1945. As a result of a series of armament modifications, her No. 2 twin-mounting main turret had been removed, while 25mm AA machine guns were drastically reinforced to improve her AA armament. Note Type 22 radar on her foremast and Type 13 radar on her mainmast. Most of her scuttles were sealed to improve her water-tightness, while degaussing was fitted to the outer hull to neutralise the magnetic effect of the ship

D. Johnson

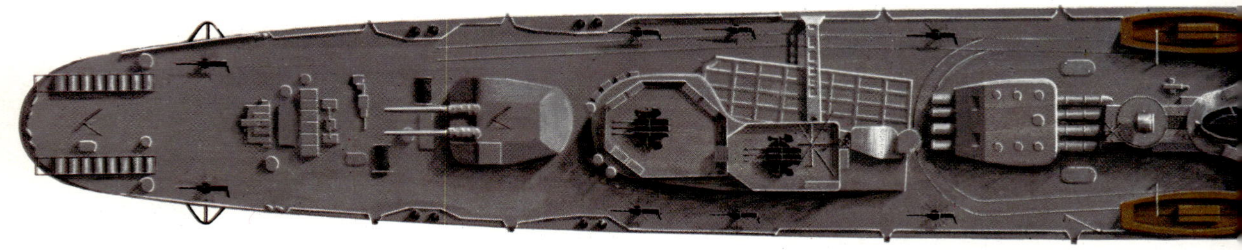

Yukikaze's silhouette in 1940 when she was completed

Yukikaze's silhouette in July 1943, after the first modificatio to her armament was made on her.
A 25cm AA machine gun platform was newly installed for'd of her bridge, while two twin-mounting 25cm machine guns, each on both sides of her second funnel, were changed into triple-mountings

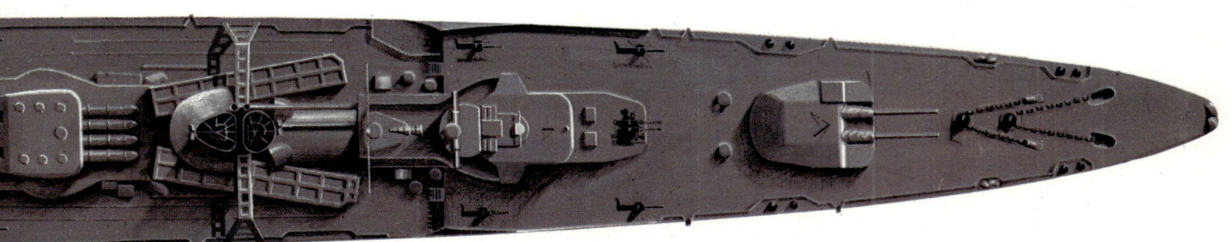

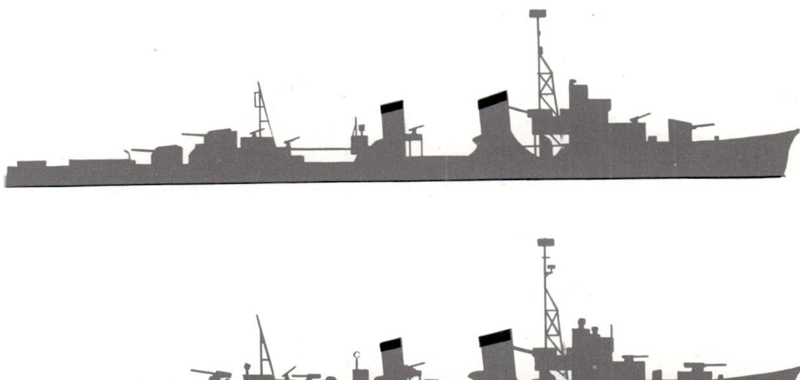

The *Tan Yang's* silhouette in 1954. She was rearmed with old Japanese weapons. A twin 12·7cm mounting was installed on her fo'c'sle and two twin 12·7cm superimposed mountings were fitted aft

The Tan Yang's silhouette in 1961. Her armament was changed into the American style and her forecastle was lengthened further aft

The Shiranuhi, *the second ship of the* Kagero-*class destroyers, under repairs in a dry dock of Maizuru Naval Yard in September 1942. She was heavily damaged by torpedo attacks from an enemy submarine on 5 July 1942 off Kiska Island. Her fore-part immediately forward of the first funnel was cut off. The box-shape installation amidships is her after quadruple 61cm torpedo-tube mounting; the platform-shaped containers abaft the tubes comprise the torpedo reloading equipment.*

Another photograph of Shiranuhi *undergoing repair in dry dock—her after part.*

the battered and starving troops from Guadalcanal. After making port in Truk Island on 23 January 1943, *Yukikaze* took part in the first evacuation on 1 February and the second on 4 February from the doomed island. In spite of tremendous odds, she and the other destroyers successfully completed their dangerous mission. The last operation on 7 February, in which *Yukikaze* did not take part, was also successful, with the result that all the remaining troops on the island were evacuated. Since this was achieved in the face of every-increasing enemy air supremacy and the constant threats from surface vessels, the successful conclusion was one of the most brilliant exploits of Japanese destroyers.

These three destroyers, from left, Hamakaze, Tanikaze *and* Isokaze *of the 17th Destroyer Division belonging to the 1st Destroyer Squadron, were at Saeki Bay in western Japan in November 1941, before they headed for Hittokap Bay in the Kurile Islands, a rendezvous point of the Pearl Harbour attack force.*

The Amatsukaze, *the ninth ship of the* Kagero-*class, destroyers, at full power under trial runs in October 1940, when she registered 34·55 knots. Because the after hull form of the* Kagero-*class destroyers was shaped differently from that of the* Asashio-*class, her stern wave was slightly different from that of the latter. In addition, the* Amatsukaze *alone employed higher pressure and temperature steam (400°C, 40kg/cm²) for trial purposes.*

Air Attack

Yukikaze's good fortune was destined to continue, although it received its biggest challenge on 5 March 1943. *Yukikaze* and seven other destroyers were escorting a convoy of eight transports, carrying reinforcements to Lae in eastern New Guinea. When they were passing through the Bismarck Sea, they were attacked by an armada of US Army Air Force B.25s using the newly-developed skip-bombing. Faced for the first time with this new technique, the Japanese destroyers were unable to evade the attackers. All eight transports and four of the eight destroyers were sunk. Only *Yukikaze* remained untouched.

Following the fall of Guadalcanal, the Japanese now attempted to reinforce a new defence line, and *Yukikaze* was assigned to a series of escort duties in that theatre. The first reinforcement was to Kolombangara in the Solomon Islands from 7 to 9 March, and the second to the same island from 12 to 14 March. Another reinforcement was escorted to Finschafen in eastern New Guinea from 10 to 12 April, and to Tuluvu on the western tip of New Britain from 13 to 14 April 1943. The undamaged *Yukikaze* was always busy because by now the Japanese destroyers had become the main work horses as the pressure of battle mounted.

The First Refit

When the Allied Powers made a surprise landing on Attu Island in the Aleutians in early May 1943, *Yukikaze* lay in her home port preparing for a counter-attack. When this plan was nipped in the bud, she was given a much needed refit at the Kure Naval Yard.

Twin mountings of 25mm machine guns were installed for'd of the bridge for the first time, and the two twin mountings of 25mm machine guns on either side of her second funnel were replaced by triple mountings. The number of 25mm AA machine guns was thus increased to eight. In addition a radar detecting device was installed on the bridge.

After the completion of the refit, *Yukikaze* made a sortie from the homeland to escort the battleship *Kongo* and her consorts to Truk atoll. In late June she escorted reinforcements to Nauru Island in the central Pacific.

The Nowaki, *the fifteenth ship of the* Kagero-*class destroyers, at full power under trial runs in April 1941. She registered a top speed of 35·1 knots*

When the Allies launched a new offensive against New Georgia on 30 June 1943, *Yukikaze* was ordered to escort the heavy cruiser *Chokai* to Rabaul. This gave the destroyer another opportunity to engage the enemy in battle.

Kula Gulf: Fight against Odds

After the Allied landings on New Georgia, the development of the situation on land and sea had been very rapid. As the Japanese attempted to send in reinforcements, a series of sea battles took place, mostly in the Kula Gulf, between the supporting Japanese force and the Allies. *Yukikaze* took part in the night engagement of 12 July in the Kula Gulf. On this occasion the Japanese force consisted of the light cruisers *Jintsu, Yukikaze,* two *Yugumo*-class, one *Shiratsuyu*-class and one *Mutsuki*-class destroyers, while the allied strength was three light cruisers and 10 destroyers.

In spite of the tremendous odds, the Japanese took up the challenge and fired their deadly torpedoes at a range of 5000m, inflicting serious damage on the US light cruiser *Leander.* Although the flagship, *Jintsu* was hit and immobilized, *Yukikaze* and the other three destroyers reloaded their torpedo tubes and, closing on the enemy again, fired their torpedoes. The enemy force, unaware of the speed with which the Japanese Navy could reload torpedoes, was taken entirely by surprise. The US destroyer *Gwin* was sunk and the USS *Honolulu* and *St Louis* severely damaged.

This was a brilliant tactical success for the Japanese Navy, and much credit must be accorded to the good fighting qualities of *Yukikaze* and the other destroyers. This engagement proved to be the last in this theatre of war in which *Yukikaze* participated.

Second Refit

In late August 1943 *Yukikaze* was ordered to make for her home port, where she arrived on 2 September for her second refit.

This time her second 12·7cm turret was removed and replaced by two triple mountings of 25mm machine guns. The total number of these weapons was thereby made up to 14.

At the same time the long-awaited radar was installed Type 22 radar for surface observation was fitted on her foremast, and Type 13 radar for aircraft detection on her mainmasts. Sonar of a new type was also installed. The refit was completed in early October.

The Marianas and the Carolines

Yukikaze was now chiefly engaged in escort duties, as the Japanese redoubled their efforts to strengthen the defence line along the Marianas and the Carolines. By April 1944 she had taken part in escort missions to Singapore, Truk, Guam and Saipan without any mishaps.

This defence line became threatened in the spring of 1944 by the now very powerful US striking force. The Japanese planned to deal with it once and for all with the carrier striking force of the main fleet. A new disposition of the fleet was made accordingly, and all ships carried out a thorough day and night action training. *Yukikaze* was once again given the task of screening the carrier force.

She joined the force at Tawitawi in the Sulu Archipelago in the middle of May, where she suffered an unexpected mishap. During a search for enemy submarines in the anchorage, she hit submerged rocks and damaged the blade of one propeller. As she was now unable to make more than 25 knots, her assignment was changed to that of escorting the 2nd Tanker Group consisting of two tankers.

While thus engaged, *Yukikaze* took part in the sea battle west of the Marianas on 19 to 20 June 1944, which resulted in the defeat of the Combined Fleet. On the evening of 20 June, the 2nd Tanker Group was attacked by enemy air strikes. One of the two tankers was sunk and the other was so seriously damaged that she had later to be sunk by torpedoes from *Yukikaze*. With a dispirited crew *Yukikaze* made her home port, although once again she had escaped untouched.

Third Refit—then Samar and Leyte

Yukikaze was under repair from 5 July to 15 August, while the third modification was carried out. *Fourteen* extra single mounting 25mm AA machine guns were installed. An attempt was made to improve the Type 22 radar for surface firing, but the

The Hamanami, *the fourteenth ship of the* Yugumo-*class destroyers, at full power during trial runs on 10 October 1943. She made a top speed of 35·4 knots.*

The midship section of the Makigumo, *the sixth ship of the* Yugumo-*class destroyers, dry-docked at Maizuru Naval Yard in early 1943. She was attacked by enemy dive bombers off Isabel Island, north of Guadalcanal Island on 1 February 1943 and sustained heavy damage. Note her starboard side patched up by temporary repairs.*

precision obtained proved to be inadequate.

The next engagement with the enemy was the sea battle off Samar in late October 1944. In a desperate attempt to stem the tide of war, the Japanese, using only surface forces, made a daring attack on the enemy beach-head on Leyte Island in the Philippines. *Yukikaze* was among the ships to break through the island chain unchallenged, only to encounter unexpectedly the enemy carrier groups during the early morning of 25 October.

The Japanese Navy was unable to launch a carrier-borne air strike because of the effects from the devastating defeat in the Philippine Sea during June. The Navy's land-based air arm, together with the Army air force, were no match for the enemy strength. In spite of this, and after identifying the carriers, the Japanese seized the chance as a golden opportunity to come to grips with their Number One enemy—the US carriers. All vessels with sufficient speed turned south-east to press home the attack. Amongst them was *Yukikaze.*

The light cruiser *Yahagi,* flagship of the 10th Destroyer Squadron, *Yukikaze* and three other sister ships then launched their torpedoes against the retreating enemy. This tactic had no success, but presently the four Japanese destroyers concentrated their fire on the US destroyer *Johnston,* who had turned to face them, and succeeded in sinking her. This proved to be the last occasion that *Yukikaze* used her guns to sink an enemy ship.

After attacking for about two and a half hours, the Japanese finally had to withdraw. Although one enemy escort carrier and a destroyer had been sunk, the Japanese force had suffered irretrievable damage. When the ships returned to Brunei in Borneo, only a remnant remained of this once powerful force. Very few ships were undamaged, but amongst this few was *Yukikaze.*

Return to the Homeland

It was then decided that the Japanese ships in Brunei should return to the homeland in separate groups. *Yukikaze* was detailed to escort *Kongo* and *Haruna,* who sailed on 16 November. On the passage *Kongo* was sunk by an enemy submarine in the Straits of Formosa on the night of 20 November. *Yukikaze* and *Haruna* reached their home port on 23 November.

After returning home, *Yukikaze* had little respite. Air and submarine attacks continued unceasingly. As one of the few serviceable destroyers, she was detailed for a series of escort duties. On one of her screening missions she was to witness the tragic end of the carrier *Shinano.* This ship had originally been built as the third of the *Yamato*-class battleships, but had been later converted to a carrier. *Shinano* left her birth-place, Yokosuka, as a newly converted carrier on the evening of 28 November 1944, bound for the Inland Sea for final fitting and training.

In the early hours of 29 November, while steaming far to the south of Japan, *Shinano* was attacked by the US submarine *Archerfish* and hit by three torpedoes. For a time the injured vessel carried on at full speed. Then leakage through her water-tight compartments proved too much for the inexperienced crew. Flooding became out of control. Potentially the most powerful carrier in the Fleet, she finally settled into the sea, and sank in the late morning of 29 November without having fired a single shot. The crew of *Yukikaze,* down-hearted at having failed in their escort duty, brought their ship to Kure on 30 November.

At Kure, *Yukikaze* underwent much needed maintenance from 30 November to 22 December when a new model Type 3 sonar was fitted. She then took part in escorting a convoy from Formosa to the homeland, and also served as a target ship for training human torpedoes. By this time, even the Inland Sea was no longer safe from enemy air attack, and *Yukikaze* occasionally had to defend herself from B.29s and carrier-borne aircraft.

Iwo-Jima and Okinawa—Desperate Defence

Japan was now exposed to increasing pressure, as the tempo of war moved towards its climax. Iwo-Jima had fallen and the invasion of Okinawa seemed imminent. With her fleet reduced to a battered remnant, the Japanese Navy had originally planned to defend the island with land-based planes alone. However, when on 1 April 1945 enemy landings started, Japan launched a last, desperate attack on the beach-head with such naval forces as could be mustered. Air attacks were strengthened by the use of 'suicide' planes (*Kamikaze*). By this drastic action Japan sought, *'to find a way to life out of a fatal situation'.*

This fatal mission was assigned to the 2nd Fleet, all that could be mobilised from the once powerful Japanese Navy. This force consisted of the battleship *Yamato,* the light cruiser *Yahagi* and eight destroyers including *Yukikaze.* In the late afternoon of 6 April they left an anchorage in the Inland Sea, and headed for a position north-west of Okinawa. As they were steaming towards their destination in the early afternoon of 7 April, the ships were subjected to repeated attacks by enemy carrier-borne aircraft. Without air cover, the Japanese ships fought back valiantly, but the odds were overwhelming. *Yamato* and *Yahagi* finally heeled over and sank. Four destroyers were also sunk. Another destroyer was crippled, and turned back for the home port of Sasebo. Only three destroyers were unscathed: amongst them was *Yukikaze.*

Defeat

This desperate but futile attempt marked the end of the Japanese Fleet. The few remaining ships sought the protection of land-based AA defences but, even so, they were sometimes damaged by the relentless enemy air offensive. *Yukikaze,* lying at Maizuru, the naval base on the Sea of Japan, had once to face a fierce attack by carrier-borne planes. She successfully repelled the assault without being hit by anything more than a single 13mm bullet.

On 15 August 1945 Japan surrendered.

At this moment in history, *Yukikaze* was still in Maizuru. She was the lone survivor of the 18 *Kagero* and 20 *Yugumo*-class destroyers. She had not only survived, but her fighting capability had not been impaired.

The Kiyoshimo, *the nineteenth ship of the* Yugumo-*class destroyers, soon after she was completed in May 1944. Because she was built in the latter part of the war, her AA armament was greatly intensified and a Type 22 radar was installed on her mainmast from the date of building.*

The Hayashima, *the eighteenth ship of the* Yugumo-*class destroyers, in February 1944, soon after she was commissioned.*

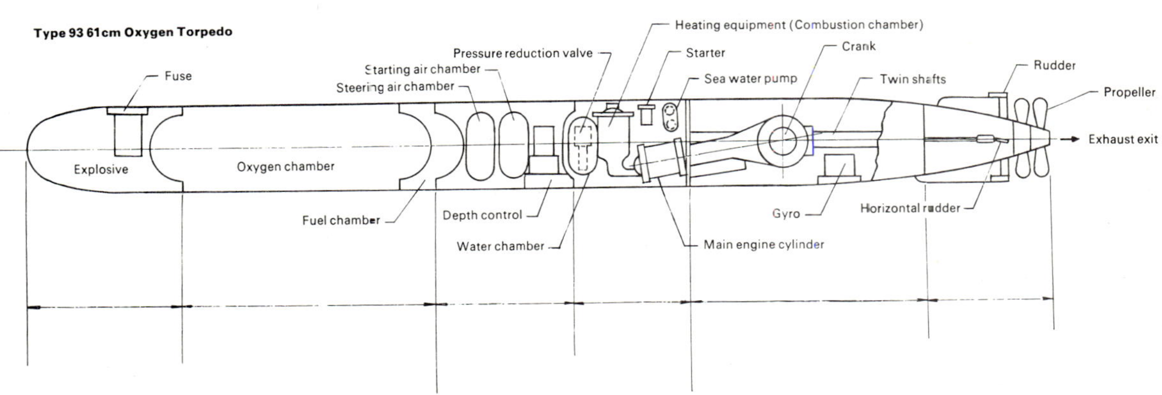

The Hayanami, *the tenth ship of the* Yugumo-*class destroyers, at full power during her trial runs in July 1943, when she made a top speed of 35·15 knots. Compared with the* Kagero-*class, her AA armament was increased and her bridge structure streamlined.*

A sortie scene of the Special Attack Force on Okinawa from the port of Kure on 28 March 1945. A sister ship of Yukikaze, *the* Isokaze *is in foreground and dimly seen in the background is* Yamato. *The picture was drawn by Mr H. Kuboki, who was then a crew member of* Yukikaze.

Opposite: *Sketch by Mr H. Kuboki showing* Yukikaze*'s bridge seen from for'd.*

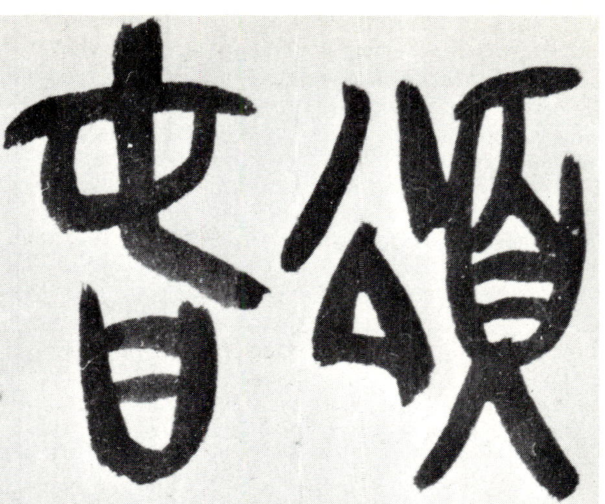

元旦

今年も先生の世界の艦船誌と
御健筆御祈致します

雪風艦橋のスケッチ

昭和十九年七月七日．サイパン沖海戦后
タウイタウイより単艦帰国．呉工广ドック内
にて防弾板を取った所（付替ノタメ）の
スケッチの写です．

Post-war Activities

After the war, warships were used to repatriate Japanese soldiers and civilians from overseas and *Yukikaze* was at once assigned for this work. At the Maizuru naval yard her armament was completely removed and suitable accommodation installed. This was completed by 10 February 1946, and by 18 December she had made 15 such missions: once to Chuanchou in China, twice to Rabaul, twice to Bangkok, once to Port Moresby in New Guinea, five times to the Ch'inhuangtao area of China, and four times to Okinawa. In all she had covered a total of 38,753 miles in moving 13,056 persons. It was some comfort to her crew, most of whom had served in *Yukikaze* during the war, to be able to contribute to the rehabilitation of post-war Japan.

Reparation Ship

The next phase was more humiliating. She was designated to be one of the reparation ships for the Allied Powers. In spite of this, her crew had maintained her so well that she enjoyed the reputation of being the best ship of the reparation vessels. *Yukikaze* was inspected by many naval attachés from a number of the victorious nations, including the US Far East Naval Commander at the Port of Tokyo in late May 1947. Her condition so impressed him that he remarked, 'It is a big surprise indeed to see a ship of the defeated navy being so well kept'.

Yukikaze was finally allotted to the Republic of China. She left Sasebo on 1 July 1947 and arrived at Shanghai on 3 July. There she was officially taken over by the Chinese Navy on 6 July and renamed the *Tang Yan*.

The End of a great Destroyer

As *Tang Yan*, she was re-armed with one unit of 12·7cm twin mounting guns placed for'd and two units of 12·7cm twin mounting guns aft, in addition to eight 25mm AA machine guns. In about 1956 her armament was replaced by three 5in single mounting guns and two 3in single mounting guns, as well as 17 40mm AA machine guns. She remained on active service until about 1965. In May 1970 she ran aground during a typhoon, and the decision was taken to scrap her. Thus ended the long and memorable career of the great destroyer.

In 1971, the Chinese Navy returned the former *Yukikaze*'s anchor and rudder to Japan, where they are preserved in the Naval Educational Museum at Etajima. Here all the facilities of the Naval Academy of the Imperial Japanese Navy have been inherited by the Maritime Self-Defence Force of Japan.

The last scene of the carrier Shinano *seen from* Yukikaze. *She finally went down in the morning of 29 November 1944. The destroyer seen to the right is* Isokaze. *The picture is by Mr H. Kuboki.*

The Yukikaze *when she was used as a transport for carrying back Japanese repatriates from overseas after the end of the war. Her armament was taken off and insignias, as designated by the Allied Powers, were painted on her funnel and sides.*

A drawing made by Mr H. Kuboki of Yukikaze *in late 1944. Note that her second 12·7cm turret was removed and a number of 25mm AA machine guns were installed to reinforce her AA armament. Around the bridge side, steel shields were fitted.*

The Isokaze's *bridge in October 1944. Note that the bridge was completely protected by steel shields. The* Yukikaze *was also provided with the same protection. The photograph was taken by Mr T. Shiraishi.*

The Yukikaze *as a transport for repatriates. Her main mountings were removed so that the accommodation could be increased by adding temporary housings fore and aft. Note that her Type 22 radar on her foremast remained as it had been during the war, while her Type 13 fire control radar on the mainmast was removed.*

The Yukikaze *of Japan's Maritime Self-Defence Force. The first Japanese-built ship of the post-war Japanese Navy, she was named after the* Yukikaze *of the Imperial Japanese Navy. Specification: displacement, 1700 tons; a maximum speed, 30 knots; three 5in AA guns; eight 40mm AA machine guns; two Hedgehogs; four depth-charge throwers (K-Gun) and two A/S torpedo launchers.*

The Yukikaze, *as renamed* Tan Yang *by the Chinese Navy. This picture was taken when she took part in the naval review on 14 December 1964. Her armament was altered to American standards and her forecastle was taken further aft.*

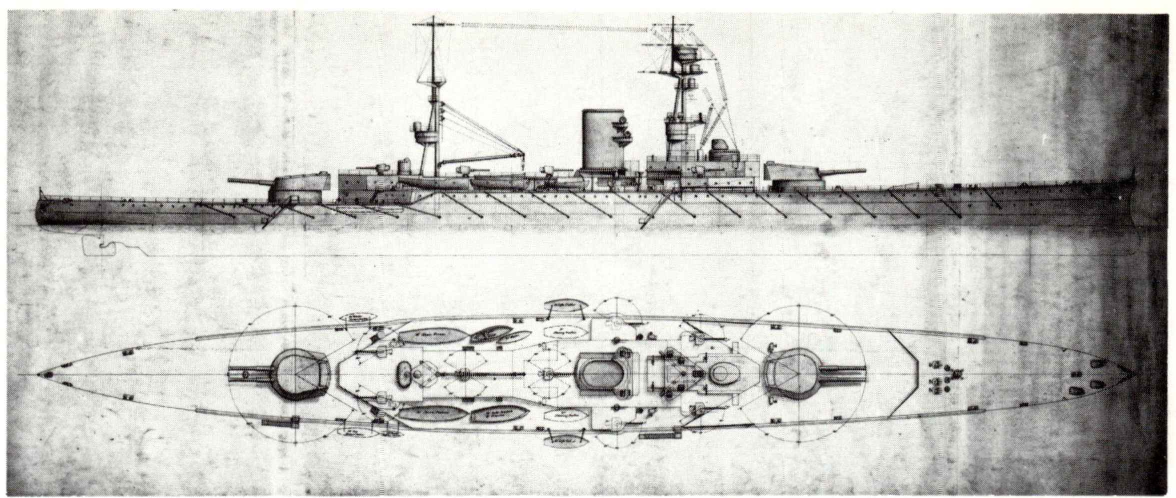

As originally designed, a 'large light cruiser'. Single 18in guns were substituted whilst the ship was building for the twin 15in shown here *(National Maritime Museum)*

HMS Furious/Aircraft Carrier 1917-1948

Part 1 : The First Eight Years

by Commander C. A. Jenkins, OBE RN

The 'Baltic Project'

Oddly enough, the ship who was destined to become, as an aircraft carrier, the nucleus around which was built so much of the history and development of naval flying was originally designed for quite a different role.

Like the history of many other ships of the First World War and the decade before it, that of HMS *Furious* starts with Admiral of the Fleet Lord ('Jackie') Fisher.

In October 1914, this energetic genius was recalled by Winston Churchill to the Admiralty as First Sea Lord, a post which he had already held from 1904 to 1910. Now 73, he enjoyed vast and almost unchallenged authority in all matters of naval administration and development, especially as to shipbuilding programmes and warship design. It was largely his personal leadership and ruthless drive during his previous period of office which had transformed the Navy and had provided the Grand Fleet on whose superiority the basic safety of the whole country depended. It was no wonder that Lord Fisher's views carried great weight and that his decisions met with little opposition.

One major scheme which he had been nursing since 1908 and into which he now threw himself with the enthusiastic backing of Winston Churchill was the 'Baltic Project'.

This plan was for three major landings, of which two were feints but capable of extension in favourable circumstances, to be made on the Pomeranian coast of Germany less than 90 miles from Berlin, with strong naval cover and aided by Russian troops.

Fisher held that such a direct thrust at the capital would mean that the enemy would have to

Lord Fisher, for whose 'Baltic Project' the Furious *was first designed, as a Vice-Admiral* *(IWM)*

withdraw a million soldiers from the Western Front and that it would force the High Seas Fleet to seek the battle in which the Grand Fleet would destroy it, the master-stroke to shorten the war.

There was no recent precedent for landings on such a scale against opposition, nor did any Naval Staff exist to make a detailed study of the proposed operation and its requirements. But Fisher never lacked either confidence or imagination, and it is astonishing how accurately he foresaw many of the requirements for specialised craft to carry and protect an assault expedition. There were minesweepers, minelayers, landing craft, monitors, and many other types of vessel, so that by the time he left the Admiralty in May 1915 he had placed contracts for no less than 612 vessels, many of them embodying ideas in advance of contemporary naval thinking.

The Ideal Fisher Fighting Ships

Fisher was always obsessed by high speed and heavy guns, maintaining that with superiority in both these factors a ship could catch any enemy and send her to the bottom without letting her approach close enough to score any hits with her own guns.

In deciding upon the design of the three vessels who were to provide the main fire power of the expedition he therefore went up to, and beyond, the limits in these two respects so far reached in any major warship.

Main Specifications

Speed and Engines

Fisher ordered the unusual speed of 32 knots—incidentally 7 knots more than that of the 'fast squadron' of the Battle Fleet. The recent invention of the all-geared turbine made this theoretically possible at a Shaft Horse Power of 90,000.

Main Armament

Although two of the ships, later named *Courageous* and *Glorious,* were to carry as their main armament four 15in guns in twin turrets—as big as any then afloat or projected even for battleships—the third, *Furious,* was to go further and mount real monsters, two 18in guns. These were to be in single turrets, one forward and one aft, and would be the heaviest naval guns in the world, capable of firing a shell of one and a half tons to a maximum range of over 20 miles.

There was much controversy, and even opposition, over the provision of guns of such a calibre. Gunnery experts pointed out that the long intervals between salvoes would make the application of spotting corrections useless by the time of the next, whilst the small number of shells would reduce the probability of a direct hit. After his emphasis on speed and surface action, Fisher seems to have been rather inconsistent in replying that '*Furious* was not built for salvoes . . . but for Berlin . . . . Her guns with their enormous shells were built to make it impossible for the Germans to prevent the Russians from landing on the Pomeranian coast'. The shells were to 'burst on reaching the ground far out of human sight, but yet with exact accuracy . . . causing craters somewhat like that of Vesuvius or Mount Etna and consequently you can easily imagine the German army fleeing for its life from Pomerania to Berlin'.

As so often, Fisher had his way. But provision was made for the substitution of four 15in guns if the 18in proved unsatisfactory.

Draught

One cannot help sympathising with her designers. Record speed and huge armament would normally call for a ship of the very largest tonnage, and yet they were at the same time ordered to keep her draught below 22ft, for the shallow waters of the Baltic, and this was five feet less than that of any capital ship of the day.

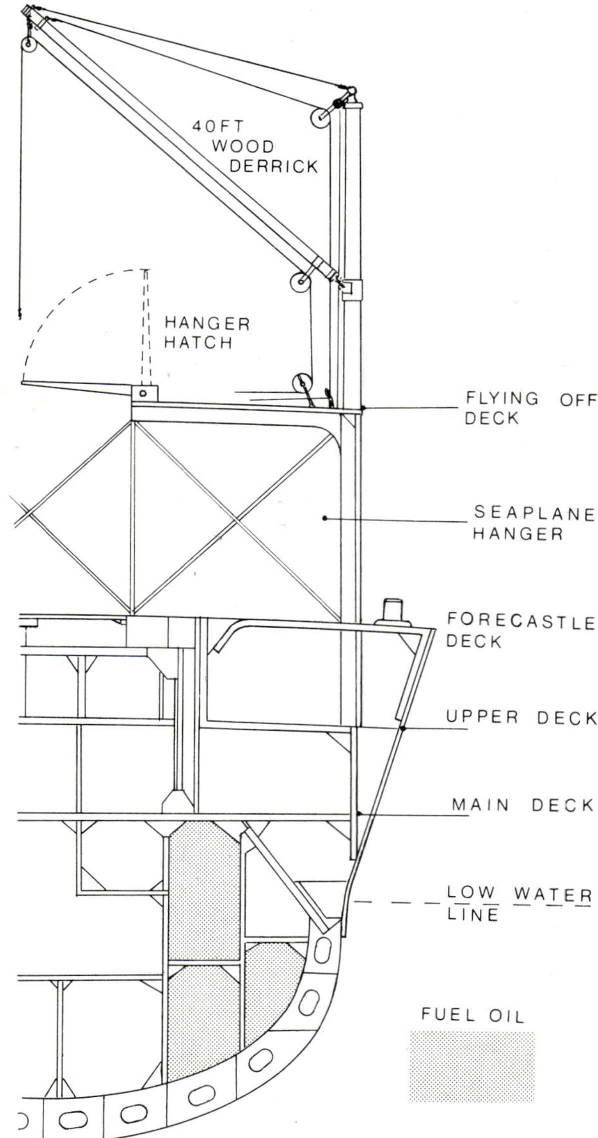

Section of the forward hangar at Frame 60, showing the structure and the aircraft derrick (1917-18)

Armour

The saving grace which made this possible was that Fisher's theory of outranging the enemy meant that armour became of secondary importance, and thousands of tons could be saved.

The Design Takes Shape

In February 1915, the Director of Naval Construction reported that his department had prepared design drawings to meet the general specifications given.

The light draught together with high speed would call for a long ship of 786ft overall, 88ft beam.

The bows would have a good flare, which would be

carried well aft.
There would be 3in side protection from 4ft 6in below the waterline to the level of the upper deck, 23ft above it, and deck armour of between 3in and 1in covering all vital parts.
Below water the hull would be bulged over a considerable length amidships as further protection against torpedoes for boilers and machinery.
The ship would be subdivided into very numerous watertight compartments.
Because the main armament of this particular ship would consist of only two guns whose interval between firing would be great, the secondary armament assumed greater importance.
Originally, eight single guns of 4in calibre were proposed, then 16 of which 12 were to be on triple mountings, but these were turned down as being too light.
Finally, after some consideration of the trusty 6in Breech Loader, an interesting suggestion by the Director of Naval Ordnance that 5·5in should be fitted was approved.
These were of a type manufactured for Greek ships which had been requisitioned, and, although no guns of this calibre had been tried in Britain, many had been satisfactorily mounted in the French Navy. Their faster rate of fire would compensate for the slight reduction in weight of projectile to 82lb compared with 100lb for the 6in.
It was therefore approved that eight of these should be fitted in *Furious.* Actually, by redistribution, this number was increased to 11.
Eighteen 21in torpedo tubes, of which two were submerged, were also incorporated in the design.
Although of greater length and heavier armament, *Furious* would approximate in many of her principal characteristics to the latest Light Cruisers and, being thus standardised, could be constructed quickly and cheaply, the estimate at the moment being just over £1,180,000.
Specially good features would be the relatively small complement needed and the large radius of action, 11,000 miles at economical speed and 6000 miles at 20 knots.
She was to be fitted as a flagship.

Approval: the 'Large Light Cruiser'

Financial approval at the moment could not be obtained for any more 'large armoured ships', so Fisher ingeniously got around the difficulty by calling the three vessels 'large light cruisers' and—probably assisted by being able to point to their light draught and lack of armour—succeeded in getting them included in the Emergency War Programme under this heading, although some official papers referred to them as 'light battle cruisers' and one well-known authority placed them in the category of 'battleships'.
After all, they were to be over 140ft longer than the *Iron Duke* or *Queen Elizabeth* and 1000 tons heavier than the *Dreadnought.*
The contract for *Furious* was placed with the well-known firm of Armstrong Whitworth, Walker Naval Yard, Newcastle-upon-Tyne, where she was built with great secrecy, being laid down in June 1915 and launched on 18 August 1916.

PARTICULARS, AS DESIGNED

Dimensions	
Length, overall	786¼ft
Beam	88ft
Draught, mean	21½ft
maximum	25ft
Displacement, normal	19,100 tons
full load	22,405 tons
Armament	
18in BL guns (after earliest design for 4 × 15in)	2
5·5in BL (after earliest design for 16 × 4in)	11
3in HA	4
3pdr	4
Weight of armament	2420 tons
Torpedo tubes (21in above water)	16
(21in submerged)	2
Protection	
Side, amidships	3in
Side, forward and aft	2in
Bulkheads, forward and aft	3in
Barbettes	7in, 6in
Turrets	9in, 5in
Conning tower	10in
Deck, over part of lower deck	3in
Deck, for most of length	1in
Deck, additional over citadel	¾in
Weight of armour	2800 tons
Machinery	
Brown-Curtis all-geared turbines, 90,000SHP	31½ knots
Yarrow boilers	18
Propellers, pitch 11ft 6in, diameter 11ft 6in	4
Fuel	
Oil, full storage	3393 tons
Anchors and cables	
Anchors, 125cwt	2
Shackles of cable on each anchor	18 of 2$\frac{11}{16}$in
Stern anchor, 60cwt	1
Kedge anchors, 16cwt and 12cwt	2
Complement, (as light cruiser)	745
Radius	
11,000 miles at economical speed, 6000 miles at 20 knots	

Those Monster Guns[1]

As the 18in gun for which *Furious* was designed was the largest ever installed in a British warship, some details may be given here.
The total revolving weight for each turret was 827 tons, made up of 152 tons for the gun, 263 tons for the shield armour and roof plates, and 412 tons for the turntable, working chamber, trunks, live roller ring, etc.
The mounting and the loading arrangements were partly of new design, partly a combination of the principles already embodied in the 15in ships.
In the shell room below, the 3600lb shell would be moved from its bin to the waiting tray by gantries with longitudinal and transverse traversing (an innovation from overhead rails). Thence an hydraulically driven chain rammer would push it on to one of two trays which could be moved by ram to a position for discharging the shell into one of two central ammunition cages. These were of a type already fitted in *Agincourt* and *Canada,* but could be worked independently or together, one ascending whilst the other descended, thus avoiding the need for any auxiliary system. These cages then brought the shell up to the working chamber, where it was loaded by ram into the lowest of three tiers of the gunloading cage.

[1] For security reasons the cover designation of '15in "B" Mounting' was adopted for these 18in guns.

1

2

3

Cordite was loaded in the two upper tiers, half a charge in each, and then the whole gunloading cage was raised to the rear of the gun and the shell rammed home. The cage then dropped so that the lower cordite charge became level with the breech for loading, similarly for the upper.

The turrets were trained by swashplate engine, capable of rotating them at a speed of 3° per second. The guns could be elevated from 5° of depression to 30° of elevation at a maximum rate of 3° per second. *Furious* only fired her after 18in gun at practice, which shook her up considerably. But they were later mounted in the monitors *General Wolfe* and *Lord Clive,* who fired them in anger. A third, spare, was at one time earmarked for mounting ashore for shelling the Ostende submarine bases if the Passchendaele offensive failed. During the Second World War it was used for test firing at Shoeburyness, being re-bored for 16in.

Changed Orders

Whether *Furious* in her original form as cruiser would have been successful was never put to the test. One may doubt the efficiency of her huge slow-firing guns in actual battle, and dread the effect of enemy fire on such a lightly armoured ship, but in any case in March 1917, shortly before she was due for completion, sudden orders were received which changed the entire conception of the role which she was to play and which therefore involved much modification.

The 'large light cruiser' was to become the 'fast seaplane carrier'.

Before studying what this meant to her, we must look at the events which led to such a decision.

The Early Days of Naval Flying

Any study of the reasons for this decision and of what was done to the *Furious,* both then and later, calls for a conscious effort to do away with hindsight and to picture at each stage nothing beyond what was then known.

Until only three years before the outbreak of war, it had not been proved sufficiently practicable for aircraft to operate from the water, much less from ships. Rigid airships from land bases were considered to be the most promising types for scouting at sea; they were able to carry greater loads, had much more endurance, and their larger crews were more efficient for observing and communicating than a single pilot in a draughty cockpit who had a busy time merely keeping his fragile machine flying. The Germans, in particular, concentrated upon Zeppelins and in the short run, but in the short run only, were right to do so.

The British Admiralty's official view had also favoured the airship, until the destruction of the navy's first completed model, nicknamed the 'Mayfly', by a gale in 1911; the first success in taking off and landing on water turned opinion to the seaplane, and several shore bases for handling these craft were set up.

From 1912 the Royal Flying Corps acted as a combined air force, with a Central Flying School but with separate Naval and Military wings. There was much goodwill, but the two Services proved to have such very different requirements for planes, equipment, armament, and training of aircrew in practice that they grew apart. It was only one month before the outbreak of war that the separation became official and the Naval Wing of the RFC became the Royal Naval Air Service.

Now that control was in his own hands, the First Lord of the Admiralty, Mr Winston Churchill, began a vigorous drive to expand the production of seaplanes.

The First Seaplanes

Amidst all the uncertainties of policy, the theories, controversies, tests, and setbacks, it is astonishing how much is owed to the personal initiative of a small band of enthusiasts who saw the advantages of being able to take off or land on the sea instead of being tied to the few shore bases then available.

One of these, Commander Oliver Schwann, bought a biplane in November 1911, fitted it with floats and took off from the water, the first man in Britain to do so.

Soon afterwards, Messrs Short collaborated with four pilots who had been taught to fly by a Mr Francis McClean—at his own expense. They took up the development of the 'hydro-aeroplane' and made good progress in improving its design.

At first, the Admiralty had given their blessing, but not their financial backing. Now they took action, and by the outbreak of war Britain possessed 31 seaplanes.

It cannot be said, however, that the full potentiality was yet realised, the principle duty laid down for them being to defend dockyards against attacks by Zeppelins. With a radius of only 70 miles at that time they were certainly limited.

The War and Earlier Seaplane Carriers

Despite this definition of the seaplanes' principal duty, the Admiralty, on the outbreak of war, were commendably quick to see the logic of solving the problem of their lack of range, by transporting them by sea as near as possible to their operational areas.

Three fast cross-channel packets, *Empress, Engadine* and *Riviera,* were converted for the purpose. They each had a hangar aft capable of housing four seaplanes, and derricks to hoist them in and out. But as yet there were no flying-off platforms, so that the ship had to be stopped and the sea calm.

Even so they made possible an attack by seven seaplanes, although without inflicting damage, on Cuxhaven on Christmas Day, 1914.

1 *From the quarterdeck, looking forward. The size of the 18in gun can be judged by comparison with the officer and men below it* (*NMM*)

2 *July 1917. As first commissioned, with flying-off deck forward and 18in gun aft. A lovely, graceful ship* (*NMM*)

3 *Also July 1917. View from the quarter. The shadows running fore and aft for much of the ship's length are unusual, the ledge or catwalk outboard having been retained although, the torpedo nets and booms had been removed and stored* (*IWM*)

These and other converted merchant ships, such as the *Ben-my-Chree* from which the first aerial torpedo attack was launched on 12 August 1915, operated with varying and limited success.
The most important advance was made when the *Campania,* a converted liner, joined the fleet. At 22 knots she was much faster than the others and more able to keep up. Although even she often lost touch after stopping to hoist out her planes, it began to be common practice for a carrier to accompany the fleet to help with spotting or scouting. But the seaplanes were still only to be used when ordered and their influence on naval warfare was very little. Big guns, and the battlefleet which carried them, were what won battles; the only priority anything else could be given depended upon its contribution towards ensuring that the fleet action should be fought under the most favourable conditions.
It was the *Campania,* in August 1915, who successfully launched a Sopwith Baby seaplane from a 120ft long flying-off deck whilst the ship was steaming at 12 knots. For this, the plane was fitted with a trolley which was jettisoned.
At last, aircraft could take off in a moderate sea and without the parent ship having to stop to hoist them out. Landing however was still a very different matter and it was worrying, to say the least, to the higher command to find that the seaplane, to which the British had given priority, still lagged behind the Zeppelin in efficiency and in independence from weather restrictions.

Above: *The earliest type of aircraft carried by* Furious. *A Sopwith Baby single-seater scout and bombing seaplane* *(From 'British Aeroplanes 1914-18', by courtesy of J. M. Bruce, Esq)*

Below: *Another view of a Sopwith Baby seaplane With a Clerget engine of 110hp, this machine could reach a speed of nearly 100mph* *(J. M. Bruce, Esq)*

The Beatty Committee

By the time he relieved Admiral Jellicoe as C-in-C at the end of 1916, Admiral Beatty had become convinced of the potential importance of aircraft to the Grand Fleet, and critical of shortcomings. He pointed out that there was no continuous reconnaissance over the North Sea to give warning of enemy units at sea, no provision for anti-U-boat patrols ahead of the fleet except at the risk of a lack of aircraft at more critical moments, nor any certainty that weather would allow of launching to shoot down Zeppelins and spot for the fleet once action was joined.
He therefore set up a Committee in January 1917 to make recommendations on these important points. This Committee produced a most valuable report.
In particular, it drew attention to the shortcomings of the ships who then operated with the Grand Fleet. *Campania* with six fighter and six reconnaissance seaplanes had done valiant service but was old and unreliable, whilst *Manxman* and *Engadine* with eight seaplanes each were too slow to keep up. The provision of new seaplane carriers was a most urgent matter.
The Admiralty had in fact already bought an Italian liner and arranged for radical modifications to her, including a flush deck to give seaplanes a long run before shedding their trolleys on take-off. But this ship, the *Argus,* would not be able to join the fleet before at least the end of the year, and time was vital. Besides, the Committee recommended that the Grand Fleet needed more aircraft than she alone would be able to carry.
Faced with this dilemma, the Committee suggested that the 'light battle cruiser' (sic) *Furious,* now nearing completion, should be converted to a seaplane carrier.
There was much to be said in favour of this. The Baltic Project had long ago been shelved, most of the craft built for it having been swallowed up in the Dardanelles operations, for which the *Furious* herself would be too vulnerable. As a seaplane carrier, she would be fast enough to overtake the fleet after stopping to recover planes, she was large and seaworthy, and reasonably able to defend herself against light craft. The forward gun would have to be sacrificed for a flying-off deck, but many officers doubted the value of a main armament of only two 18in guns, with their long delays between salvoes and their lack of spread.
There was some natural opposition from the gunnery world, but the conversion was approved and the order given. The role of the *Furious* for the next 29 years had been decided.

1917, the Seaplane Carrier

It had already been approved in July 1916 that *Furious,* like several other units, should be fitted to carry two single-seater seaplanes, by a modification of design which would provide a small hangar

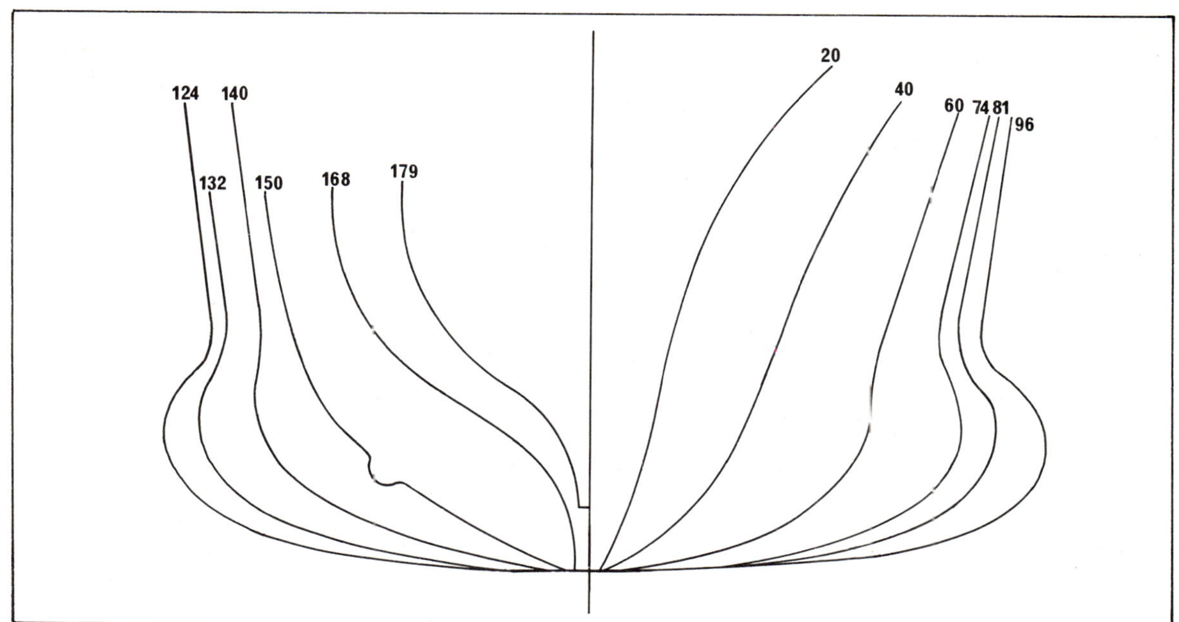

Hull section, as completed in 1917

forward. But, now that her primary role was to be as seaplane carrier, more extensive alterations would be necessary so that she could carry and operate larger numbers.

On 15 and 31 March 1917, therefore, the DNC issued orders to Mr A. Nicholls, Resident Overseer responsible for her construction, that *Furious* was to be fitted for the carrying of four two-seater reconnaissance seaplanes and four single-seater fighters,[1] fitted with land undercarriages, as first operated by *Manxman* in the following month. This was to involve the following:

The foremost 18in gun and mounting were to be removed.[2]

A large new seaplane hangar was to be built, using the space thus provided, with weather doors forward and special arrangements for ventilation, heating, and lighting. The shellroom could be turned into bomb storage.

A flying-off platform was to be made on the top of the hangar.

Carpenters' workshops would be required, and stowage for 600 two-gallon cans of petrol.

All work on net defence should be stopped, and the booms stored.

The Captain would be instructed that it would not be possible to drive the ship at the highest speed without injury to the flying-off deck except in fine weather—surely a sad limitation on a ship whose high speed for regaining station had been the reason for her selection.

Stability

An important incidental benefit came from the removal of the topweight of the foremost gun and

A Sopwith 2F1 Camel taking off from another carrier in 1918 (Fleet Air Arm Museum, Yeovilton)

turret. In the previous October DNC had expressed himself worried as to stability and as to the large angle of heel to be expected when turning at high speed, due to the small metacentric height. He now reported that stability would be 'ample'.

Commissioning and Trials

Great priority was given to completing the ship in her new form, and the delays caused by the alterations were cut to only one month.

She was commissioned at Walker-on-Tyne on 26 June 1917 by Captain Wilmot S. Nicholson. As well as the ship's company of 796, there were borne, additional 14 officers and 70 ratings of the Royal Naval Air Service under Squadron Commander E. H. Dunning. A week later she sailed for the Firth of Forth and trials.

[1] Later improved to a total of 10 aircraft.
[2] For some time the huge gun had been lying on the dockside, guarded by sentries for reasons of secrecy.

There had been some anxiety as to her performance at speed because the *Courageous* had developed signs of weakness a few feet before her forward 15in turret when steaming fast into head seas and had required strengthening by adding double plates. *Furious,* however, had a different form of midship section, a more pronounced bulge and a simpler form of main framing and structure of the hull. In the event, neither during these first trials nor at any time in her long career did she suffer from structural defects, and a speed of 31½ knots at full power was maintained without difficulty.

Joining the Fleet

On 4 July 1917, trials completed, *Furious* joined the Grand Fleet at Scapa Flow, being inspected by Admiral Beatty on 6 July.

Amongst the huge assembly of battleships, cruisers and destroyers there were at this time only two vessels available for air work with the Fleet, the old *Campania* and the slow *Manxman,* now capable of carrying 11 and 8 seaplanes respectively. *Argus* would have a speed of 21 knots and could fly off her 18 machines from a lengthy flush deck, but she would not join until October, 1918.

Furious, better armed than any other carrier, larger and more capable of keeping the seas, 10 knots faster, and with a flying-off deck of 228 by 50ft which was big enough for any seaplane or aeroplane of the day to take off, was therefore an important reinforcement. At this time she carried three Short Seaplanes and five Sopwith Pups.

Those were busy days for her Captain and officers and men. To work up any new ship to full efficiency is always strenuous, yet for them there were the additional complications of learning the new technique of handling aircraft, constant calls for experiments, official and unofficial; problems arising from a complicated system of higher organisation for the manufacture and supply of spare parts by the Ministry of Munitions; and above all the urgent need to become ready as soon as possible for war operations.

For the remainder of July and all of August they were kept hard at it, exercising either under way in the Flow or at anchor.

The First Decklanding

Now that a ship capable of providing 31 knots of wind over the deck existed, Squadron Commander Dunning gave it as his belief that in a strong steady wind it would be perfectly possible to land on the flying-off platform forward by flying parallel to the ship, then slipping in sideways past the superstructure and centring the plane over the deck. After successful trials without actually landing, whilst the ship lay at anchor, it was approved that this experiment should be carried out.

Clearly the senior officers at Scapa Flow were alive to the great advantages if aircraft became no longer one-shot. On the day selected for the trials, an eye-witness reported that the ship was 'weighed down with brass hats and gold braid'.

Conditions on 2 August were perfect. The wind was steady and strong at 21 knots, so that, with the ship steaming at 10 knots, Dunning was able to handle his Sopwith Pup at a very slow relative speed. He brought her in close past the port side of the upperworks, lined her up correctly and touched down gently. Waiting officers rushed out and held on to special toggles and other parts of the machine and brought her to a standstill: a perfect demonstration. To have made history after only five weeks was surely an unique start to a commission. But tragedy followed.

Two Sopwith Pups on the flying-off deck. This photograph shows the collapsible wind-breaks on either side and the trolley for seaplanes in the foreground

(Real Photographs, Ltd)

Five days later, in more gusty conditions, Dunning made a second successful landing, but at a cost of some minor damage to the elevator. He changed planes and tried again. This time, however, his approach was a little higher. A line had been painted athwartships on the deck to show the furthest safety-point for touch down. Seeing that he was passing it, Dunning waved the deck party away and opened up to go round again, but the engine choked and the aircraft stalled. It came down heavily on its starboard wheel and cartwheeled over the ship's side before it could be grabbed, the pilot being drowned.[1]

New Proposals and First Active Service Operations

Although this tragedy put a stop to attempts to land by sideslipping past a superstructure on to a fore deck, the advantages which would follow if aircraft could thus operate continuously with the fleet in all reasonable weather conditions had become clear.

The whole matter was carefully looked into on 18 September at a conference of the Captain and officers under the Chairmanship of Rear-Admiral R. F. Phillimore. They reported that only very

[1] During the research for this Profile, new evidence of this incident came to light through the donation to the IWM of notes and photographs of an eye-witness pilot, Flight Sub-Lieutenant Acland.

To help the reader to follow the many changes to Furious *in her lifetime these six silhouettes show her appearance from inception to World War II*

1 As designed in 1915, with 15-inch or 18-inch guns forward and aft

2 As completed in mid-1917, with a hangar and flying-off deck forward

3 As modified in 1918 with a landing-on deck replacing the after 18-inch gun

4 As a flush-decked carrier in 1925, on completion of her reconstruction

5 As modified in 1932, with the quarterdeck raised and the HA armament altered

6 As modernised in 1939, with a small island and armament of 4-inch AA guns

Another view of the flying-off deck, trolley in groove, derricks, bridge and foremast (IWM)

Lowering aircraft through the hatch, a slow process before lifts were installed (IWM)

skilled pilots would be able to land by the side-slipping method, and only in Sopwith Pups at that, but gave their opinion that any moderate pilot should be able to do so on a long flush deck aft in any fighting or reconnaissance machine.

They went on to make constructive suggestions. Such a deck could be built abaft the funnel, giving a length of not less than 300ft and full width, if the after gun, turret, and mainmast were hoisted out and the Torpedo Control Tower removed. Lifts instead of hatches and derricks would be a vast improvement. The arrangement should still be considered experimental.

The report ended by saying that they realised the complications of taking away the only efficient fleet carrier whilst such alterations were being made.

Whilst these important recommendations were being considered at higher and technical levels, the ship spent much time at sea on operations and sweeps, her function being covered by the revised Grand Fleet Battle Orders issued in August 1917.

These showed growing realisation of the importance of aircraft, mainly seaplanes for scouting. They were still, however, supplementary to blimps and light cruisers. Now there was also a role for fighters, which were to be launched to shoot down enemy aircraft before they sighted the Grand Fleet, protect our own seaplanes and blimps when required, and establish air superiority over the battle area.

With these instructions, *Furious* operated constantly throughout September, October and early November, escorted by light cruisers and destroyers nearly to the coast of Denmark. Few opportunities for success came her way, however.

It must be remembered that her aircraft were still 'one-shot', and any decision to fly off could only be taken if the risk of their not being available later when more urgently required could be accepted. For instance, when two German light cruisers struck at a Scandinavian convoy outside the range of shore-based aircraft and *Furious* alone was within striking distance, permission for her to mount an attack was refused on the grounds that the weather was too bad to recover seaplanes, whilst wheeled planes must be retained in case Zeppelins approached the fleet.

There was particular disappointment on a very early occasion, her second sweep with other units, when on 11 August a Zeppelin was reported in sight. Flight-Commander Moore took off at once in a Sopwith Pup, but could not gain enough altitude before the enemy escaped in thick cloud.

The *Furious's* contribution therefore during these months can be said to have been potential rather than actual, an assurance that in a crisis the fleet would be able to see further ahead than from the bridge of a screening light cruiser and that the enemy airships would no longer be unchallenged when beyond the range of shore-based aircraft.

On 14 November, the ship was ordered to Walker-on-Tyne. The recommendations of the conference on 18 September had borne fruit and fresh alterations awaited her.

Winter 1917-18: Another Major Change—the 'after landing deck'

Higher authority had moved commendably fast. The C-in-C approved and forwarded his recommendations only 10 days after the original meeting; DNC's department submitted their technical proposals a fortnight after that; the Controller in consultation with Armstrong Whitworth's agreed the following week; and the final approval of the Board of Admiralty was given on 30 October.

In all, it had taken only 42 days for a decision, at a critical stage of the war, which involved the acceptance of a reduction in the tactical support of the Grand Fleet for some months: the removal from a ship of her heaviest armament; the assessment of the prospects for deck-landing of aircraft only a few weeks after an early success and subsequent failure; and a good many major structural alterations.

Orders were given for the following:

(i) The after 18in gun, turret, and top ring of armour to be taken out and also the TCT.

(ii) The mainmast to be removed.

(iii) The 5·5in guns, now to be the main armament, to be rearranged, those on the shelter deck aft being moved to the lower level of the fo'c'sle deck. Although at first a reduction to eight guns was proposed, later resiting resulted in the loss of only one, leaving 10 instead of the original 11.

(iv) On the space thus made available, an after landing deck 26ft above the quarter deck was to be built, extending from the funnel to a spot 75ft before the stern, 300ft long in all with a minimum width of 50ft at the after end.

(v) Another hangar, 70ft by 38ft, to be made under this flight deck.

(vi) Electric lifts, 48ft by 18ft, to be provided forward and aft. The Captain considered that these were the most important modifications of all.

(vii) To reduce the risk of aircraft over-running into the funnel, a structure somewhat resembling a large football goal was to be built, with strong rope nets hanging from the crosspiece. Wires, with sandbags attached, placed athwartships were also tried but were found to be too unpredictable.

(viii) Fore and aft wires were to be rove to keep the aircraft straight, for which purpose it was fitted with skids. Doglead catches to pick up these wires were also tried.

(ix) Narrow gangways, 170ft long and 11ft wide, were to be built on either side of the superstructure and funnel to connect the flying on and flying off decks.

She would in future be able to carry 16 aircraft, Sopwith Pup and Camel fighters and 1½-Strutter two-seater reconnaissance planes. Sea-planes were no longer part of her complement, although occasionally operated.

Her original building and alterations to date had by now cost just over £6,000,000. Additions in weight for the flying decks and their supports totalled 1481 tons, but 2758 tons had been saved by the removal of the two turrets and guns, mainmast, net defence and by the provision of smaller boats now that they must be hoisted by davit instead of derrick.

An incidental but useful advantage arose from the building of the high flying deck aft, since from now onwards the ship carried considerable weather helm. This meant that she practically steered herself, even at slow speed, when dead into the wind's eye for flying on or off. No bad helmsmanship need worry the approaching pilot after he had lined up.

Experiments and Operations, 1918

Tremendous efforts were made to get the ship back into service as quickly as possible, and the original estimate of six months was in the result reduced to four.

Above: *The only ship ever to combine an 18in gun and a flying-off deck* (*Ministry of Defence*)

Below: *Another photograph of* Furious *as hybrid; under way in 1917* (*IWM*)

HMS *Furious* is here depicted as she was in 1918. Her starboard battery of 5·5in is visible, as also is the crash netting slung from abreast the level of the funnel top at Station 102 to where it reaches the deck at Station 128. The aircraft on the for'd flight deck of the plan drawing is a Sopwith Pup.
A Submarine Scout blimp is illustrated flying-off, over the bows, in the side-view.

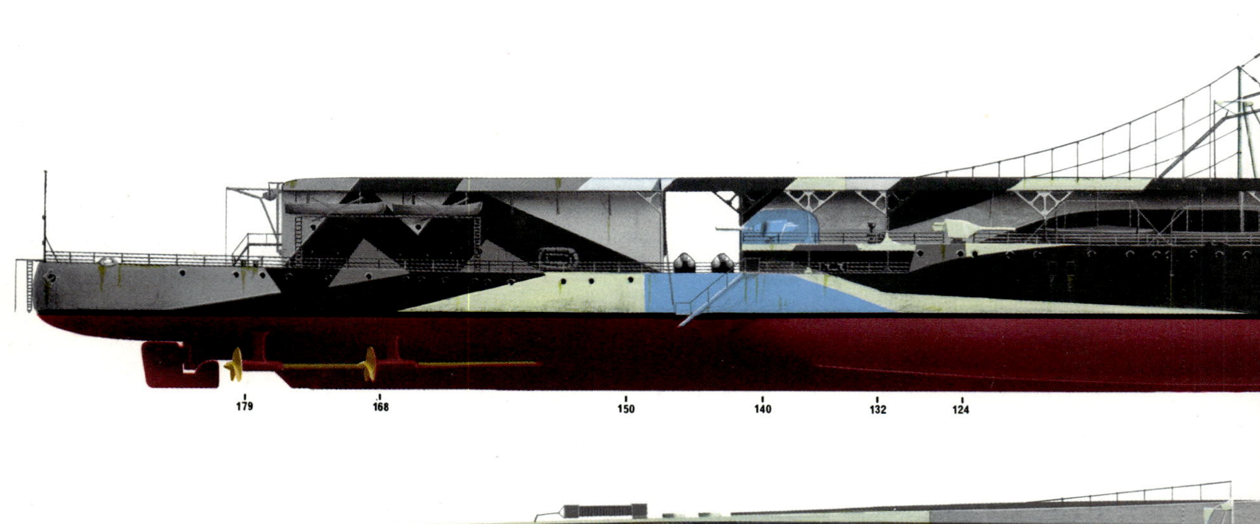

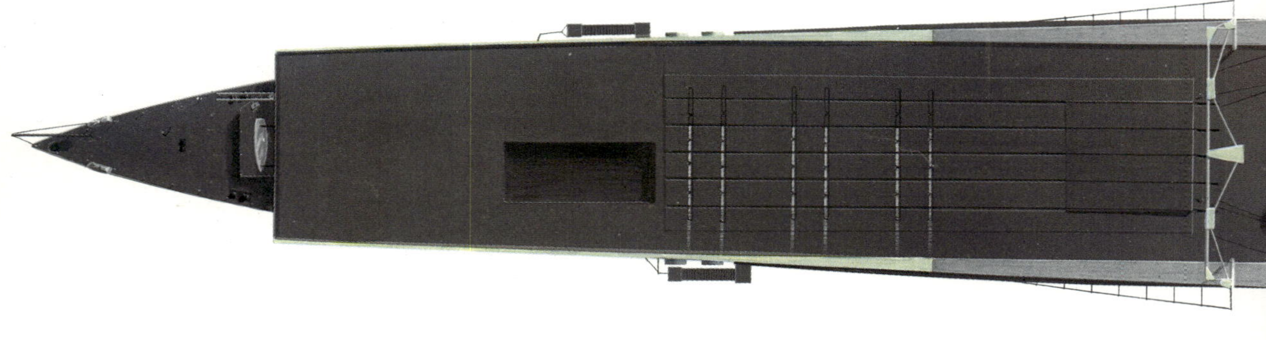

1

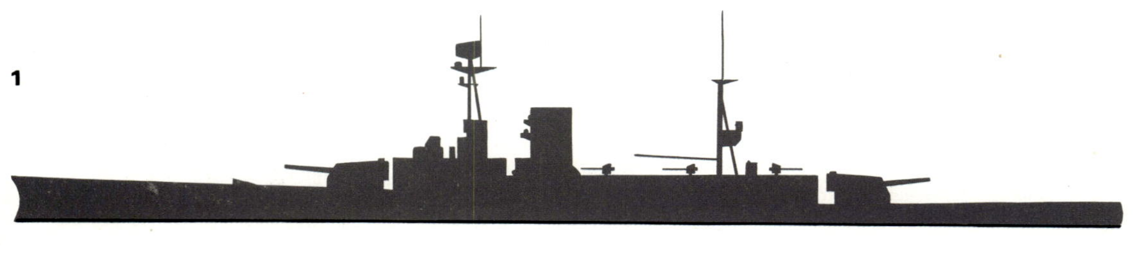

2

1 *1915 As designed, a large light cruiser. Two 18in guns (originally four 15in), eleven 5·5in (originally sixteen 4in, then eight 5·5in), four 3in AA*

2 *1917 As completed, a hybrid seaplane carrier with forward flying-off deck. One 18in gun, eleven 5·5in, four 3in AA. Aircraft complement—10*

3 *1918 As first modified to aircraft carrier with after landing-on deck. Ten 5·5in guns, four 3in AA. Aircraft complement—16*

4 *1925 As flush-deck carrier, plus lower flying-off deck. Ten 5·5in guns, six 4in AA. Aircraft complement—36*

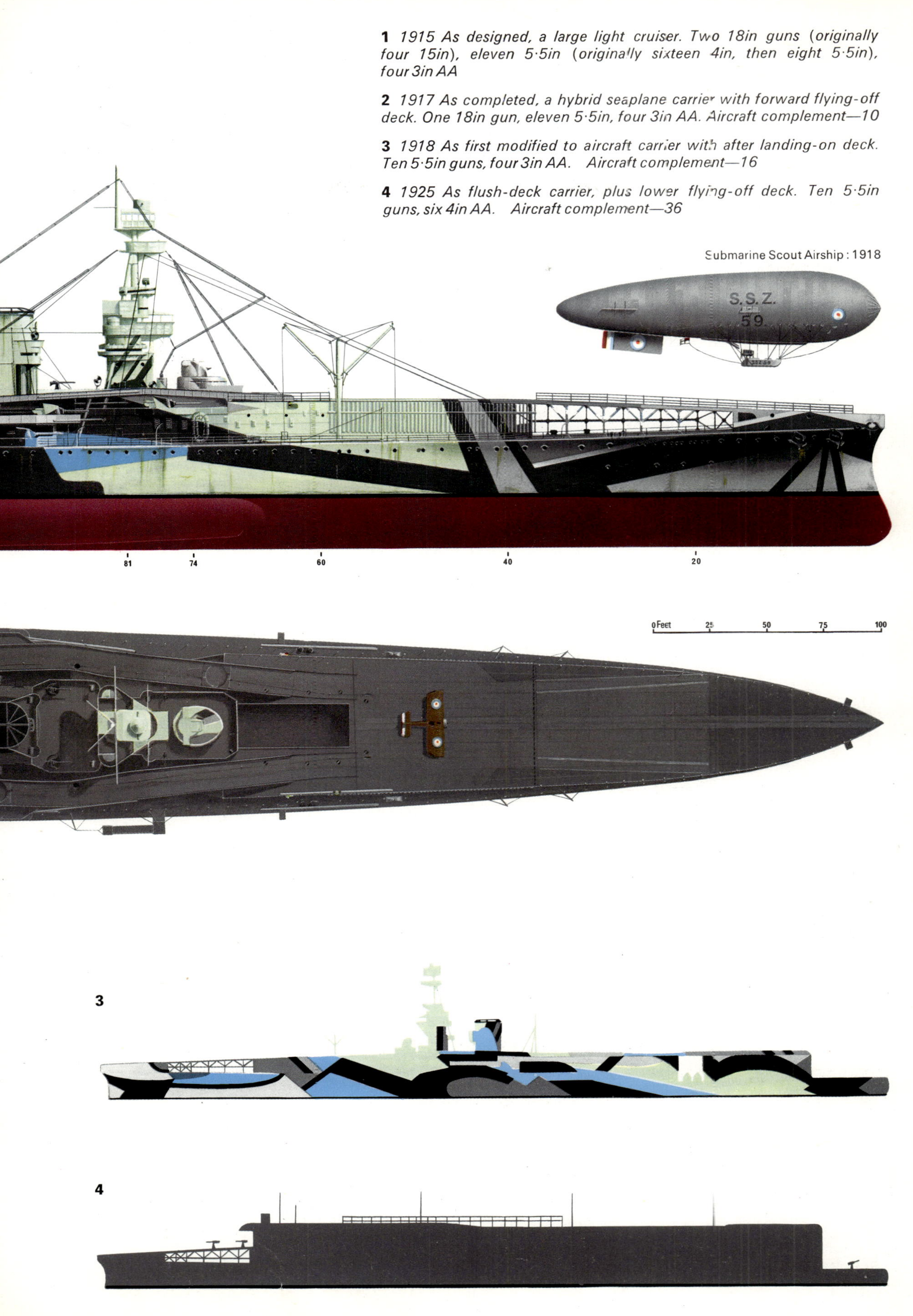

1

2

3

1 *The first deck landing by Squadron Commander Dunning on 2 August 1917. Officers running to catch loops and toggles to help hold the machine*
(FAA Museum, Yeovilton)

2 *The moment of triumph. Dunning leaving his Sopwith Pup after the landing* *(NMM)*

3 *Just before disaster*
(Papers of Wing Cdr Acland at IWM)

4 *The moment of disaster. Dunning's aircraft toppling over the side, the pilot being drowned*
(Papers of Wing Cdr Acland at IWM)

On 15 March, *Furious* completed to full complement and hoisted the flag of Rear-Admiral Phillimore, commanding the 'Flying Squadron' of the Grand Fleet. W. S. Nicholson was still her Captain, and the Squadron Commander was F. J. Rutland, pilot of the only seaplane to operate at Jutland and more recently pioneer of flying off from platforms on top of gun-turrets.

She came to sea at a moment of important change in the higher organisation. After wasteful duplication in the design and supply of airframes and engines, and many arguments as to the control of flying personnel, the War Cabinet had decided to set up an Air Council on 3 January 1918, and to bring the Royal Air Force into official existence on 1 April to control absolutely the existing Air Services.

The RNAS thus came to an end and the officers and men found themselves transferred as 'Air Force Contingents' to a new service. For the moment, it made little difference to them individually except for the possession of new ranks such as 'Lieutenant-Colonel RAF', but to exercise later their right to revert to the RN would mean to give up flying. Naturally only a few did so, and the navy lost many of the oustanding officers who later reached high rank in the RAF, such as Air Chief Marshals Sir Arthur Longmore, Sir Frederick Bowhill, Sir W. Dickson, and Sir Christopher Courtney.

For the remaining eight months of the war, *Furious* again sustained her double role of part experimental, part operational. It involved much steaming, a total of 72 days under way.

The experiments were mostly those of deck-landing and of improving arrester gear. Rutland himself undertook many of these tests, and his reports are interesting reading, though disappointing.

He pointed out that the eddies formed by the passage of any body through the air were bound to be complicated by obstructions such as bridges and funnels, and reported that the air was uniform along the ship's side or over the fo'c'sle but that the maximum effects were always felt—just at the very worst spot—from 150 to 180ft abaft the funnel. Here the approaching aircraft would suddenly drop dangerously, if not disastrously.

In spite of the skill of Rutland and his fellow-pilots, it became clear that landing on the deck of the *Furious* under these circumstances was too dangerous an operation. In May there were a few successful attempts, 12 in all, but there were far too many crashes, with planes over-running into the net abaft the funnel, smashing their undercarriages, or toppling over the side. Reluctantly it was concluded that except when the situation required the taking of great risks her aircraft must still be looked upon as one-shot until modifications to the ship made landing on deck safer.

Both at the Admiralty and on board the *Furious* herself there was a great determination to master the problem. Experiments were carried out in a wind tunnel ashore, using a model of the ship, and various ingenious suggestions were put forward including:

To land on at an angle, presumably on the foremost deck as this was first mooted by the Captain of *Furious* in September 1917. The Director of Air Services turned this down as a 'highly dangerous proposal, which should be discouraged'.

To move the funnel right aft as landing-on forward appeared to meet with less turbulence; another suggestion from the Captain, in March 1918.

To move the funnel to starboard. This proposal got as far as the production of full General Arrangement Diagrams by DNC, dated September 1918.

To do away with the mast and funnel altogether. The technical difficulties were, however, great although a Lt-Cdr Holmes RNVR, had suggested ducting as long ago as 1916, without much notice being taken apparently of his proposals at the time.

One-shot or not, the ship herself could not be spared for further modification. Although nine battle cruisers and several of the cruisers, including *Courageous* and *Glorious*, now carried aircraft for flying off gun-turrets, she was the only actual carrier operating with the fleet until *Vindictive* (seaplane

4

A good view of Furious *in 1917. Comparison of this with the last photograph in this Profile shows the astonishing structural changes made to this ship* (*Real Photographs*)

The flying-off deck with Sopwith Camels ranged, taken from the bridge during a break from maintenance work (*IWM*)

carrier) and *Argus* should join in October 1918. Even these had not the speed to keep up with the Battlecruiser squadron when required.

So throughout the summer and autumn *Furious* accompanied units of the fleet on various operations, primarily to provide fighters to drive off enemy Zeppelins or seaplanes. There were submarine attacks on her and her escorts but otherwise contact with the enemy only rarely came her way.

On 19 June she scored her first kill. The squadron with which she was operating was attacked by German seaplanes. *Furious* launched two Camels who succeeded in shooting down one of the enemy, the crew being picked up by the destroyer *Valentine.*

The First Successful Carrier-Borne Raid

This, interspersed with experiments in handling airships on deck, was all very well, but the officers of the *Furious* were too keen and had too much initiative to be content with waiting for the enemy to show himself. They pressed to be allowed to attack Zeppelins at their main base, now identified as Tondern at the mouth of the Elbe.

The scheme was approved, and the ship sailed on 17 July with an escort of light cruisers and destroyers and covered by a squadron of battleships.

Two days later she flew off seven Sopwith Camel 2F1s in two flights from only 80 miles off Tondern. Each machine carried two 50lb bombs and its pilot had been carefully rehearsed by mock attacks at Turnhouse, near Edinburgh.

Surprise was complete and the target correctly identified. Soon the sheds were blazing fiercely, with two Zeppelins—L54 and L60—totally destroyed inside. It had been a perfect example of what could be done by making proper use of the mobility and striking power offered by carrier-borne aircraft.

Unfortunately only three of the Camels returned safely, ditching near the fleet for rescue by destroyers. Three others landed in Denmark, whilst the fate of the seventh has never been discovered.

Armistice, and the First Post-war Year

If the war had continued, this outstanding success might well have been followed by further bomb raids on bases or ships; or perhaps by attacks by torpedo for which Beatty had been pressing strongly now that trials had proved that this weapon could be carried and launched by seaplanes, as well as by Sopwith Cuckoo land planes destined for *Argus.*

It is interesting to speculate upon the effect which success by air operations at this time might have had upon the degree of priority to be given to naval aviation in the years between the wars.

All through August, September and October the ship did a great deal of sea-time on operations and exercises. There were exciting moments such as on 1 August when enemy submarines made several unsuccessful attacks on her and her escorts, but no major sorties by her planes were mounted.

In October the *Argus* completed her trials and joined the fleet. Arguments became heated between the relative merits of a flush-deck carrier such as she, in which the funnel gases were kept clear of the approach path and more space was available for hangars, and one with an island to one side, which was considered to lessen the interference by air eddies and which gave a mark to help aircraft judge their position. Whichever was to prove the better design, that of the *Furious* with her central funnel was in any case right out of favour.

Another view of the flying-off deck in 1918, showing wind breaks and the hatch to the hangar (*IWM*)

No decision on these matters had been taken by the time of the Armistice or when she accompanied the Grand Fleet 10 days later to escort the High Seas Fleet to Rosyth. Nor, except by a few far-thinking officers, was the air yet thought of as more than an aid to spotting and reconnaissance and, as a weapon, a very minor one.

A conference to assess post-war aerial requirements was held at the Admiralty on 4 December, with the Deputy First Sea Lord in the chair. This laid down that '*Furious* and five seaplane carriers' should be retained as a 'Flying Squadron' and distributed amongst the larger fleets. A decision on the future of *Eagle* and *Hermes,* both due to complete in 1919, was deferred.

Furious therefore changed her wartime scheme of dazzle painting for the dark grey of the Atlantic Fleet, with which she served for the next 12 months, including a period in the Baltic where a naval force was assisting the White Russians against the Bolsheviks. Although her own ship's company remained disciplined, they were uneasy months for everyone, with bickering at higher levels over the future of naval aviation and a good deal of discontent on board most ships as a reaction after the strain of war, which broke into open mutiny on board another carrier, the *Vindictive.*

1

2

3

4

1 *Types of aircraft. A hangar view of a BE2, a Camel, and a (crashed) Pup* (*IWM*)

2 *In May 1918, dazzle-painted, now with the 18in gun aft replaced by a flying-on deck* (*NMM*)

3 *This view from the port side shows a different dazzle scheme from that on the starboard. German submarine officers denied that dazzle-painting of ships ever confused them* (*IWM*)

4 *Proof of success. The Zeppelin sheds at Tondern well alight (with L54 and L60 inside)* (*IWM*)

At last, with her future still uncertain, she received orders to reduce to Reserve at Rosyth on 21 November 1919. Flush-deck, island to starboard, scrapheap—it might turn out to be any of these.

Uncertainty, then Decision

It must be admitted that at this time the *Furious* was looked upon as a white elephant in spite of some isolated successes to her credit, such as the first deck landing; the proof that she could handle airships;[1] and the Tondern Raid. Nor is this to be wondered at; an aircraft carrier on which landing was virtually impossible was no longer an asset.

Even the acceptance in principle that she should be converted, much less how, was not agreed until July 1920, and then only on the grounds that this would cost less than a new hull. The Admiralty had even brushed aside a suggestion made by Armstrong's in October 1919 that she should be flush-decked. 'Quite impossible', they minuted, 'the flat portion would be subject to most extreme heat and would collapse . . . flames from the funnel openings would sweep across the deck and destroy any aeroplanes or living creature'.

So Rosyth Dockyard stripped her of all inessentials and awaited developments. The turning point came on 23 March 1921 from a paper submitted by DNC, Sir Eustace Tennyson d'Eyncourt.

The scheme provided for clearing the vessel down to the level of the present hangar and building a double-decked hangar along whose sides the funnels would be led aft, eventually discharging near the stern. The upper hangar would be able to take 33 Sopwith Torpedo-carrying aircraft and the lower 28 if their wings were folded.

On top would be a continuous flight deck, and machines could also be taken out through large hinged doors from the upper hangar on to the fore deck and flown off from there.

Now that there would be no superstructure, navigation would be from either of two platforms outboard with a good view aft, connected by a gangway running athwartships below the flight deck. The control positions for the armament of 10-5·5in and six 4in HA guns would also be on each side.

This general design was immediately approved, on 21 April, with the comment that *Furious* should be a really valuable carrier, and high priority was given.

The white elephant period was over.

[1] Experiments just before the Armistice in landing airships on the after flight deck had been successful (see photograph).

An Anxious Passage

Devonport Dockyard was better able to undertake this extensive work, but the problem was how to get her there in her present state. She had been lightened down to 15,600 tons, was relatively long for a draught of only 18ft. and had still high upperworks to catch the wind. Towing would be difficult and dangerous.

Eventually it was decided to put her into steaming condition with one boiler-room, temporary uptake and funnel, a temporary bridge, telegraphs and steering gear. In this peculiar form, with head-shakings from DNC in case her structural strength would not stand up to the voyage, she safely steamed from Rosyth to Devonport in June 1922.

A Further Major Change, 1922-25

By now, all details for this huge reconstruction had been worked out. And huge it was, calling for replanning of nearly all the internal arrangements of the ship, and ingenuity and imagination needed at every level in meeting problems many of which were new in naval design. It was no wonder that DNC complained that he was desperately short of constructors.

Details were worked out by his department in consultation with flying and gunnery experts, and the following were approved:

(i) The upper flight deck would be 576ft long and 91½ft wide. The length of the lower flying-off deck would be 200ft.

(ii) The extreme breadth of the ship would now be 107ft, the overhang being a matter of some concern.

With the Rear-Admiral's flag at the masthead. A view along the flying-on deck, showing the crash-barrier gallows (*IWM*)

A Sopwith Pup slewing on landing, in spite of her skids and the carrier's fore and aft guiding ropes. The more distant ropes outboard were rigged in 1918 and 1919 to lessen losses overboard, predecessors of the palisades of 1927 (IWM)

Although saving total damage, the ropes of the crash-barrier have cut into the fabric of the wings of this plane, on which is prophetically painted the words, 'Excuse me!' (IWM)

1

1 *Early deck-landing gear. A Sopwith Pup, shipboard version, with skid undercarriage and V-shaped hooks to engage in the guide-ropes which were hauled taut by tackles* (IWM)

2 *In 1918, with two aircraft ranged aft and one forward. Note the gallows abaft the funnel from which ropes were hung as crash barrier* (NMM)

3 *This view from the air in 1918 shows the ship's graceful lines. Note the gangways on either side of the funnel, by which aircraft could be wheeled from the after to the fore flying-deck* (MOD)

2

3

A close-up of the forward superstructure as completed, 1917 (see also p. 248) (IWM)

In 1919. Now painted the dark grey of the Atlantic Fleet (NMM)

Just before the Armistice in 1918. With all landings by wheeled planes cancelled as too dangerous, Furious *carried out a successful experiment by landing a Submarine Scout airship on her after deck* (IWM)

(iii) Safety nets outboard would be provided for the deck party.

(iv) The nose of the upper flight deck to be rounded off, as experiments had proved that this was better aerodynamically.

(v) The hangars to be 50ft wide, the lower being 550ft long and the upper 520ft, both divided for fire purposes by steel roller blinds or curtains.

(vi) The armament in future would be 10-5·5in and six 4in. Torpedo tubes to be removed.

(vii) There would be a retractable navigating position on the centre-line, for use when not flying.

(viii) There should be 25ft telescopic signalling masts each side, also short horizontal spars for communication with aircraft.

(ix) Wireless masts should be hinged and so could be lowered to horizontal during flying.

(x) Because of the raised freeboard, heavier anchors and cables would be needed, 160cwt and $3\frac{1}{4}$in instead of 125cwt and $2\frac{11}{16}$in.

(xi) Bulk storage for 24,000 gallons of petrol and 4000 of lubricating oil would be required, with steam pumps to deliver to the hangars and flight deck.

(xii) Ample accommodation would be provided for the extra 65 RAF officers and 260 men required for flying and maintenance, the total complement being now 1218.

Virtually a New Ship, 1925

Work went ahead fairly steadily. But it was peacetime now and national economy came first, so that the two years originally estimated for her completion grew to three.

The Devonport 'dockyard maties' watched with interest and a good deal of criticism as this new-fangled ship with her towering sides, her flat flight-deck and her spacious hangars, her guns and navigating positions in most unusual spots, took shape. They vowed that she would not even float the right way up, and when the undocking was arranged for the dinner-hour on 8 December 1924 a strong rumour arose that this timing was to minimise the casualties when she inevitably turned turtle.

Safely afloat nevertheless, she was commissioned with a ship's company from Portsmouth on 1 September 1925 by Captain J. L. Pearson, who had supervised her rebuilding. Steaming, navigation, and extensive flying trials proved very successful.[1]

She now carried 36 aircraft, Fairey Flycatchers (fighters), Blackburns and Avro Bisons (Spotter/Reconnaissance), all fairly recently in service. An interesting and powerful unit was joining the Atlantic Fleet.

As yet *Furious* had been mainly experimental, trying out new techniques and being modified as ideas developed. Now, although many improvements and changes were still to come, the broad pattern of naval flying had become clear.

A long career in peace and war lay ahead.

[1] Fuller details of these will be given in Profile 24.

In 1919. A view from the quarter, in her Atlantic Fleet grey. The landing-on deck had no round-down at that time. The signal, Red Ensign above M International, denotes HM Ship under way within the limits of a dockyard port (NMM)

As she emerged in 1925, flush-decked with retractable central navigating position and hinged wireless masts. The 'egg-box' plating over the horizontal funnel ducts, shown here, caused excessive heating aft and was later removed (Real Photographs)

MAIN TYPES OF AIRCRAFT OPERATED FROM FURIOUS 1917-1919

Maker and Type	Date of first production	Powerplant (maximum output)	Maximum speed (mph)	Endurance	Armament Forward (F) Rear (R) Bombs (B)	Weight empty	Weight loaded	Remarks
Sopwith Baby (Single-seater scout and bombing seaplane)	1915	110hp Clerget	100	2¼hrs	(F) 1 Lewis MG (B) 2×65lb	1226lb	1715lb	
Sopwith Pup (Official name, Sopwith Scout) (Single-seater fighter scout)	1916	80hp Le Rhone	111	3hrs	1 Lewis MG	787lb	1225lb	1st decklanding
Sopwith 1½-Strutter (Single-seater bomber, or two-seater fighter/reconnaissance)	1916	110hp Clerget	106	4½hrs	(F) 1 Vickers MG (B) 4×65lb or (F) 1 Vickers MG (R) 1 Lewis MG (B) 2×65lb	1259lb	2149lb	
Sopwith Camel 2F1 (Single-seater fighter scout)	1917	130hp Clerget, or 150hp Bentley BR1	124	2½hrs	(F) 1 Vickers MG (synchronised) (R) 1 Lewis MG (B) 2×50lb	1036lb	1530lb	Tondern Raid
Sopwith Cuckoo (Single-seater torpedo carrier)	1917	200hp Sunbeam-Arab	103½	4hrs	(B) 1×18in Mk IX torpedo	2199lb	3883lb	
Beardmore WB III D (Single-seater scout). Based on Pup design	1917	80hp Le Rhone or Clerget	103	2¾hrs	(F) 1 Lewis MG	890lb	1289lb	

Flush-decked. As Furious *emerged in 1925 from her drastic reconstruction. The 'egg box' plating over the side funnel ducts, shown here, caused excessive heating aft and was soon removed* (*Real Photographs, Ltd*)

HMS Furious/Aircraft Carrier, 1917-1948

Part II: 1925-1948

by Commander C. A. Jenkins, OBE RN

Flat-topped: Virtually a New Ship

When, on 1 September 1925, the *Furious* recommissioned after four years of drastic reconstruction at Rosyth and Devonport dockyards, she was entering the fourth stage of her long and much-modified career.

In the previous issue of this series, we traced her from the original conception of an heavily-armed cruiser through one period as land-and-seaplane carrier with a forward flying-off deck only; and another as aircraft carrier with also a landing-on deck abaft her central funnel. Now, with the box-like effect of her towering sides and flush flight deck misleading the eye of any unskilled observer from the beauty of her lines, she was in the form in which, with only comparatively minor modifications, she was to serve for another fourteen years of peace and five of war.

Five months earlier, she had been put through a series of most extensive trials, whose results had been awaited with unusual interest. For she embodied many ingenious innovations in discharge of funnel gases, internal lay-out, methods of handling aircraft, navigation and signalling arrangements, armament control positions, and fire-fighting. Above all, there was anxiety whether her earlier problems of interference with landing aircraft by air eddies had been solved.

Sea Trials

Captain J. L. Pearson, who had been watching over her reconstruction since June 1923, took her to sea with a reduced complement on 29 March 1925 for 4/5ths power trials. In a full gale, the ship proved remarkably steady and made good a speed of 28·65 knots.

In her full-power trials on 3 April, the *Furious* averaged 30·03 knots with a shaft horse power of 90,895. Although not so fast as originally designed, this was described by the Chief Constructor as 'good, for four months out of dock and a shallow course.'

Turning trials were carried out on the 7th off the Isle of Wight, this time with the sea smooth. With a mean speed, during the circle, of 25 knots and using 35° of helm, the tactical diameter worked out at 1320 yards and the advance at 1070 yards. The angle of heel was only 5°.

So the handling qualities in her new form, which of course remained unchanged throughout the rest of her life, were clear,—a huge turning circle but little heel, great steadiness in a seaway, ease of steering when head to wind, very little vibration. To these, although not mentioned in the reports on trials, might be added considerable leeway in a beam wind, quick steadying on a course, and the capacity to come to rest under reversed engines in a remarkably short distance.

To help the reader to follow the many changes to Furious *in her lifetime these six silhouettes show her appearance from inception to World War II*

1 As designed in 1915, with 15-inch or 18-inch guns forward and aft

2 As completed in mid-1917, with a hangar and flying-off deck forward

3 As modified in 1918 with a landing-on deck replacing the after 18-inch gun

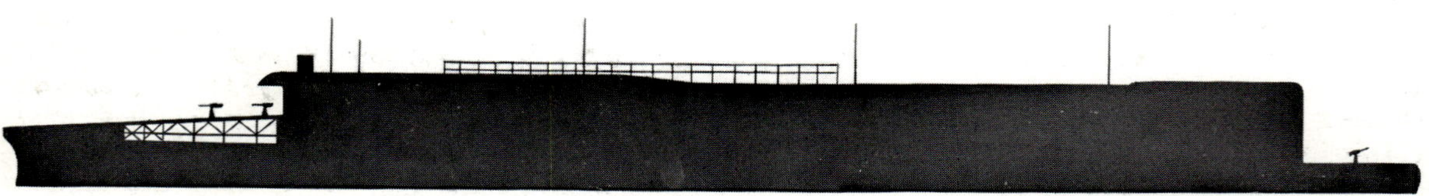

4 As a flush-decked carrier in 1925, on completion of her reconstruction

5 As modified in 1932, with the quarterdeck raised and the HA armament altered

6 As modernised in 1939, with a small island and armament of 4-inch AA guns

Weighing anchor at Plymouth after the egg-boxing and the forward AA guns had been removed (Public Record Office)

Flying Trials

These were carried out off the Isle of Wight on 6 April in fine weather, with a wind over the deck of 27 knots, and thoroughly tested both the ship and aircraft of various types in handling, landing, and flying off.

(i) First a Fairey Flycatcher (Flight-Lieutenant W. Jones) landed satisfactorily and was arrested in 110 feet, flying off in 70 feet.

(ii) The same plane landed again but slewed due to falling hurdles pinching an arrester wire. These collapsible hurdles held the fore-and-aft arrester wires 6in above the deck. Fittings on the plane's axle engaged the wires on landing.

(iii) A much heavier plane, a Blackburn Dart loaded to 4200lbs (Fl-Lt Riddle) landed safely, stopping in 176 feet.

(iv) A Fairey IIID, weighing 4700lbs, (Fl-Lt Boyer with Air Commodore Masterman as passenger), stopped on deck after a run of 160 feet.

(v) A Fairey Flycatcher was flown off the Upper Hangar Deck below, after a run of only 20ft.

(vi) A Blackburn Blackburn weighing 5000lbs came next, stopping after 215 feet.

(vii) Heavier still, a Blackburn Dart with a torpedo of 1421lbs landed safely. Although the arresting wires had been braced down, the skid gathered one wire which had a slewing effect before becoming detached. The plane lifted off after 110 feet.

(viii) A Fairey IIID took off from the forward lift position in 65 feet.

The Captain's terse summary 'all satisfactory' was justified. *Furious* had shown her ability to handle any naval aircraft of the day.

Gunnery Trials

The gun trials for the foremost guns were also entirely satisfactory. Those for the after guns were, however, found to be too much affected by funnel duct gases and were not completed.

Aircraft Carriers of the Twenties

In September 1925, when *Furious* rejoined the Fleet, there were in commission *Argus*, whom she relieved in the Atlantic Fleet and who then paid off into Reserve, *Eagle* and *Hermes* in the Mediterranean, the latter being shortly afterwards diverted to China. *Courageous* and *Glorious* were in hand for conversion to carriers, completing in February 1928 and January 1930 respectively. When these two became operational the total tonnage of British carriers would still be within the limit of 135,000 laid down by the Washington Naval Conference of 1921-2.

Carrier-operated Planes of the Twenties[1]

The fighter on which the navy primarily relied from 1923 until 1933 was the remarkable and popular Fairey Flycatcher, a strong single-seater of 133mph which handled easily.

The main spotter-reconnaissance plane was the 3-seater Fairey IIID of 106mph, gradually superseded after 1926 by the Fairey IIIF of 120mph. There were also the Avro Bison and the Blackburn Blackburn of the early twenties, both considerably heavier than the IIID.

The torpedo carrier of the day was the Blackburn Dart, an ugly machine but one which fulfilled its role competently for nine years until the arrival of the Blackburn Ripon in 1929.

The fore-and-aft system of arrester gear had never been satisfactory, and was abandoned in late 1925. Until the development of athwartship wires after 1929, aircraft landing on carriers had to rely upon a strong head wind and slow landing speed.

Manning and Control of Naval Aviation in the Twenties

It is not necessary here to examine closely the controversies over naval aviation which bedevilled the period between the wars, except where the resulting decisions and reversals of decisions affected the *Furious* herself.

Basically, the Admiralty claimed that the air arm

[1]For details of these and later planes flown from *Furious*, see Appendix.

of the Navy was part of the fighting fleet, and that its personnel required specialised training in navigation over the sea, ship recognition, naval tactics, gunnery requirements and the like.
The Air Ministry, on the other hand, claimed that there needed to be 'unity of the air' to achieve the best results as to general policy, aircraft design and production, training of flying and ground personnel, and (the Trenchard doctrine) that the capital weapon of the future was the long-distance bomber.
Throughout the twenties and most of the thirties the result may perhaps be summed up as: battles and skirmishes in the background, co-operation afloat.
In 1925, when *Furious* recommissioned, the organisation was based on compromise arrangements recommended the year before by the Balfour Committee, although these took time and were only gradually being made good. 70% of the pilots were to be naval officers, the initial training being by the RAF, the pilots holding double rank. The point that all observers from carriers should be naval had already been won by the Admiralty in 1922. Design, provision and maintenance of aircraft were the business of the Air Ministry, on Admiralty recommendation as to requirements. Aircraft allocated for operations from HM ships were to be called the Fleet Air Arm of the RAF, paid for by the naval vote.
Thus throughout the years between the wars *Furious* usually had an RAF Wing Commander, light and dark blue uniforms mingled in the Wardroom, and her messdecks included RAF engineers, fitters and storekeepers. It was 1937 before it was finally decided that naval personnel should take over completely, and only a few months before the war that the last RAF officer left her.

The Flush-deck Aircraft Carrier

In *Furious* some Captains and Navigating Officers disliked the draughtiness and inaccessibility of the Central Navigating Position so much that they refused to make use of it. In any case, it had to be retracted whenever flying was taking place: the ship was then conned from the Starboard Navigating Position, and her flight deck was therefore clear of all obstacles.
By comparison with the other carriers, which all had islands, the two flush-deck ships, *Furious* and *Argus*, had unusual problems as well as some advantages.
From the 'starboard nav', the height of eye was only some two feet above the level of the flight deck so that, whenever the ship heeled, as for instance whilst turning or with a wind on the port beam, the vast surface of the deck rose and cut off all view of the sea or other ships on that side.
There were difficulties for the signal staff, too: the rising flight deck would sometimes interfere with the reading of a signal, even in mid-sentence, and skilful co-ordination was needed for signalmen on the port side to take over from those on the starboard, or vice versa: whenever the telescopic masts were lowered during flying operations, messages had to be passed by lamp to every ship concerned or else a repeating ship arranged, where a flag hoist would have sufficed.
On the other hand, the navigating positions were excellent viewpoints for those bringing the ship alongside: all the spaces for planning, information, navigation and signals could be on the same level because the horizontal passage which ran the entire

A Fairey IIIF, three-seater spotter-reconnaissance aircraft. Furious *operated this type of plane from 1927 to 1936* (*Fleet Air Arm Museum, Yeovilton*)

1926. The Blackburn Dart on the deck of Furious *after the first night deck-landing in history* (*Imperial War Museum*)

In 1927. An impression of the size of Furious *by comparison with the destroyer* Tyrian *alongside. The door through which aircraft could be brought direct from the upper hangar to the foremost flying-off deck is partly open* (NMM)

In 1927. This shows the ramp on the flight deck, just above a carley float. The wind-break on the lower flying-off deck has been raised (NMM)

width of the ship under the fore round-down linked the wing positions with the meteorology office, plotting office, observers' room, charthouse, Captain's and Navigating Officer's sea cabins, and the Signal Distributing Office: communication and discussion between their various users was much easier than if on different decks.

A flush flight deck brought another, incidental, benefit. Because of it, the Captain and navigating party were not aloof olympians on a high bridge far above everything and everybody, but mortals with their heads (brass hat and all), only a couple of feet above the flight deck. The men in the nettings overside, with the seas rushing past 56 feet below, could look forward and see the Captain or the Wing Commander similarly situated. In an interval from flying, a signalman might leap onto the flight deck to make a signal by hand flags, the Wing Commander might run across and lean over to talk to the Captain, and the Yeoman of Signals write his message whilst lying flat on the armoured lid abreast the 'starboard nav' to be nearer the officer dictating. All this made for a glorious feeling of informality and intimacy, so that all through her life the *Furious* was an outstandingly happy ship.

Slow Progress for the Fleet Air Arm

The years between the wars were not marked by many important advances in the Fleet Air Arm. Heavily squeezed financially and of minor importance in the eyes of the controlling Air Ministry, it was inevitable that the development of carrier-based aircraft during this period should be slow, particularly by comparison with the USA. It was a case of making do with whatever was handed out rather than of reaching ahead for what was desirable.

The First Night Deck-landing, 1926

Amongst the things that could be done with what was available were training and experimenting in deck-landing. Here, again, *Furious* became the setting for a major step forward.

After some preliminary night-flying training at Gosport, Squadron Leader Howe and Flight-Lieut. Boyce (462 Flight Commander) flew over the ship at Spithead on 5 May 1926 to inspect her deck lighting from the air and report on the possibility of landing in the dark.

The ship happened to be swung dead into a light westerly breeze. This tempted Howe to glide in and actually touch down before having to open up because of lack of space for pulling up in so little wind.

On the following evening, the first proper night landings were successfully carried out, with the *Furious* under way off the Isle of Wight, by Howe and Boyce alternately, flying Blackburn Darts.

It is interesting to know the arrangement of lights on the deck at this time, confirmed in July after a series of trials off the Firth of Forth as being very satisfactory, with the sole recommendation that dimming would be an improvement:

20 Concave projector Posterlites on each side, 6 yards apart and standing 2 feet above the deck.
58 Amber lights spaced round the after ramp.
84 Amber lights spaced round the forward ramp.
'Miscellaneous' white lights.

1925-1930

Throughout these five years, *Furious* carried a mixed complement of spotter reconnaissance and torpedo-carrying aircraft with, usually, only one flight of fighters.

With these and under a succession of three energetic and enthusiastic Captains—J. L. Pearson[1], R. G. H. Henderson[3], and the Hon A. R. M. Ramsay[2], —she took part in all the exercises of the Atlantic Fleet, including the annual spring cruises to the Mediterranean, in one of which three carriers—*Furious, Courageous* and *Eagle*—operated together.

Three carriers together for the first time, in 1929. Eagle, *(left) in the lighter Mediterranean colour, is passing* Furious *(right) and* Courageous, *(centre) in Atlantic Fleet dark grey, who are already moored* *(FAA Museum, Yeovilton)*

It is unfortunate the the records of the Fleet Exercises of those years have been destroyed as a result of damage by bombing whilst in storage. But from what documents and memories are available it is clear that the ship worked hard. Training and practice in deck-landing went steadily ahead, experiments were made to speed up the handling and operating of aircraft, and the role of her planes was demonstrated in several fleet exercises.

The Naval Staff History sums up her activities: '. . . by 1927 she had demonstrated the success and potentialities of large carriers.'

Experiments and Improvements

Of the experiments which she carried out, some are particularly interesting. Successful trials with aircraft wheel brakes in August 1927 showed major possibilities which were later realised: tests were

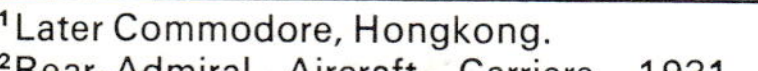

[1]Later Commodore, Hongkong.
[2]Rear-Admiral Aircraft Carriers, 1931. Vice-Admiral and Controller, 1934. Primarily responsible for the *armoured* carriers.
[3]Rear-Admiral Aircraft Carriers, 1933. Vice-Admiral, Commander-in-Chief East Indies 1936. Admiral, 1939.

Unusually funnel smoke is coming at the same time from both the side duct and the grating at the after end of the flight deck *(IWM)*

1 *March 1930. After 1926 the side was painted black aft because of smoke from the discharge ports. This view also shows the after HA guns, the cranes in stowage position and a glimpse of the hangar through the open door* (*Wright and Logan*)

2 *December 1931 before the raising of the quarterdeck* (*Wright and Logan*)

3 *The palisades were fitted in 1927 to reduce losses of planes from toppling overboard on landing* (*NMM*)

made of an undercarriage with rubber balls which, when compressed, gripped the sides of their containing tubes, also of Oleo undercarriages and pneumatic tyres.

Some further improvements to the ship herself had to be made as time went on:

The foremost lift, which had been strained by heavy weights unevenly placed, gave much trouble until 1929.

After a series of losses of planes overboard, a proposal from the ship's officers that palisades be fitted outboard was adopted in 1927, and very soon afterwards successfully passed an unrehearsed test in a bad landing. These palisades were fixed 10 feet apart, 15 feet in length, angled at 45°, and were joined by four fore-and-aft wires.

The worst difficulty was the great heat aft when 'smoking down', as happened whenever the ship turned into wind for flying. Orders were then passed from the 'starboard nav' to men in the waist, who turned handwheels operating valves which diverted the funnel gases from the flight deck to the side ducts. The after part of the ship was at times quite uninhabitable, fumes were always objectionable, and smoke hung low around the stern. Over the years this problem was vastly reduced, especially when the 'egg box' plating was removed, but was never completely solved.

Criticism was made of the 'hump', an athwartships ramp where the higher fore deck was gradually levelled off to join the lower after part of the flight deck. But it was retained as an effective help in bringing machines to rest.

The Refit of 1930 to 1931

Furious was reduced to Reserve on 1 July 1930 for a further refit at Devonport. The main items were retubing, raising of the quarterdeck, revision of bomb stowage, fitting of advanced hangar spraying

arrangements and the provision of up-to-date anti-aircraft armament.
Three 4in HA guns were now mounted, two forward on the lower flying-off deck and one aft, where the quarterdeck was too narrow to allow of two abreast, as originally hoped. To site these further forward would have interfered with the clearance of the cranes lifting aircraft for the lower hangar.

1931-1939. Peace, but the Growing Threat of War

Furious recommissioned with reduced complement in May 1931 under Captain C. F. S. Danby, the ship being brought up to full complement in November when she joined the Home Fleet as second operational carrier with *Courageous.* Apart from six months with the Mediterranean Fleet in 1934 she remained in that capacity throughout the last years of peace.
The thirties were a time of growing awareness of the importance of air power, coupled with perplexity as to its best use. Should its primary role be offensive with torpedo and bomb attacks, or to provide efficient reconnaissance? Could fighters be considered a worth-while defence against enemy aircraft?
Stimulated by the appointment of Rear-Admiral R. G. H. Henderson, once Captain of *Furious*, to the new post of Flag Officer (Air), each of the fleets which contained carriers tried out these and similar problems by tactical exercises, notably the successful massed attacks from aircraft of *Courageous, Furious* and *Glorious* on the combined Atlantic and Mediterranean fleets in 1933. Out of 32 torpedoes fired, 21 scored hits, surely a warning of the powers of the new arm.
Technically, the main advances in this period were the development of efficient arrester gear, the practice of night flying and some improvements in aircraft design.
Attempts to find the best arrester gear had been continuous since the earliest days of decklanding, not only in the British Navy but in those of the USA and Japan. Many devices had been tried—sandbags in pairs on raised ropes stretched taut athwartships, curved sprung skids instead of wheels, horns or V-shaped hooks on wheel axles of planes to catch fore-and-aft wires, comb-like fittings to landing gear and a main hook to engage wires which pulled against friction brakes[1]. Yet none had proved really satisfactory until the installation in *Courageous* in 1933, and in *Furious* soon after, of hydraulic cylinders giving a constant braking effect when a hook caught the wire.
This, and the introduction from 1937 of the Deck Landing Control Officer, or 'Batsman', to signal instructions to the pilot, proved to be the answer.

Aircraft Carried, 1933-39

The main changes in composition of the aircraft in *Furious*,[2] usually numbering 33, during these years were:

Fighters. In 1933, 401 Flight became 801 Squadron. Its Fairey Flycatchers at last gave way to the faster Hawker Nimrod and the two-seater Hawker Osprey, followed just before the war by the first naval monoplane, the Blackburn Skua, a combined fighter dive-bomber.
Spotter reconnaissance. The Fairey IIIF of 822 Squadron was superseded by the Fairey Seal (first aircraft with both wheelbrakes and proper arrester hook).
Torpedo-bombers. Starting with the Ripon, 811 Squadron changed to the Blackburn Baffin.
Torpedo-spotter-reconnaissance. When these functions were combined in 1935, *Furious* carried the Sharks of 821 Squadron and then many succeeding Squadrons of Swordfish, that slow, hardy, ubiquitous maid-of-all-work.

Deck-Landing Training

In 1937 the Admiralty regained control of the FAA and took energetic steps to deal with the shortage of trained personnel and aircraft. As far as the *Furious* was concerned, this meant an increase in sea time whilst successions of pilots, now all RN, were trained in deck-landing. From the time of the Coronation Review, at which she was present, until the outbreak of war this became her main duty.
There was, however, a break during the Munich crisis when she re-embarked her squadrons—801 821 and 822—and joined the Fleet at Scapa Flow, on the way being struck a glancing blow aft in thick fog by the destroyer *Encounter*, with little damage except to the port 'smoke-down' shutters.
After Munich, *Furious* returned to Rosyth packed with reservists bound for their homes, disembarked squadrons, and resumed decklanding training.
'D.L.T.' involved getting under way in darkness so as to reach open waters by daylight, steaming until dark on whatever courses and at whatever speeds the wind dictated for ideal landing conditions, then returning to the nearest anchorage. A faithful destroyer on her starboard quarter followed her throughout, with seaboat manned at the davit-head in instant readiness for life-saving.
A certain number of crashes in the sea or on deck was inevitable when training inexperienced pilots, but over the months great numbers qualified in the art of deck-landing and so could play their vital part from *Furious* herself and other carriers in the coming war.

MORE MODIFICATIONS: 1936 to 1939

In 1936 it was decided that the ship's armament must be further improved to meet the growing need for anti-aircraft defence.
As the *Furious* could not be spared for the lengthy stay in dockyard hands which this involved, the work was done in 'penny numbers' in order of priority and availability of material during normal periods alongside in 1936 and 1938 and at a longer refit in the winter of 1938-39. When, therefore, she recommissioned in May 1939 she had been once again extensively changed:
The ten 5·5in guns had gone. There were now twelve 4in HA/LA in twin mountings, capable of a broadside of eight either side. Mountings, supply

[1]Some of these devices can be seen in photographs in Profile 23.
[2]For more detail of types and performances, see Appendix.

1 *7 March 1932. Perhaps not beautiful, but businesslike. Note the metal screens which could be raised on their hinges to act as wind baffles for the flight deck* (Wright and Logan)

2 *1 March 1932. Now with AA guns and multiple pompoms (covered) forward. The ship is being conned from 'Wilfred' whilst leaving HM Dockyard* (Wright and Logan)

3 *Also 1 March 1932. Note the duct opening, from which emerged the funnel gases when 'smoking down' during flying* (Wright and Logan)

arrangements, directors, deck strengthening and supports had all been modified accordingly.

A small 'island' structure was in place on the starboard side of the flight deck, reducing the clear width for flying to 79 feet but providing a combined HA/LA Control System Director, two Pompom Directors, six Anti-Aircraft lookout sights, some shelter for personnel, and an aircraft homing beacon.

Two 2pdr eight-barrelled multiple pompoms were mounted on the flight deck, one just before and one just abaft this island. Unlike those of other carriers, this island was not for navigation: the ship was still conned usually from the starboard navigating position, with the alternative of the central, retractable, position.

Unofficially, the port (Flying Control) position was known as 'Pip', the starboard (Navigating) as 'Squeak', and the Central (also Navigating) as 'Wilfred'.

The forward section of the deck had been raised, an HA Control Position provided on the centre-line and two multiple pompoms mounted on sponsons, one either side. There would be no more flying from here even in emergency, but the guns could now be fought except in unusually heavy headseas.

The doors at the forward end of the upper hangar had been plated in.

Air defence positions had been built on each side of the navigating positions.

The palisades had been removed.

The two after wireless masts had been repositioned, as had one searchlight, to clear the arcs of the 4in guns.

These extensive changes and improvements in armament were completed four months before the outbreak of war.

British Carrier Strength at the Outbreak of War

In 1936 the Washington Treaty, with its limitations on carrier tonnage, expired and six ships were authorised within the next three years: *Illustrious, Formidable, Victorious, Indomitable, Implacable* and *Indefatigable.*

So on the outbreak of war these ships were building. But the *Ark Royal*, who had been authorised in 1934 within the Treaty limits, was the only really up-to-date aircraft carrier yet completed and operational: all the others were now elderly, having been launched over twenty years before.

Ark Royal, Courageous, and *Furious* were in home waters, *Glorious* in the Mediterranean, *Eagle* in the Far East, *Argus* in Reserve and *Hermes* newly commissioned.

Between them, these carried 176 of the Fleet Air Arm's 232 operational aircraft—26 Skuas, 10 Sea Gladiators and 140 Swordfish.

War: Early Days

The first few months of the war were far from phoney, for the *Furious.*

Until 2 October she continued training and DLT with anti-submarine sweeps, in the exposed waters of the East Coast of Scotland. Then she was summoned to join the Home Fleet at Loch Ewe as the only carrier, *Courageous* having been sunk and *Ark Royal* detached. Embarking Swordfish and crews to form 816 Squadron and retaining Training Squadrons 767 and 768, later formed into 818, she sailed on the 8th with the main body to search between the Shetlands and Norway, thence nearly to Iceland, for the *Gneisenau, Koln* and nine destroyers who had been sighted under way off South Norway.

1

2

3

4

5

1 *In 1932. The small diamond-shaped object abaft 'Wilfred' on the flightdeck is 'George', the retractable direction-finder* (NMM)

2 *1935. At this time* Furious *left the Mediterranean to rejoin the Atlantic Fleet* (NMM)

3 *13 June 1936. An interesting comparison with the photograph dated December 1931 from the same angle. There are now multiple pompoms and 4in HA guns on the forward deck, and the quarterdeck has been raised* (Wright and Logan)

4 *The Swordfish, the most famous of all Fleet Air Arm planes. A torpedo-spotter-reconnaissance, flown from* Furious *and other British carriers for most of the Second World War* (FAA Museum, Yeovilton)

5 *May 1937. With the Central Navigating Position lowered, showing the open-air wing navigating positions and the fore round-down* (NMM)

On return to Scapa, *Furious* luckily sailed from the berth next to the *Royal Oak* just before Prien's U-boat attack on the 13th.

After further vain searches from 13 to 22 October, which reached over 150 miles into the Arctic Circle north of Iceland to cover a reported break-out of the *Deutschland, Furious* was detached on the following day to form with *Repulse* a Hunting Group based on Halifax, Nova Scotia; this Group was to cover convoys and to search for raiders, mainly working in conditions of gales or fog. Leaving Halifax on 10 December *Furious* acted as Senior Officer's ship bringing the first Canadian troops safely to Britain in a fast convoy of large trans-Atlantic liners, in spite of a near-collision off North Ireland on 17 December with *SS Samaria*, outward bound and routed by Liverpool along the track selected by the Clyde authorities for the incoming convoy.[1]

In all, she was at sea for 71 days out of the first four wintry months of the war. All this was from a standing start. Yet a ship, especially an aircraft carrier, does not become an integrated weapon of war at one stroke.

Furious's first sweep with the Fleet in far Northern waters had been only five days after her first squadron, 816, was formed. Officers and men accustomed to peacetime deck-landing training now had to face the staggering risks called for in flying in wartime even when not in the physical presence of the enemy. There was no more waiting for things to be just right for new pilots, no more cancellation of flying because the round-down was rising and falling as the ship pitched or because the wind over the deck was not thirty knots or the visibility five miles.

NORWAY, APRIL 1940

When Germany invaded Norway, *Furious* was in the Clyde, her Swordfish on shore at Campbeltown for intensive squadron training. One splendid Captain, M. L. Clarke, had recently been relieved by another, T. H. Troubridge[2].

Embarking 816 and 818 squadrons on 9 April[3], the ship sailed north at speed to join the Fleet, making 27½ knots. She was, as before, the only carrier available, so that it was upon this now elderly vessel and her aircrews that the first major test fot the FAA fell.

On the 11th she flew off her Swordfish for a torpedo attack on the *Hipper* off Trondheim, but the target had to be switched to a destroyer in a different anchorage when the cruiser was found to have sailed. This, the first large-scale torpedo attack, was well carried out but unsuccessful because of intervening shoals.

Next day, *Furious* flew off nine Swordfish of 818 Squadron at 1615 to attack enemy ships at Narvik. In bad conditions of snow and sleet, with cloud ceiling averaging 1000 feet and often descending to only 200 feet, the aircraft managed to find and attack five enemy destroyers, two hits being claimed. Six merchant ships were also reported and valuable information collected as to the positions of sunken ships, mines and shore batteries. Six of the Swordfish were damaged. 816 Squadron also flew off, at 1705, but ran into such low cloud that it was forced to return, landing-on just before dark.

On 13 April, *Warspite* and nine destroyers entered Ofot Fjord, and the second battle of Narvik was fought, in which eight German destroyers and one U-boat were sunk at a cost of damage to two British destroyers. *Furious* flew off an A/S patrol ahead of our forces, and ten Swordfish for a synchronised attack. In spite of adverse weather conditions, this striking force arrived at the pre-arranged time and dive-bombed from 2000 feet in a moment of partial clearance, dropping thirty-five 250lb bombs and seventy of 20lbs. Two hits were claimed but were later proved to be only near misses: two aircraft were lost.

When the Fleet returned to Scapa on the 15th, *Furious* remained behind and continued to carry out patrols and photographic reconnaissance with as many aircraft as could be kept serviceable, the ship working in and out of the fjords as far north as Tromso in spite of a defective A-bracket.

All the odds were against the Swordfish crews. There were steep mountains on either side to run into; there were no proper maps, only photographed copies of the ship's navigational charts which had no contours; there were unsuspected electric power cables here and there over the fjords; there were snow squalls and fog, often suddenly reducing visibility to nothing; there were targets to be found which were dwarfed and hidden by mountains; and a return to a slush-decked, often pitching, carrier.

When the *Furious* was at last relieved on 25 April, she had only 8 serviceable aircraft remaining and was herself only able to steam at a much reduced speed because of stripping of turbine blades through the whipping of her hull by the concussion from a very near miss, sustained on the 18th when a single Heinkel attacked her in a fjord near Tromso too narrow to permit of drastic manoeuvring.

In 14 days her aircraft had flown 23,870 miles, dropped 18 torpedoes and 409 bombs totalling over 15 tons, and had taken 295 photographs. 17 Swordfish had been hit by enemy fire, 9 being lost, with 12 casualties of which 3 were fatal.

The results cannot be accurately assessed. But the aircraft had brought back much useful information as well as making many attacks on ships, ports and the railway, and destroying several enemy transport aircraft parked on a frozen lake. For good measure, the ship herself had captured a modern trawler, the *Rhein* of Wessermunde.

There was justification for the signal from the Fifth Sea Lord, 'Am very proud of the way in which the

---

[1]In pitch darkness *Samaria* passed unseen through the destroyer screen, passed so close to the starboard side of *Furious* as to carry away the horizontal wireless masts, removed five overhanging lifeboats from the port side of the *Aquitania* and only just missed the third and fourth ships in the line. When one remembers the size and speed of all these vessels, crowded with troops, the narrowness of the escape can be realised.

[2]Later Vice-Admiral Sir Tom Troubridge

[3]Captain Troubridge asked by signal whether fighters should also be embarked. But the Admiralty replied in the negative, probably because of the urgency to get all units to sea and because 801 Squadron had only been reformed six days earlier and was at Evanton near Invergordon, earmarked for other operations.

HMS *Furious*, August 1941, in her operational wartime appearance. A Seafire IB is shown on her flight deck; her HA/LA armament is now twin 4in and her close range armament has been brought up to date.
An aircraft homing beacon and a 285 HA Director have been fitted in the new island. Note that the flight deck is camouflaged.

1 Flycatcher, No 405 Flight HMS *Furious*—1928/9

2 822 Squadron Fairey IIIF aboard *Furious* between 1933 and 1935

3 818 Squadron Fairey Swordfish 1—lost 13 April 1940 during 2nd Battle of Narvik

4 Supermarine 'Hooked Spitfire' of 801 Squadron, November 1942 (note gold winged trident below cockpit sill)

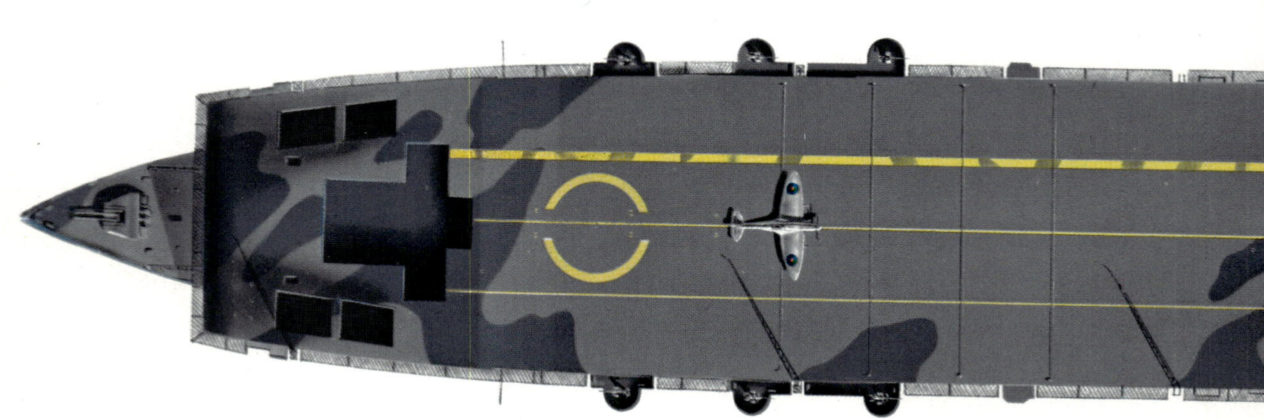

1932. With quarterdeck raised and modifications to armament. Ten 5·5in guns, three 4in HA, three multiple pompoms. Aircraft complement—36 (reduced to 30 in 1933)

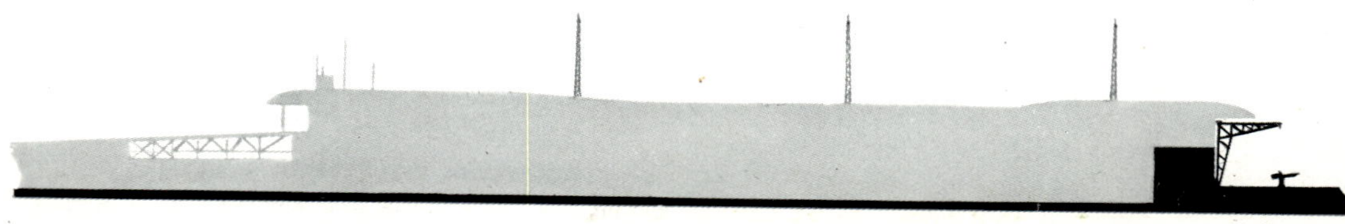

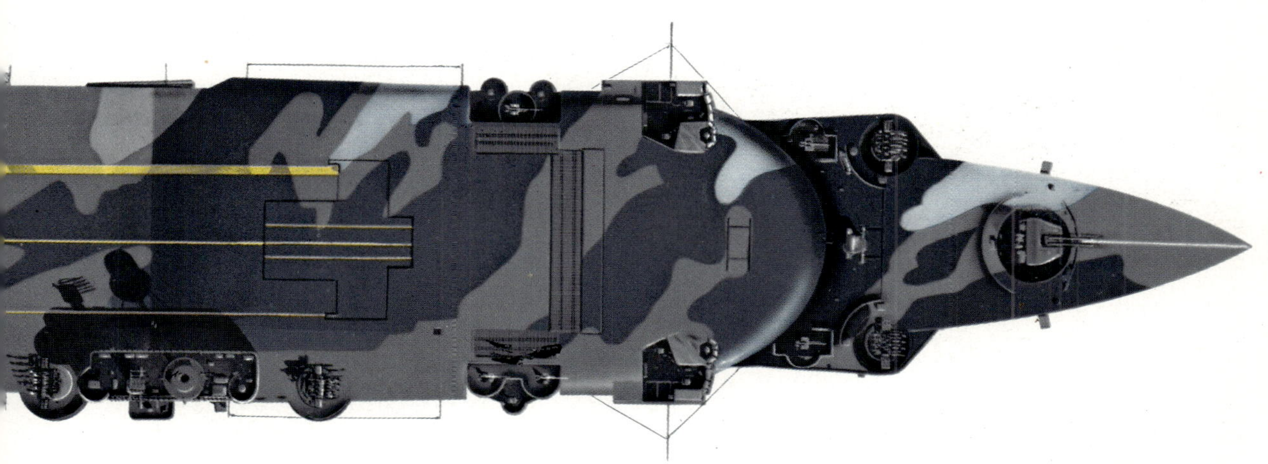

1939. With small island and improved AA armament. Twelve 4in HA/LA, three multiple pompoms. Aircraft complement—30

1 *Although this is the flight deck of* Ark Royal, *not* Furious, *the photograph shows a typical scene with Swordfish ranged* *(Charles W. Cain Archives)*

2 *There are an infinite number of ways of landing on a carrier*
(Courtesy of Instructor Captain C. R. Benstead, RN)

3 *The 'starboard nav' after being hit by an aircraft which crashed into the sea (pilot saved, uninjured). The Navigating Officer's binoculars are 'posed' for the photograph, after reassembly of portions recovered from the fo'c'sle and flight deck* *(Author's collection)*

4 *August 1939.* Furious *leaving Devonport for her War Station. Her armament has been altered and improved, and an 'island' fitted on the starboard side of her flush deck to provide High Angle and Pompom Directors and a homing beacon*

1

old ship has carried out her difficult task. The FAA has done magnificently.' Other signals of congratulation were received from the First Lord and from the Chief of the Air Staff.

In Norwegian Waters, May 1940

After her defects had been put right, partly by cutting out several rows of loose turbine blades, (for which some of her engineroom ratings swore that she ran all the better), *Furious* returned to Norwegian waters. The hopelessness of operations without fighters was clear. So, although her own aircraft still provided strikes and reconnaissance, she and the *Glorious* (who had been summoned from the Mediterranean) ferried RAF Gladiators and Hurricanes. These were flown off from an offshore position and were guided by ships' Swordfish to improvised landing strips, from where they did splendid service, as well as heartening our troops ashore by their presence.

It was on her way home after re-embarking some of these RAF fighters that *Glorious* was sunk on 8 June. Now only *Furious* remained of the three sister, or near-sister, ships.

Other Operations, Active and Supporting, of 1940 and 1941

An aircraft carrier has to be both versatile and far-ranging. Especially, it may be added, one who is getting on in years and therefore more likely to be spared for the odd task.

So for the next 18 months, *Furious* so much mixed active service with supporting duties that only a summary is possible.

2

3

4

14 June 1940. Embarked half of 816 squadron for her own protection. Relying on this and high speed, sailed unescorted for Halifax carrying £18,000,000 of gold bullion, with her ship's company joking that she was now officially recognised as being 'safer than the Bank of England.'

1 July 1940. Left Halifax, covering *Empress of Canada,* who was carrying Canadian troops for Iceland. *Furious* brought to Liverpool 5 Curtis dive-bombers, 21 Brewster fighters, 23 Northrops, 268 cases of spares and innumerable bombs. Further, on Captain Troubridge's initiative, all available space was filled with sugar for rationed Britain.

July to October 1940. Re-embarking squadrons 801, 816 and 825[1], she made a succession of attacks on shipping in Norwegian waters, sinking several merchant vessels for the loss of six aircraft, and on a seaplane base and oil tanks near Tromso.

November 1940 to February 1941. Now under Captain A. G. Talbot, ferried crated Hurricanes and

[1] Under Lt-Cdr Esmonde, later to win a posthumous VC leading the Swordfish against German heavy ships in their dash up-Channel. See Aircraft Profile No 212.

1 *The informality of the 'starboard nav'. The Commander kneels on top to be near the Captain during some anxious moments, in case a neighbour (dummy battleship) drags on to* Furious *at Scapa Flow*
(Courtesy of Inst Capt C. R. Benstead RN)

2 *Detail of the island and starboard boat deck*
(Crown copyright)

Fairey Fulmars for reassembly and flying off to Takoradi. From there, the aircraft crossed Africa and were in action in the Middle East within a week, at a critical period.

In all *Furious* and *Argus* ferried 142 aircraft in two operations.

Christmas Day, 1940. Hipper attacked Convoy WS5A, in which were *Furious* and *Argus* full of crated aircraft and so with only three Skuas and two Swordfish operational between them. When the heavy cruiser withdrew after an engagement with the *Berwick* and the latter rejoined the convoy, the two unaccompanied carriers chased to the westward for several hours in visibility of under a mile without being able to obtain contact, on the offchance of inflicting damage before being sunk themselves.

April 1941. Off Gibraltar. Transferred much-wanted aircraft to *Ark Royal*.

May 1941. At Belfast during two heavy air-raids, a few yards off Bryant and May's match factory. Only one small bomb scored a direct hit, but a parachute mine lifted *Furious*'s stern bodily and a near-miss peppered the port funnel duct. Belfast still remembers the ship's impressive anti-aircraft fire in reply.

12 May 1941. Arrived Gibraltar with 48 Hurricanes. In company with *Ark Royal* and Force H ferried aircraft to Malta.

30 June 1941. Whilst on one such operation, a Hurricane taking off hit the island, causing 14 casualties including several pilots.

30 July 1941. Back to the Arctic on an expedition, undertaken at Russia's request, so dangerous that the C-in-C protested. With *Victorious* and a strong escort, sailed to attack lines of communication at Kirkenes and Petsamo.

Furious flew off 9 Swordfish, 9 Fairey Albacores, 6 Fulmars and 4 Sea Hurricanes. Finding Petsamo practically empty of shipping, they torpedoed piers, sank the MV *Rottver* and set oil tanks on fire. Eleven of *Victorious*'s Albacores were shot down by enemy fighters: *Furious* lost one Albacore and two Fulmars. Losses had been heavy and disproportionate.

August 1941. Took part in anti-shipping operations in Varanger Fjord.

September 1941. In two sorties with *Ark Royal*, flew off 45 Hurricanes to Malta.

7 October 1941. Arrived Philadelphia, USA for refit.

Reinforcements to Malta, 1942

Returning to home waters in April, *Furious* spent the next three months working-up.

Her Captain was now T. O. Bulteel, the first aviator to command a major carrier. Unfortunately, however, he was to die of pneumonia within a year.

In August, a supreme effort was made to save Malta. 41 warships and 14 merchant ships took part in 'Operation Pedestal', a desperate venture in face of 600 enemy aircraft as well as submarines, MTBs and the threat of the whole Italian Fleet.

This was the convoy in which the heroic *Ohio* was to earn undying fame.

Indomitable, Victorious and *Eagle* carried fighters and torpedo planes in defence of the convoy. *Furious* was to accompany the fleet until within 550 miles of Malta, when she would fly off 38 Spitfires vitally needed for the island's defence.

The convoy reached this position without loss on the afternoon of the 11th but, just as *Furious* was flying off her Spitfires, the *Eagle* was hit by four torpedoes from a U-boat and sank in eight minutes. Saddened by the loss of yet another of the older carriers *Furious* turned back to Gibraltar, to be somewhat heartened en route by the news that all 37 Spitfires (one had force-landed on *Indomitable* shortly after take-off) had successfully reached Malta; and by the sinking of an Italian submarine by *Wolverine,* one of her escorting destroyers.

Furious remained with Force H and made two more such sorties, in August and October, delivering 29 Spitfires on each occasion. With *Indomitable* damaged, *Victorious* refitting and *Illustrious* in the Indian Ocean, she again was the only carrier available, with a justified reputation as a lucky ship.

'Torch', the North African Landings, November 1942

For the landings at Oran and Algiers in November, air cover and support depended entirely upon the carriers until shore airfields should become available. Until the evening of the 7th, *Furious* remained with *Formidable* and *Victorious* as part of Force H, to guard the huge expedition against interference by the Italian Fleet. Then, as there was no sign of this, she was detached to join the Centre Task Group off Oran.

Her aircraft for these operations consisted of 801 and 807 Squadrons of the Supermarine Seafires and 822 Squadron of Albacores. Incidentally, this was the first use of Seafires, converted for naval purposes from Spitfires, which proved successful as fighters but fragile for deck-landing.

Taking off at first light on 8 November to neutralise La Senia and Tafaroui, *Furious*'s Albacores made successful precision attacks by dive-bombing, particularly one in which 47 aircraft were destroyed at the former airfield. By the end of the day, the USAAF Spitfires were able to use these landing grounds, so her own aircraft were diverted to assist the Army by reconnaissance and bombings on call, until Oran capitulated on 10 November.

Furious had been the only Fleet carrier operating in this sector. Hurricanes from the Escort carriers *Biter* and *Dasher* had provided escort for the initial Albacore strike and thereafter top cover for the assault beaches. Much of the credit for the speedy end to hostilities must go to these three ships and their aircrews.

She remained with Force H and *Formidable* until January 1943, in case of a break-out by the Italian Fleet. She then rejoined the Home Fleet to replace *Victorious.*

With the Home Fleet, 1943

Captain G. T. Philip, who was to remain in command for the rest of *Furious*'s active career, joined her in February.

Under him, she spent the next few months with the Home Fleet, sailing to cover North Russian convoys. An interesting sortie took place in July, when the Fleet demonstrated in strength off Norway, to pin down enemy forces before the invasion of Sicily.

1

2

3

4

1 *Captain T. H. Troubridge, in the starboard navigating position. A photograph taken only a few seconds after a very near miss from a bomb* (*Courtesy of Inst Capt C. R. Benstead RN*)

2 *A view along the flight deck which shows the conditions under which* Furious *operated aircraft during the Norwegian campaign* (*Author's collection*)

3 *A Swordfish touching down on a carrier, with the 'Batsman' (Deck-landing Control Officer) signalling instructions* (*IWM*)

4 *With Earl Mountbatten. Captain Troubridge as a Rear-Admiral* (*IWM*)

A German aircraft was carefully allowed to make a sighting report before being shot down by *Furious*'s fighters.

On relief by *Illustrious, Furious* spent the autumn refitting at Liverpool and working-up afterwards.

The Attack on Tirpitz in Kaa Fjord, April 1944, (Operation 'Tungsten')[1]

The influence of the 42,900 ton *Tirpitz* on British naval resources was tremendous.

With eight 15in, 12-5·9in, and over 40 of the latest anti-aircraft guns, with a speed of 30 knots, very heavy armour and excellent water-tight subdivision, the mere threat of her—even if she never moved—meant that every convoy to North Russia required cover by huge forces including battleships and carriers.

She had been damaged in September by midget submarines, but by April was again ready for sea. It was vital that she be eliminated; but at her anchorage in Kaa Fjord there were booms to protect her against submarines, nets against torpedoes, and smoke defences to screen her. Dive-bombing offered the best chance, although it would be a most difficult operation.

The main attacks, by Fairey Barracudas with armour-piercing bombs of up to 1600lb, were to be mounted from *Victorious* and *Furious*, supported by Corsairs, Wildcats and Hellcats from them and four escort carriers, 121 aircraft in all. *Furious*, whose aircraft had practised rigorously on a dummy lay-out ashore at Loch Eriboll, would have to handle more planes and bombs of varying weights than ever before. In order that the Wings which had rehearsed together should strike together, the Fleet carriers exchanged a Barracuda Squadron apiece before the force sailed.

Flying off at 0416 on 3 April from a position 120 miles away, the first flight under Lt-Cdr Baker-Faulkner arrived over the target at 0528. Leaving Corsairs as top cover, Hellcats and Wildcats flew in from all directions, machine-gunning the shore AA batteries and the *Tirpitz* herself. Only one minute later, the 20 Barracudas of the first wave dived at the target.

They caught the *Tirpitz* as she was weighing to proceed on trials, her AA armament only partially ready to open fire, and before her protecting smoke screen had time to thicken enough to hide her. Within one minute the attack was over, heavy explosions and flames came from nine direct hits, and she broke away from her moorings.

Weaving their way through anti-aircraft fire from defences now fully alerted, the 19 Barracudas of the second strike made a masterly attack at 0635,

[1] Warship Special Profile No 29: HMS *Belfast*.

diving at three-second intervals and scoring five direct hits.

Carefully planned and practised, beautifully synchronised and gallantly executed, this operation is often classed with Taranto as the two finest Fleet Air Arm attacks of the war. Certainly, for the loss of only three aircraft, the mighty *Tirpitz* had been put out of action for three months, with her decks, superstructure and fire control systems extensively damaged and 422 of her crew dead or wounded. There was only one imperfection; the attacks had been pressed home too well and most of the bombs had been released from below 2000ft instead of 3000 as intended, so that the armoured deck had not been penetrated before they exploded.

Off the Norwegian Coast, 1944

During the next six months, *Furious* took a major part in eight operations in Norwegian waters, usually with other carriers, three more being cancelled at the last moment because of weather.

These were major efforts, escorted by large forces, and in June the veteran carrier was fittingly selected to fly the flag of the Commander-in-Chief, Home Fleet, Admiral Sir Henry Moore.

Three of the attacks were on the *Tirpitz*, by combined forces flown from *Furious*, *Indefatigable*, and *Formidable*. Smoke screens made accurate bombing impossible and only one direct hit was obtained, on 24 August by a 1600lb bomb: this penetrated

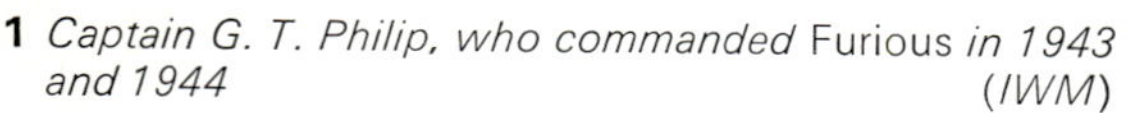

1

2

1 *Captain G. T. Philip, who commanded* Furious *in 1943 and 1944* *(IWM)*

2 *Late in the war. Ready to turn into wind and land aircraft on her pitching deck, although spray is nearly reaching the 'port nav'* *(NMM)*

3 *July 1942. In Disruptive Camouflage; even the line of the black colour aft, by the smoke duct, has been angled* *(MOD)*

4 *Another view taken in July 1942* *(MOD)*

3

4

6

7

5 *After her refit at Philadelphia, in 1942. This aerial view shows in particular her foremost guns and, right aft, the funnel outlets on the flight deck, only used when 'smoking up'* (MOD)

6 *1942* (MOD)

7 *Puzzle: find the* Furious. *Her camouflage successfully hides her outline. Photograph taken at Gibraltar* (Courtesy of Lt-Cdr C. E. Mills RN)

the armour, but failed to explode[1]. Eleven planes in all were lost.

The other operations were against shipping in the fjords, ranging from Bergen to the Arctic Circle. Between April and September 1944, in spite of opposition from fighters, *Furious*'s aircraft assisted in the destruction of over 25,000 tons of enemy shipping with damage to a further 21,000 tons.

In a country where nearly all communications have to be by water, *Furious* had caused serious disruption to the enemy.

Ageing at Last, late 1944

In all these operations, *Furious* had never failed. But it was 27 strenuous years since her first commissioning, and over three years since her Engineer Commander had reported that in peacetime he would have had no hesitation in saying that the ship was unfit for service. He and others had devotedly kept her going throughout all the extra calls made in wartime upon a ship such as she.

Now, at last, on 31 August 1944, DNC reported firmly to the Controller that the ship was worn out

[1] *Tirpitz* was finally destroyed on 12 November by huge 12,000lb bombs dropped by 30 Lancasters from Lossiemouth.

5

from all points of view, her stability no longer up to the required standard and her subdivision such that she was specially vulnerable to torpedo attack. In spite of a plaintive Minute that 'all sorts of duties are being considered for her' the Controller agreed, and orders were given for her to become non-operational on 15 September.

She was offered to the C-in-C, British Pacific Fleet, as accommodation ship, but was not required in this capacity and so was reduced to Reserve.

From 1945 to 1948, *Furious* was berthed at Loch Striven, near Rothesay, and used for Ship Target Trials. Primarily, these were to test the effects of aircraft explosives under varying conditions of hits and near misses, and were conducted by experts sent from the gunnery school at Whale Island, Portsmouth.

In 1948, she was sold for breaking up and was towed to Troon for final demolition, completed in 1954.

A Proud Record

So ended the long career of HMS *Furious.* What had she achieved?

Few other ships since the days of sail have spanned the years like she, none have been so closely linked with the evolution and history of naval flying, nor been so frequently and radically modified to meet changes in techniques and improvements in aircraft. Nor is it likely that any other warship has steamed so many miles in a lifetime. For even in the years of peace she was probably the hardest-worked ship in the Navy, constantly at sea whilst she trained pilots in deck-landing and often travelling at high speed if the wind was light.

She lived to wield the weapon which she had forged. For from her own deck, as from those of many another carrier, there flew against the enemy the officers and men whom this ship had trained in peacetime years for this very eventuality.

If a school can be judged by its 'Old Boys', so may a ship. Amongst those who served in *Furious,* are many famous names—R. G. H. Henderson, the Hon A. R. M. Ramsay, M. L. Clarke, and T. H. Troubridge amongst her Captains; A. M. Longmore, A. N. Dowding, F. W. Bowhill, C. L'E. Malone, E. H. Dunning, F. J. Rutland, R. Bell-Davies, VC, and E. Esmonde VC amongst her flying crews. Over the years there were many others, RAF and RN, who at one time or another had occupied her huge wardroom or teeming messdecks.

From all of these she earned a tremendous affection. Some people hold that it is nonsense to say that a ship has an aura, a personality: they can never have served in the fascinating, unorthodox, thoroughly human *Furious.*

She had been the scene of many experiments and

Left: *In dawn twilight, Barracuda 5A takes off from* Furious *to attack the* Tirpitz, *watched by the Wing Commander and others in the 'port nav.'* (*IWM*)

Below: *Barracuda 6M of 830 squadron getting airborne on 17 July 1944 in Operation 'Mascot'. Note the ramp rigged to increase length of take-off* (*IWM*)

technical achievements, notably the first landing on a British warship in 1917 and the first deck-landing by night in 1926.

She had handled nearly every type of aircraft ever carried in ships—one-shot seaplanes, unwieldy airships, aeroplanes unable to land-on again once airborne; then limited to landings in daylight only, up to the latest and most versatile machines of the days of victory in 1944.

Her operational record in the two world wars, although including highlights like the attacks on the Zeppelins at Tondern in 1918 and on the *Tirpitz* at Kaa Fjord in 1944, was perhaps less spectacular than that of some other ships whose names became legendary. But, veteran though she was in World War Two, she never failed; and the record of strikes and reconnaissances mounted from her deck is one of which any future holders of her name can well be proud.

The flight deck, island, and homing beacon. Gunnery Radar 285 is also visible (IWM)

The Launching of a Typical Attack, 1940

In this year, *Furious* mounted many attacks on shipping and other targets, her aircraft usually taking off before dawn to arrive at first light.

A Seafire taking off past the 'starboard nav'. In the left foreground can be seen the hinged wind-shields, in the down position (IWM)

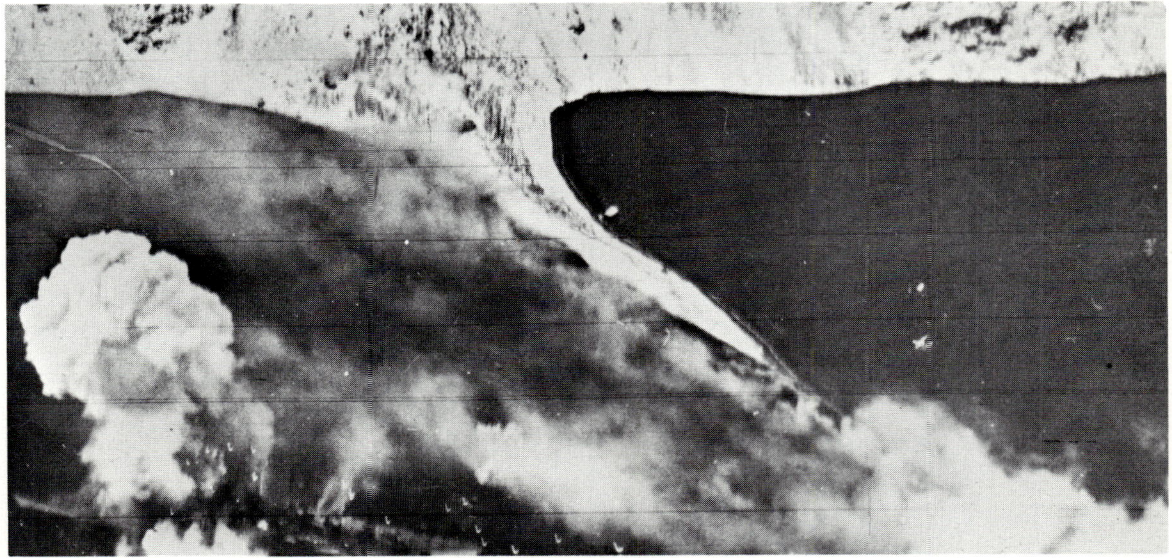

Operation 'Tungsten'. One of the hits on Tirpitz *(bottom left). Smokescreens vainly try to cover her from the attacking aircraft* (IWM)

Overnight, everything possible would have been prepared, the aircraft in the hangars checked, tuned, and armed, and aircrews given their main briefing.

For hours, the carrier and her escorting destroyers steam through the darkness at speed, making for the flying-off position.

At last, the ship springs to life. Lifts descend, to emerge loaded with planes which the flight-deck party manhandle to their ranging positions aft, sometimes a dangerous job if the ship is rolling, the wind strong, or the deck slippery. Observers muster in the Observers' Plotting Room under the fore round-down for final briefing and weather reports, guns' crews emerge from the warmth and lights below-decks and grope their way to their dawn Action Stations.

The Captain presses a buzzer and speaks down the voice-pipe to the Commander (Flying). The sound of the explosive starting charges, flashes of flame, and the roar of engines show that the aircraft are starting up and warming through. Grotesquely padded figures emerge on to the flight-deck and

August 1941, with even the flight deck camouflaged *(Ministry of Defence)*

make their precarious way aft to the waiting machines as the Observers take their places. In the darkness ahead, destroyers move to their new stations ready to screen the carrier when she turns into wind.

In wind. An increased roar of engines, and the first plane comes lumbering down the flight-deck, increasing speed as she approaches the watchers in the navigating positions. The air becomes heavy as the squadrons circle and form up before finally taking their departure and leaving a sudden silence. The ship turns to her next course, the flight-deck party disappear below, perhaps 'cooks to the galley' is sounded over the loudspeaker, guns' crews note with approval that the sky is getting lighter and so the hope of reverting to Cruising Stations is growing. For the next three hours or so, the everyday life of the ship continues—breakfast, gun drills, maintenance and cleaning jobs. But, all the time, everyone is in reality thinking or saying the same thing, 'I wonder how they're getting on'.

When the time of return draws near, this tension grows. There is no need for silence to be ordered. Officers, signalmen, lookouts are intent; searchlights are burning behind closed shutters in case they should be required to draw attention to the carrier's position; 'George', the diamond-shaped retractable D/F Aerial in the centre of the flight-deck, is rotating slowly to catch a vital bearing if a plane should make a wireless signal; there is no radar; the sky is horribly empty and the clouds hostile.

At last comes a welcome report, 'Aircraft in sight bearing green two-oh, Sir,' followed by 'Nine of them, Sir,' and perhaps someone else calls out, 'Another four coming up from astern, Sir'. The count brings its own tension. Casualties?

Sometimes, in low visibility, the waiting is more dramatic still. In the anxious silence someone hears an aircraft's engine, then suddenly the air is full of throbbing sound and the sky crowded with speeding planes circling and banking impatiently.

Hastily the carrier turns into wind. 'George', his job over, folds up and sinks below the flight-deck, his hinged covering plate closing behind him with a satisfied bang. Men count how many of the planes have released their bombs or torpedoes. A signalman may be specially detailed never to take his eye off a damaged Swordfish, which is lurching drunkenly but gallantly insisting on landing-on last to make certain that others are not held up.

The Squadron Leader lands on first, fights his way against the wind to the 'starboard nav', leans over, and makes a brief report to the Captain. Fuller assessment of damage inflicted and of reconnaissance results will be made later by a committee of officers, and the findings signalled.

31 March 1944. One of the last photographs taken of the 27-year-old ship, showing her slim lines and the length of the flight deck (*MOD*)

Acknowledgments

The author is indebted to the following, who have all helped him greatly, either in general or over points of detail:

The National Maritime Museum, Greenwich, especially Antony Preston who gave his time and expert knowledge without stint, and Mr Squires; the Imperial War Museum, especially Messrs R. Suddaby and G. Osbon; the Public Record Office, especially A. J. Norris Esq; the Ministry of Defence, especially J. D. Brown Esq, and Miss Joll; the Oxfordshire County Library, especially Miss Ross; Lt-Cdr L. A. Cox, RN, Curator of the FAA Museum, Yeovilton; Captains G. A. French, H. A. King, M. P. Lawson, C. R. Benstead, M. B. Laing, Commanders W. R. Gilbert, H. P. Bramwell, and Lt-Cdr C. E. Mills, all RN; James Dixon Esq; Dr I. L. Buxton; Miss Sheila Reid.

Bibliography

Unfortunately, there is no longer a 'Ship's Book' for *Furious*, whilst the records of her modifications and refits at Devonport were destroyed by enemy air-raids in 1941. So her story has had to be pieced together from no less than 48 references, ranging from major books to memoirs, too numerous to list here.

The main ones were:

The 'Ship's Covers' at the NMM, Greenwich.
'Naval Construction during the War'. Paper read by Sir Eustace Tennyson d'Eyncourt, and printed in 'Engineering' on 11 April 1919.
Summary of Logs of HMS *Furious*.
Hydraulic Manual 15in 'B' Coast Defence Mounting (security cover title for the 18in gun).
'The Naval Air Service' 1908-18. Edited by Captain S. W. Roskill (Naval Records Society).
'Aircraft and Sea Power', by Vice-Admiral Hezlet (Peter Davies).
'Into Wind', by Hugh Popham (Hamish Hamilton).
'Aircraft Carriers', by Norman Polmar (Macdonald & Co).
Naval Staff Histories.
The papers of Wing Cdr W. R. D. Acland and Air Commodore T. E. B. Howe at the IWM, Lambeth Road, London.
Sketches by Richard Perkins Esq at the NMM, Greenwich.
'British Naval Aircraft since 1912' by Owen Thetford.

Main types of aircraft operated from Furious 1925-45

Manufacturer & Service Type Landplane (L), Amphibian (A), Seaplane (S)	Initial Production	Powerplant (maximum output)	Maximum Speed (mph)	Range (miles)/ Endurance (hours)	Armament Forward (F) Rear (R) Bombs (B)	Weights (lb.) Empty/Loaded	Flights (Flts) and Squadrons (Sqns) Period Embarked
Avro Bison (L/A) ¾-seat spotter-reconnaissance	1921	450hp Napier Lion II	110	360	(F) 1×0·303in Vickers (R) 1×0·303in Lewis	4,163/6,336	421, 421A, 447 Flts 1925 to 1927
Fairey Flycatcher (L/S) 1-seat fighter	1923	400hp Armstrong-Siddeley Jaguar III/IV	133	263	(F) 2× Vickers (B) 4×20lb	2,039/2,979	401, 402, 405, 407 Flts 1925-1933
Fairey (L/S) IIID ¾-seat spotter-reconnaissance	1920	450hp Napier Lion II	106	550	(F) 1×Vickers (R) 1×Lewis	3,248/4,918	443A Flt 1925-1927
Blackburn Dart (L/S) 1-seat torpedo-bomber	1920	450hp Napier Lion IIB/V	110	256	(F) 1×Vickers (B) 1×18in Mk IX torpedo or 1100lb bombs	3,843/6,400	461, 462 Flts 1926-1928
Blackburn Blackburn (L) 3-seat spotter-reconnaissance	1920	450hp Napier Lion II	100	210	(F) 1×Vickers (R) 1×Lewis	4,034/6,112	420, 449 Flts 1926-1931
Fairey IIIF (L/S) 3-seat spotter-reconnaissance/ 2-seat bomber	1926	450/570hp Napier Lion VA/XIA	120	3-4hrs	(F) 1×Vickers (R) 1×Lewis (B) up to 500lb	3,923/6,301	442, 443, 447, 449 Flts 822 Sqn 1927-1936
Blackburn Ripon (L/S) 2-seat torpedo-bomber	1929	570hp Napier Lion XIA	126	3hrs	(F) 1×Vickers (R) 1×Lewis (B) 1×18in Mk VII/X torpedo or 1,500lb bombs	4,255/7,405	462, 465, 466 Flts 811 Sqn, 1929-1935
Hawker Nimrod (L) single-seater fighter	1929	525/640hp Rolls-Royce Kestrel	181	1·65hrs	(F) 2×Vickers (B) 4×20lb	3,065/4,258	801 Sqn, 1933-1936
Hawker Osprey (L/S) 2-seat fighter-reconnaissance	1932	640hp Rolls-Royce Kestrel	176	2·25hrs	(F) 1×Vickers (R) 1×Lewis	3,020/4,150	801 Sqn, 1933-1938
Fairey Seal (L/S) 3-seat spotter-reconnaissance	1933	525hp Armstrong-Siddeley Panther	138	4·25hrs	(F) 1×Vickers (R) 1×Lewis (B) up to 500lb	3,800/6,000	822 Sqn, 1934
Blackburn Baffin (L/S) 2-seat torpedo-bomber	1934	565hp Bristol Pegasus	136	450	(F) 1×Vickers (R) 1×Lewis (B) 1×18in torpedo or up to 2000lb bombs	4,180/7,610	811 Sqn, 1935
Blackburn Shark (L/S) 2/3-seat torpedo-spotter-reconnaissance	1935	700hp Armstrong-Siddeley Tiger	152	4·9hrs	(F) 1×Vickers (R) 1×Lewis/ Vickers (B) 1×18in torpedo or up to 1500lb bombs	4,333/8,050	821 Sqn, 1936-1938
Fairey Swordfish (L/S) 3-seat torpedo-spotter-reconnaissance	1933	690/750hp Bristol Pegasus	139	546	(F) 1×Vickers (R) 1×Lewis/ Vickers (B) 1×18in torpedo or up to 1500lb bombs	5,200/8,250	810, 811, 812, 816, 818, 822, 825, 835, 842 Sqns 1936-1944
Blackburn Skua single-seater fighter and dive-bomber monoplane	1937	905hp Bristol Perseus	225	4·5hrs	4×Browning 1×Lewis (B) 1×500lb 8×30lb	5,490/8,228	801 Sqn, 1939-41
Fairey Fulmar 2-seater fighter monoplane	1940	1080hp Rolls-Royce Merlin	280	800	8×Browning 1×Vickers (sometimes)	5,955/9,800	800, 804, 807 Sqns 1940-1942
Fairey Albacore 3-seater torpedo-bomber	1938	1065hp Bristol Taurus	160	710	1×Vickers 1×Twin Vickers 1×18in torpedo or 2000lb bombs	7,200/12,600	817, 822, 823 Sqns 1941-1943
Fairey Barracuda 3-seater torpedo and dive-bomber monoplane	1942	1260hp Rolls-Royce Merlin	235	524 (1320 light)	Twin Vickers 1×1610lb torpedo or up to 2000lb bombs	8,700/13,500	827, 830, 831 Sqns 1943-1944
Grumman Martlet (L) 1-seat fighter	1940	1,200hp Pratt & Whitney R-1830 'Twin Wasp'	315	1,150	(F) 4×0·50in Browning M-2s	4,649/6,100	881 Sqn, 1943
Supermarine Seafire Mks I-III (L) 1-seat fighter-bomber/ tactical reconnaissance	1942	1,340/1,470hp Rolls-Royce Merlin	365	490 (or 770)[1]	(F) 2×20mm Hispano cannon 4×0·303in Brownings	5,000/6,700	801, 807, 880 Sqns 1942-1944
Hawker Sea Hurricane Mks 1-II (L) 1-seat fighter	1941	1,030/1,260hp Rolls-Royce Merlin	315	510	(F) 8×0.303in Brownings	5,000†/6,589	804, 825, 880A Sqns 1941-1942
Grumman Hellcat (L) 1-seat fighter	1943	2,000hp Pratt & Whitney R-2800 'Double Wasp'	376	370[2]	(F) 6×0·50in Brownings	9,238/12,740	1840 Sqn, 1944

[1]drop tank range [2]approx (for Sea Hurricane Mk 1A/Grumman Hellcat Mk II)

Index

C

D

E

F

G

H

I

J

K

L

U

V

W

Y

Warships in Profile 1
Warships in Profile 1
PROFILE